F

THE BRITISH ACADEMY
CLASSICAL AND MEDIEVAL LOGIC TEXTS
General Editors: P.T. *Geach and* W. *Kneale*

PAUL OF VENICE
LOGICA MAGNA
PART II
FASCICULE 8

PAULI VENETI
LOGICA MAGNA

SECUNDA PARS

TRACTATUS DE OBLIGATIONIBUS

---

*Edited with an English Translation
and Notes by*
E. JENNIFER ASHWORTH

Published for
THE BRITISH ACADEMY
by the
OXFORD UNIVERSITY PRESS
1988

Oxford University Press, Walton Street, Oxford OX2 6DP
Oxford   New York   Toronto
Delhi   Bombay   Calcutta   Madras   Karachi
Petaling Jaya   Singapore   Hong Kong   Tokyo
Nairobi   Dar es Salaam   Cape Town
Melbourne   Auckland

and associated companies in
Beirut   Berlin   Ibadan   Nicosia

Oxford is a trade mark of Oxford University Press

Published in the United States
by Oxford University Press, New York

© 1988 The British Academy

All rights reserved. No part of this publication may be reproduced,
stored in a retrieval system, or transmitted, in any form or by any means,
electronic, mechanical, photocopying, recording, or otherwise, without
the prior permission of The British Academy

British Library Cataloguing in Publication Data

Paulus, Venetus, d. 1429
[Logica Magna, English and Latin]. Pauli Veneti Logica Magna.—(Classical
and medieval logic texts, 5).
Secunda pars : Tractatus de obligationibus.
1. Logic—Early works   I. [Logica Magna, English and
Latin]   II. Title   II. Ashworth, E.J. (Earline Jennifer)   IV. British
Academy   V. Series 160

ISBN 0-19-726065-9

Produced by Alan Sutton Publishing
Gloucester
Printed in Great Britain

CONTENTS

INTRODUCTION	vii
Life	vii
Works	viii
The Development of the Theory of Obligations	x
Paul's sources	xii
The Purpose of Obligations Treatises	xiii
A Note about this edition	xiv
A Note about this translation	xv
Acknowledgements	xvi
Sigla et Abbreviationes	xvi
PART ONE	
Section One: Informal Definitions of Terms	3
Section Two: Preliminary Assumptions	31
Section Three: Rules	51
Section Four: Theses	75
PART TWO: CONCERNING *POSITIO*	
CHAPTER ONE: AGAINST THE RULES	101
Against Rule One	101
Against Rule Two	123
Against Rule Three	147
Against Rule Four	171
Against Rule Five	195
Against Rule Six	223
Against Rule Seven	235
Against Rule Eight	249

Against Rule Nine	261
Against Rule Ten	285
Against Rule Eleven	303
Against Rule Twelve	315

CHAPTER TWO: ON CONJUNCTIONS — 327

CHAPTER THREE: ON DISJUNCTIONS — 335
Rules	335
Sophism	343

CHAPTER FOUR: ON SIMILARS AND DISSIMILARS — 345
Sophisms	345
Rules for Similars	351
Rules for Dissimilars	361

PART THREE: CONCERNING *DEPOSITIO*

CHAPTER ONE: RULES — 369

CHAPTER TWO: THESES — 379

CHAPTER THREE: SOPHISMS — 379

BIBLIOGRAPHY

I. OBLIGATIONS TREATISES — 393
1. Manuscripts and early printed texts	393
2. Editions	394

II. OTHER SOURCES — 394

INDEXES
Index of sophisms	398
Index of names	401
Index of doctrines	404

INTRODUCTION

Life

PAUL OF VENICE, otherwise known as Paulus Nicolettus Venetus, O.E.S.A., was probably born in Udine, Italy between 1369 and 1372, though the earlier date is most likely.[1] He became a Hermit of Saint Augustine in S. Stefano Convent, Venice; and on December 9, 1387, was assigned as a student to the Padua Convent. By an order dated August 31, 1390, he was sent to study in Oxford, where he remained until at least 1393. He probably visited Paris before returning to Padua where he had become a lecturer in philosophy at the University of Padua by about 1395. In May 1408 he became Doctor of Arts and Theology, and in the same year he became professor of arts at the University of Padua. Thereafter his career was both successful and varied. He was active in three spheres. First, and most important, he was an academic. He taught at the Universities of Parma (1412), Siena (1420 and 1427), and Bologna (1424), but he still retained an association with the University of Padua for much of his life. Indeed it was in Padua that he died on June 15, 1429, having returned there from Siena the previous year. Second, he was a religious leader. He was first Rector and Vicar General of the Hermits of Saint Augustine and then Prior Provincial of the Order in Lombardy from 1409 to 1410; he was Prior Provincial in Siena (1420), Prior Provincial of Marche Tarvisine (1420–1421), and Regent at the Siena Convent (1422). Finally, he was a diplomat who undertook a number of missions on behalf of the Council of Venice. In 1410 he visited Hungary and Germany, and in 1412 he went to Poland. Later, however, he found himself in trouble with the Venetian government on more than one occasion, and was even banished to Ravenna in 1420, though it is not known why.

As a philosopher he enjoyed wide fame. In 1417 the Venetian republic recognized his eminence by granting the friars of S. Stefano's Convent the privilege of wearing the black biretta of the patricians; and in 1420 he was made '*artium monarcha*' at Padua. Both his reputation and something of his personality are captured by the words of Gaspar of Verona when writing of his own student days at Bologna:[2]

---

[1] The material in the section is taken from three sources: Alan R. Perreiah, 'A biographical introduction to Paul of Venice', *Augustiniana*, 17 (1967), 450–461; Charles H. Lohr, 'Medieval Latin Aristotle commentaries: Authors Narcissus–Richardus', *Traditio*, 28 (1972), 314; Francesco Bottin, 'Logica e filosofia naturale nelle opere di Paolo Veneto', in *Scienza e Filosofia all' Università di Padova nel Quattrocento*, edited by A. Poppi, (Trieste: Lint, 1983), 85–124.

[2] 'Florebat et Paulus Venetus, ordinis heremitarum frater, omnium arrogantissimus homo quos unquam noverim, philosophus tamen non ignobilis, simul et theologus, lector cathedrae compositissimus.' Gaspar Veronensis in: Giuseppe Zippel, *Le Vite di Paolo II di Gaspare da Verona e di Michele Canensi*, Rerum Italicarum Scriptores T.III, P. XVI (Città di Castello, 1904), p. XXII. I would like to thank W. Keith Percival for drawing my attention to this passage.

Paul of Venice . . . also flourished, the most arrogant man of all those I have ever been acquainted with, but not unknown as a philosopher and theologian. . . .

Works

Paul of Venice was a prolific writer, and the complete canon of his philosophical and theological works has yet to be established. The task is difficult both because he wrote *quaestiones* and commentaries in addition to independent works, and because some of the works attributed to him may be *reportationes*, or notes by his students, rather than material he himself prepared for circulation.

One group of works consists of commentaries on Aristotle. Here we find:

1. *Expositio in libros Posteriorum Aristotelis.*
2. *Expositio super VIII libros Physicorum necnon super Commento Averrois* (1409).
3. *Expositio super libros De generatione et corruptione.*
4. *Lectura super librum De Anima.*
5. *Conclusiones Ethicorum.*
6. *Conclusiones Politicorum.*
7. *Expositio super Praedicabilia et Praedicamenta* (1428).

The attribution to Paul of a commentary *In Perihermenias* is doubtful, as is the status of *De motu animalium* and *Quaestiones metaphysicales*.[3] The *Quaestio de Universalibus* seems to be part of a much longer work rather than a commentary on Aristotle.[4]

Other works by Paul include:

1. *Super Primum Sententiarum Johannis de Ripa Lecturae Abbreviatio* (1401).
2. *Summa philosophiae naturalis* (1408).
3. *De compositione mundi.*
4. *Quaestiones adversus Judaeos.*
5. *Sermones.*

There are four independent logical works:

1. *Logica Parva* or *Tractatus Summularum* (1395–96).
2. *Logica Magna* (1397–98).

---

[3] My information on Paul's works is taken from Lohr, op. cit., 315–320; Bottin, op.cit.; Bottin, 'Alcune correzioni ed aggiunte al censimento dei codici di Paolo Veneto', *Quaderni per la Storia dell' Università di Padova*, 14 (1981), 57–60. For details of the printed editions of these works, see Wilhelm Risse, *Bibliographia Logica. Verzeichnis der Druckschriften zur Logik mit Angabe ihrer Fundorte. Band I. 1472–1800.* (Hildesheim: Georg Olms, 1965).

[4] See Francesco Bottin, 'Paolo Veneto e il problema degli universali', in *Aristotelismo Veneto e Scienza Moderna* (Saggi e Testi, 17), (Padova; Antenore, 1983), 459–68.

3. *Quadratura*.
4. *Sophismata Aurea*.

The *Logica Parva* was undoubtedly the most popular of the logical works, since it survives in more than 150 manuscripts and more than 40 printed editions.⁵ It differs in doctrine from the *Logica Magna* on various points, such as the definition of *obligatio* (see below), and it is probable that it consists of material put together by Paul at Oxford.⁶ It was succeeded by the *Logica Magna* (1397–98) which Francesco Bottin has been able to date through references in the correspondence of Pietro Tomasi.⁷ It was obviously not as successful as the *Logica Parva* since it survives in just one manuscript, Codex Vaticanus Latinus 2132,⁸ and just one printed edition, Venetiis, 1499.⁹ The *Sophismata* and the *Quadratura* were modestly successful, each receiving three printed editions.¹⁰ They are supplementary to the *Logica Magna* in that they go over much of the same material. As its title suggests, the *Sophismata* is a collection of sophisms; whereas the *Quadratura* contains a series of logical problems, each of which is to be solved with the aid of four theses postulated in relation to that particular problem. The four chapters which make explicit reference to obligational material have little to add to the *Logica Magna* discussion,¹¹ so I shall not refer to the *Quadratura* below.

---

⁵ Bottin, 'Alcune correzioni', 59–60.

⁶ Bottin 'Logica e filosofia naturale', 90–91. In 1476 Antonio Cittadini da Faenza wrote: 'Ferunt autem quidam non auctoritate indigni, hunc libellum in Britannia, ubi olim et dialecticae et philosophiae studia floruerunt, in antiquissimis litteris compertum esse, ut ex illis constaret, prius opusculum hoc extructum fuisse quam Paulus Venetus natus esset. Quod eo magis a non nullis creditur, quod certum est Paulum apud Britanos visendorum gymnasiorum gratia aliquando commoratum esse, ac postea in Italiam revertentem multos libros secum detulisse, quorum auctores Italis penitus erant incogniti.' Bruno Nardi, *Saggi sull'aristotelismo padovano dal secolo xiv al xvi*, (Firenze: Sansoni, 1958), p. 76.

⁷ Bottin, 'Logica e filosofia naturale', 91–93.

⁸ The manuscript is described by Anneliese Maier, *Codices Vaticani Latini. Codices 2118–2192* (Città del Vaticano: In Bibliotheca Vaticana, 1961), 27–28. Lohr lists a number of other manuscripts: Charles H. Lohr, 'A note on manuscripts of Paulus Venetus, Logica', *Bulletin de philosophie médiévale*, 15 (1973), 145–146. However Francesco del Punta reports that only one of these contains any material from the *Logica Magna* (Paul of Venice, *Logica Magna Part II Fascicule 6*, edited with notes on the sources by Francesco del Punta, translated into English with explanatory notes by Marilyn McCord Adams (Oxford, Published for the British Academy by the Oxford University Press, 1978), p. viii, note 5). See also Bottin, 'Alcune correzioni', p. 58.

⁹ Risse, op.cit., gives a second edition under the year 1559, and Del Punta, op.cit., p. viii specifies that the 1559 edition 'does not represent an independent edition but only a reissuing of the first'. However, Bottin, 'Logica e filosofia naturale', 92–93, n. 34, reports that the 1559 edition is the *Logica Parva*. This fits in with Risse's description of the book as *in octavo*, an unlikely format for so massive a work.

¹⁰ For details see Risse, op. cit.

¹¹ Paul of Venice, *Quadratura* (Venetiis, 1493): Dubium secundum, cap. 11, De propositionibus contradictoriis concedendis vel negandis in arte obligatoria, fol. 30 $^{\text{ra-va}}$; Dubium tertium, cap. 6, De propositionibus concedendis et negandis in arte obligatoria, fol. 47vb–fol.48rb [printed as fol.53vb–fol.42rb]; cap.23, De negatione veritatis ac proprii actus in tempore obligationis, fol.54$^{\text{rb-va}}$; cap.29, De negatione veri et concessione falsi extra materiam obligationum et insolubilium, fol.56$^{\text{rb-vb}}$.

Nor shall I refer to the *Sophismata*, since there is little overlap between this work and the sophisms presented in the *Tractatus de Obligationibus*.

The Development of the Theory of Obligations

The history of the theory of obligations may be traced as far back as the late twelfth century.[12] However, for the purposes of this study we may take as our starting point the *Tractatus de Obligationibus* written by Walter Burley in about 1302,[13] both because Burley presents the theory in a fully developed form, and because his treatise sets the stage for later developments. The other major figure of the first half of the fourteenth century is Roger Swyneshed, whose *Obligationes* was probably written between 1330 and 1335.[14] His peculiar importance for this study is that he introduced new doctrines, especially to do with conjunction,[15] the reaction to which enables us to organize and assess other treatises on obligations.

Let us first consider the English scene after Swyneshed.[16] Martinus Anglicus, who clearly approved of Swyneshed's views, wrote a treatise in which he carefully distinguished between the *antiqua responsio* of Burley and

---

[12] For the early period see: Lambertus Marie de Rijk, 'Some thirteenth century tracts on the game of obligation', *Vivarium*, 12 (1974), 94–123; continued, ibid., 13 (1975), 22–54; continued, ibid., 14 (1976), 26–49. See also Lambertus Marie de Rijk, editor, *Die mittelalterlichen Traktate De modo opponendi et respondendi*. Einleitung und Ausgabe der einschlägigen Texte. Beiträge zur Geschichte der Philosophie und Theologie des Mittelalters, Neue Folge, Band 17. (Münster: Aschendorff, 1980).

[13] For Burley's text, see Romuald Green, *The Logical Treatise 'De Obligationibus'. An Introduction with Critical Texts of William of Sherwood and Walter Burley*. (St. Bonaventure, N.Y.: Franciscan Institute, forthcoming). I would like to thank Paul Vincent Spade for providing me with a copy of Green's manuscript, and Romuald Green for permission to use it. For discussion, see Eleonore Stump, 'William of Sherwood's Treatise on Obligations', *Historiographia Linguistica*, 7 (1980), 249–264; Paul Vincent Spade and Eleonore Stump, 'Walter Burley and the *Obligationes* attributed to William of Sherwood', *History and Philosophy of Logic*, 4 (1983), 9–26. For a general account of the early development of the theory of obligations, see Eleonore Stump, 'Obligations. A. From the beginning to the early fourteenth century' in *The Cambridge History of Later Medieval Philosophy*, edited by Norman Kretzmann, Anthony Kenny, Jan Pinborg (Cambridge: Cambridge University Press, 1982), 315–334. [Hereinafter cited as CH.]

[14] For the text, see Paul Vincent Spade, 'Roger Swyneshed's *Obligationes*: edition and comments', *Archives d'histoire doctrinale et littéraire du moyen âge*, 44 (1977), 243–285. For discussion of Swyneshed, see Paul Vincent Spade, 'Three theories of *obligationes*: Burley, Kilvington and Swyneshed on counterfactual reasoning', *History and Philosophy of Logic*, 3 (1982), 1–32; Eleonore Stump, 'Roger Swyneshed's theory of obligations', *Medioevo*, 7 (1981), 135–174. For a more general account of developments during the fourteenth century, see Paul Vincent Spade, 'Obligations. B. Developments in the fourteenth century' in *CH*, 335–341.

[15] For discussion of Swyneshed's doctrines and the reaction to them see text and notes, Part 1, section 3, rule 12.

[16] I shall not discuss Pseudo-Dumbleton, Richard Brinkley or John Tarteys, though I would like to thank Norman Kretzmann for sending me a copy of his transcription of Dumbleton(?) and Paul Spade for providing me with his own partial transcription of Brinkley. There are other English treatises which I have not seen. For a fairly complete list of manuscripts on obligations, both English and non-English, see Romuald Green, op.cit. For an overview of English logic, see Paul Vincent Spade, 'Logic in late medieval Oxford 1330–1500' in *The History of the University of Oxford. Volume II* (forthcoming).

the *nova responsio* of Swyneshed.[17] Robert Fland's treatise is very similar to that of Martinus, and it is impossible to say who influenced whom. Richard Lavenham who summarized Swyneshed's doctrines later in the century, should also be mentioned here. Richard Billingham, who was a fellow of Merton College, Oxford, in 1344 and regent master of arts in 1349, wrote an *Ars obligatoria* containing a rule for conjunction which was not Swyneshed's though it could be seen as related to his rule (see below, Part 2, chapter 1, against rule 12, sophism 3). This rule also appeared in an obligations treatise by John of Holland, who began his regency of arts at Prague in 1369, but seems to have studied at Oxford. Billingham's lengthy section on *positio* was reproduced almost without change in a series of obligations texts which belong to the *Logica Oxoniensis*.[18] I have mainly cited the version printed in the *Libellus Sophistarum ad Usum Oxoniensium*, supplemented by a longer version of the same text found in Oxford, Bodleian Library MS Lat. misc.e 79, fols.18ra–24ra. Billingham's definitions and rules, together with some of his sophisms, were used by John Wyclif, whose *Logica* may have been written before 1362. The same definitions and rules reappear in the obligations treatise belonging to the *Logica Cantabrigiensis*, which is found in Cambridge, Gonville and Caius College MS 182/215, pp. 42–47, and was printed in the *Libellus Sophistarum ad Usum Cantabrigiensium*.[19] This treatise is unlike the Oxford logic both in the complete absence of sophisms and in the presence of a section on *impositio*. Last but not least, there is Ralph Strode, who was a contemporary of Wyclif at Merton College. He explicitly rejected Swyneshed's views in a treatise which is lively, interesting, and seems to have no very close links either with continental authors or with Burley's treatise. Many of his sophisms appear to be original.

Let us now turn to the University of Paris. Here, the first great figure is Albert of Saxony (1316–1390) who taught in Paris from about 1351 to 1362, when he went to the University of Vienna. In the section on obligations he

---

[17] De Rijk has argued that Martinus Anglicus must be Martin of Alnwick, O.F.M., who died in 1336 after a long career: see L.M. de Rijk, *Some 14th Century Tracts on the Probationes Terminorum* (Nijmegen: Ingenium Publishers, 1982), pp. 6*–7*. However, I do not think this identification is plausible, and N.J. Green-Pedersen has independently suggested a date of c.1350 for the *Consequentiae* by Martinus Anglicus: see N.J. Green-Pedersen, 'Early British treatises on consequences' in *The Rise of British Logic* edited by P.O. Lewry, O.P., (Toronto: Pontifical Institute of Medieval Studies, 1985), p. 303.

[18] For further details, see E.J. Ashworth, 'English *Obligationes* texts after Roger Swyneshed: The tracts beginning "Obligatio est quaedam ars",' in *The Rise of British Logic*, 309–333. See also L.M. de Rijk, 'Logica Oxoniensis. An attempt to reconstruct a fifteenth century Oxford manual of logic', *Medioevo*, 3 (1977), 121–164; and E.J. Ashworth, 'The "Libelli Sophistarum" and the use of medieval logic texts at Oxford and Cambridge in the early sixteenth century', *Vivarium*, 17 (1979), 134–158. De Rijk's hypothesis ('Logica Oxoniensis', p. 164) that these texts go back to Martinus Anglicus is mistaken, as is his identification (*Some 14th Century Tracts*, p. 40*) of the tract in Corpus Christi College, Cambridge MS 378, fols.48^r–57^r with the tract by Martinus.

[19] See L.M. de Rijk, 'Logica Cantabrigiensis – A fifteenth century Cambridge manual of logic', *Revue internationale de philosophie. Grabmann*, 29e année 113 (1975), 297–315.

follows Burley very closely, and uses a number of Burley's sophisms, but he also discusses Swyneshed. Albert in his turn was used, albeit critically, by William Buser, a Dutchman from Heusden who was a prominent member of the English nation at the University of Paris and who wrote his treatise on obligations in 1360.[20] His discussion was original and interesting, and much of it was reproduced in the treatise by Marsilius of Inghen (c.1340–1396) who incepted under William Buser in 1362.[21]

To end, I should like to mention two Italian authors. Peter of Mantua, who taught at the University of Bologna from 1392 until his death in 1399, included a rather unreadable section on obligations in his *Logica* in which he made use of Strode. Peter of Candia (d.1410) judging by the sophisms, also made use of Strode in a short, eclectic treatise.

Paul's Sources

The question of sources for a medieval logician has to be approached with some caution, since quotations were rarely acknowledged, and since identical passages in two authors may have been taken from an unknown common source, rather than from the earlier of the two in question. However, given these caveats, Paul's main sources are quite clear. He used Albert of Saxony, William Buser,[22] Ralph Strode, some version of the *Logica Oxoniensis*, and Peter of Candia. He probably read some other authors, including Peter of Mantua, but in various places where he summarizes alternative views he is merely quoting from the authors I have mentioned (see notes, passim.) He has occasional flashes of originality, as when he classifies *obligatio* as a relation; but in general his tract on obligations is a patchwork of earlier sources, with some passages quoted verbatim and others neatly summarized. Even the overall organization that Paul imposed on his material is not entirely different from that of his sources, as can be seen from the following tables of contents for Buser and Strode respectively.

I. *William Buser: Treatise on Obligations.*

1. Introductory material.
    Informal definitions of terms.
    Preliminary assumptions.
    General rules.
    On the species of *obligatio*.
2. *Impositio*: rules and sophisms.

---

[20] The details of Buser's life and work have recently been established for the first time by C.H. Kneepkens in 'The mysterious Buser again: William Buser of Heusden and the *Obligationes* tract *Ob Rogatum*' in *English Logic in Italy in the 14th and 15th Centuries*, edited by Alfonso Maierù (Napoli: Bibliopolis, 1982), 147–166.

[21] Kneepkens, op.cit., p. 152.

[22] My evidence for the claim that Paul used Buser rather than Marsilius of Inghen is presented in the notes to the text, *passim*. See also Kneepkens, op.cit., pp. 161–165.

3. Simple *positio*: rules and sophisms.
4. Composite *positio*: conjunctions and disjunctions.
5. Dependent *positio*.
6. On *depositio*.
7. On *petitio*.

II. *Ralph Strode: Treatise on Obligations*.

1. Introductory material.
    Informal definitions of terms.
    Preliminary assumptions.
    Theses (including rules).
2. Arguments and sophisms designed to test the theses and preliminary assumptions.
3. Composite *positio*: conjunctions and disjunctions.
4. On *depositio*.
5. On the variation of signification (*impositio*).
6. Similars and dissimilars.

The Purpose of Obligations Treatises

A contentious and as yet unresolved issue has to do with the purpose of obligations treatises. The treatises themselves do not offer much discussion of this point, being content to remark that the opponent in a disputation is to try to push the respondent into accepting a contradiction, whereas the respondent has to resist this, even when faced with the curious consequences of granting such a *propositum* as 'You do not exist.'[23] In the process both participants would have their knowledge of valid inferences thoroughly tested, for each proposition put forward would be such that it followed from preceding steps, or such that its negation followed, or such that neither it nor its negation followed. In this third case either it or its negation would enter the sequence as an extra premiss for further conclusions or non-conclusions. It should also be emphasized that the bulk of almost all treatises on obligations consisted of a series of sophisms which, as Edith Sylla has argued of the 'physical' sophisms, formed an integral part of logic teaching, at least in fourteenth century Oxford, and were designed to develop a student's subtlety and skill in handling logical rules.[24] These remarks suggest that obligational disputations (if such were ever in fact held) had the primary function of providing oral exercise in formal logic, and hence were of mainly pedagogical significance.

This solution has been adopted by a number of authors; but reflection on the complex and sophisticated nature of the controversy between Swyneshed and others has led P.V. Spade to suggest that obligations treatises offer us an

---

[23] For detailed references, see Part 1, section 2, note 3.
[24] Edith Dudley Sylla, 'The Oxford calculators' in *CH*, 540–563.

account of counterfactual reasoning.[25] This theory in turn has been criticized by E. Stump, who points out that the treatises reflect a number of diverse concerns, including 'epistemic logic, indexicals, propositional attitudes, and other issues in the philosophy of language.'[26] She also points out that in Burley at least there was 'a concern with special sorts of difficulties in evaluating consequences or inferences as a result of the disputational context in which the inferences occur.'[27]

My own view is that there is probably something to be said for all these accounts. Insofar as the treatises described a routine to be followed in class-room disputations, the purpose could only have been that of testing a student's skill in formal logic, since truth was explicitly not an issue;[28] but the authors and readers of such treatises obviously welcomed the opportunity to discuss other matters in some depth. Paul himself was particularly concerned with the difference between use and mention, as will be seen from many of his sophisms. One must also bear in mind the often-noted link between treatises on obligations and treatises on insolubles. They go together not only in Paul, but in Swyneshed, Albert of Saxony and Strode, to mention but three names. This suggests a general interest in discussing all kinds of paradoxes, both semantic and non-semantic. Whatever the final answer is, reading Paul of Venice should help us to arrive at it, since his *Tractatus de Obligationibus* is a compendium of all the main views current in the second half of the fourteenth century.

A Note about this edition

I have used a microfilm of the Vatican manuscript and the Bodleian Library copy of the printed edition, as well as photocopies of both texts supplied by the Editor, P.T. Geach.

The differences between the two texts are minor, though they are enough to show that the printed edition was not based on the Vatican manuscript. Where a choice had to be made, I have followed the manuscript unless the reading in the edition was obviously preferable.

I have listed all significant variants in the critical apparatus. I have not noted simple inversions and transpositions which do not affect the sense, obvious scribal errors, and useless repetitions of words or phrases. I have ignored the frequent cases in which the manuscript has '*ille*' in place of the edition's '*iste*' (or vice versa), and the edition has '*ergo*' in place of the manuscript's '*igitur*' (or vice versa). I have also ignored a number of places

---

[25] See Spade, 'Some theories', pp. 1–2, for an account of the literature, and throughout for a defence of his thesis about counterfactual reasoning.

[26] See Stump, 'Roger Swyneshed', pp. 169–174: 'The purpose and function of obligations', p. 171 n. 45 is particularly important for her discussion of Spade's thesis.

[27] Stump in *CH*, p. 328.

[28] For an account of the distinction between doctrinal disputations, which were designed to arrive at the truth of some claim, and obligational disputations, see E.J. Ashworth, 'Renaissance man as logician: Josse Clichtove (1472–1543) on disputations', *History and Philosophy of Logic*, 7 (1986), 15–29.

where the manuscript has *'huius'* (with no additional sign of contraction) in place of the edition's *'huiusmodi'*.

The spelling has been standardized except for the forms 'Sortes' (for 'Socrates') and 'Parisius' as a locative.

A Note about this translation

Medieval logicians frequently used words drawn from common speech in a special, technical sense. A prime example of this practice is the word *'obligatio'* itself which in non-logical contexts has much the same force as the English 'obligation'. In order to focus attention on the technical aspect of Paul's terminology I have not translated the word *'obligatio'*, nor have I translated such words as *'positio'*, *'admissio'*, *'depositio'* and *'suppositio'*. In addition I have retained the Latin words *'obligatum'*, *'admissum'*, *'positum'*, and *'depositum'*, partly for the reason already given, and partly for ease of expression, since there are no precisely corresponding terms in English. An *obligatum* is the proposition put forward by the opponent at the beginning of an obligational disputation, and which has been admitted by the respondent to be a legitimate starting-point. An *admissum* is the proposition so put forward which has been admitted. A *positum* is the proposition put forward by the opponent at the beginning of an obligational disputation with the proviso that, if admitted, it must be granted. A *depositum* is put forward with the proviso that it must be denied.

I have coined the term 'deposit' to express the activity of putting forward a proposition with the proviso that it must be denied, since I could not find an appropriate English word which could be paired with 'posit' in the way that *'ponere'* and *'deponere'* are paired in Latin. I also use the term 'imposit' for *'imponere'*, i.e. the activity of putting forward a new meaning for a term or proposition. However, I translate *'supponere'* as 'assume' rather than as 'supposit' in order to avoid confusion with the more usual employment of that term in medieval logic.

I have translated *'Nihil est tibi positum'* and other similar propositions with present-tense verbs. ' . . . *est tibi positum'* could be read as 'was posited to you', but it could also be read as ' . . . is the *positum* put to you'. I have compromised by using 'is posited to you', which seems to suit most contexts.

Strictly speaking both *'sequens'* and *'repugnans'* should be expanded in English to read ' . . . following from a previous proposition or propositions' and ' . . . inconsistent with a previous proposition or propositions'. I decided that these expansions would make my translation too wordy in comparison with the Latin.

In other matters I have tended to follow the usages of Patricia Clarke in her translation of *Logica Magna Part 1 Fascicule 7*, though I found it more convenient to retain the verb 'doubt' for *'dubitare'*.

Acknowledgements

I would like to thank Rega Wood for her advice on editing Latin texts; Francesco Bottin, C.H. Kneepkens and Eleonore Stump for the generous way in which they have shared their research with me; Paul Vincent Spade not only for generously sharing his research with me over the years but also for reading and criticizing my first draft; and the Editor of the series, P.T. Geach, who persuaded me to undertake this task, and who gave me invaluable help with tricky points of translation and interpretation.

Finally, I owe a great debt of gratitude to Alexander Broadie who undertook the thankless task of copy-editing my typescript.

I would also like to thank the Social Sciences and Humanities Research Council of Canada for the research grants which enabled me to visit libraries in Oxford, Cambridge, London and Cracow, and for the Leave Fellowship which enabled me to complete this project.

SIGLA ET ABBREVIATIONES

M = Codex manuscriptus Vaticanus Latinus 2132 (saec.xv, ante an. 1443).

M^2 significat lectionem aut ab ipsomet scriptore aut ab alia manu correctam esse.

E = Editio typographica Venetiis 1499.

add. = addidit.

corr. = correxit.

in marg. = in margine.

om. = omisit.

s.lin. = supra lineam.

⟨. . .⟩ includunt verba ab editrice addita.

SIGNS AND ABBREVIATIONS USED IN THE TRANSLATION

⟨. . .⟩ enclose words added by the translator.

ABBREVIATIONS COMMON TO THE EDITION AND THE TRANSLATION

R = Responsum, Reply
O = Obiectio, Objection

A sequence of numerals and symbols is used to abbreviate explanatory headings. For instance ⟨1R2OR⟩ would abbreviate either 'Responsum ad obiectionem ad secundum responsum ad primum argumentum' or 'Reply to the objection against the second reply to the first argument'.

DE OBLIGATIONIBUS[1]

---

[1] De Obligationibus] Incipiunt obligationes M

⟨PARS PRIMA: QUATTUOR ARTICULI⟩

(216^{va}M, 177^{ra}E) Tractaturus de obligationibus quattuor articulos propono in serie procedendi in sequentibus viam radiantes:

In primo ponentur quorumdam terminorum descriptiones.

In secundo praeambulae suppositiones.

In tertio adnectentur[2] regulares observationes.

In quarto concludentur utiles propositiones.

⟨*Articulus Primus: Descriptiones Terminorum*⟩

⟨I⟩ Quantum ergo[3] ad primum, sit haec prima descriptio:
Positio est enuntiatio composita implicite vel explicite ex posito et signis positionis. Verbi gratia: haec tota oratio

Pono tibi istam: 'Tu es Romae'

est positio. Ly .Tu es Romae. est positum. Signa[4] positionis sunt ista: 'pono'[5], 'sit rei veritas', 'sit ita', et huiusmodi.

Et notanter dicitur 'implicite vel explicite', quia aliqua est positio quae non habet huiusmodi signa explicite, sicut quaelibet talis:

Moveatur Sortes;

Alteretur B. calidum;

vel

Stet oppositum consequentis cum antecedente.

Verumtamen habent implicite huiusmodi signa. Prima enim subordinatur uni istarum:

Pono quod Sortes moveatur,

vel

Pono tibi istam: 'Sortes movetur';

et sic quaelibet aliarum modo proposito[6].

---

[2] adnectentur] autem E
[3] ergo]autem E
[4] Signa]autem *add*.E
[5] pono]tibi istam *add*.E
[6] proposito]consimili E

⟨PART ONE. FOUR SECTIONS.⟩

In order to treat of *obligationes* I propose four sections which, in sequence, will shed light on the way of proceeding in the following:
 1. Informal definitions of terms.[1]
 2. Preliminary assumptions.
 3. Rules.
 4. Useful theses.

⟨*Section One: Informal Definitions of Terms.*⟩
⟨I⟩ First section, first informal definition: A *positio* is a statement implicitly or explicitly formulated from the *positum* and the marks of a *positio*.[2] For instance, this entire sentence:
 I posit this to you: 'You are in Rome',
is a *positio*. The expression 'You are in Rome' is the *positum*. The marks of a *positio* are these: 'I posit', 'Let it be true', 'Let it be the case', and so forth.

It should be noted that I say 'implicitly or explicitly', because there can be a *positio* which does not contain explicit marks of this sort, as in the following cases:
 Let Socrates be moved,
 Let degree B of heat be altered,
or
 Let the opposite of the conclusion be consistent with the premiss.[3]
These statements do indeed implicitly contain marks of the appropriate sort. The first is subordinated to one of these sentences:
 I posit that Socrates is moved
or
 I posit this to you: 'Socrates is moved';
and the same holds for each of the other examples.

---

[1] Albert of Saxony, Marsilius of Inghen, and William Buser all began with *Descriptiones*, and all used the same list of nine. Albert's list is ordered as follows: 1. Obligatio; 2. Obligatum; 3. Tempus obligationis; 4. Pertinens; 5. Impertinens; 6. Pertinens obligationi tantum; 7. Pertinens obligationi et admissioni simul; 8. Pertinens obligato tantum; 9. Pertinens obligato et bene concesso vel concessis, bene negato vel bene negatis. Marsilius and Buser alter the list only by placing 'impertinens' ninth. See Albert of Saxony, *Perutilis Logica* (Venetiis, 1522. Reprinted: Hildesheim, New York: Georg Olms, 1974) fol. 46va–47ra; Marsilius of Inghen, *Tractatus de Obligationibus*, Cracow, Biblioteka Jagiellońska MS 2602, fols. 70^v–72^v; and William Buser, *Obligationes*, Oxford, Bodleian Library MS Canon.Class.Lat.278, fols. 72ra–72vb.

The main difference between Paul's list and those mentioned above is that Paul begins with *positio* and related notions which did not appear in Albert's list, and he leaves the lengthy and important discussion of *obligatio* to seventh place. This difference in organization reflects a difference in doctrine. For Albert and the others, the definition of *obligatio* was just a general

Ex quibus sequitur quod aliqua est positio quae est idem cum posito, sicut patet de illa:

   Moveatur Sortes,

quae simul est positio, cum subordinetur uni positioni, et positum, cum tale admissum postmodum concedatur⁷, congruitate servata.

⟨II⟩ Secunda descriptio est ista: Positum est enuntiatio implicite vel explicite signis positionis (217ʳᵃM) immediate coniuncta.

Ponitur hic et superius 'enuntiatio'⁸ loco generis; 'implicite vel explicite' propter causam dictam. Dicitur autem 'immediate', quia si poneretur ista:

   Omnis homo est animal,

ista:

   Homo est animal

non esset posita licet esset sequens, sed ista solummodo

   Omnis homo est animal (177ʳᵇE)

quae suis signis est immediate coniuncta.

⟨III⟩ Tertia descriptio est ista: Depositio est enuntiatio implicite vel explicite composita ex deposito et signis depositionis. Verbi gratia:

   Depono tibi istam: 'Tu es homo'.

Haec tota oratio vocatur depositio; ly .Depono tibi istam. dicuntur signa depositionis; et 'Tu es homo' dicitur depositum.

⟨IV⟩ Quarta descriptio est ista: Depositum est enuntiatio implicite vel explicite immediate coniuncta signis depositionis.

Declaretur⁹ haec descriptio sicut et secunda.

⟨V⟩ Quinta descriptio est ista: Admissio est enuntiatio implicite vel explicite composita ex admisso et signis admissionis. Verbi gratia:

   Admitto illam: 'Tu es Romae'.

Haec tota oratio dicitur admissio; 'Tu es Romae' dicitur admissum; et illa duo 'admitto illam' dicuntur signa admissionis.

Et notanter dicitur 'implicite vel explicite', quia stat admissionem esse sine admisso dicendo

---

⁷ concedatur]conceditur E
⁸ enuntiatio] *om*.E
⁹ Declaretur]declaratur E

---

formula which could be used to generate the definition of *positio* by certain simple substitutions, such as 'marks of *positio*' for 'marks of *obligatio*'. In Paul's view, as will be seen from Definition 7, the relationship between *obligatio* and *positio* was more complex; and it is possible that he began with *positio* in order to underline the sharp distinction he made between *obligatio* and its species.

² For the antecedents of this definition, see note 13 on the third definition of *obligatio*.

³ Here Paul seems to be expanding some remarks by Ralph Strode, *Obligationes* in *Consequentie Strodi etc*. (Venetiis, 1517 fol. 78ʳᵇ: 'Sed certificatio fit communiter per verbum subiunctivi modi, ut cum dicitur "Stet oppositum consequentis cum antecedente" vel "Transeat A punctus B lineam" vel "Alteretur Sortes sic vel sic"; et solet talis certificatio reputari vel sustineri ut positio. . . .'

From these remarks it follows that there can be a *positio* which is identical with a *positum*, as is obvious from the example

Let Socrates be moved.

This is at one and the same time a *positio*, because it is subordinate to a *positio*, and a *positum*, because once it has been admitted it can be granted, allowing for the appropriate grammatical changes.

⟨II⟩ Second informal definition: A *positum* is a statement which immediately follows the marks of a *positio*, either implicitly or explicitly.

Both here and above 'statement' is used in place of the genus; and 'implicitly or explicitly' for the reason already given. 'Immediately' is used, because if

Every human being is an animal

were posited, this:

⟨A⟩ human being is an animal

would not be the *positum*, although it would follow from it. Only this ⟨is the *positum*⟩:

Every human being is an animal,

because it immediately follows the appropriate marks.

⟨III⟩ Third informal definition: A *depositio* is a statement implicitly or explicitly formulated from the *depositum* and the marks of a *depositio*. For instance:

I deposit this to you: 'You are a human being'.

This whole sentence is called a *depositio*; the words 'I deposit this to you' are called the marks of a *depositio*; and 'You are a human being' is called a *depositum*.

⟨IV⟩ Fourth informal definition: A *depositum* is a statement which immediately follows the marks of a *depositio* either implicitly or explicitly.

This definition should be explained in the same way as the second.

⟨V⟩ Fifth informal definition: An *admissio* is a statement implicitly or explicitly formulated from the *admissum* and the marks of an *admissio*.[4] For instance:

I admit this: 'You are in Rome'.

This whole sentence is called an *admissio*; 'You are in Rome' is called an *admissum*; and these ⟨three words⟩ 'I admit this' are called the marks of an *admissio*.

It should be noted that I say 'implicitly or explicitly' because it is possible for an *admissio* to exist without an *admissum*, as when one says

---

[4] Note that not every *positum* was admissible: for details see rule 1 and thesis 6. Other authors did not give a separate account of *admissio*, but took it for granted that everyone knew what it was.

Admissio was the second step in an obligational disputation, being preceded by *positio* (or *depositio*, etc.) and succeeded by *propositio* (not defined here) in which the initial *positum* was repeated. Peter of Candia put the matter clearly when he wrote: 'Advertendum autem est quod quandocumque dicitur "Pono tibi istam propositionem", si sit possibilis semper respondetur per hoc verbum "admitto". Quando autem postea dicitur "Tibi propono eadem", debeo respondere per hoc verbum "concedo".' See Peter of Candia, *Obligationes*, Oxford, Bodleian Library MS Canon.Class.Lat. 278, fol. 65ra.

Admitto hoc[10] verum.

Est[11] implicite[12], sed explicite[13] nullo modo.

⟨VI⟩ Sexta descriptio: Admissum est enuntiatio implicite vel explicite signis admissionis immediate coniuncta.

Patet haec descriptio ex prioribus.

Ex praedictis[14] sequitur quod nihil est positum, depositum vel admissum nisi per habitudinem ad signa quibus implicite vel explicite immediate coniungitur.

Item sequitur quod eadem propositio quae nunc est posita, alias erit deposita ex sola mutatione suorum signorum. Quare[15] etc.

⟨VII⟩ Septima[16] descriptio et principalis in tota materia est ista: Obligatio est relatio limitans ad aliquod enuntiabile vel sibi consimile[17] aliqualiter sustinendum.

Volo dicere quod obligatio est relatio, qua quis sustinere tenetur enuntiabile aliquod affirmative vel negative.

Ponitur enim 'relatio' loco generis, quia ly .obligatio. non videtur esse in alio[18] praedicamento quam in praedicamento relationis.

⟨1⟩ Non enim est in praedicamento substantiae, ut patet, quia non est formaliter materia, forma, aut compositum.

⟨2⟩ Nec in praedicamento quantitatis, quia non quantitas continua[19]; nec quantitas discreta, quia aut numerus, quod non videtur possibile, aut oratio, quod aliqualiter verisimile apparet. Sed probo quod non, quia si obligatio esset oratio, aut igitur ⟨i⟩ positio sola aut depositio, aut ⟨ii⟩ admissio sola, aut ⟨iii⟩ compositum ex hiis.

⟨i⟩ Non est dicendum quod positio aut depositio sola, quia positio sine admissione non obligat, similiter nec depositio sine huiusmodi.

⟨ii⟩ Nec etiam admissio sola, quia si aliquid admitterem[20], non praecedente positione aut depositione, non essem[21] obligatus.

⟨iii⟩ Nec est dicendum tertium, videlicet quod positio et admissio simul constituant obligationem aliquam[22].

---

[10] hoc]haec E
[11] Est]esset E
[12] implicite]explicite M,E *correxi*
[13] explicite]implicite M,E *correxi*
[14] praedictis]quibus E
[15] Quare etc.]*om*.E
[16] Septima]Alia E
[17] consimile]simile E
[18] alio]aliquo E
[19] quia . . . continua]continua ut patet M
[20] admitterem]admitteretur E
[21] essem]esset E
[22] aliquam]*om*.E

I admit this truth.

⟨The *admissum*⟩ exists implicitly but in no way explicitly.

⟨VI⟩ Sixth informal definition: An *admissum* is a statement which immediately follows the marks of an *admissio*, either implicitly or explicitly.

The previous definitions make this one obvious.

From what has been said it can be inferred that nothing counts as a *positum*, *depositum*, or *admissum* except by virtue of a relationship to the marks which it immediately follows, either implicitly or explicitly.

It can also be inferred that the same proposition which is now posited will at another time be deposited solely by virtue of a change in the appropriate marks. Therefore etc.

⟨VII⟩ The seventh and most important informal definition for this entire topic is the following: An *obligatio* is a relation limiting one to uphold some statement, or its equiform, in some way.[5]

I mean to say that an *obligatio* is a relation through which someone has to uphold a statement affirmatively or negatively.

'Relation' is put in place of the genus because the expression '*obligatio*' seems to belong to no category other than that of relation.

⟨1⟩ It does not belong to the category of substance, as is obvious, because it is not formally matter, form, or a composite.

⟨2⟩ Nor does it belong to the category of quantity, because it is not a continuous quantity. Nor is it a discrete quantity, because it would be either number, which does not seem possible, or speech, which does seem somewhat plausible. But I can prove that this is not the case. If an *obligatio* were a speech,[6] it would either be ⟨i⟩ a *positio* alone or a *depositio*; or ⟨ii⟩ an *admissio* alone, or ⟨iii⟩ a composite of these.

⟨i⟩ One should not say that it is a *positio* or a *depositio* alone, because a *positio* without an *admissio* does not obligate; and the same holds for a *depositio*.[7]

⟨ii⟩ Nor can it be an *admissio* alone, since if I were to admit something in the absence of a preceding *positio* or *depositio*, I would not be obligated.

⟨iii⟩ Nor can one adopt the third choice, whereby an *obligatio* is made out of a *positio* and an *admissio* together.

---

[5] This definition appears to be original. Notice that Paul omits '*dubitative*' as one of the ways in which a proposition could be sustained. Cf.Marsilius, op.cit., fol. 71^r; Buser, op.cit., fol. 72ra. Cf. Definition 4 below.

[6] The view that an *obligatio* was an *oratio* was found in various authors: for details, see below, notes 11 and 13. I use the word 'speech' in this paragraph because of the reference to Aristotle, *Categories* 6, 4b20–25.

[7] A similar sequence of arguments to (i) and (ii) is found in Peter of Mantua, *Logica* ([Venice] 1492), sig.G ii^{rb}. About point (iii) and the claim that there can be no *obligatio* on the grounds that *positio* and *admissio* can never exist at the same time, given the disappearance of the first utterance, he comments (sig.G ii^{rb}–^{va}) 'In hac arte praesupponimus gratia argumenti eandem propositionem remanere vel unam sic significantem sicut significavit illa quam intendebat ponere ponens.'

⟨a⟩ Nam corrupta positione et admissione, remanente tempore obligationis remanet obligatio; sed tunc non remanet talis enuntiatio composita ex positione et admissione, igitur etc.

⟨b⟩ Secundo sic. Et pono tibi istam: Tu es Romae, quae manet[23] tibi posita praecise pro tempore admissionis; quam admittas. Facta admissione, quaero numquid sis obligatus vel non.

Si non, habeo intentum, videlicet quod ex positione et admissione non resultat obligatio tamquam ex partibus integralibus.

Si sic, contra: ista:

Tu es Romae,

non manet tibi posita post tempus admissionis, igitur tunc non es obligatus. Consequentia tenet, quia tunc aliter ex sola admissione consurgeret obligatio, cuius oppositum est manifestum ex dictis.

Nec est dicendum quod dum admittitur[24] est obligatio. Hoc non est verum, quia non est obligatio aliqua nisi facta admissione; aliter sequeretur[25] quod aliqua obligatio esset, et nullus obligaretur, immo quod nullum obligatum esset.

Et si dicitur quod aliquis obligatur dum fit[26] talis admissio, sequitur ista conclusio, quod aliquis obligatur pro hoc instanti et tamen poterit esse (217^{rb}M) quod ille numquam obligabatur pro eodem instanti. Patet dato quod pro isto instanti compleverit mediam partem[27] illius verbi 'admitto'. Quia ergo poterit non complere, poterit non admisisse illud, et per consequens nec[28] obligatum fuisse.

⟨3⟩ Item non est dicendum quod obligatio sit in praedicamento qualitatis, cum non sit formaliter qualitas corporalis nec spiritualis. Consideretur namque species praedicamenti qualitatis, et videbitur in nulla earum formaliter collocari.

⟨4⟩ Item nec in praedicamento actionis vel passionis, quia actio prout est praedicamentum est respectus dicens a quo esse aliud; et passio dicit esse ab alio. Modo patet quod obligatio non est[29] primum nec secundum volenti subtiliter speculari.

Oppositum huius ponit unus magister dicens quod obligatio est in praedicamento actionis; et non adsignat aliam causam nisi quia est actus obligandi. Sed

---

[23] manet]maneat E
[24] admittitur]admittit E
[25] sequeretur]sequitur E
[26] fit]sit E
[27] mediam partem]mediantem M,E, *correxi*
[28] nec]non E
[29] est]dicit M

⟨a⟩ If the *positio* and the *admissio* pass away, the *obligatio* still remains during the period of the *obligatio*; but in this case no statement formulated from the *positio* and the *admissio* still exists. Therefore etc.

⟨b⟩ Second: I posit this to you: You are in Rome.
It is to stay posited to you exactly for the period of the *admissio*. You admit this. After the *admissio* has been made, I ask whether you are obligated or not.

If not, I have proved my point, namely that an *obligatio* does not result from a *positio* and an *admissio* as if from integral parts.

If the answer is 'Yes', I argue against it. This proposition
    You are in Rome
does not stay posited to you after the period of the *admissio*; therefore you are not then obligated. The inference holds, because otherwise an *obligatio* would arise solely from an *admissio*, and the opposite of this is obvious from what has been said.

Nor should one say that an *obligatio* exists while the *admissio* is being made. This is not true, because no *obligatio* exists unless an *admissio* has been made. Otherwise it would follow that some *obligatio* would exist without anyone being obligated; indeed, without any *obligatum* existing.

And if it is said that someone is obligated while he makes such an *admissio*, this conclusion follows: someone may be obligated at this moment and yet it may later be true that he was never obligated at that very moment. This is obvious, given that he had completed just half of the word 'admit' at that moment. Because he will be in a position not to complete ⟨the word⟩, he will be in a position not to have made an *admissio* and, as a result, not to have been obligated.

⟨3⟩ Likewise one should not say that an *obligatio* belongs to the category of quality, since it is not formally either a corporeal quality or a spiritual. If you consider the species falling under the category of quality, you will see that ⟨an *obligatio*⟩ cannot be formally allocated to any of them.

⟨4⟩ Likewise it does not belong to the category of action or passion. Action, as a category, is that in respect of which another thing's existence is explained, and passion is that which is said to arise from another thing. But it is clear to anyone wishing to examine the matter with discrimination that an *obligatio* is not the first or the second.

A certain master[8] put forward the opposite of this when he said that an *obligatio* did belong to the category of action; and he gave no reason other than that there is an act of obligating. But this is a scandalous reason, since it

---

[8] 'Unus magister' must be William Buser who, in rejecting the first three definitions of *obligatio* (see below) wrote: 'Omnes tres definitiones deficiunt in hoc quia non dantur per genus proprium obligationis, quia est de praedicamento actionis, cum sit actus obligandi.' Buser, op.cit., fol. 72ra. Marsilius made no similar remark, though he did describe *obligatio* as an *actus*: op.cit., fol. 70^v. Peter of Mantua also wrote: 'Iste terminus "obligatio" est de praedicamento actionis' (op.cit., sig.G ii^{rb}; and it was he who used the example of heat in explaining the nature of *obligatio* as an act: 'Si obligatio est, aliquis obligatur. Patet consequentia, quia sequitur: "Calefactio est, igitur calefaciens est".' Peter of Mantua, op.cit., sig.G ii^{ra}.

turpis causa est, quia per idem caliditas est[30] in praedicamento actionis, quia est actus calefaciendi. Consequens est falsum, quia est in praedicamento qualitatis.

⟨5⟩ Item non est dicendum (177^{va}E) quod ly .obligatio. sit in aliis praedicamentis, videlicet 'ubi', 'quando', 'situs' et 'habitus[31]', ut patet cuilibet consideranti rationes formales obligationis et talium praedicamentorum.

Dicatur ergo quod[32] obligatio est in praedicamento relationis, et est formaliter relatio fundata in obligante et obligato: in obligante, ratione positionis vel depositionis; in obligato, vero ratione admissionis. Non enim videtur quare plus in obligato quam in obligante et e contra, cum aeque consurgat ab actu obligantis, qui est positio vel depositio, sicut ab actu obligati, qui est admissio.

Ex hoc tamen non habetur quod semper obligatio consurgat ex positione et admissione; et hoc ubi est repugnantia non permittens, ut patet in ponendo aliquid et illud non maneat positum nisi pro tempore admissionis. Ubi tamen tolleretur haec repugnantia vel alia similis potens impedire, concedo semper ex positione vel depositione simul et admissione obligationem oriri, non quidem existentem enuntiationem[33] ut dictum est, sed solum relationem modo declarato. Et hoc est verisimile quia obligans refertur ad obligatum et e contra, et non nisi per obligationem quae debet[34] esse utriusque relatio.

Ex praedictis sequitur quod licet[35] idem sit ponens vel[36] deponens et obligans, tamen prius tempore est ponens vel deponens quam obligans. Patet quia nullus est obligans nisi facta admissione. Similiter idem est admittens et obligatus, et per[37] prius admittens quam obligatus.

Item sequitur quod quam primo[38] est obligans tam primo est obligatus et e contra. Patet, quia in fine admissionis est unus primo obligans et alter primo obligatus.

Ex eisdem sequitur quasdam descriptiones obligationis insufficienter processisse.

⟨1⟩ Prima fuit[39] ista: Obligatio est oratio composita ex signis obligationis et posito vel deposito una cum admissione qua tenetur obligatus in tempore obligationis concedere positum et negare depositum.

---

[30] est]esset E
[31] et 'habitus']om.M
[32] quod]ly add.E
[33] enuntiationem]talem add.E
[34] debet]oportet E
[35] licet] om.E
[36] vel]et E
[37] per]om.E
[38] primo] primum E
[39] fuit]est M

would also make heat belong to the category of action, for there is an act of heating. This conclusion is false, for ⟨heat⟩ belongs to the category of quality.

⟨5⟩ Likewise one should not say that the expression '*obligatio*' belongs to any other category, i.e. 'where', 'when', 'position' and 'state', as will be obvious to anyone considering the formal characteristics of an *obligatio* and of these categories.

Let it be said then, that an *obligatio* belongs to the category of relation, and it is formally speaking a relation based on the obligater and the obligated. It is based on the obligater, by virtue of the *positio* or the *depositio*; and on the obligated, by reason of his *admissio*. Nor does it seem to rest more on the obligated than on the obligater, or the reverse, since it arises as much from the act of the obligater, which is the *positio* or the *depositio*, as from the act of the obligated, which is the *admissio*.

However, it does not follow from this that an *obligatio* always arises from the *positio* and the *admissio*, for there may be an inconsistency which debars this, as is clear when something is posited with the proviso that it will be the *positum* only during the period of the *admissio*. However, when this inconsistency, or some similar impediment is removed, I always grant that an *obligatio* arises from the *positio* or the *depositio*, together with the *admissio*; not indeed as an existent statement, as has been said, but only as a relation of the sort described. And this is a plausible account because the obligater is concerned with the one obligated, and the reverse. Such a state of affairs can only come about through the *obligatio*, which must be the relation between them.

From what has been said it follows that although the one who posits or deposits and the obligater are the same person, the one who posits or deposits temporally precedes the obligater.[9] This is clear because no one is an obligater unless an *admissio* has been made. Similarly, the same person is the one who admits and the one who is obligated, but he admits before he is obligated.

It also follows that when the obligater begins his task, so does the one who is obligated, and vice versa. This is obvious, because as the *admissio* ends one person begins to obligate and the other to be obligated.

From the same remarks it follows that some of the informal definitions of an *obligatio* are inadequate.[10]

⟨1⟩ The first was this: An *obligatio* is a spoken sentence formulated from the marks of an *obligatio* and the *positum* or the *depositum*, together with the *admissio*, by means of which the one who is obligated is bound during the period of the *obligatio* to grant the *positum* and deny the *depositum*.[11]

---

[9] For these remarks on time, cf. Peter of Mantua, op.cit. sig.G ii^{rb}.

[10] Both Marsilius and Buser have a lengthy section in which they examine and reject the following three definitions of *obligatio* before they accept the fourth: Marsilius, op. cit., fols. 70^v–71^r; Buser, op.cit., fol. 72ra.

[11] This is Buser's first definition and Marsilius's second. For other versions see: Roger Swyneshed in Paul Vincent Spade, 'Roger Swyneshed's *Obligationes*: edition and comments', *Archives d'histoire doctrinale et littéraire du moyen âge*, 44 (1977), p. 251, §6; Richard

Haec descriptio falsa est, quia obligatio non est oratio sed relatio ut dictum est.

⟨2⟩ Secunda descriptio fuit ista: Obligatio est quaedam ars mediante qua opponens ligat[40] respondentem ad sui voluntatem.

Haec descriptio falsa est:

⟨i⟩ Primo quia obligatio non est ars, cum obligans non sit formaliter artifex nec obligatus artificiatum aliquod.

⟨ii⟩ Secundo quia opponens non ligat respondentem; sed potius respondens[41] ligat seipsum, quia per positionem vel depositionem non ligatur respondens sed bene per admissionem. Admissio autem est actus respondentis[42]; positio autem vel depositio est actus opponentis.

⟨3⟩ Tertia descriptio fuit ista: Obligatio est oratio composita ex signis obligationis et obligato.

Verbi gratia, ait auctor huius descriptionis, dicat opponens respondenti
Pono tibi istam: 'Tu sedes.' (217^{va}M)
Ista tota oratio
Pono tibi istam: 'Tu sedes'
vocatur obligatio[43]; ly .Pono tibi istam. vocantur signa obligationis; et ly .Tu sedes. vocatur obligatum.

Descriptio in se est falsa quia obligatio non est oratio sed relatio. Declaratio vero istius descriptionis continet tria falsa:

⟨i⟩ Primum est quod ly .Pono tibi istam:'Tu sedes'.sit obligatio, quia dato quod obligatio esset oratio, adhuc obligatio numquam esset positio, sed compositum ex positione vel depositione et admissione. Numquam enim aliquis obligatur nisi admittat.

⟨ii⟩ Secundum falsum est quod ly .Pono tibi istam. sunt signa obligationis, quia sicut ly .Pono tibi istam: 'Tu sedes'. non est obligatio, ita ly .Pono tibi istam. non sunt signa obligationis in positione illa. Sed facta positione et admissione, tunc primo signa positionis et signa admissionis dicuntur signa obligationis.

---

[40] ligat]obligat E
[41] respondens]opponens E
[42] respondentis]et *add*.M
[43] obligatio]et *add*. E

Lavenham in 'Richard Lavenham's *Obligationes* (Edition and comments by Paul Vincent Spade)', *Rivista Critica di Storia della Filosofia*, 33 (1978), p. 227 §1; Strode, op.cit., fol. 78ra; Peter of Candia, op.cit., fol. 65ra. Cf. John of Holland, *Obligationes*, Cracow, Biblioteka Jagiellońska MS 2132 fol. 103^v. Marsilius rejected the definition because it did not apply to *dubie positio*; Buser rejected it because it did not apply to *impositio* or *petitio*. Paul could not employ these arguments because he did not recognize *dubie positio* etc. as separate species of *obligatio*: see below, section 2, assumption 8.

This informal definition is false, because an *obligatio* is not a speech, but a relation, as has been said.

⟨2⟩ The second informal definition was this. An *obligatio* is an art whereby the opponent binds the respondent to his will.[12]

This informal definition is false:

⟨i⟩ first, because an *obligatio* is not an art, since the one who obligates is not formally a craftsman, nor is the one who is obligated an artifact;

⟨ii⟩ second, because the opponent does not bind the respondent, but rather the respondent binds himself. He is not bound by the *positio* or the *depositio*, but by the *admissio*. But the *admissio* is the act of the respondent; whereas the *positio* or the *depositio* is the act of the opponent.

⟨3⟩ Third informal definition: An *obligatio* is a spoken sentence formulated from the marks of an *obligatio* and the *obligatum*.[13]

For instance, says the author of this definition, let the opponent say to the respondent:

I posit this to you: 'You are sitting down'.
This whole sentence:

I posit this to you: 'You are sitting down'
is called the *obligatio*; the words 'I posit this to you' are called the marks of an *obligatio*; and the expression 'You are sitting down' is called the *obligatum*.

The definition in itself is false because an *obligatio* is not a speech but a relation. Moreover, the explanation of the definition contains three falsehoods:

⟨i⟩ First falsehood: The expression 'I posit to you: "You are sitting down"' is an *obligatio*. Even if an *obligatio* were a spoken sentence, an *obligatio* would never be a *positio*, but a combination of a *positio* or a *depositio* and an *admissio*. No one is ever obligated unless he makes an *admissio*.

⟨ii⟩ Second falsehood: The words 'I posit this to you' are the marks of an *obligatio*. Just as the expression 'I posit this to you: "You are sitting down"' is not an *obligatio*, so the words 'I posit this to you' are not the marks of an *obligatio* in that *positio*. But when the *positio* and the *admissio* have been completed, then the marks of a *positio* and the marks of an *admissio* can first be called the marks of an *obligatio*.

---

[12] This is Buser's second definition and Marsilius's third. For other versions see: [*Obligationes*], Oxford, Bodleian Library MS *Lat. misc.e 79*, fol. 18ra; *De Obligationibus* in *Libellus Sophistarum ad Usum Oxoniensium [Lib.Soph.Oxon.]*, (Londoniis, 1510), sig.C vr; *De Obligationibus* in *Libellus Sophistarum ad Usum Cantabrigiensium [Lib.Soph.Cantab]*, (Londoniis, 1524), sig.C iv; Martinus Anglicus [*Obligationes*] Cracow, Biblioteka Jagiellońska MS 2602, fol. 127r; John Wyclif, *Tractatus de Logica*, edited by M.H. Dziewicki, Vol. I (London: Trübner & Co., 1893), p. 69.

Marsilius gave the essence of both Paul's arguments against this definition, but Buser gave only the second.

The opponent was the person who opened an obligational disputation. He had the task of proposing a series of propositions to the respondent. The respondent's only duty was to reply to each member of the series in accordance with the rules for such disputations.

[13] This is Buser's third definition and Marsilius's first. It has been omitted from the Cracow manuscript, but is found in the printed edition: *Tractatus de arte obligandi. Editus a magistro Petro de Alliaco* (Parisius, 1489) sig.A iira. However, the manuscript goes on to speak of three definitions, so the omission was obviously an error.

⟨iii⟩ Tertium dictum est falsum, videlicet quod 'Tu sedes' sit obligatum in positione illa. Nulla enim propositio vocatur obligatum nisi facta fuerit admissio. Quare etc.

⟨4⟩ Quarta descriptio fuit ista: Obligatio est praefixio alicuius enuntiabilis ad sustinendum secundum aliquem statum, videlicet affirmativum, negativum vel dubitativum[44].

Ista descriptio non valet. Nam dicendo

Propono tibi istam: 'Tu es animal',

haec tota oratio est praefixio alicuius enuntiabilis, videlicet .Homo est animal. ad sustinendum secundum aliquem statum, scilicet affirmativum, eo quod est digna sustineri secundum istum statum. Igitur descriptio non est convertibilis cum descripto, et per consequens descriptio ista non est sufficiens.

Auctor huius descriptionis contra tres praecedentes arguit ostendendo ipsarum insufficientiam ex hoc quia[45] non dantur[46] per genus proprium obligationis. Sed haec obiectio non procedit, quia in descriptionibus non expedit tale genus proprium adsignare. Secus est in definitionibus pure quidditativis. Unde in tertio *Physicorum* Philosophus describens motum ait: 'Motus est actus entis in potentia secundum quod in potentia', ubi patet quod ly .actus. qui ponitur ibi[47] loco (177^{vb}E) generis est terminus praedicamenti relationis; et non ly .motus[48]., sed praedicamenti passionis secundum aliquos, et secundum Commentatorem de genere termini ad quem, qui non potest esse relatio, etc[49]. Item quarto *Physicorum* Philosophus describens locum ait: 'Locus est terminus corporis continentis immobilis primum', ubi patet quod ly .locus. est de genere quantitatis et ly .terminus. de genere relativo[50]. Et ita consimile posset reperiri in multis locis philosophiae, eo quod naturalis philosophus non semper habet dare huiusmodi definitiones pure quidditativas.

⟨VIII⟩ Octava descriptio est ista: Obligatum est enuntiatio implicite vel explicite immediate coniuncta signis obligationis.

---

[44] dubitativum]dubium E
[45] quia]quod E
[46] dantur]dicantur E
[47] ibi]in E
[48] motus]modus sed praedicamenti motus M
[49] etc.]*om*.E
[50] relativo]relationis E

The definition comes from Albert of Saxony, op.cit., fol. 46va. 'Obligatio prout hic sumitur est oratio composita ex signis obligationis et obligato. Verbi gratia: dicat opponens respondenti: "Pono tibi illam 'Tu sedes'." Illa tota oratio "Pono tibi istam 'Tu sedes'" vocatur obligatio; et ly .pono tibi. vocantur signa obligationis; et ly .tu sedes. vocatur obligatum.'

Marsilius rejected this definition because it was too wide, and Buser because it did not manifest the nature of the defined. If one were to ask what the *obligatum* was, one would only get the reply that it was part of the *obligatio* 'et sic iterum revertitur quaestio prima, videlicet quid sit obligatio.' (Buser, loc.cit.)

Note that the very same definition is accepted in the *Logica Parva:* Paul of Venice, *Logica* ([Venice] 1472. Reprinted Hildesheim, New York: Georg Olms, 1970), p. 118.

⟨iii⟩ Third falsehood: 'You are sitting' is the *obligatum* in that *positio*. No proposition can be called an *obligatum* unless an *admissio* has been made. Therefore etc.

⟨4⟩ Fourth informal definition: An *obligatio* is a preface to some statement which shows that it should be upheld in some way, i.e. affirmatively, negatively, or with uncertainty.[14]

This informal definition does not hold. When one says

I propose this to you: 'You are an animal',[15]

this whole sentence is the preface to some statement, i.e. 'A human being is an animal', showing that it should be upheld in some way, i.e. affirmatively, given that it is worthy to be upheld in this way. Therefore the definition is not interchangeable with the thing defined, and as a result this informal definition is not adequate.

The author of this informal definition[16] argued against the three which precede it by revealing their inadequacy, which he based on the fact that they were not given in terms of the proper genus of an *obligatio*. But this objection does not work because in informal definitions it is not necessary to assign such a proper genus. It is quite otherwise with strict definitions. In *Physics* III.1. 201a 10 Aristotle, defining motion, said: 'Motion is the act of what exists potentially, in so far as it exists potentially.' Here it is obvious that the word 'act' which is put in place of the genus, is a term belonging to the category of relation; whereas the word 'motion' is not. It belongs to the category of passion according to some, and according to Averroes, to the genus of *terminus ad quem* which cannot be a relation.[17] Similarly in *Physics* IV.4. 212a 20 Aristotle, defining place, said: 'Place is the first motionless boundary of the containing body.' Here it is obvious that the word 'place' belongs to the genus of quantity and the word 'boundary' to the genus of relation. Similar examples can be found in many philosophical sources, since the natural philosopher does not always have to offer strict definitions.

⟨VIII⟩ Eighth informal definition: An *obligatum* is a statement which immediately follows the marks of an *obligatio* either implicitly or explicitly.

---

[14] This fourth definition was adopted by both Marsilius, who described it as *more antiquorum*, and Buser, who ascribed it to *primitivi*. It is found in Walter Burley: Romuald Green, *The Logical Treatise 'De obligationibus'. An Introduction with Critical Texts of William of Sherwood and Walter Burley*, (Franciscan Institute, forthcoming) 0.02; and in William Ockham, *Summa Logicae*, edited by Philotheus Boehner, Gedeon Gál, and Stephen Brown (St. Bonaventure, N.Y.: Franciscan Institute, 1974), p. 732. For a thirteenth century source, see Lambertus Marie de Rijk, 'Some thirteenth century tracts on the game of obligation', *Vivarium*, 12 (1974), p. 103: 'Per hoc patet quod positio est prefixio alicuius enuntiabilis ad sustinendum tamquam verum ut videatur quid inde sequatur.'

[15] Cf. Paul's remarks on the third definition of *obligatum*. His point may rest on the fact that if one grants 'You are an animal', one will then be committed to granting 'A human being is an animal', which follows from it. The definition of *obligatio* is too wide, because it turns the entire initial statement into a prefix, and turns a completely new statement into the *obligatum*.

[16] This argument is found in both Marsilius and Buser, though it is more clearly presented by the latter. As note 14 shows, neither claimed to be 'auctor huius descriptionis'.

[17] The Commentator is Averroes. For some relevant discussion by Averroes, see *Aristotelis de Physico Auditu libri octo cum Averrois Cordubensis variis in eosdem Commentariis*, (Venetiis, 1562: Reprinted, Frankfurt am Main: Minerva G.m.b.H., 1962), fol. 87^{ra-vb}. Note that in 1409

Hic ponitur 'enuntiatio' loco generis et non eiusdem cum descripto, quia non oportet ut dictum est. Unde ly .obligatum. est de genere relationis sicut ly .obligatio., et ly .enuntiatio. est de genere qualitatis.

Dicitur notanter 'implicite vel explicite' propter causas superius dictas; et 'immediate' similiter. Ultimo dicitur 'signis obligationis' et non 'positionis vel[51] depositionis aut admissionis', quia illa signa prius sunt signa positionis, depositionis, vel admissionis quam obligationis. Quam primo enim ex positione et admissione oritur relatio quae est obligatio, tam primo ista signa sunt signa obligationis; et hoc loquendo de prioritate durationis, quia forte prioritate naturae prius est obligatio quam illa sint signa obligationis, et prius illa sunt signa obligationis quam propositio aliqua sit obligatum.

Sed hic[52] est notandum de quo obligato adsignatur descriptio, quia in obligatione quattuor considerantur, videlicet, illud quod obligat; illud quod obligatur; illud a[53] quo vel ad quod obligatur; et obligatio. Illud quod obligat est ponens vel deponens. Illud quod obligatur est admittens. Illud vero a[54] quo vel ad quod fit obligatio est enuntiatio talis coniuncta. Obligatio vero (217^{vb}M) est relatio ut dictum est. De obligato, ergo, quod se habet in ratione termini obligationis non datur descriptio illa; sed solum de obligato quod se habet tamquam illud a quo vel ad quod fit obligatio, et illud non est nisi enuntiatio.

Ex ista descriptione cum alia immediate praecedente sequitur quod licet possibile sit positum aut depositum vel admissum esse obligatum; impossibile est tamen positionem, depositionem vel admissionem esse obligationem[55]. Patet prima pars eo quod idem quod est positum, depositum vel admissum sit obligatum. Secunda pars patet eo quod impossible est orationem aut enuntiationem esse relationem.

Item sequitur quod omnis descriptio sonans quod positio, depositio, impositio, petitio vel huiusmodi est obligatio est falsa et impossibilis, loquendo semper de tali obligatione quae obligat formaliter et relative, quia forte diceretur quod haec est obligatio, videlicet

    Obligo te ad istam: 'Tu es Romae.'

---

[51] vel] om.E
[52] hic]hoc M
[53] a]om.M
[54] a]om.M
[55] obligationem]obligationes E

Paul wrote *Expositio super VIII libros Physicorum necnon super commento Averrois*, a work which survives in four manuscripts and one printed edition: see Charles H. Lohr, 'Medieval Latin Aristotle commentaries: Authors Narcissus-Richardus', *Traditio*, 28 (1972), p. 318.

Here 'statement' is given in place of a genus, and it is not of the same sort as what is being defined. It does not have to be, as has been explained. The expression '*obligatum*' belongs to the genus of relation, as does the expression '*obligatio*'; and the expression 'statement' belongs to the genus of quality.

It should be noted that 'implicitly or explicitly' is added for the reasons given above; and so too for 'immediately'. Finally, I say 'marks of an *obligatio*' and not 'marks of a *positio* or a *depositio* or an *admissio*' because these marks are marks of a *positio*, a *depositio*, or an *admissio* before they are marks of an *obligatio*. The moment when the relation which is an *obligatio* arises from the *positio* and the *admissio* is the moment when these marks become the marks of an *obligatio*. In saying this, I am speaking of temporal priority, for perhaps by natural priority an *obligatio* exists before these marks are marks of an *obligatio*, and these are the marks of an *obligatio* before some proposition is an *obligatum*.

At this point one should note what kind of *obligatum* is being defined, since in an *obligatio* there are four things to be considered, i.e. that which obligates; that which is obligated; that by which or to which one is obligated; and the *obligatio* itself. That which obligates is the one who posits or deposits. That which is obligated is the one who admits. That by which or to which the *obligatio* is directed is the added statement. The *obligatio* itself is a relation, as has been said. The present definition is not concerned with the *obligatum* which is one of the relata of an *obligatio*, but only with the *obligatum* which plays the role of that by which or to which the *obligatio* is directed, and this is nothing other than the statement.

From this definition together with the other which immediately precedes it, it follows that although it is possible for a *positum* or a *depositum* or an *admissum* to be an *obligatum*, it is quite impossible for a *positio*, *depositio* or *admissio* to be an *obligatio*. The first clause is obvious because one and the same thing which is the *positum*, *depositum* or *admissum* is the *obligatum*. The second clause is obvious because it is impossible for a sentence or a statement to be a relation.

Likewise it follows that every definition which suggests that a *positio*, *depositio*, *impositio*, *petitio*, or anything like these, is an *obligatio* is false and impossible.[18] I speak here of the kind of *obligatio* which obligates formally and relationally, since it might perhaps be said that the following is an *obligatio*, namely:

I obligate you to this: 'You are in Rome'.

---

[18] Paul seems to be attacking all other authors here.

Sed de tali non est sermo, quia non est nisi positio quaedam non obligans, sicut[56] patet.

Ex eadem descriptione sequitur quasdam descriptiones obligati insufficienter similiter processisse:

⟨1⟩ Prima fuit ista: Obligatum est altera pars obligationis, vel oppositum depositi, ad quod concedendum infra tempus obligationis mediante obligatione et admissione respondens obligatur.

Ista descriptio insufficiens est:

⟨i⟩ Primo quia superflue ponitur ly .oppositum depositi., quia ex quo omne depositum admissum sine repugnantia est obligatum, non debet poni in descriptione obligati. Item[57] superflue ponitur ly .admissione., quia sola obligatione[58] quis tenetur respondere et non admissione, ut dictum est.

⟨ii⟩ Secundo ista descriptio est falsa in hoc quod ponit obligatum esse alteram partem obligationis, cum obligatum sit enuntiatio et obligatio relatio.

⟨iii⟩ Tertio arguo contra intentionem suam, dato adhuc quod obligatio sit oratio composita ex positione vel depositione et admissione. Nam omne depositum et admissum sine impedimento est obligatum; et tamen non est altera pars obligationis vel oppositum depositi ad quod concedendum infra tempus obligationis mediante obligatione et admissione respondens obligatur, quia suum oppositum est verum[59] cum nullum depositum sit concedendum sed negandum; et si sic, patet quod descriptio non est convertibilis cum descripto.

⟨2⟩ Secunda descriptio fuit ista: Obligatum est illa pars obligationis ad quam sustinendam secundum aliquem statum infra tempus obligationis mediante obligatione et admissione respondens obligatur. Haec descriptio damnatur[60] sicut prima: primo, propter falsitatem; secundo, propter superfluitatem.

⟨3⟩ Tertia descriptio fuit ista: Obligatum est[61] praefixum enuntiabile ad sustinendum secundum aliquem statum.

---

[56] sicut]bene *add*.E
[57] Item]similiter E
[58] obligatione]positione M
[59] verum]falsum M,E, *correxi*
[60] damnatur]datur E
[61] est]obligationis *add*.E

But I am not speaking of such an example, for it is nothing other than a *positio* which does not obligate, as is obvious.

From the same definition it follows that certain other informal definitions of the *obligatum* which have been put forward are inadequate.

⟨1⟩ First informal definition: An *obligatum* is the other clause of an *obligatio*, or the opposite of the *depositum*, which the respondent is obligated to grant during the period of the *obligatio* because of the *obligatio* and the *admissio*.[19]

This definition is inadequate:

⟨i⟩ first, because the expression 'the opposite of the *depositum*' is redundant. Since every *depositum* which is admitted without inconsistency is an *obligatum*, it should not be referred to in the definition of an *obligatum*. The expression '*admissio*' is also redundant, because it is only by virtue of an *obligatio* and not of an *admissio* that anyone is bound to reply, as has been said.

⟨ii⟩ second, this definition is false because it puts forward an *obligatum* as the other clause of an *obligatio*, whereas an *obligatum* is a statement, and an *obligatio* is a relation.

⟨iii⟩ third, I can argue against his intention even if one grants that an *obligatio* is a sentence formulated from a *positio* or *depositio* and an *admissio*. Every *depositum* which is admitted without any impediment is an *obligatum*,[20] yet it is not the other clause of the *obligatio* or the opposite of the *depositum* which the respondent is obligated to grant within the period of the *obligatio* because of the *obligatio* and *admissio*. The opposite of this is true, for no *depositum* should be granted, but rather denied. And if this is so, it is obvious that the informal definition is not interchangeable with the thing to be defined.

⟨2⟩ Second informal definition: An *obligatum* is that clause of an *obligatio* which the respondent is obligated to uphold in a particular manner during the period of the *obligatio* because of the *obligatio* and the *admissio*.[21] This definition can be condemned like the first. First, because it is false; second, because it is redundant.

⟨3⟩ Third informal definition: An *obligatum* is a statement which has been so prefaced that it should be upheld in a particular manner.[22]

---

[19] See Albert of Saxony, op.cit., fol. 46va. Cf. Marsilius's third definition, op.cit., fol. 71^v, and Buser's first, op.cit., fol. 72^{ra-rb}. Buser argued against it because it excludes *dubitatio*, and it is inconsistent with *depositio*, a point which Paul picks up in argument ⟨iii⟩ below.

[20] Albert of Saxony held that the opposite of the *depositum* was the *obligatum*. He wrote, op.cit., fol. 46va: 'Et tunc illa "Tu sedes" est deposita et eius opposita est posita et obligata.' Lavenham held the same view: op.cit., p. 227, §3. For further discussion, see Part 3, Chapter 2, note 2.

[21] See Marsilius, op.cit., fol. 71^r and Buser, op.cit., fol. 72rb. Both accepted this definition.

[22] See Marsilius, op.cit., fol. 71^v. 'Aliter et brevius describitur sic: Praefixum enuntiabile ad sustinendum secundum aliquem statum infra tempus obligationis. . . .' Buser, op.cit., fol. 72rb wrote: '. . . sic brevius et magis proprie: Obligatum est praefixum enuntiabile ad sustinendum secundum aliquem.'

Haec descriptio minus declarat naturam definiti quam (178^{ra}E) aliqua praecedentium, quia haec propositio

Homo est animal,

est praefixum enuntiabile sustinendum secundum aliquem statum, videlicet affirmativum, et tamen non est obligatum. Quare etc.

⟨IX⟩ Nona descriptio est ista: Tempus obligationis est adaequata mensura ipsius secundum prius et posterius. Volo dicere quod tempus obligationis durat usque ad desitionem obligationis, puta talis relationis.

Et si quaeritur quando desinit haec obligatio, dico quod in pluribus casibus:

⟨1⟩ Primus[62], si opponens dicat

Cedat tempus obligationis;

et respondens dicat

Admitto;

tunc obligatio desinit esse; ita quod secundum istum modum non sufficit ad desitionem obligationis quod dicatur ab opponente 'Cedat tempus', nec sufficit dicere 'Admitto', sed requiritur utrumque. Sicut enim nec ex positione praecise nec ex admissione praecise[63] solum oritur obligatio, sed ex ambabus simul; ita in proposito in sui desitione.

⟨2⟩ Secundus[64] est ubi opponens poneret oppositum prioris positi, et respondens admitteret. Tunc cessat prima obligatio et oritur nova. Duae enim obligationes repugnantes non possunt simul esse, nec se in eodem (218^{ra}M) compati.

⟨3⟩ Tertius casus est ubi opponens et respondens se transferrent ad aliam materiam. Verbi gratia, si poneretur illa

Tu curris,

et admitteretur; qua admissa post aliqualem moram intrarent materiam physicam disputando de cursu utrum distingueretur[65] a re currente, dico quod statim desinit[66] obligatio, cum materiam particularem dimittunt[67]. Idem dico si intrarent materiam moralem, sibi ipsis dicendo vituperium vel ignominiam[68].

---

[62] Primus]prius M
[63] praecise]om. E
[64] Secundus]secundo M
[65] distingueretur] distinguetur E
[66] desinit]esse add.E
[67] dimittunt]ideo add.E
[68] ignominiam]ignorantiam M

This definition is even less successful in explaining the nature of the thing to be defined than any of the preceding, for this proposition

A human being is an animal

is a statement so prefaced that it should be upheld in a particular manner, i.e. affirmatively, and yet it is not an *obligatum*[23] Therefore etc.

⟨IX⟩ Ninth informal definition: The period of an *obligatio* is an appropriate measuring of the *obligatio* with respect to before and after.[24] I mean to say that the period of an *obligatio* lasts until the *obligatio*, that is the relation, ends.

If someone asks when an *obligatio* ends, I reply that there are several cases.

⟨1⟩ First case: If the opponent says

Let the period of the *obligatio* come to an end

and the respondent says

I admit this

then the *obligatio* ceases to exist.[25] In this case it is not enough for the opponent to say 'Let the period come to an end', nor is it enough to say 'I admit this' but both ⟨speech acts⟩ are required. Just as an *obligatio* arises neither from the *positio* alone nor from the *admissio* alone, but from both of them, so it is with respect to the ending of an *obligatio*.

⟨2⟩ Second case: When the opponent posits the opposite of something posited earlier and the respondent admits it, then the first *obligatio* comes to an end and a new one arises. This is because two incompatible *obligationes* cannot exist at once, nor can they agree in anything.

⟨3⟩ Third case: The opponent and the respondent move on to another topic. For instance, if

You are running

were posited and admitted, and then after some delay the disputants were to embark on the topic of physics by arguing about whether running should be distinguished from the thing running, I would say that the *obligatio* should end at once, since the initial topic has been abandoned. I would say the same if they embarked on moral matters by trading insults.

---

[23] Cf. note 15.
[24] Other authors devoted little space to this definition: see Albert, op.cit., fol. 46va; Marsilius, op.cit., fol. 71^v; Buser, op.cit., fol. 72rb; Strode, op.cit., fol. 78^{rb-va}.
[25] Cases 1 and 2 were standard. Case 3 is mentioned by Strode, loc.cit., in these words: '. . . vel se transferat ad disputandum in alia materia.'

⟨4⟩ Quartus modus: ubi ex turbatione vel aliqua alia causa dimitterent disputationem sicut pluries contingit[69].

⟨5⟩ Quintus[70] casus: ubi fiat positio vel admissio usque ad tale instans vel sub conditione. Verbi gratia, dicat opponens[71] respondenti

 Pono tibi istam: 'Tu es Romae' usque ad A instans.

Qua admissa, dico quod ly .usque. tenetur inclusive[72]. In A instanti obligatio desinet[73] esse per remotionem de praesenti. Si vero exclusive[74], tunc desinet esse per positionem de praesenti.

 Similiter dicat opponens

  Pono tibi istam: 'Tu curris'

et[75] respondens dicat

  Admitto eam usque ad B instans,

patet quod obligatio[76] ista desinet esse in B instanti per positionem vel remotionem secundum quod ly .usque. inclusive vel exclusive tenetur.

 Notanter dicitur 'vel sub conditione', quia si poneres mihi illam

  Tu curris,

et admitterem sub hac conditione quod numquam mihi proponeres impossibile vel faceres hoc vel[77] illud, dico quod si contingat te mihi impossibile proponere, obligatio desinet esse ita quod proposito impossibili non amplius sum obligatus.

⟨6⟩ Sextus[78] casus est ubi unum fundamentorum desineret esse, ita quod si opponens vel respondens infra disputationem desineret esse, et obligatio desineret esse[79], quia non potest manere in uno solo fundamento. Quare etc.

Ex praedictis sequitur quod tempus obligationis non incipit a positione nec ab admissione sed ab obligatione sive ab instanti quo primo oritur obligatio.

Item sequitur quod si positio et admissio manerent pro toto tempore obligationis, tempus positionis maius esset quam admissionis, et tempus admissionis maius quam obligationis. Patet, quia positio secundum se vel aliquid sui prius incipit esse quam admissio, et admissio quam obligatio; et hoc loquendo de prioritate durationis.

---

[69] Quartus . . . contingit]*om*.M
[70] Quintus]quartus M
[71] opponens . . . inclusive]*om*. M
[72] inclusive]exclusive, E, *correxi*
[73] desinet]desinat M
[74] exclusive]inclusive M, E, *correxi*
[75] et]*om*.E
[76] obligatio . . . tenetur]*om*.M
[77] vel]aut E
[78] Sextus] quintus M
[79] et . . . esse]*om*.M
[75] et]*om*.E
[76] obligatio . . . tenetur]*om*.M
[77] vel²]aut E
[78] Sextus quintus M
[79] et . . . esse]*om*.M

⟨4⟩ Fourth case: They give up the disputation because of a disturbance or some other cause, as often happens.[26]

⟨5⟩ Fifth case: the *positio* or *admissio* is made until such and such a moment, or under some condition.[27] For instance, let the opponent say to the respondent:

I posit this to you: 'You are in Rome', until moment A.

When this has been admitted, I say the word 'until' is to be taken in the inclusive sense. At moment A the *obligatio* will cease to be as the present moment ⟨A⟩ passes away. If 'until' had been taken in the exclusive sense, then the *obligatio* would cease to be as the present moment ⟨A⟩ begins.[28]

Similarly let the opponent say

I posit this to you: 'You are running',

and the respondent say

I admit it until moment B.

It is obvious that this *obligatio* will cease to exist at moment B, either through its arrival or its passing, according as the expression 'until' is taken inclusively or exclusively.

Note that I have said 'or under some condition', because if you posit this to me:

You are running;

and I admit it on the condition that you never propose anything impossible to me, or that you do this or that, then I say that if it does happen that you propose something impossible to me the *obligatio* will cease to be, because once the impossible has been proposed I am no longer obligated.

⟨6⟩ Sixth case: one of the relata ceases to exist. If the opponent or the respondent expires during the disputation, the *obligatio* too will cease to exist, since this relation cannot be based on only one person. Therefore etc.

From what has been said it follows that the period of the *obligatio* does not begin with the *positio* or the *admissio*, but with the *obligatio*, or with the moment at which the *obligatio* first arises.

Likewise it follows that if the *positio* and the *admissio* remain throughout the period of the *obligatio*, the period of the *positio* will be longer than that of the *admissio*, and the period of the *admissio* longer than that of the *obligatio*. This is obvious because the *positio* as such, or some part of it, begins to exist before the *admissio*, and the *admissio* before the *obligatio*. I am speaking here of temporal priority.

---

[26] For details of such disturbances, see Anthony Kenny and Jan Pinborg, 'Medieval Philosophical Literature' in *The Cambridge History of Later Medieval Philosophy [CH]*, edited by Norman Kretzmann, Anthony Kenny, Jan Pinborg (Cambridge: Cambridge University Press, 1982), p. 24. Despite its title, this section of the *Cambridge History* contains much useful information about the origins, purpose, and nature of disputations.

[27] This kind of *positio* was known as *positio dependens*, and was discussed by Burley, op.cit., 3.148–3.169; Albert of Saxony, op.cit., fol. 51^{ra-rb}; Marsilius, op.cit., fols. 96^r–97^r; Buser, op.cit., fol. 77^{va-vb}. *Positio dependens* was divided into *positio cadens*, whereby the *positio* ceased when the condition was fulfilled, and *positio renascens*, whereby a *positio* which had ceased could be reintroduced. We find an example of *positio cadens* on p.22, line 5.

[28] The distinction between 'inclusively' and 'exclusively' is explained by Albert of Saxony,

Item sequitur quod si positio duraret solum per tempus mensurans illam enuntiationem, et admissio similiter, staret tempus positionis vel[80] admissionis esse minus vel aequale aut maius tempore obligationis. Patet, dato quod positio aut admissio fieret sub conditione aut usque ad talem instans aut aliquo aliorum modorum, ut patebit conclusio volenti speculari et commensurare talia tempora[81].

⟨X⟩ Decima descriptio: Impertinens alicui dicitur esse illud quod neque[82] ad ipsum sequitur neque sibi repugnat; sicut illa

　　Tu curris,

quae[83] non sequitur ad hanc

　　Tu es grammaticus,

nec sibi repugnat; ideo est sibi impertinens.

⟨XI⟩ Undecima descriptio est ista: Pertinens alicui dicitur esse illud quod ad ipsum sequitur vel sibi repugnat.

　Verbi gratia: sicut huic

　　Tu es Romae

est quaelibet istarum pertinens

　　Tu non es Parisius

et

　　Tu es Parisius,

sed prima est pertinens sequens et secunda[84] pertinens repugnans. Sed hic est notandum quod de numero propositionum pertinentium sequentium in arte obligatoria, alia est pertinens[85] positioni tantum; alia est pertinens positioni et admissioni simul; alia est pertinens obligato tantum; alia est pertinens obligato et bene concesso vel[86] bene concessis vel bene negato vel bene negatis simul.

⟨XII⟩ Ideo sit haec duodecima descriptio: Pertinens sequens positioni tantum dicitur illud quod ex sola positione sequitur.

　Verbi gratia, dicat opponens (178^{rb}E)

　　Pono tibi istam: 'Tu es Romae';

tunc ista propositio:

---

[80] positionis vel] *om*. E
[81] talia tempora] talium tempus E
[82] neque . . . repugnat] ad ipsum non sequitur vel sibi non repugnat E
[83] quae] *om*. E
[84] secunda] alia E
[85] pertinens] sequens *add*. M
[86] vel] et E

---

op.cit., fol. 51rb, in terms of the example 'Ponatur tibi Sortem esse album donec proponatur tibi aliquod negandum.' If 'donec' is taken inclusively the *positio* cannot cease until a sentence which should be denied has been proposed. If 'donec' is taken exclusively, then the *positio* can only continue until something which should be denied begins to be proposed. The difficulties caused by the exclusive interpretation are discussed below: see Part 2, chapter 1, against rule 4, sophism 5.

Likewise it follows that if the *positio* were to survive only for the time measuring that statement, and similarly for the *admissio*, it would be consistent for the period of the *positio* or the *admissio* to be less than, equal to, or greater than the period of the *obligatio*. This is obvious, given that the *positio* or the *admissio* can be put forward with a condition attached, or until some particular moment, or in some other way. This thesis will be plain to anyone who wishes to examine it and to proportion these periods one to another.

⟨X⟩ Tenth informal definition: A proposition is said to be irrelevant to another when it neither follows from it nor is inconsistent with it. Just as this

  You are running

does not follow from

  You are a grammarian,

so it is not inconsistent with it, and hence it is irrelevant to it.

⟨XI⟩ Eleventh informal definition: A proposition is relevant to another when it follows from or is inconsistent with it.

 For instance, both of these propositions

  You are not in Paris

and

  You are in Paris

are relevant to

  You are in Rome,

but the first is relevant as following, and the second is relevant as inconsistent. But it should be noted here that of the kinds of propositions which are relevant as following that one finds in the art of *obligatio*, one kind is relevant only to the *positio*; another is relevant to the *positio* and the *admissio* together; another is relevant only to the *obligatum*; and another is relevant to the *obligatum* together with a correctly granted proposition (or propositions) or a correctly denied proposition (or propositions).[29]

⟨XII⟩ Twelfth informal definition. A proposition relevant as following only to the *positio* is one which follows from the *positio* alone.

 For instance, let the opponent say:

  I posit this to you: 'You are in Rome'.

Then this proposition,

---

[29] This analysis is also found in Albert, op.cit., fols. 46vb–47ra; Marsilius, op.cit., fols. 71^{v}–72^{v}; Buser, op.cit., fols. 72rb–72vb; though only Albert explicitly discusses *pertinentia repugnantia* as well as *pertinentia sequentia*. See also John of Holland, op.cit., fols. 101^{v}–102^{r}. In the subsequent discussion of each type of relevant proposition, Paul follows his sources quite closely.

The definition of *pertinens sequens* is of major importance for the history of obligations. Swyneshed had defined the notion only in terms of relationship to the *positum*, and it was this that enabled him to introduce his new rules for conjunction and disjunction (see below, Part 1, section 3, notes 15 and 16; Swyneshed, op.cit., p. 251, §7; Lavenham, op.cit., p. 230, §10). Swyneshed rejected Definition 16 below, and would have described Paul's examples as irrelevant propositions.

>   Aliquid[87] est tibi positum

est pertinens sequens tantummodo positioni. Ex ipsa solummodo sequitur sic arguendo:

>   Pono tibi istam: 'Tu es Romae'; igitur aliquid est tibi positum.

⟨XIII⟩ Tredecima descriptio: Pertinens sequens positioni et admissioni simul dicitur esse illud quod ex positione et admissione simul sumptis sequitur, et ex neutra per se.

>   Verbi gratia: si[88] pono tibi istam
>
>   Tu es Romae,

et tu eam admittis, tunc ista

>   Tu es obligatus

est sequens ex positione et admissione simul, dato quod non sit impedimentum impediens obligationem, et non ex aliqua parte per se.

>   Similiter ista:
>
>   Aliquid est tibi positum et a te admissum

sequitur ex positione et admissione simul et non ex aliquo de per se. Unde bene sequitur:

>   Pono tibi A et tu admittis[89] idem; igitur aliquid est tibi positum et a te admissum.

Sed non sequitur:

>   Pono tibi A; (218^{rb}M) igitur aliquid est tibi positum et a te admissum.

Nec sequitur:

>   Tu admittis A; igitur aliquid est tibi positum et a te admissum.

⟨XIV⟩ Quartadecima descriptio est ista: Pertinens sequens obligato tantum dicitur esse illud quod ex solo obligato sequitur.

>   Verbi gratia, si pono tibi istam:
>
>   Tu es Parisius,

illa

>   Tu non es Romae

est pertinens sequens obligato tantum. Sequitur enim:

---

[87] aliquid]aliquod E
[88] si]*om.* E
[89] admittis]admittas E

Something is posited to you,

is relevant as following only to the *positio*. It follows from the *positio* alone by virtue of the following argument:

I posit this to you: 'You are in Rome'; therefore something is posited to you.

⟨XIII⟩ Thirteenth informal definition. A proposition relevant as following to both the *positio* and the *admissio* together is one which follows from the *positio* and the *admissio* taken together, and from neither by itself.

For instance, if I posit this to you:

You are in Rome,

and you admit this, then

You are obligated

follows from the *positio* and the *admissio* together, given that there is no impediment to the *obligatio*; and it does not follow from either clause taken alone.

In the same way

Something is posited to you and admitted by you

follows from the *positio* and the *admissio* together, and not from either one by itself. Thus one can argue validly

I posit A to you and you admit it; therefore something is posited to you and admitted by you.

But this inference is not valid:

I posit A to you; therefore something is posited to you and admitted by you.

Nor is this inference valid:

You admit A; therefore something is posited to you and admitted by you.

⟨XIV⟩ Fourteenth informal definition: A proposition relevant as following only to the *obligatum* is one which follows from the *obligatum* alone.

For instance, if I posit this to you

You are in Paris,

this

You are not in Rome

is relevant as following only to the *obligatum*. This inference:

Tu es Parisius; igitur tu non es Romae.

Sed non sequitur

Pono tibi istam: 'Tu non es Parisius'; igitur tu[90] non es Romae.

⟨XV⟩ Quintadecima descriptio: Pertinens sequens tam obligato quam positioni dicitur esse illud quod ex utroque divisim sequitur.

Sicut ista:

Aliquid est tibi positum

ita est sequens ad illam:

Aliquid est tibi positum

sicut ad illam:

Pono tibi istam: 'Aliquid est tibi positum'

et e contra. Unde[91] ex qualibet illarum sequitur formaliter.

⟨XVI⟩ Sextadecima descriptio et ultima sit ista: Pertinens sequens ex obligato et bene concesso vel bene concessis vel bene negato vel[92] bene negatis simul, dicitur esse[93] quod ad ea simul sumpta sequitur.

Verbi gratia:

Pono tibi istam: '"Deus est" et "Homo est asinus" convertuntur.'

Postea propono tibi illam:

Haec[94] est vera: 'Deus est.'

Concedenda est, ut patebit, quia vera et impertinens. Tunc:

Haec est vera: 'Homo est asinus'

sequitur ex obligato et bene concesso[95] simul sumptis. Sequitur:

'Deus est' et 'Homo est asinus' convertuntur, et haec est vera: 'Deus est';

igitur haec est vera: 'Homo est asinus';

sed non sequitur ex obligato praecise, nec ex concesso, ut patet formanti consequentias.

Exemplum de sequente ex obligato et bene concessis simul: quia ponatur illa:

Omnis homo albus est Romae,

deinde propono illam[96]:

---

[90] tu]*om*.M
[91] Unde]Bene E
[92] vel]aut M
[93] esse]*om*.E
[94] Haec est vera]*om*.E
[95] concesso]concessis E
[96] illam]*om*.E

You are in Paris; therefore you are not in Rome

is valid, but this inference is not:

I posit this to you: 'You are not in Paris'; therefore you are not in Rome.

⟨XV⟩ Fifteenth informal definition. A proposition relevant as following both to the *obligatum* and to the *positio* is one which follows from each of them separately.[30]

For instance

Something is posited to you,

follows from this:

Something is posited to you,

just as it does from this:

I posit this to you: 'Something is posited to you';

and the reverse. Hence, it follows formally from each of them.

⟨XVI⟩ Sixteenth and last informal definition: A proposition relevant as following to the *obligatum* and a correctly granted proposition (or propositions) or a correctly denied proposition (or propositions) together is one which follows from them taken together.

For instance

I posit this to you: '"There is a God" and "A human being is a donkey" are interchangeable'.

Afterwards I propose this to you:

'There is a God' is true.

This should be granted, as is obvious, because it is true and irrelevant. Then:

'A human being is a donkey' is true

follows from the *obligatum* and the correctly granted proposition together, for this is a valid inference:

'There is a God' and 'A human being is a donkey' are interchangeable, and 'There is a God' is true; therefore 'A human being is a donkey' is true.

But the conclusion does not follow from just the *obligatum*, nor from the previously granted proposition, as is obvious to anyone who formulates the inferences.

An example of a proposition which follows from the *obligatum* and some correctly granted propositions together: Let this be posited:

Every white human being is in Rome.

Then I propose this:

---

[30] In his definition of *pertinens obligationi tantum* Albert, loc.cit., had added the rubric 'cum non est obligatum' in order to exclude 'Aliquid est tibi positum' from falling into this category of relevant propositions. Marsilius, loc.cit., omitted this rubric, and remarked in the corollary to his seventh description that the same proposition could be both 'pertinens obligationi tantum' and 'pertinens obligato tantum'; though Buser, loc.cit., had said that this 'apparet multis inconveniens'. Paul dodges the issue by introducing a separate definition.

Tu es homo.

Concedatur⁹⁷ quia vera et impertinens. Deinde:

Tu es albus.

Concedatur⁹⁸, propter eandem causam. Tunc proponatur illa:

Tu es Romae.

Et debet concedi quia sequitur ex obligato et illis duobus concessis 'Tu es homo' et 'Tu es albus'. Nam⁹⁹ sequitur:

Omnis homo albus est Romae, tu es homo et tu es albus, igitur tu es Romae.

Sed non sequitur ex obligato praecise, nec ex illis concessis praecise, nec ex obligato cum aliquo illorum, ut patet intuenti.

Modo proportionabili possunt exempla formari de pertinente sequente ex obligato et bene negato vel bene negatis aut opposito negati vel bene negatorum sed haec in processu magis clarebunt.

Item quaecumque dicta sunt in his ultimis descriptionibus de positione et posito vel obligato, possunt correspondenter dici ⟨de⟩ depositione et deposito, admissione vel admisso, exempla formando suis modis¹.

⟨*Articulus Secundus: Praeambulae Suppositiones*⟩

Secundus articulus est quarumdam praeambularum suppositionum intrinsice contentivus.

⟨I⟩ Quarum prima est ista: videlicet quod non intendo in hoc tractatu aliter loqui de possibilitate², impossibilitate, necessitate vel contingentia, sequela³, repugnantia, vel impertinentia quam me praecedentes in hac materia locuti sunt. Longus enim sermo esset continue explicare quae diffuse suis locis tradita sunt, videlicet de possibilitate vel impossibilitate, necessitate aut contingentia consurgente ex terminis vel ex suo significato, similiter de sequela vel repugnantia quae regulariter⁴ declaratur, ut primitus ostensum est.

---

⁹⁷ Concedatur]conceditur E
⁹⁸ Concedatur]conceditur E
⁹⁹ Nam . . . tu es albus]*om*.E
¹ modis]etc. *add*.E
² possibilitate]et *add*.E
³ sequela]*om*.M
⁴ regulariter]gradualiter E

You are a human being.

This is granted because it is true and irrelevant. Then

You are white.

This is granted for the same reason. Then let this be proposed:

You are in Rome.

It ought to be granted because it follows from the *obligatum* and the other two propositions which were granted, i.e. 'You are a human being' and 'You are white'. This is a valid inference:

Every white human being is in Rome, you are a human being and you are white; therefore you are in Rome.

But this conclusion does not follow from just the *obligatum*, nor from just the previously granted propositions, nor from the *obligatum* with one of the propositions, as is obvious to anyone who thinks about it.

In a similar way one can formulate examples of propositions which are relevant as following to the *obligatum* and a correctly denied proposition (or propositions) or to the opposite of a correctly denied proposition (or propositions); but more light will be shed on these matters as we proceed.

Whatever has been said in the last definitions about a *positio* and a *positum* or an *obligatum* can be said in a corresponding way about a *depositio* and a *depositum*, an *admissio* and an *admissum*; and appropriate examples can be formulated.

⟨*Section Two: Preliminary Assumptions*⟩

The second section contains some preliminary assumptions.

⟨I⟩ First assumption.[1] In this tract I do not intend to speak of possibility, impossibility, necessity or contingency, inferred propositions, inconsistent propositions, or irrelevant propositions, in any way other than did those who have written before me on this topic. My discourse would indeed be long if I were to keep on explaining those things which have been extensively discussed in their proper place, namely the possibility or impossibility, necessity or contingency which arises from terms or their significates. The same applies to matters concerning inference and inconsistency which have to be explained through rules, as was shown previously.

---

[1] See Marsilius, assumption 1, op.cit., fols. 72^v–73^r; Buser, assumption 1, op.cit., fols. 72vb–73ra. Since they were writing independent treatises, they both gave an elaborate analysis of what was meant by a 'possible proposition'. For Paul's discussion, see *Logica Magna* II.12, *Tractatus de necessitate, contingentia, possibilitate et impossibilitate propositionum*.

⟨II⟩ Secunda suppositio est ista: Quod omnes regulae superius adsignatae in *Tractatu Consequentiarum* de consequentia bona vel non bona sunt hic fundamentaliter sustinendae. Et ratio quia materia obligationum non est nisi materia consequentiarum stilo subtiliori procedens, et an respondens sit sani capitis gressu deceptorio temptativa; nam per huiusmodi casus obligationis[5], sive veri sint sive falsi, stabilem sustentationem docetur infallibiliter et invariabiliter sustinere. Quare iam causam finalem huius artis verus indagator poterit adsignare.

⟨III⟩ Tertia suppositio est ista: Infra tempus obligationis sunt omnes (178^{va}E) responsiones ad idem instans retorquendae, id est responsiones continue dandae sunt pro illo instanti quo casus est primo positus vel saltim obligatio orta est; ita quod omnes responsiones factae infra tempus obligationis (218^{va}M) intelligendae sunt ac si fierent pro eodem instanti.

Ista suppositio fundatur super oppositum redargutionis, quia nisi sic esset, non esset causa quare infra tempus obligationis per lapsum temporis non concederentur ⟨contradictoria⟩ ita bene sicut extra, vel idem concederetur et negaretur, cuius tamen oppositum omnes testantur.

---

[5] obligationis]obligatorios E

⟨II⟩ Second assumption: All the rules concerning valid and invalid inferences which were given in the *Tract on Inferences* should be basically upheld here as well.² The reason for this is that the topic of *obligationes* is nothing other than the topic of inferences presented in a more subtle manner, in a way intended to test whether the respondent has a good head ⟨for logic⟩ by setting a deceptive course before him.³ By means of the kind of puzzle-cases, whether they are real or fictional,⁴ which the theory of *obligationes* presents, the respondent is taught to keep up his side of the argument steadily and without error. From what has been said the genuine investigator will be able to work out the true aims of this art.

⟨III⟩ Third assumption: During the period of an *obligatio* all replies are to be referred back to the same moment.⁵ That is, replies should continue to be related to that moment in which the case was first posited, or at least when the *obligatio* began; so that all replies given during the period of one *obligatio* are to be understood as if they were given at the same moment.

This assumption is based on the opposite of *redargutio*,⁶ for unless it were as assumed, there would be no reason why during the period of an *obligatio* ⟨contradictories⟩ should not be granted owing to the lapse of time, as they are outside the period; or why the same proposition should not be granted and denied – something which all witnesses reject.

---

² Paul's discussion of inference in general is found in *Logica Magna* II.9, *De hypotheticis propositionibus*, fols. 139rb–147rb.

³ This short passage gives us Paul's view of the purpose of obligational disputations. The only other author who mentions inferences in this context is Peter of Candia, op.cit., fol. 66ra, who wrote that the opponent was to proceed 'ut decipiat respondentem per consequentias apparentes et non tamen existentes.' Strode, op.cit., fol. 78ra, spoke of the testing function of obligational disputations. Burley had been more explicit about this testing function: the opponent was to try to lead the respondent into contradiction, and the respondent was to resist: Burley, op.cit., 0.01. This view is found in the Oxford logic: in Bodleian MS *Lat.misc.e 79*, fol. 19ra, we read: 'Opus autem opponentis est oppositionem et proponere propositiones quousque viderit respondentem male respondere. Opus autem respondentis sustinere et servare illud ne videatur deduci ad aliquid inconveniens.' For similar remarks, see *Lib.Soph. Oxon.*, sig.C v^v; *Lib.Soph.Cantab.*, sig.C ii^r; Wyclif, op.cit., p. 71.

Buser wrote, op.cit., fol. 73rb: 'Pro tanto fuerunt obligationes inventae ut sciamus sustinere aliquod possibile licet falsum nec ex isto cogemur ad concedendum impossibile simpliciter.'

The use of the word 'temptativa' on p. 32, line 5 (cf. p. 48, line 3 'oratio temptativa', p. 78 line 4 from bottom 'disputatio temptativa') is interesting because it suggests a link with the Examination argument of Aristotle (*De Sophisticis Elenchis* 165 b1–10) which appears as 'disputatio temptativa' in the Latin versions (see *Aristoteles Latinus VI 1–3. De Sophisticis Elenchis*, edited by Bernard G. Dod (Leiden: E.J. Brill, Bruxelles: Desclée de Brouwer, 1975), p. 7). However, to the best of my knowledge commentators on Aristotle did not refer to the subject of *obligationes*, with the single exception of Boethius of Dacia in his commentary on Topics 8: see *Boethii Daci Opera. Topica. Opuscula. Vol. 6, Pars 1. Quaestiones super Librum Topicorum*, edited by N.J. Green-Pedersen and Jan Pinborg (Hauniae: G.E.C. Gad, 1976), pp. 329–331. Nor did writers on *Obligationes* make reference to the relevant Aristotle texts.

⁴ Note that Paul writes 'sive veri sint sive falsi'. Originally it had been assumed that only false propositions could serve as *posita*. E.g. *Lib.Soph.Cant.*, sig.C i^v: 'Solum falsum et possibile est admittibile in positione.' Cf.Ockham, op.cit., p. 736; De Rijk, 'Some thirteenth century tracts', p. 98. Later authors tended to speak as if the *positum* would probably be false, but not to insist on this: Strode, op.cit., fol. 78vb, wrote: 'Solemus enim communiter falsos casus ponere, ut discat homo consequenter respondere in vero casu consimili.' (Text corrected from Oxford, Bodleian Library MS *Canon.misc.219*, fol. 37va.)

⟨IV⟩ Quarta suppositio est ista: Numquam propositiones sibi invicem contradictoriae infra idem tempus obligationis sunt concedendae ab eodem.

Patet ex priori, nam impossibile est[6] talium adaequata significata simul et semel verificari.

⟨V⟩ Quinta suppositio est ista: Quod una propositione semel concessa infra idem tempus obligationis quotienscumque proponitur est semper concedenda.

Patet ex prioribus quia si primo loco concederetur et secundo loco proposita negaretur, oporteret tertio loco concedere suum contradictorium. Et cum ipsa fuisset prius concessa et eius contradictorium nunc concederetur, tunc duo contradictoria infra idem tempus obligationis essent ab eodem concedenda, quod est contra quartam suppositionem.

⟨VI⟩ Sexta suppositio est ista: Extra tempus obligationis rei veritas est fatenda quia cum quis concedit[7] falsum vel negat[8] verum non obligatus, male respondet.

Ita quod fatendum est extra tempus obligationis si quaeratur quomodo respondebatur infra tempus[9]. Et per hunc modum poterit examinari[10] si bene sit responsum vel non, penes regulas subsequentes.

⟨VII⟩ Septima suppositio est ista: Quod in hoc capitulo vel sequenti aut in tota arte obligatoria non sumitur 'concedendum'[11], 'negandum' vel 'dubitandum' participialiter pro eo quod concedetur[12], negabitur aut dubitabitur[13]; sed nominaliter pro eo quod est dignum concedi, negari vel dubitari. Nam forte haec

    Homo est asinus

est concedenda participialiter quia concedetur[14], quae tamen non est concedenda nominaliter, quia non est digna concedi. Quare[15] etc.

---

[6] est]*om*.M
[7] concedit]concederet E
[8] negat]negaret E
[9] tempus]*om*.M
[10] examinari]exanimari E
[11] concedendum]vel *add*.E
[12] concedetur]concederetur aut E
[13] dubitabitur]dubitatur E
[14] concedetur]concederetur M
[15] Quare etc.]*om*.E

---

[5] For this rule see Burley, op.cit., 3.84; Marsilius, assumption 4, op.cit., fol. 74ᵛ; Buser, assumption 4, op.cit., fol. 73ʳᵇ; Strode, assumption 5, op.cit., fol. 78ᵛᵃ. Buser wrote: 'In ista regula omnes conveniunt et nisi sic esset non esset causa quare infra tempus per lapsum temporis non deberemus concedere contradictoria, ita bene sicut extra, vel idem concedere et negare, cuius oppositum tamen omnes concedunt.' It will be seen how closely Paul follows Buser, and accordingly I have restored the word 'contradictoria' to the text.

Peter of Mantua, op.cit., sig.G iiᵛᵃ, gave a revised version of the rule: 'Omnes propositiones concessae et contradictoriae negatorum debent facere copulativam possibilem: et hoc est quod aliqui voluerunt dicere cum dixerunt quod omnes responsiones in arte obligatoria sunt retorquendae ad idem instans.'

[6] For *redargutio*, see Stump in *CH*, pp. 315–316. 'In the first half of the thirteenth century, in the work of the terminists, the investigation of fallacies tends to contain a long discussion of disputation, and one of the species of disputation discussed there has as its goal *redargutio*: the forced denial of something previously granted or the granting of something previously denied in

⟨IV⟩ Fourth assumption: One person during the period of one *obligatio* should never grant two propositions which are mutually contradictory.

This is obvious from the above, since it is impossible for the adequate significates of such propositions to be verified for one and the same time.[7]

⟨V⟩ Fifth assumption: When a proposition has once been granted, then whenever it is proposed during the period of one *obligatio*, it should still be granted.

This is obvious from the things said above, for if a proposition was granted at its first appearance and was then denied when it was proposed in a second place, one would have to grant its contradictory in the third place. And since it was granted at first, and its contradictory is now to be granted, then two contradictories would be granted by one person during the period of one *obligatio*, which is against the fourth assumption.

⟨VI⟩ Sixth assumption: Outside the period of an *obligatio* one must tell the truth, since he who grants a falsehood or denies a truth when he is not obligated to do so, replies incorrectly.[8]

Thus ⟨we see⟩ what is to be acknowledged outside the period of an *obligatio* if someone asks how we replied during the period. And in this way, one is enabled to investigate whether the replies were correct or not, in accordance with the rules which will be given below.

⟨VII⟩ Seventh assumption: In this chapter and the following, and indeed in the entire art of *obligatio*, the expressions 'to be granted', 'to be denied', 'to be doubted' are not to be taken participially for that which will be granted, denied or doubted, but nominally, for that which is worthy of being granted, denied or doubted.[9] For perhaps this:

   A human being is a donkey

is to be granted in the participial sense because it will be granted, but it is not to be granted in the nominal sense, since it is not worthy of being granted. Therefore etc.

---

one and the same disputation. . . .' Cf. Strode's opening words, op.cit., fol. 78ra: 'Redargutum dicimus respondentem qui solius argumentationis virtute respectu propositionis alicuius responsionem suam priorem variare cogitur. . . .'

Here we find another link with Aristotle, since 'redargutio' was the word used in the Latin versions (*Aristoteles Latinus* VI 1–3, p. 7) for refutation, the first aim of those who argue: see *De Sophisticis Elenchis* 165 b14–16.

[7] The notion of *adaequatum significatum* was thoroughly discussed by Paul in his *Tractatus de Significato Propositionis*: see Paul of Venice, *Logica Magna Part II Fascicule 6*, edited by Francesco del Punta and translated by Marilyn McCord Adams (Oxford: published for the British Academy by the Oxford University Press, 1978). See especially the Doctrinal Index, pp. 284–285.

[8] See Strode, assumption 4, op.cit., fol. 78va; Peter of Mantua, op.cit., sig.G ii^{va}. Burley, op.cit., 3.38 described this as 'alia regula antiquorum'. He makes the point of the rule clear by explaining that it is only outside the obligational disputation that we can assess what went on within that disputation.

[9] This distinction was sketched by Strode, op.cit., fol. 78rb; and explained in terms of 'nominaliter' versus 'participialiter' by Peter of Mantua, op.cit., sig.G ii^{va}.

⟨VIII⟩ Ultima suppositio est ista et[16] principalis in hac materia: Tres sunt species obligationum et non plures non[17] coincidentes in respondendo, videlicet suppositio, positio et[18] depositio.

Suppositio est enuntiatio implicite vel explicite composita ex signis suppositionis et suppositi; a qua simul cum admissione egreditur obligatio relativa limitans ad suppositum[19] concedendum tamquam verum necessarium aut per se notum.

Verbi gratia: Dicat opponens respondenti

> Suppono quod Antichristus sit.

Quo admisso, habet respondens illam:

> Antichristus est

concedere et sustinere pro vero. Ita quod si proponitur[20]

> Antichristus est,

concedatur[21]. Et si proponitur

> Ipsa est vera,

concedatur. Et si arguitur more aliarum obligationum:

> Ipsam esse veram non sequitur ex supposito, nec ante suppositionem concessisses ipsam esse veram; igitur non habes concedere ipsam esse veram,

non valet argumentum eo quod iste modus arguendi tenet in positione et non in[22] suppositione. In positione enim est concedendum positum licet sustineatur ipsum esse falsum, et in depositione negatur depositum, quorum nullum in suppositione contingit.

---

[16] et]*om.*M
[17] non]*om.*E
[18] et]*om.*M
[19] suppositum]supponendum M
[20] proponitur]propono E
[21] concedatur]conceditur E
[22] in]*om.*E

⟨VIII⟩ Last and most important assumption:[10] There are three species of *obligatio* and no more which can be distinguished by the replies they allow, namely *suppositio, positio*, and *depositio*.[11]

A *suppositio* is a statement implicitly or explicitly formulated from the marks of a *suppositio* and the *suppositum*. From it, together with an *admissio*, there arises a relational *obligatio* which limits one to granting a *suppositum* as true, necessary, or known *per se*.

For instance, let the opponent say to the respondent:

I assume that Antichrist exists.

When this has been admitted, the respondent must grant

Antichrist exists,

and uphold it as true. Thus, if

Antichrist exists

is proposed, it should be granted. And if this is proposed:

The above is true,

it too should be granted. And if someone argues in the manner of other types of *obligatio*,

That it is true does not follow from the *suppositum*; nor did you grant its truth before the *suppositio*; therefore you do not have to grant its truth,

the argument does not hold, because this kind of argument applies only in a *positio* and not in a *suppositio*. In a *positio*, the *positum* must be granted even though one can uphold its falsehood, and in a *depositio* the *depositum* is denied, none of which happens with a *suppositio*.

---

[10] The question of the different species of *obligatio* was dealt with in a separate chapter by Albert, op.cit., fol. 48rb, and Marsilius, op.cit., fols. 76^v–77^v. Buser, op.cit., fol. 74ra, also devotes a short but distinct section to the matter.

[11] It was a fairly common view that there were three species of *obligatio*. (See below, note 16 for the view that there were six.) However, no one else gave Paul's list. Marsilius, op.cit., fol. 77^r, had argued for *positio, depositio*, and *dubie positio* on the grounds that granting, denying and doubting were the only three possible responses to any proposition. Paul does not mention these arguments, and they do not appear in Buser, who argued for six species. The usual list of three was *positio, depositio* and *impositio*: see Swyneshed, op.cit., pp. 249–250, §1; Richard Billingham, [*Obligationes*], Salamanca Univ.MS 1735, fol. 89^v; Lavenham, op.cit., p. 227 §1; John of Holland, op.cit., fol. 101^v; Bodleian MS *Lat.misc.e* 79, fol. 18ra. Other sources preferred just two species, *positio* and *depositio*: see *Lib.Soph.Oxon.*, sig.C v^r; Wyclif, op.cit., p. 69; Strode, op.cit., fol. 78^{ra-rb}; Peter of Mantua, op.cit., sig.G ii^{ra}, sig.G iiii^{vb}–G v^{ra}; Peter of Candia, op.cit., fol. 65ra; *Logica Parva*, p. 118. Martinus, op.cit., fol. 127^r, discusses only these two species but hints that there may be others. For the possibility of reduction to just one species, see Part 3, chapter 2, note 2.

We have seen that in giving *suppositio* (not to be confused with the theory of terms) as a special kind of *obligatio* Paul was doing something unusual. Nevertheless there are hints in his sources. Strode, op.cit., fol. 78rb wrote: 'Sed utimur tali termino "suppono" [vel "suppositio" *add*. MS fol. 37rb] disputando non solum ut suppositam propositionem sustineat respondens concedendo, sicut conceditur aliquod contingens, sed sicut necessarium vel verum de se notum.' Peter of Mantua, op.cit., sig.G v^{ra} wrote: 'Modus obligandi per ly .suppono. aut .praesuppono. continetur sub positione. ... Per istam notam .praesuppono. solemus obligare respondentem ad sustinendum suppositum non solum tamquam verum, sed frequenter tamquam necessarium.' Billingham, op.cit., fol. 89^v, said 'et aliqui dant suppositio.' For more details about *suppositio* see below p. 40, p. 46–48, and notes 18 and 19, this section.

Notanter dicitur in suppositione 'non coincidentes in respondendo', quia plures sunt species obligationum quam tres nominatae. Verum coincidunt in suis regulis et modis respondendi cum praedictis. Unde praeter praedictas sunt impositio, petitio, dubitatio, sit verum, obligatio, volitio, nolitio, et huiusmodi. Unde species obligationis adsignantur penes multiplicitatem[23] notarum et signorum; modo notae talium distinguuntur specie; igitur etc.

Non tamen dico quod huiusmodi species obligationum a speciebus positionis vel suppositionis distinguantur; unde quaelibet impositio, petitio, sit verum et huiusmodi, est positio, si non subsequatur formaliter vel virtualiter alia positio vel depositio. Ita quod hae nominatae se habent inter se ut species specialissimae, et positio ad omnes illas ut genus. Cum enim dico

Peto te respondere ad A,

adserit haec petitio sicut ista positio:

Pono quod tu respondeas ad A.

Ita breviter quod ad omnes huiusmodi species respondendum est sicut ad positionem. Unde si dicit[24] opponens (218^{vb}M) respondenti

Peto te concedere illam 'Homo est asinus'

et proponitur

Homo est asinus,

negatur quia illud est impossibile et non petitum; licet sit petitum concedere. Propterea si proponitur

Tu concedis hominem esse asinum,

concedatur, quia positum et petitum.

Et ita dicatur de aliis, dummodo[25] sint positiones. Et notanter hoc dico quia aliquae harum specierum possunt ita esse suppositiones sicut positiones. Sunt enim positiones quando enuntiabile ipsarum per opponentem intenditur fieri obligatum disputandum; et hoc contingit quando (178^{vb}E) ipsis propositis non subsequitur[26] alia positio. Verbi gratia: si ego dicerem[27]

Sit ita quod tu sis[28] Romae[29],

nihil plus ponendo; et procederem facta admissione cum illa

---

[23] multiplicitatem]multitudinem E
[24] dicit]dicat E
[25] dummodo]dum E
[26] subsequitur]subsequatur E
[27] si ego dicerem]*om*.E
[28] sis]es M
[29] Romae]vel depono formaliter aut virtualiter *add*.E

It should be noted that in stating the assumption I said 'which can be distinguished by the replies they allow', for there are more species of *obligatio* than the three named above. However, they are not distinguished from the aforesaid by their rules and ways of replying. These other species include *impositio, petitio, dubitatio, sit verum*, obligation,[12] wanting, not wanting, and so on. One can see that the species of *obligatio* are listed in accordance with the multiplicity of marks and signs; but these marks are themselves of different sorts; therefore etc.

However, I do not claim that these kinds of *obligatio* are to be distinguished from the species of *positio* or *suppositio*. Each instance of *impositio, petitio, sit verum*, and the like is a *positio*,[13] unless it formally or virtually follows another *positio* or *depositio*. Thus the types which have been named are related to each other as most particular species, and *positio* stands as a genus to all of them. For when I say

I ask you to reply to A,

this *petitio* makes the same claim as this *positio*:

I posit that you reply to A.

Thus, in short, one should reply to all these species just as one would to a *positio*. Hence if the opponent says to the respondent:

I ask you to grant this: 'A human being is a donkey',

and then this is proposed:

A human being is a donkey,

it should be denied because it is impossible and it is not the *petitum*, although one was asked to grant it. Therefore if

You grant that a human being is a donkey

is proposed, it is granted because it is both the *positum* and the *petitum*.

Similar remarks are to be made about the other types of *obligatio*, so long as they count as examples of *positio*. It should be noted that I say this because some of these types can be examples of *suppositio* just as much as of *positio*. They count as examples of *positio* when the relevant statement is intended by the opponent to be the sort of *obligatum* which is the object of dispute; and this happens when no other *positio* follows the initial proposals. For instance, if I were to say

Let it be the case that you are in Rome,

positing nothing further; and if I were to proceed after the *admissio* had been made by offering this

---

[12] '*Obligatio*' here presumably refers to the case in which 'obligo te' is used as a prefix: see p. 16. For mention of the various possible species, see Marsilius, op.cit., fol. 77^r ('percipit, nego, affirmo, consentio, suppono, contendo') and Peter of Mantua, op.cit., sig.G iiii^{vb}–G v^{ra}: 'Si enim dubitare pro dubie respondere esset species distincta obligationis sic concedere, negare, credere, essent species distinctae obligationis.'

[13] Cf. Marsilius, op.cit., fol. 77^v. He argued that *impositio, petitio* and *sit verum* are related to *positio* as inferior to superior species, just as human being and animal are related to body (i.e. corporeal substance). Marsilius, op.cit., fol. 77^r, also argues that *petitio* can be reduced to *positio* in the way suggested by Paul.

Tu es Romae

disputative, dico quod tunc[30] sit verum est[31] positio vel[32] depositio formaliter aut virtualiter; et quaelibet aliarum specierum quae tali modo ponentur praeter suppositionem et depositionem.

Si autem proponitur aliqua illarum cum alia[33] specie obligationis subsequente, prima remanet suppositio et secunda positio vel depositio. Verbi gratia: Dicat opponens respondenti:

Sit rei veritas quod tu sis Romae.

Qua admissa, proponat idem opponens positionem istam:

Pono tibi istam: 'Tu non es Romae'.

Debet admitti. Qua admissa, dicat opponens quod illae non sunt positiones nec obligationes oppositae, quia prima est suppositio et secunda positio. Et ita dicatur de aliis suo modo.

Notanter dico 'virtualiter' quia aliquando suppositio sequitur[33] situaliter. Ponitur post positum, sed tamen virtualiter praecedit, quia semper intelligitur praecedere. Verbi gratia:

Pono tibi istam: 'Tu curris' quae sit A.

Ecce quomodo suppositio postponitur positioni et nulla alia positio vel depositio situaliter sequitur, sed bene virtualiter, quia expressa positio.

Ex praedictis sequitur quod ponentes aliter respondendum[34] ad petitionem, dubitationem, vel sit verum quam ad suppositionem, positionem vel depositionem, insufficienter loquuntur.

Unde dato quod petas concedere hominem esse asinum, dicunt aliqui quod non est admittenda petitio, quia petit unum impossibile. Alii dicunt quod admittenda est, et cum proponitur

Homo est asinus,

---

[30] tunc]est *add*.E
[31] est]et E
[32] vel ... virtualiter]*om*.E
[33] alia]aliqua E
[33] sequitur situaliter]situatur situaliter M, virtualiter E, *correxi*
[34] respondendum]respondent M

You are in Rome

in a disputatious manner, I would say that here *sit verum* is formally or virtually a *positio* or a *depositio*. This is so for every other type of *obligatio* which is posited in a similar way, except for *suppositio* and *depositio* themselves.

If, however, the statement was proposed with some other type of *obligatio* following it, the first proposal would count as a *suppositio* and the second would be a *positio* or a *depositio*. For instance, let the opponent say to the respondent

Let it be true that you are in Rome.

Once this has been admitted, let the same opponent put forward this *positio*:

I posit this to you: 'You are not in Rome'.

This ought to be admitted. When it has been admitted, the opponent may say that these are not conflicting examples of a *positio* or an *obligatio*, for the first is a *suppositio* and the second is a *positio*. The same can be said of other examples, with appropriate changes.

It should be noted that I say 'virtually', because sometimes a *suppositio* follows with respect to its place. It is posited after the *positum*, but nevertheless virtually precedes it, because it is always understood to precede. For instance:

I posit this to you: 'You are running', which is A.

You can see how the *suppositio* is placed after the *positio*, and no other *positio* or *depositio* follows it with respect to place, but in fact the *positio* follows it virtually, for the *positio* has been made explicit.

From what has been said it follows that those who claim that one should reply in another way to a *petitio*, *dubitatio* or *sit verum* than to a *suppositio*, *positio* or *depositio*, have an inadequate theory.

Hence, given that you ask someone to grant that a human being is a donkey,[14] some people[15] say that this *petitio* is not to be admitted, because someone is asked ⟨to grant⟩ an impossible proposition. Others say that it is to be admitted, and when

A human being is a donkey

---

[14] Here a special problem about *petitio* is raised, namely its relation to an impossible *positum*. Although both Burley and Ockham had allowed an impossible *positum*, no later author did. (See Burley, op.cit., 3.179–3.186; Ockham, op.cit., pp. 739–741; discussed by Stump in *CH* pp. 332–334.) Yet the notion does seem to make sense in some contexts. One can ask the respondent to grant an impossible proposition, and the respondent may allow this. Burley wrote, op.cit., 2.06: 'Nec est inconveniens concedere impossibile, facta petitione ut concedatur impossibile.' He was echoed by Ockham, op.cit., pp. 734–735, and Albert, op.cit., fol. 51va: 'Circa istam speciem obligationis pro regula teneatur quod impossibile non est concedendum nisi fiat petitio ut impossibile concedatur. . . .' The question was then discussed by Marsilius, who devoted article 6 of chapter 4 to *petitio* as a species of *positio* (fols. 97^r–99^r) and raised the problem of the impossible, op.cit., fols. 97^v–98^r. Buser treated *petitio* as a separate species of *obligatio* at the end of his treatise, op.cit., fol. 78^{ra-rb}. As usual, Marsilius's discussion follows Buser's, as does Paul's. Paul's version is more condensed and streamlined. Another difference is that Marsilius and Buser omit arguments 1(ii) and 2(ii).

[15] Paul writes 'dicunt aliqui'. I do not know who these people were, but it is unlikely Paul himself knew. He is quoting Buser, op.cit., fol. 78ra: 'Ad istud respondent aliqui dicendo quod

ipsi concedunt, dicendo quod non est inconveniens in petitione concedere impossibile.

⟨1⟩ Prima responsio est insufficiens propter duo.

⟨i⟩ Primo quia petitio non petit impossibile, immo possibile. Non enim petit hominem esse asinum, sed petit te concedere hominem esse asinum. Et[35] hoc est possibile, videlicet te concedere hominem esse asinum.

⟨ii⟩ Secundo quia per idem haberet haec responsio non admittere illam positionem, videlicet

Pono quod tu concedas hominem esse asinum,
quia deberet dicere consequenter[36] quod positio haec ponit impossibile. Sed certum est quod si concesserit positionem istam ponere solum possibile, necessario idem dicet[37] de petitione priori.

⟨2⟩ Secunda responsio etiam est insufficiens:

⟨i⟩ Primo quia non habet concedere nisi sit[38] petitum vel sequens; modo hominem esse asinum non est petitum nec sequens.

⟨ii⟩ Secundo quia per idem haberet consimiliter respondere in positione, dato quod poneretur te concedere hominem esse asinum. Consequentia patet, quia non videtur ratio quare mutaretur responsio. Nam nulla ratio sufficiens dari potest quare impossibile concedendum sit in petitione et non in positione.

Item sequitur ex eisdem[39] quod plures quam sex sunt species obligationum, cuius oppositum ponunt aliqui. Sunt enim illae sex, quas ipsi ponunt, videlicet: positio, impositio, depositio, sit verum, petitio et dubitatio; et aliae plures, videlicet[40] suppositio, nolitio, scientia[41], credulitas et huiusmodi. Non enim videtur quare illa sit una species obligationis[42]

Dubitet[43] istam 'Sortes currit'
quin sit[44] etiam quaelibet[45] istarum

Sciat Sortes[46] te currere,

Credat Plato te disputare
et huiusmodi.

Contra ista[47] arguunt aliqui probando istum sextum numerum specierum

---

[35] Et ... asinum]*om*.M
[36] consequenter]*om*. E
[37] dicet]dicit E
[38] sit]*om*.M
[39] eisdem]eis E
[40] videlicet]scilicet M
[41] scientia]et *add*.E
[42] obligationis]obligationum E
[43] Dubitet]dubita M
[44] sit]*om*.M
[45] quaelibet istarum]*om*.M
[46] Sortes te currere]Sortem currere M
[47] ista]istam E

---

petitio non est admittenda simpliciter et absolute, quia petit unum impossibile.' Marsilius also quoted Buser: op.cit., fol. 97^v: 'Hic aliqui respondent non admittendo positum ideo quia dicunt non est possibile.'

is proposed, they grant it, saying that it is not awkward to grant something impossible in the case of a *petitio*.

⟨1⟩ The first reply is inadequate for two reasons:

⟨i⟩ first, because the *petitio* does not seek ⟨the granting of⟩ something impossible, but rather something possible. The opponent does not ask for a human being to be a donkey, but he asks you to grant that a human being is a donkey. And this is possible, namely that you should grant that a human being is a donkey.

⟨ii⟩ second, because the person giving this reply would not be able to admit the following *positio*, namely

I posit that you grant a human being to be a donkey,

for the same reason. He would have to say as a result ⟨of his earlier reply⟩ that this *positio* puts forward an impossible proposition. But it is certain that if one were to grant that this *positio* posits only what is possible then necessarily the same should be said about the above *petitio*.

⟨2⟩ The second reply is also inadequate:

⟨i⟩ first, because one need grant only the *petitum* or what follows from it; but that a human being is a donkey is neither the *petitum* nor what follows from it;

⟨ii⟩ second, because in accordance with this view one would have to reply in a similar manner in cases of *positio*, given that it was posited that you grant a human being to be a donkey. The inference is obvious, because there seems to be no reason why the reply should be changed. No adequate reason can be given why the impossible should be granted in cases of *petitio* but not in cases of *positio*.

Likewise it follows from the same views that there are more than six species of *obligatio*, a claim which some people deny. For there are those six types which they themselves put forward, i.e. *positio, impositio, depositio, sit verum, petitio* and *dubitatio*; and then there are many others, i.e. *suppositio*, not wanting, knowledge, belief, and so on. There seems to be no reason why

You should doubt this: 'Socrates is running'

should count as a species of *obligatio* without each of these also counting:

Socrates should know that you are running

Plato should believe that you are disputing

and so forth.

Some people argue against these claims by offering the following proof that

obligationum per hunc modum. Nam aliud[48] est obligare ad actum, aliud ad habitum. Obligare ad actum est facere obligationem in qua exprimitur aliquis actus exercendus a respondente circa obligatum. Verbi[49] gratia: ut si dicerem

Peto te concedere[50] primum proponendum a me.

Obligare vero ad habitum est facere obligationem in qua non exprimitur aliquis actus exercendus a respondente circa obligatum, ut si dicerem (219^{ra}M)

Pono tibi istam: 'Tu es Romae'.

Secundo est notandum. Dicunt quod actuum quidam dicitur incomplexus, ut respondere vel tacere; et[51] quidam complexus, sicut[52] est te scire, te currere, te dubitare, te respondere.

Istis notabilibus praesuppositis, arguunt sufficientiam illarum[53] specierum sic. Omnis obligatio vel obligat ad actum vel ad habitum. Si ad actum: hoc dupliciter: vel ad actum incomplexum, sic est petitio; vel ad actum complexum, sic est sit verum. Verbi gratia: si opponens peteret a respondente

Peto te respondere affirmative ad primum proponendum a me,

sic est petitio. Exemplum de[54] sit verum: ut si opponens dicit[55] respondenti

Sit verum te scire te respondere.

Si autem obligat ad habitum, vel igitur cadit super[56] complexum vel super[57] incomplexum indifferenter, et[58] sic est impositio; vel super[59] complexum solum, et hoc est tripliciter: vel ad sustinendum pro vero, et sic est positio; vel ad sustinendum pro falso, et sic est depositio; vel ad sustinendum pro dubio, et sic est dubitatio.

Horum doctorum[60] notabilia praemissa sufficienter transeunt, sed divisio facta ex eisdem involvit seipsam.

⟨1⟩ Nam cum dicitur in principio quod omnis obligatio obligans ad actum incomplexum est petitio et omnis (179^{ra}E) obligatio[61] obligans ad actum[62] complexum est sit verum, sequitur quod petitio est sit verum. Probatur quia[63] quaero utrum illa oratio

---

[48] aliud]aut M
[49] Verbi . . . obligatum]*om*.E
[50] concedere]ad *add*.M
[51] et]*om*.E
[52] sicut]ut E
[53] illarum]illam M
[54] de]*om*.M
[55] dicit]dicat E
[56] super]supra E
[57] super]supra E
[58] et]om.M
[59] super]supra M
[60] doctorum] dictorum M
[61] obligatio]*om*.M
[62] actum]*om*.E
[63] quia]et M

there are just six species of *obligatio*:[16] It is one thing to obligate to an act, another to obligate to a disposition. To obligate someone to an act is to produce an *obligatio* in which mention is made of some act to be exercised by the respondent with respect to the *obligatum*. ⟨This would come about⟩ if I were to say

I ask you to grant the first proposition to be proposed by me.

But to obligate someone to a disposition is to produce an *obligatio* in which no mention is made of any act to be exercised by the respondent with respect to the *obligatum*. ⟨This would come about⟩ if I were to say:

I posit this to you: 'You are in Rome'.

Second, this is to be noted. They say that some acts are called simple, e.g. to reply or to be silent, and some complex, e.g. for you to know, for you to run, for you to doubt, for you to reply.

Once they had assumed these distinctions, they argued the adequacy of their list of species in this way. Every *obligatio* obligates a person either to an act or to a disposition. If it obligates a person to an act, this can happen in two ways. Either it obligates a person to a simple act, and this is a *petitio*, or to a complex act, and this is a *sit verum*. For instance, if the opponent were to ask the respondent:

I ask you to reply affirmatively to the first proposition to be proposed by me,

this would be a *petitio*. An example of *sit verum* is when the opponent says to the respondent:

Let it be true that you know you are replying.

If however ⟨the *obligatio*⟩ obligates a person to a disposition, then either it applies to a complex or a simple indifferently, and this is an *impositio*; or to a complex alone, and this can occur in three ways. Either the complex must be upheld as true, and this is a *positio*; or it must be upheld as false, and this is a *depositio*; or it must be upheld as uncertain, and this is a *dubitatio*.

I have said enough about the premisses on which these doctors are operating. The division based on these premisses leads to contradictions:

⟨1⟩ Because it is said in the beginning that every *obligatio* which obligates a person to a simple act is a *petitio* and every *obligatio* which obligates a person to a complex act is a *sit verum*, it follows that a *petitio* is a *sit verum*. This is proved by asking whether this sentence:

---

[16] These arguments for six species are from Burley, op.cit., 0.02. They were reproduced by Albert, op.cit., fol. 48rb and by Buser, op.cit., fol. 74ra. However, these authors only discussed four of the six species, omitting *dubitatio* and *sit verum*. Buser wrote, op.cit., fol. 74ra: 'Utrum autem sex sint species obligationis aut non et utrum ista probatio valet aut non, non multum curo ad praesens cum de omnibus non propono tractare. Istud tamen recitavi quia famosum et vere ab omnibus est concessum.'

Te respondere ad primum proponendum a me

dicat actum complexum vel actum[64] incomplexum. Si complexum, tunc haec enuntiatio

Peto te respondere ad primum proponendum a me

est sit verum, cuius oppositum dicitur. Si incomplexum, sequitur quod haec oratio

Sit verum te respondere ad primum proponendum a me

esset petitio, quod est falsum, cum nihil petatur ibidem.

⟨2⟩ Dicitur secundo quod omnis obligatio obligans ad habitum complexum vel incomplexum indifferenter est impositio, sed hoc iterum est falsum. Nam quaero utrum haec oratio

Ly .homo. significat adaequate asinum,

sit habitus complexus vel incomplexus. Si incomplexus, sequitur quod haec oratio

Pono tibi illam: 'Ly .homo. significat adaequate asinum'

est impositio. Consequens est[65] contra eos cum sit enuntiatio composita ex posito et signis positionis.

⟨3⟩ Tertio dicunt quod si obligatio cadit super habitum[66] complexum, hoc est tripliciter: vel ad sustinendum pro vero et sic est positio etc. Ista falsa sunt, quia in positione positum non habet sustineri pro vero, immo potius pro falso; et in depositione non habet sustineri pro falso; licet depositum semper sit[67] negandum.

⟨4⟩ Item sequitur quod suppositio est[68] positio, quod est falsum[69]. Consequentia patet iuxta istas regulas, dicendo

Suppono quod Sortes currat.

Etiam quod sit depositio patet[70] dicendo

Suppono quod Sortes non currat.

Utrobique enim cadat obligatio super complexum, ad istorum modum loquendi, quorum primum est sustinendum pro vero et secundum sustinendum pro falso.

---

[64] actum] *om*.M
[65] est] *om*.M
[66] habitum] *om*.E
[67] sit] sic E
[68] est] sit E
[69] falsum] et *add*.E
[70] patet] quia *add*.E

... that you reply to the first proposition to be proposed by me represents a complex act or a simple act. If the answer is 'complex', then this statement

I ask that you reply to the first proposition to be proposed by me

is a *sit verum*; yet the opposite of this claim is expressed. If the answer is 'simple', it follows that this sentence

Let it be true that you reply to the first proposition to be proposed by me

would be a *petitio*; and this is false, since nothing is requested here.

⟨2⟩ Secondly it is said that every *obligatio* which obligates a person indifferently to a complex or simple disposition is an *impositio*, but this again is false. For I ask whether this sentence

The expression 'human being' adequately signifies a donkey

represents a complex or a simple disposition. If the answer is 'simple', it follows that this sentence

I posit to you: 'The expression "human being" adequately signifies a donkey'

is an *impositio*. The conclusion is contrary to their view, since the statement is formed from a *positum* and the marks of a *positio*.

⟨3⟩ Thirdly they said that if an *obligatio* applied to a complex disposition, this happened in one of three ways: either the complex should be upheld as true and this is a *positio*; and so on. These claims are false, because in a *positio* the *positum* does not have to be upheld as true; indeed, more often it is upheld as false. In a *depositio* it does not have to be upheld as false, even though the *depositum* should always be denied.[17]

⟨4⟩ Likewise it follows that a *suppositio* is a *positio*, which is false. The inference is obvious, given these rules, if one says:

I assume that Socrates is running.

One can also infer that ⟨a *suppositio*⟩ is a *depositio* by saying:

I assume that Socrates is not running.

In each of these cases the *obligatio* applies to a complex, given their way of speaking, the first of which should be upheld as true and the second of which should be upheld as false.

---

[17] The point here involves the distinction between mention and use (see below, section 4, note 3). If P is the *positum*, then P must always be granted (provided it is possible) but 'P is true' can be denied. Similarly if P is the *depositum*, then P must always be denied (provided it is not necessary), but 'P is false' can also be denied.

Ex quibus patet quod ista divisio est in toto falsa. Quare etc.

De prima specie obligationis[71] non procedam in sequentibus, nisi forte de per accidens ratione positionis vel depositionis, quia non est oratio temptativa nec per quam fit disputatio deceptoria[72], sed sola[73] positio vel depositio est huiusmodi. Est igitur pro hac specie regulariter observandum quod[74] suppositum admissum absque impedimento ad ortum[75] obligationis est concedendum simpliciter propositum et similiter esse verum. Et hoc infra tempus suppositionis quod dicitur esse mensura adaequata suppositionis secundum prius et posterius quae quidem mensura mensurat, ut dictum fuit de positione vel suo opposito. Et hoc quod dico 'concedendum simpliciter et[76] esse verum similiter concedendum', intelligendum est quando proponitur suppositio sine positione vel depositione posteriori[77]. Quando sibi adnectitur positio vel depositio, respondeatur secundum quod dicetur infra iuxta modum positionis vel depositionis.

Verbi gratia: dicat opponens

Suppono quod Antichristus sit.

Qua admissa, respondens habet illam concedere et eandem esse veram quousque fit positio vel depositio. Quae si fiat dicendo

Pono tibi istam: 'Nullus[78] Antichristus est',

admittenda et concedenda est; sed negandum (219^{rb}M) est istam esse veram. Ecce quomodo suppositum in positione negandum est, et concedendum est ipsum esse verum. Negandum est, quia oppositum positi. Concedendum est ipsum esse verum quia hoc est impertinens posito, remanente suppositione.

Aliquando autem oportet negare suppositum et concedere ipsum esse falsum ubi hoc sequatur ex posito. Tamen ex hoc non desinit obligatio suppositionis, quia cum dicitur

Cedat tempus

in positione vel depositione deliberatur[79] homo a secunda obligatione et revertitur ad primam quae est suppositionis. Verbi gratia: dicat opponens respondenti

---

[71] obligationis]obligationum M
[72] deceptoria]deceptatoria E
[73] sola]solum E
[74] quod]quia E
[75] ortum]actum E
[76] et]vel E
[77] posteriori]quod *add*.M
[78] Nullus]*om*.M
[79] deliberatur]deliberabitur M

From these remarks it is obvious that the proposed division is completely unfounded. Therefore etc.

In what follows, I shall not discuss the first species of *obligatio*, unless perhaps accidentally in the context of a *positio* or *depositio*, since it is not a sentence used to test ⟨logical skills⟩, nor are misleading disputations produced through it. Only a *positio* or *depositio* is of this sort. The rule for this species of *obligatio* is that a *suppositum* which has been admitted without any impediment to the arising of an *obligatio* should be granted simply when it is proposed, and its truth should also be granted.[18] And this should happen during the period of a *suppositio* which is said to be the appropriate measuring of the *suppositio* with respect to before and after. ⟨Before and after⟩ is what the measuring measures, as was said of a *positio* or of its opposite. And when I say 'should be granted simply and its truth should also be granted', my words are to be understood of the circumstances in which a *suppositio* is proposed without any subsequent *positio* or *depositio*. When a *positio* or *depositio* is added to the *suppositio*, one should reply in accordance with what will be said below about the mode of *positio* or *depositio*.[19]

For instance, let the opponent say:

I assume that Antichrist exists.

When this has been admitted, the respondent must grant it and must also grant it to be true until some *positio* or *depositio* has been produced. If this is done in the following words:

I posit to you: 'No Antichrist exists',

it should be admitted and granted; but one should deny that ⟨the posited statement⟩ is true. Here we see how a *suppositum* should be denied when it appears in a *positio*, and how it should be granted that it is true. It should be denied because it is the opposite of the *positum*. While the *suppositio* remains in force, it should be granted that it is true, because this is irrelevant to the *positum*.

Sometimes, however, one ought to deny the *suppositum* and to grant it to be false where this follows from the *positum*. But this does not end the *obligatio* of the *suppositio*, for when

Let the period come to an end

has been said during a *positio* or a *depositio*, the second *obligatio* is ended for the participant, and he is returned to the first *obligatio*, which is that of the *suppositio*. For instance, let the opponent say to the respondent

---

[18] Paul's discussion of *suppositio* should be compared to Ockham's discussion of *casus*, op.cit., pp. 735–736; though unlike Paul, Ockham said that *casus* did not obligate (p. 735). What Paul seems to be doing here is formalizing the standard procedure whereby an initial set of circumstances was specified in order to make it possible to view the propositions uttered during the course of a disputation as having a specific truth value. This procedure was, of course, particularly important for those writing about obligational disputations. At the beginning of an actual disputation all the participants know whether they are in Rome or not, but in a theoretical discussion of how to handle the *positum* 'You are in Rome' it is necessary to make some initial remark such as 'Let it be the case that you are actually in Paris.' Most authors made such remarks without reflecting on them any further.

[19] By treating *suppositio* as if it obligates, Paul allows the possibility of two obligational

Sit rei veritas quod Sortes currit.
Quo admisso dicat idem
Pono tibi istam: 'Nullus Sortes currit.'
Quo admisso, proponatur positum et sic ultra arguatur quousque dicat opponens
Cedat tempus obligationis.
Quo admisso, deobligabitur[80] a secunda obligatione, sed non a prima. Patet, quia si post deliberationem huius proponatur
Sortes currit,
concederetur[81], et hoc est ratione obligationis[82] suppositionis. Ubi vero diceret opponens
Cedat similiter tempus huius obligationis,
demonstrando obligationem egredientem partialiter a suppositione, et admitteretur, patet quod respondens totaliter deliberatus est et ad hanc
Sortes currit,
non habet ipse respondere nisi sicut ante suppositionem, videlicet dubitando eam. Et si proponitur
Ipsa est vera aut ipsa est falsa,
concedatur[83] tota disiunctiva et quaelibet pars dubitaretur[84]. Quare etc.

⟨*Articulus Tertius: Regulae*⟩
Tertius articulus principaliter declarandus est quarumdam regularum declarativus.
⟨I⟩ Prima est ista: Omne possibile aut per accidens impossibile scitum ab aliquo esse tale, eidem positum est admittendum.
Patet nam quodlibet tale est admittendum ex quo non sequitur contradictio. Sed[85] ex nullo tali possibili aut impossibili sequitur contradictio[86], (179^{rb}E) sicut est ostensum in *Tractatu Consequentiarum*, igitur etc.
Notanter dicitur 'per accidens impossibile', quia si poneretur impossibile simpliciter non admittendum esset; quia tunc oportet concedere contradictoria in

---

[80] deobligabitur]deobligat E
[81] concederetur]conceditur E
[82] obligationis]*om*.E
[83] concedatur]conceditur E
[84] dubitaretur]dubitetur E
[85] Sed . . . contradictio]*om*.M
[86] contradictio]igitur etc. *add*.E

---

disputations, one embedded within the other. However, he has been careful to set things up so that the admission of the *suppositum* cannot conflict with the admission of the *positum*. Here he is unlike Swyneshed, who allowed for the possibility of a respondent being bound by two *posita*, the second of which has been introduced half way through a disputation: Swyneshed, op.cit., p. 273, §98. For a discussion of Swyneshed, see Eleonore Stump, 'Roger Swyneshed's theory of obligations', *Medioevo*, 7 (1981), 135–174, especially in the section 'Roger Swyneshed: an evaluation', pp. 167–169.

Let it be true that Socrates is running.

When this has been admitted, let the same person say:

I posit this to you: 'No Socrates is running'.

When this has been admitted, let the *positum* be proposed, and let the argument go on until the opponent says:

Let the period of the *obligatio* come to an end.

When this has been admitted, the respondent is released from the second *obligatio*, but not from the first. This is clear, because if after the ending of the ⟨second *obligatio*⟩

Socrates is running

is proposed, it should be granted, by reason of the *obligatio* of the *suppositio*. But when the opponent says

Let the period of this *obligatio* similarly come to an end,

indicating the *obligatio* which arises partially from the *suppositio*, and this is admitted, it is clear that the respondent is completely free and he need not reply to this:

Socrates is running

in any way other than before the *suppositio*, that is, by doubting it. And if

This is true or this is false

is proposed, then the whole disjunction is granted while each clause is doubted. Therefore etc.

⟨*Section Three: Rules.*⟩

The main object of the third section is to lay out various rules.[1]

⟨I⟩ First rule: Every possible or *per accidens* impossible proposition, known by someone to be such, should be admitted when posited to him.[2]

This is clear because everything of that sort from which a contradiction does not follow should be admitted. But no contradiction does follow from a possible or impossible proposition of that sort, as was shown in the *Tract on Inferences*.[3] Therefore etc.

It should be noted that I said '*per accidens* impossible' because if the simply impossible were posited, it would not be admitted, because ⟨if it were⟩,

---

[1] On the whole, this set of rules for *obligatio* was standard. Paul has his own organization.

[2] Cf. Bodleian MS *Lat.misc.e* 79, rule 2, fol. 18ra; Peter of Mantua, rule 1, op.cit., sig.G ii^{va}. Apart from these two sources, Paul's first rule was not usually offered as a rule. It appears in Marsilius, op.cit., fol. 73^r, as assumption 3; and in Buser, op.cit., fol. 73rb as a corollary to assumption 2.

'Aut per accidens impossibile' is added by Paul. For definitions of this and related notions, see *Logica Magna* II.12, fols. 169va–170ra. For a simpler discussion, see Albert, op.cit., fols. 47vb–48ra. In the standard view, a proposition was impossible *simpliciter* if it was false at all times of utterance, whereas a proposition was impossible *per accidens* if it had at some time been true, though all subsequent utterances in the recent past, the present and the future are false. Thus, had God said 'Adam non fuit' on the second day of creation, his utterance would have been true, since it would have been a negative proposition with a non-referring subject. For further discussion of the definition of modality in terms of time, the so-called statistical interpretation, see Simo Knuuttila, 'Modal Logic', in *CH*, pp. 345–346.

[3] See *Logica Magna* II.9, fols. 143vb–144va. The principle that an impossible proposition implies any proposition is found ibid., fol. 140rb.

eodem tempore obligationis, quod est contra quartam suppositionem. Et consequentia patet quia ex impossibili simpliciter[87] sequitur quodlibet materialiter vel formaliter, sicut superius fuit declaratum. Unde si poneretur quod homo esset asinus non admittendum esset, sed bene admitteretur ista

 Adam non fuit,

non obstante quod sit impossibilis, quia per accidens est talis. Ex ipsa enim nihil sequitur nisi quod sequebatur quando fuit vera. Aliter aliqua esset consequentia falsa quae posset esse bona sic significando adaequate, quod est contra sanam doctrinam valentium logicorum.

⟨II⟩ Secunda regula est ista: Omne positum obligatum sub forma positi in tempore obligationis propositum scitum esse tale est continue ab eodem concedendum.

 Verbi gratia: si ponatur talis propositio

  Tu es Romae,

admittenda[88] est quia possibilis. Deinde stante tali positione, si proponatur talis propositio

  Tu es Romae,

quam scis esse tibi positam, tunc debes ipsam concedere.

⟨1⟩ Dicitur primo notanter 'omne positum[89] obligatum' et non 'omne positum et admissum', quia per ea quae dicta sunt in primo articulo potest esse positio et admissio sine obligatione; et per consequens in tali positione et admissione, aliquid esset positum et admissum et tamen non esset concedendum quia non obligatum.

⟨2⟩ Dicitur secundo 'sub forma positi propositum', quia si proponeretur aliquod simile posito et non in forma ipsius[90], non oporteret illud concedere. Verbi gratia: Pono tibi illam:

  Reliquum istorum est verum,

demonstratis illis contradictoriis

  Rex sedet

et

---

[87] simpliciter]*om*. E
[88] admittenda]concedenda E
[89] positum]*om*.M
[90] ipsius]ipsum E

one would then have to grant contradictories during the period of one *obligatio*, which violates the fourth assumption. The inference is obvious because from the simply impossible any proposition follows materially or formally, as was explained above. Hence, if it is posited that a human being is a donkey, this is not to be admitted; but
> Adam did not exist

can certainly be admitted, even though it is impossible, because it is only *per accidens* impossible. Only what followed from it when it was true can now be inferred from it. Otherwise there would be a false inference which could be valid without losing its adequate signification, a claim which conflicts with the reasonable theories of all worthwhile logicians.

⟨II⟩ Second rule: Every *positum obligatum* which is proposed in the form of the *positum* during the period of the *obligatio* and is known to be such ⟨by someone⟩ should keep on being granted by that person.

For instance, if this proposition
> You are in Rome,

is posited, it should be admitted, because it is possible. Then, while the same *positio* is in force, if
> You are in Rome,

which you know to have been posited to you, is proposed, you must grant it.

⟨1⟩ It should be noted first that I said 'every *positum obligatum*' and not 'every *positum* and *admissum*' because, in accordance with the things said in the first section, one can have a *positio* and an *admissio* without an *obligatio*; and as a result in such a *positio* and *admissio* something is a *positum* and an *admissum* which nevertheless should not be granted because it is not an *obligatum*.

⟨2⟩ Secondly I said 'proposed in the form of the *positum*' because if something similar to the *positum* but not of the same form were proposed, one ought not to grant it. For instance: I posit this to you
> The other of these is true,[4]

indicating these contradictories
> A king is sitting down

and

---

[4] For the sophism 'Reliquum istorum est verum' see Burley, op.cit., 3.07, 3.09; Bodleian MS *Lat.misc.e 79*, fol. 18^{va-vb}; Martinus, op.cit., fol. 127^{r-v}; John of Holland, op.cit., fols. 103^v–104^r; and Buser, op.cit., fol. 76ra.

> Nullus rex sedet

Quo posito et admisso, propono tibi istam

> Alterum istorum est verum.

Concedenda est, quia vera et impertinens. Deinde propono istam

> Reliquum istorum est verum.

Si conceditur arguo[91] sic.

> Alterum istorum est verum et reliquum istorum est verum; igitur utrumque istorum est verum. Et illa sunt duo contradictoria, igitur duo contradictoria sunt (219^{va}M) simul vera.

Antecedens est concedendum a te, igitur et consequens, quod est contra quartam suppositionem.

Ideo debet negari ista

> Reliquum istorum est verum;

et licet sit similis posito, tamen non proponitur in forma positi. Nam in posito tenetur ly .reliquum. infinite, et dum proponitur tenetur relative.

⟨3⟩ Dicitur tertio 'infra tempus obligationis', quia extra tempus obligationis[92] respondens non tenetur concedere positum.

⟨4⟩ Dicitur quarto 'scitum esse tale', quia si non sciretur non oporteret ipsum concedere. Verbi gratia: si ponerem tibi istam:

> Haec est vera: 'Tu es Romae'

et tibi proponerem eandem post admissionem, et tu crederes istam

> Tu es Romae

primo[93] fuisse positam non oporteret[94] te illam concedere, videlicet:

> Haec est vera: 'Tu es Romae'.

⟨III⟩ Tertia regula est ista: Omne sequens ex posito obligato scitum esse tale in[95] tempore obligationis est concedendum.

Verbi gratia: Pono tibi istam:

> Tu es Romae.

Qua posita et admissa, propono tibi[96] istam:

---

[91] arguo]arguitur E
[92] obligationis]*om*.E
[93] primo]*om*.M
[94] oporteret]oportet E
[95] in tempore obligationis]*om*.M
[96] tibi]*om*.M

No king is sitting down.

When the above has been posited and admitted, I propose this to you:

One of these is true.

This should be granted, because it is true and irrelevant. Then I propose this:

The other of these is true.

If it is granted, I argue like this:

One of these is true and the other of these is true; therefore both of these are true. And they are two contradictories; therefore two contradictories are true at the same time.

The premisses should be granted by you; therefore the conclusion should also be granted, which violates the fourth assumption.

For this reason one must deny

The other of these is true.

Although it is similar to the *positum*, it is nevertheless not proposed in the form of the *positum*. In the *positum* the expression 'the other' is taken in an indefinite sense;[5] but when the sentence is proposed, the expression is taken in a relative sense.

⟨3⟩ Thirdly, I say 'during the period of the *obligatio*' because outside the period of the *obligatio* the respondent does not have to grant the *positum*.

⟨4⟩ Fourthly I say 'known to be such' because if something is not known, no one ought to grant it. For instance, if I were to posit this to you:

This is true: 'You are in Rome'

and if I were to propose the same to you after your *admissio*, and you believed that

You are in Rome

had been posited in the first place, you ought not to grant the following:

This is true: 'You are in Rome'.

(III) Third rule: Everything which follows from the *positum obligatum* and which is known to do so should be granted during the period of the *obligatio*.

For instance, I posit this to you:

You are in Rome.

When this has been posited and admitted, I propose this to you

---

[5] Buser, loc.cit., explains 'infinite' thus: 'ly .reliquum. stabat infinite cum nihil per se praecessit ad quod potest referri.'

Tu es alicubi;

aut istam:

Tu non es Parisius,

et patet quod quaelibet istarum est concedenda quia sequens.

Et dicitur notanter 'scitum esse tale', quia si poneretur tibi illa:

Marcus currit;

qua admissa et concessa proponeretur tibi illa[97]:

Tullius currit,

si nescis illos terminos 'Marcus' et[98] 'Tullius' esse nomina synonima nec adinvicem converti, non expedit quod tu concedas eam[99], sed debes dubitare illam quousque sciveris tales terminos synonimos esse.

⟨IV⟩ Quarta regula est ista: Omne posito obligato repugnans scitum esse tale in tempore obligationis est negandum.

Verbi gratia: si[1] ponatur tibi ista[2]:

Tu sedes,

admittatur. Qua posita et admissa, si proponatur

Tu stas,

neganda est non obstante quod sit vera, quia repugnat posito[3].
Sequitur enim[4]

Tu sedes, igitur tu non stas.

⟨V⟩ Quinta regula est ista: Omne sequens ex posito obligato et bene concesso vel[5] bene concessis scitum esse tale infra tempus obligationis est ab eodem concedendum.

Exemplum primi: pono tibi istam:

Omnis homo est Romae.

Qua posita et admissa, propono tibi[6] istam:

Tu es homo.

Concedenda est quia vera et impertinens. Deinde:

Tu es Romae.

Concedenda est quia sequens ex posito obligato cum uno bene concesso.

---

[97] illa]*om*.M
[98] et]*om*.E
[99] eam]illam E
[1] si]dicatur vel *add*.E
[2] ista]*om*.M
[3] posito]quia *add*.E
[4] enim]*om*.E
[5] vel bene concessis]*om*.E
[6] tibi]*om*.M

You are somewhere,
or this
   You are not in Paris.
It is obvious that each of these should be granted because it follows.
   And it should be noted that I say 'known to be such' because if
   Marcus is running
were posited to you, and when it had been admitted and granted
   Tullius is running
were proposed to you, if you did not know that the terms 'Marcus' and 'Tullius' were synonymous, or that they were interchangeable, it would not be in your interest to grant the proposal. Instead, you must doubt it until you do come to know that the terms are synonymous.[6]

⟨IV⟩ Fourth rule: Everything which is inconsistent with the *positum obligatum* and is known to be such should be denied during the period of the *obligatio*.

   For instance, if this is posited to you:
   You are sitting down,
it should be admitted. When it has been posited and admitted, if this is proposed:
   You are standing up,
it should be denied, despite the fact that it is true, for it is inconsistent with the *positum*. This is a valid inference:
   You are sitting down; therefore you are not standing up.

⟨V⟩ Fifth rule: Everything which follows from the *positum obligatum* together with a correctly granted proposition (or propositions) and is known ⟨by someone⟩ to follow should be granted by that person during the period of the *obligatio*.[7]

   An example of the first case: I posit this to you:
   Every human being is in Rome.
When it has been posited and admitted, I propose this to you:
   You are a human being.
This should be granted because it is true and irrelevant. Then:
   You are in Rome.
This should be granted because it follows from the *positum obligatum* together with a correctly granted proposition.

---

[6] Burley used Marcus Tullius Cicero, op.cit., 3.06, in order to explain the rubric 'sub forma positi', and so did Albert, op.cit., fol. 47rb. Albert, loc.cit., uses the example a second time to explain the rubric 'scitum esse tale'. For a discussion of Burley's view, see Hermann Weidemann, 'Ansätze zu einer Logik des Wissens bei Walter Burleigh', *Archiv für Geschichte der Philosophie*, 62 (1980) 32–45.

[7] Rule 5 and those following were not accepted by Swyneshed since he claimed that a proposition could be relevant only by virtue of its relation to the *positum*: see section 1, note 29.

Exemplum secundi: Nam pono tibi istam
> Omnis homo disputans est Parisius.

Qua posita et admissa, propono[7] tibi:
> Tu es homo.

Concedenda est[8] quia vera et impertinens. Deinde:
> Tu es disputans.

Concedenda est[9] per idem. Ultimo proponitur
> Tu es Parisius.

Concedenda est quia sequens ex posito[10] obligato et duabus concessis. (179^{va}E)

⟨VI⟩ Sexta regula est ista: Omne repugnans posito et concesso vel[11] concessis scitum esse tale infra tempus obligationis est ab eodem negandum.

Verbi gratia de primo: Pono tibi istam:
> Omnis homo currit.

Qua posita et admissa, propono tibi istam:
> Tu es homo.

Concedenda est[12], quia vera et impertinens. Deinde propono:
> Tu non curris.

Neganda est[13] quia repugnat posito et uno concesso. Patet eo[14] quod ex eadem cum concesso sequitur oppositum positi, sic arguendo:
> Tu non curris et tu es homo, igitur non omnis homo currit.

Item ex posito et illo[15] concesso[16] sequitur oppositum illius[17]
> Tu non curris;

igitur illa
> Tu non curris

repugnat eisdem. Consequentia tenet et antecedens probatur. Nam bene sequitur in tertio primae
> Omnis homo currit, tu es homo; igitur tu curris.

Exemplum secundi: Pono tibi istam
> Tu moveris.

Qua posita et admissa, propono tibi:

---

[7] propono]pono E
[8] est]*om*.M
[9] est]*om*.M
[10] posito ... et]*om*.M
[11] vel concessis]*om*.E
[12] est]*om*.M
[13] est]*om*.M
[14] eo]quia *add*.M
[15] illo]*om*.E
[16] concesso]illius *add*.E
[17] illius]*om*.E

An example of the second case: I posit this to you
> Every disputing human being is in Paris.

When it has been posited and admitted, I propose this to you:
> You are a human being.

It should be granted because it is true and irrelevant. Then
> You are disputing.

It should be granted for the same reason. Finally, this is proposed:
> You are in Paris.

It should be granted because it follows from the *positum obligatum* together with the two previously granted propositions.

⟨VI⟩ Sixth rule: Every proposition which is inconsistent with the *positum* and a previously granted proposition (or propositions), and is known to be such ⟨by someone⟩ should be denied by that person during the period of the *obligatio*.

An example of the first case: I posit this to you:
> Every human being is running.

When this has been posited and admitted I propose this to you:
> You are a human being.

It should be granted because it is true and irrelevant. Then I propose:
> You are not running.

This should be denied because it is inconsistent with the *positum* and a previously granted proposition. This is obvious because, by the argument below, the opposite of the *positum* follows from this proposition together with the previously granted proposition:
> You are not running and you are a human being; therefore it is not the case that every human being is running.

Likewise from the *positum* and the same previously granted proposition one can infer the opposite of this:
> You are not running.

Therefore this:
> You are not running

is inconsistent with them. The inference holds and the premiss can be proved, for the following is a valid example of the third mood of a first figure syllogism:
> Every human being is running, you are a human being; therefore you are running.

An example of the second case: I posit this to you:
> You are moving.

When this has been posited and admitted I propose to you

Tu non moveris localiter.

Concedenda est quia vera et impertinens. Deinde:

Tu non moveris augmentative.

Concedenda est per idem. Deinde tertio:

Tu non moveris alterative.

Neganda est quia repugnat posito obligato et[18] duobus concessis, cum ex eisdem sequatur[19] oppositum ipsius. Sequitur enim:

Tu moveris, et non motu locali[20] nec motu augmentationis, igitur motu alterationis.

E contra etiam negative sequitur cum eisdem concessis oppositum positi. Nam sequitur:

Tu non moveris (219^{vb}M) alterative nec localiter nec augmentative, igitur tu non moveris.

⟨VII⟩ Septima regula est ista: Omne sequens ex posito obligato et opposito bene negati vel bene negatorum scitum esse tale infra tempus obligationis est ab eodem concedendum.

Exemplum primi: Pono tibi istam:

Omnis homo est Romae.

Qua admissa, propono

Tu es Romae.

Neganda est, quia falsa non sequens. Deinde propono:

Tu non es homo.

Concedenda est quia sequens ex posito et opposito bene negati, nam bene negata fuit ista:

Tu es Romae,

et eius oppositum est illud:

Tu non es Romae.

Tunc[21] bene sequitur:

Omnis homo est Romae, tu non es Romae, igitur tu non es homo in[22] quarto modo secundae figurae.

---

[18] et]cum E
[19] sequatur]sequitur E
[20] locali]et *add*.E
[21] Tunc]*om*.M
[22] in . . . figurae]*om*.M

You are not moving with local motion.

This should be granted because it is true and irrelevant. Then:

You are not moving with the motion of augmentation.

This should be granted for the same reason. Then thirdly:

You are not moving with the motion of alteration.[8]

This should be denied because it is inconsistent with the *positum obligatum* and the two previously granted propositions, since its opposite can be inferred from these taken together. This is a valid inference:

You are moving, and you are not moving with local motion or with the motion of augmentation; therefore you are moving with the motion of alteration.

On the other hand, the opposite of the *positum* follows in a negative manner from the previously granted propositions, for this is a valid inference:

You are not moving with the motion of alteration or with local motion or with the motion of augmentation, therefore you are not moving.

⟨VII⟩ Seventh rule: Everything following from a *positum obligatum* and the opposite of a correctly denied proposition (or propositions) and known to be such ⟨by someone⟩ should be granted by that person during the period of the *obligatio*.

An example of the first case: I posit this to you:

Every human being is in Rome.

When this has been admitted, I propose:

You are in Rome.

This should be denied, because it is false and does not follow. Then I propose:

You are not a human being.

This should be granted because it follows from the *positum* and the opposite of a correctly denied proposition, for this was correctly denied:

You are in Rome,

and its opposite is this:

You are not in Rome.

The following is a valid example of the fourth mood of a second figure syllogism:

Every human being is in Rome, you are not in Rome; therefore you are not a human being.

---

[8] For local motion, augmentation and alteration see Aristotle, *Physics* V.2. 226 a23–226 b9. For further discussion and references, see J.A. Weisheipl, 'The interpretation of Aristotle's *Physics* and the science of motion' in *CH*, pp. 521–536.

Exemplum secundi: Et pono tibi istam:
> Antichristus est coloratus.

Qua posita et admissa, quia possibilis est, propono
> Antichristus est albus.

Neganda est, quia falsa et impertinens. Deinde propono istam:
> Antichristus est niger.

Etiam neganda est propter eandem causam. Ultimo propono tibi istam:
> Antichristus est medio colore coloratus.

Concedenda est, quia sequitur ex posito obligato et oppositis bene negatorum. Nam bene sequitur:
> Antichristus est coloratus, sed[23] nullus Antichristus est albus nec aliquis Antichristus est niger, igitur Antichristus est medio colore coloratus.

⟨VIII⟩ Octava regula est ista: Omne repugnans posito obligato et opposito bene negati vel bene negatorum scitum esse tale infra tempus obligationis est negandum.

Exemplum primi: Ponatur ista:
> Omnis homo est Romae.

Deinde:
> Tu es Romae.

Neganda est[24] quia falsa et impertinens. Ulterius
> Tu es homo.

Neganda est[25] similiter, quia repugnat posito obligato[26] et opposito bene negati, cum suum oppositum ex eisdem sequatur[27]. Sequitur enim:
> Omnis homo est Romae, tu non es Romae, igitur tu non es homo.

Exemplum secundi: Pono tibi istam:
> Aliquis istorum est Romae

demonstratis te et me et[28] Platone hic existentibus[29]. Qua posita et admissa, propono tibi istam:
> Ego sum Romae.

Neganda est[30], quia falsa et impertinens[31]. Deinde propono tibi[32] istam:
> Tu es Romae.

---

[23] sed]et E
[24] est]*om*.M
[25] est]*om*.M
[26] obligato]bene negato E
[27] sequatur]sequitur E
[28] et]*om*.M
[29] existentibus]existente E
[30] Neganda est]*om*.E
[31] impertinens]ideo neganda est *add*.E
[32] tibi]*om*.M

An example of the second case: I posit this to you:
> Antichrist is coloured.[9]

When this has been posited and admitted because it is possible, I propose:
> Antichrist is white.

This should be denied because it is false and irrelevant. Then I propose this:
> Antichrist is black.

This should also be denied, for the same reason. Finally I propose this to you:
> Antichrist has a colour between white and black.

This should be granted, because it follows from the *positum obligatum*, together with the opposite of correctly denied propositions. This is a valid inference:
> Antichrist is coloured, but no Antichrist is white, nor is any Antichrist black; therefore Antichrist has a colour between white and black.

⟨VIII⟩ Eighth rule: Everything which is inconsistent with the *positum obligatum* and the opposite of a correctly denied proposition (or propositions) and is known to be such should be denied during the period of the *obligatio*.

An example of the first case: Let this be posited:
> Every human being is in Rome.

Then:
> You are in Rome.

This should be denied because it is false and irrelevant. Further:
> You are a human being.

This should be denied as well, because it is inconsistent with the *positum obligatum* and the opposite of a correctly denied proposition, since its own opposite follows from them. This is a valid inference:
> Every human being is in Rome, you are not in Rome; therefore you are not a human being.

An example of the second case: I posit this to you:
> One of them is in Rome,

indicating you, me and Plato, all of whom are existent here. When this has been posited and admitted, I propose this to you:
> I am in Rome.

This should be denied because it is false and irrelevant. Then I propose this to you:
> You are in Rome.

---

[9] Like the examples involving running or sitting, being in Rome or being in Paris, 'Antichristus est coloratus' is standard fare. Cf. Burley, op.cit., 3.28; Albert, op.cit., fol. 47va; Bodleian MS *Lat.misc.e 79*, fol. 18vb.

Neganda etiam est propter eandem causam. Ultimo propono istam:

> Iste non est Romae,

demonstrando tertium, et patet quod neganda est quia repugnans posito obligato cum duobus oppositis bene negatorum, cum suum oppositum ex eisdem sequatur[33]. Sequitur enim:

> Aliquis istorum trium est Romae, sed ego non sum Romae nec tu es Romae, igitur iste est Romae, (demonstrando Platonem),

a disiunctiva cum destructione duarum partium principalium ad tertiam eiusdem.

⟨IX⟩ Nona regula est ista: Ad omne impertinens respondendum est secundum sui qualitatem, id est, si est verum scitum esse tale est concedendum; si est falsum scitum esse falsum, est negandum; et si est[34] dubium, dubitandum.

Et huiusmodi verbi gratia: Pono tibi istam

> Tu es Romae.

Qua admissa, propono tibi istas tres propositiones:

> Tu es homo;
>
> Tu curris;
>
> Rex sedet.

Prima concedenda est; secunda neganda; tertia dubitanda, quia[35] quaelibet istarum talis est et impertinens, quia non sequitur nec repugnat.

⟨X⟩ Ex ista regula cum prioribus sequitur decima quae est ista: Omne falsum non sequens scitum esse tale infra tempus obligationis est (179^{vb}E) negandum et omne verum non repugnans est concedendum.

Patet quia[36] illud falsum ex quo est non[37] sequens vel est impertinens vel repugnans. Si impertinens, negandum per regulam immediatam. Si repugnans, negandum similiter secundum quod ostendunt priores regulae mentionem de repugnantia facientes. Secunda pars similiter patet quia si illud est verum et non repugnans, igitur impertinens vel sequens, et per consequens iuxta regulam concedendum.

⟨XI⟩ Undecima regula est ista: Possibili obligato licet falso, non propter hoc est negandum necessarium per se, nec est concedendum impossibile per se.

---

[33] sequatur]sequitur E
[34] est]*om.*E
[35] quia]et M
[36] quia]nam M
[37] est non]*transp.*E

This should also be denied, for the same reason. Finally I propose this:
>He is not in Rome,

indicating the third. It is obvious that this should be denied because it is inconsistent with the *positum obligatum* and the two opposites of correctly denied propositions, since its opposite follows from them. The following is a valid inference from a disjunction with the denial of two of its principal clauses to the assertion of the third principal clause:

>One of these three is in Rome, but I am not in Rome, nor are you in Rome; therefore he is in Rome (indicating Plato).

⟨IX⟩ Ninth rule: One must reply to each irrelevant proposition in accordance with its status. That is, if it is true and known to be such it should be granted; if it is false and known to be such, it should be denied; and if it is uncertain, it should be doubted.

Here are some examples. I posit this to you:
>You are in Rome.

When this has been admitted, I propose the following three propositions to you:
>You are a human being;
>You are running;
>A king is sitting down.

The first should be granted, the second denied, and the third doubted because each of them has the appropriate status, and each is irrelevant since it neither follows from nor is inconsistent with ⟨the *positum*⟩.

⟨X⟩ From this rule together with the previous ones, there follows a tenth rule, which is this: Every false proposition which does not follow, and is known not to, should be denied during the period of the *obligatio*; and every true proposition which is not inconsistent should be granted.[10]

This is obvious because, given that the false proposition does not follow it must be either irrelevant or inconsistent. If it is irrelevant, it should be denied by virtue of the rule immediately above. If it is inconsistent, it should also be denied in accordance with those earlier rules which deal with inconsistency. The second clause is also obvious, because if a proposition is true and not inconsistent, then either it is irrelevant or it follows, and as a result it should be granted in accordance with the rule.

⟨XI⟩ Eleventh rule: A proposition which is necessary *per se* should not be denied because of an *obligatum* which is possible, even if it is false, nor should a proposition which is impossible *per se* be granted.[11]

---

[10] Rule 10 is not standard. It is found in Strode, op.cit., fol. 78vb: 'Servetur igitur pro principio quasi potissimo in hac arte, quod omne scitum esse verum non repugnans est concedendum, et omne scitum esse falsum non sequens est negandum; et scitum esse dubium et impertinens est dubitandum.'

[11] This standard rule is crucial for the theory of *obligationes*. As the Dominicans of Cologne put it in their commentary on an anonymous *Tractatus obligatoriorum* in the fifteenth century: '. . . principium ex quo iste tractatus obligatoriorum elicitur, sumitur ex nono Metaphysicae et primo Priorum, ut dicit Aristoteles quod possibili posito inesse, nullum sequitur impossibile. Et ideo tota scientia ista in illo principio fundatur quia scientia obligatoriorum in hoc consistit quod

Probatur, nam omne per se necessarium ex quolibet sequitur ut supra patuit. Si ergo negatur[38] necessarium per se infra tempus obligationis, negaretur (220^{ra}M) sequens ex posito, et per consequens male iuxta tertiam regulam.

Similiter, quodlibet per se impossibile cuilibet repugnat, cum oppositum ex quolibet sequatur[39]. Si ergo possibili posito obligato concederetur[40] per se impossibile, concederetur[41] repugnans posito, quod non est fiendum iuxta doctrinam quartae regulae.

Et notanter dicitur 'impossibile per se' et 'necessarium per se', quia obligato possibili admisso non est inconveniens concedere impossibile per accidens et negare necessarium per accidens. Verbi gratia: sit ita in rei veritate quod A sit illa

Deus est,

ad quam numquam respondisti. Quo supposito et admisso, pono tibi istam:

Tu es Romae.

Admittenda est[42] quia possibilis. Deinde propono tibi illam:

Tu numquam respondisti ad A.

Et patet quod est concedenda, quia vera et impertinens. Ulterius propono[43] tibi istam:

Deus est.

Concedenda est, quia per se necessarium. Ultimo propono:

Tu respondisti ad A.

Et[44] patet quod neganda est quia repugnans uni prius concesso, et tamen ipsa est necessaria per accidens quia vera de praeterito non[45] dependens a futuro, cuius significatum adaequatum non poterit esse falsum ut patet[46]. Similiter si proponitur suum contradictorium[47]

Tu numquam respondisti ad A,

patet quod est concedenda, quia idem non conceditur et negatur in eodem tempore, ex quinta suppositione alterius articuli; et tamen illa est impossibilis per accidens. Quid autem sit impossibile per se, necessarium per se, impossibile per accidens, necessarium per accidens, patet clarissime in *Tractatu de Veritate Propositionis*.

---

[38] negatur]negaretur M
[39] sequatur]sequitur E
[40] concederetur]concederet E
[41] concederetur]concederet E
[42] est]*om.*M
[43] propono]pono E
[44] Et]*om.*E
[45] non]*om.*E
[46] ut patet]*om.*E
[47] suum contradictorium]sua contradictoria M

---

aliquis concedat multa possibilia secundum conditionem obligationis, et illa sic defendat ne cogatur ex illis concedere aliquod impossibile, licet aliquando et saepe cogatur concedere aliquod falsum.' *Copulata super omnes tractatus parvorum logicalium Petri hispani ac super tres tractatus modernorum.* . . . ([Cologne], 1493), fol. lxxxi^v.

This can be proved because every proposition which is necessary *per se* follows from every other proposition, as was made clear above.¹² If, therefore, a proposition which is necessary *per se* is denied during the period of an *obligatio*, something which follows from the *positum* is denied, and as a result it is denied incorrectly according to the third rule.

Similarly, every proposition which is *per se* impossible is inconsistent with every other proposition, since its opposite follows from every proposition. If therefore a proposition which is *per se* impossible were to be granted on the basis of a possible *positum obligatum*, a proposition which is inconsistent with the *positum* would be granted, and this should not be done according to the teaching of the fourth rule.

It should be noted that I say 'impossible *per se*' and 'necessary *per se*' because when a possible *obligatum* has been admitted there is no awkwardness in going on to grant a *per accidens* impossible proposition and to deny a *per accidens* necessary proposition. For instance, let it be true that A is this proposition:

There is a God,

to which you have never replied.¹³ When this has been assumed and admitted, I posit this to you:

You are in Rome.

It should be admitted because it is possible. Then I propose this to you:

You have never replied to A.

It is clear that this should be granted because it is true and irrelevant. Further I propose this to you:

There is a God.

It should be granted because it is necessary *per se*. Finally I propose:

You have replied to A.

It is clear that it should be denied because it is inconsistent with a proposition granted earlier, and yet it is itself necessary *per accidens* because it is a truth about the past, not dependent on the future, whose adequate significate cannot be false in the future as is obvious. Similarly if its contradictory:

You have never replied to A

is proposed, it is obvious that it should be granted, because the same proposition cannot be granted and denied during the same period, according to the fifth assumption of the other section, and yet it is impossible *per accidens*. However, what it is for a proposition to be impossible *per se*, necessary *per se*, impossible *per accidens*, and necessary *per accidens* is laid out most clearly in the *Tract on the Truth of the Proposition*.¹⁴

---

¹² Cf. note 3. This principle is the converse of the principle that an impossible proposition implies any proposition, since the negation of an impossible proposition is a necessary proposition.

¹³ 'Tu numquam respondisti ad "Deus est"' is a standard sophism: see Burley, op.cit., 3.50; Albert, op.cit., fol. 48ra; Buser, op.cit., fol. 73vb. Marsilius had a similar sophism, op.cit., fols. 75^v–76^r. For discussion of an earlier use of the sophism, see Eleonore Stump, 'William of Sherwood's Treatise on Obligations', *Historiographia Linguistica*, 7 (1980), pp. 259–260.

¹⁴ The *Tractatus de Veritate et Falsitate Propositionis* has been edited and translated in *Logica Magna Part II Fascicule 6*.

⟨XII⟩ Ultima regula est ista: Qualibet parte copulativae concessa, concedenda est copulativa cuius illae vel consimiles sunt partes principales.

Verbi gratia: Si ponatur talis propositio

Tu es Romae,

qua posita et admissa, proponatur illa

Tu es homo,

concedenda est, quia vera et impertinens. Qua concessa et proposita, proponatur ista copulativa:

Tu es Romae et tu es homo.

Concedenda est, quia ex quo utraque pars fuit concessa, concedenda est.

⟨1⟩ Sed quia aliqui tenent oppositum huius regulae quasi omnes antiqui, ideo[48] pro maiori regulae declaratione arguo contra eos primo sic. Et pono illam:

Aliquis homo est Romae.

Qua posita[49], admissa et concessa, propono tibi istam:

Tu es homo[50].

Concedenda est quia vera et impertinens. Deinde propono tibi istam copulativam:

Aliquis homo est Romae et tu es homo.

Si conceditur, habeo intentum. Si negatur, propono suum oppositum, videlicet:

Nullus homo est Romae vel tu non es homo,

quae concedenda est consequenter. Deinde propono tibi illam:

Tu es homo

quae[51] concedenda est quia semel concessa est. Ultimo propono illam:

Nullus homo est Romae.

Vel concedis vel negas vel dubitas illam. Non est concedenda nec dubitanda, quia repugnans posito. Deinde suum oppositum est concessum. Si negas eam: contra:

---

[48] ideo] *om.* E
[49] posita] et *add.* E
[50] homo] quae *add.* E
[51] quae concedenda est] *om.* E

⟨XII⟩ Last rule: When each clause of a conjunction has been granted, the conjunction of which these, or equiform propositions, are the principal clauses should be granted.

For instance, if a proposition like this:
   You are in Rome,
is posited and if when it has been posited and admitted, this is proposed:
   You are a human being,
it should be granted because it is true and irrelevant. After it has been granted and proposed, let this conjunction be proposed:
   You are in Rome and you are a human being.
This should be granted, because on the basis that each of its clauses has been granted, the ⟨whole conjunction⟩ should be granted.

⟨1⟩ But because some people, indeed almost all the logicians of the past, hold to the opposite of this rule, I will present some arguments against them in order to explain the rule more clearly.[15] First argument: I posit this:
   Some human being is in Rome.
When this has been posited, admitted and granted, I propose this to you:
   You are a human being.
This should be granted because it is true and irrelevant. Then I propose the following conjunction to you:
   Some human being is in Rome and you are a human being.[16]
If this is granted, I have made my point. If it is denied, I will propose its opposite, namely:
   Either no human being is in Rome or you are not a human being.
This should be granted as a consequence of the previous move. Then I propose this to you:
   You are a human being.
This should be granted because it has already been granted once. Finally I propose this:
   No human being is in Rome.
Either you grant this or you deny it or you doubt it. It should not be granted, nor should it be doubted, for it is inconsistent with the *positum*. Then its opposite is granted. If you deny it, I argue against you like this:

---

[15] The view under discussion here is that of Roger Swyneshed. For an account of Swyneshed's position and of the reactions to him, see Paul Vincent Spade, 'Three theories of *obligationes*: Burley, Kilvington and Swyneshed on counterfactual reasoning', *History and Philosophy of Logic*, 3 (1982), 1–32; Stump, 'Roger Swyneshed'; E.J. Ashworth, 'The problems of relevance and order in obligational disputations: some late fourteenth century views', *Medioevo*, 7 (1981), 175–193.

Swyneshed's position was accepted by Lavenham, op.cit.; discussed favourably by Martinus Anglicus, op.cit., fols. 127^r–131^r; and discussed without condemnation by Robert Fland in Paul Vincent Spade, 'Robert Fland's *Obligationes*: an edition', *Mediaeval Studies*, 42 (1980), 41–60. The position was firmly rejected by Albert, op.cit., fol. 47^{ra-rb}; Marsilius, op.cit., fols. 86^r–87^r; Buser, op.cit., fol. 76^{rb-va}; Strode, op.cit., fol. 79^{rb-vb}; Peter of Candia, op.cit., fol. 66^{rb-va}. Cf. Peter of Mantua, op.cit., sig.G iii^{vb}–G iiii^{ra}.

For a note on the reading of 'quasi omnes antiqui', see Paul Vincent Spade, 'Obligations: B. Developments in the fourteenth century' in *CH*, p. 339, note 25. Spade suggests 'almost all [of them were] ancients' in place of 'almost all the ancients' which suggests a false assessment of the

Tu negas sequens ex duobus[52] concessis, igitur male.
Consequentia tenet[53] per regulas, et antecedens patet quia sequitur:
> Nullus homo est Romae vel tu non es homo, sed tu es homo, igitur nullus homo est Romae.

Consequentia tenet a disiunctiva[54] cum destructione unius partis ad alteram partem.

Sed forte diceretur hic iterum ut prius, concedendo[55] quamlibet partem antecedentis et negando[56] totam copulativam sicut negabatur[57] illa
> Aliquis homo est Romae et tu es homo

et concedebatur quaelibet pars eius.

Contra: tota ratio quare negatur illa copulativa est quia est falsa, ratione unius partis falsae, et impertinens, quia non sequitur ex suis partibus nec repugnat eisdem, ut dicit ista opinio. Sed sic non est hic, quia copulativa ista ultimo facta est impertinens, ut habet dicere opinio, et vera quia quaelibet eius pars est vera. Igitur concedenda est, et sic nulla est fuga.

⟨2⟩ Secundo arguitur[58] sic. Et pono tibi istam:
> Nullus homo est Parisius.

Haec est possibilis igitur admittenda. Qua admissa, ponatur alia:
> Nullus homo est Romae.

Haec est admittenda (220^{rb}M) cum prima, cum non repugnet[59] eidem, igitur per admissionem secundae non cessat prima. Istis ergo (180^{ra}E) admissis, propono illam copulativam:
> Aliquis homo est Parisius et aliquis homo est Romae.

Et patet quod ista copulativa est ab ipsis concedenda, quia vera ut notum est, et impertinens secundum eos, quia secundum ipsos totum est impertinens suis partibus. Tunc arguitur sic:
> Aliquis homo est Parisius et aliquis homo est Romae, igitur aliquis homo est Parisius.

Consequentia bona[60]; antecedens est concedendum ab eis, igitur et consequens. Sed consequens est oppositum positi; igitur oppositum positi est

---

[52] duobus]duabus E
[53] tenet]patet E
[54] a disiunctiva]*om*.M
[55] concedendo]concedo M
[56] negando]nego M
[57] negabatur] negabitur E
[58] arguitur]arguo E
[59] repugnet]repugnat M
[60] bona]patet et E

---

number of those holding Swyneshed's views. However, if I am correct in thinking that Paul's main sources were Albert, Buser, Strode, and the *Logica Oxoniensis* Paul may well have had the impression that everybody before Albert held a strange view about conjunctions.

[16] Swyneshed claimed that a conjunction could be denied, even though both parts had been granted. In this example, the false *positum* is granted because it is possible, and the proposition 'You are a human being' is granted because it is true and irrelevant. The conjunction of these two propositions has to be classified as irrelevant, given Swyneshed's restricted definition of relevance. Since it is also false, on account of the false *positum*, it must be rejected. A corollary is that the disjunction which is equivalent to the negated conjunction must be accepted. Hence we obtain Swyneshed's second rule that a disjunction can be granted even though both its parts are to be denied, since these are the negations of propositions already granted. Note the use made here of De Morgan's Law: '-(P.Q)' is equivalent to '-P v -Q.' See Swyneshed, op.cit., p. 257, §32; and Lavenham, op.cit., pp. 230–231, §11.

You deny what follows from two previously granted propositions, therefore you reply incorrectly.

The inference holds by virtue of the rules, and the premiss is obvious because this is a valid inference:

Either no human being is in Rome or you are not a human being, but you are a human being; therefore no human being is in Rome.

The inference holds from a disjunction with the denial of one clause to the assertion of the other clause.

But perhaps the same reply as before may be offered once again, by granting each clause of the premiss and denying the whole conjunction,[17] just as

Some human being is in Rome and you are a human being

was denied even though each of its clauses was granted.

An argument against the above: according to the view in question the full explanation of why that conjunction was denied was that it was false, by virtue of one false clause, and irrelevant, because it neither followed from its clauses nor was inconsistent with them.[18] But this situation does not obtain here, for the conjunction finally formed above is irrelevant, as the view in question must hold, and true, because each of its clauses is true. Therefore it should be granted and no escape route has been found.

⟨2⟩ Second argument: I posit this to you:

No human being is in Paris.

This is possible, therefore it should be admitted. When it has been admitted, let another proposition be posited:

No human being is in Rome.[19]

This should be admitted together with the first proposition, since it is not inconsistent with it. Thus by the *admissio* of the second proposition the first ⟨*positio*⟩ does not come to an end. When these propositions have been admitted, I propose this conjunction:

Some human being is in Paris and some human being is in Rome.

It is obvious that this conjunction should be granted by the people ⟨I am attacking⟩ because it is true, as we know; and it is irrelevant according to them, because in their view the whole is irrelevant to its parts. Next I argue like this:

Some human being is in Paris and some human being is in Rome, therefore some human being is in Paris.

The inference is valid; the premiss should be granted by them; hence the conclusion should be granted as well. But the conclusion is the opposite of the *positum*; therefore the opposite of the *positum* should be granted by

---

[17] This approach was adopted by Martinus Anglicus, op.cit., fol. 129^{r-v}. He used the same sequence of propositions, with the substitution of 'Tu es Romae' for 'Aliquis homo est Romae' as the initial *positum*. Similar sequences are found in Fland, op.cit., pp. 45–46, §14, §18, §19; and Strode, op.cit., fol. 79^{va-vb}. See also Peter of Candia, op.cit., fol. 66rb. Martinus Anglicus thought that it was all right to deny the last conjunction because this enabled one to avoid discordant results; and Fland denied it without comment. Strode and Peter of Candia, on the other hand, rejected this move, and Peter commented that it would lead to the rejection of all fundamental rules in the *ars obligatoria*.

concedendum ab eis, quod est falsum, quia tunc duo contradictoria essent concedenda ab eis in eodem tempore obligationis, videlicet positum et oppositum positi.

⟨3⟩ Tertio arguitur sic. Extra tempus obligationis concessa qualibet parte copulativae concedenda est copulativa; sed non aliter se habet copulativa respectu suarum partium principalium infra tempus obligationis quam extra. Igitur etc.

Idem dicatur de disiunctiva, videlicet quod negata utraque eius parte, debet ipsa negari, quia sic sit extra tempus obligationis. Licet enim copulativa vel disiunctiva quaecumque possit concedi vel negari non concessis vel negatis eius partibus, quia potest aliter significare quam ex compositione suarum partium; tamen[61] quia modo nulla significat nisi ex compositione suarum partium, non ideo debet copulativa aliqua negari, concessis partibus illius, nec disiunctiva concedi, negatis partibus eiusdem.

⟨4⟩ Ulterius dicit haec opinio quod haec non est consequentia:

Aliquis homo currit, tu es homo, igitur aliquis homo currit et tu es homo

nisi ponatur coniunctio copulativa inter partes; quod si fiet conceditur consequentia et negatur antecedens[62].

Et si quaeratur pro qua parte, dicunt quod pro nulla sed pro tota copulativa quae facta est ex posito falso et impertinenti vero.

Contra hoc dictum arguitur:

⟨4.O1⟩ Ex illo dicto sequitur quod ille non est syllogismus nec consequentia[63]:

Omnis homo currit, tu es homo, igitur tu curris.

Consequens est contra Aristotelem *Primo Priorum*, qui sic describit syllogismum:

Syllogismus est oratio in qua quibusdam positis et concessis necesse est conclusionem invenire[64], id est esse concedendam

ubi patet quod solae[65] praemissae absque huiusmodi nota copulationis sufficiunt conclusionem inducere.

⟨4.O2⟩ Secundo arguitur sic. Haec adinvicem repugnant

---

[61] tamen . . . partium]*om*.M
[62] antecedens]sicut et consequens *add*.E
[63] nec consequentia]*om*.E
[64] invenire]evenire E
[65] solae]solum E

---

[18] Here Paul is echoing Strode who wrote, op.cit., fol. 79vb: 'Sed forte negatur antecedens pro tota copulativa. Sed contra: illa copulativa est vera et impertinens, scita a te esse vera, ergo secundum istam viam deberet concedi.'

[19] In this argument two *posita* are employed: see section 2, note 19. The argument is taken from Marsilius, op.cit., fol. 86^v; Buser, op.cit., fol. 76^{rb-va}. The examples are Buser's.

them. This must be false, for then two contradictories, namely the *positum* and its opposite, would have to be granted by them during the period of one *obligatio*.

⟨3⟩ Third argument: outside the period of an *obligatio* a conjunction should be granted when each of its clauses has been granted; but a conjunction is not related to its principal clauses in any other way during the period of an *obligatio* than it is outside the period of the *obligatio*.[20] Therefore etc.

The same can be said of a disjunction, namely that it should be denied when each of its clauses has been denied, for this is the case outside the period of an *obligatio*. It is true that any conjunction or disjunction might be granted or denied without its clauses having been granted or denied, because it could be given some meaning other than the one which arises from the composition of its clauses. However, as things are, no conjunction or disjunction does have a meaning other than the one which arises from the composition of its clauses; and as a result no conjunction should be denied when its clauses have been granted, nor should any disjunction be granted when its clauses have been denied.

⟨4⟩ Further, the view in question holds that the following:
> Some human being is running, you are a human being; therefore some human being is running and you are a human being,

will not count as an inference unless a conjunction-operator is placed between the clauses ⟨of the premiss⟩.[21] But if this is done, they grant the inference and deny the premiss.

And if someone asks on account of which clause, they say on account of neither. It is the whole conjunction ⟨which causes the denial⟩, because it is formulated from a false *positum* and an irrelevant truth.

⟨4.O1⟩ An argument against that above claim: from the claim it follows that
> Every human being is running, you are a human being, therefore you are running,

does not count either as a syllogism or as an inference. But this conclusion flies in the face of Aristotle, who defined a syllogism like this (*Prior Analytics* I.1. 24b18–20):
> A syllogism is a discourse in which when certain things have been posited and granted, it is necessary for a conclusion to be reached, that is, to be granted.

Here it is obvious that the premisses alone, without any special conjunction-operator are enough to induce the conclusion.

⟨4.O2⟩ Second argument: the following propositions are mutually inconsistent:[22]

---

[20] This argument is similar to one found in Marsilius op.cit., fols. 86ᵛ–87ʳ; and Buser, op.cit., fol. 76ʳᵇ. Marsilius wrote: 'Quia copulativa non significat aliud a suis partibus, istis partibus pro eodem instanti concessis, concedenda est copulativa.'

[21] See Swyneshed, op.cit., pp. 260–261, §43. Strode briefly mentions Swyneshed's claim: op.cit., fol. 79ᵛᵃ.

[22] Peter of Mantua used these examples, op.cit., sig.G iiiᵛᵇ, to show that propositions can be inconsistent even if they are not conjoined.

> Omnis homo currit,
> Tu es homo,

et

> Tu non curris.

Igitur ex uno sequitur oppositum alterius, et per consequens ex illis praemissis sequitur quod tu curris.

⟨4.03⟩ Tertio arguitur sic. Ex ista opinione sequitur quod nihil sequitur nec repugnat posito et concesso aut opposito bene negati. Patet cum tam positum quam concessum successive proponantur[66] absque copulatione media. Modo si aliquid repugnaret illis, oppositum illius sequitur ex eisdem, quod non concedit haec opinio.

Magis apparebit huius opinionis insufficientia cum contra hanc regulam propria solventur argumenta.

⟨*Articulus Quartus: Conclusiones*⟩

⟨I⟩ Quartus articulus est plurium conclusionum illativus[67], quarum prima est ista: Non sequitur:

> Tu concedis scitum a te esse falsum vel tu[68] negas scitum a te esse verum vel tibi dubium, igitur male respondes.

Haec conclusio patet ex secunda et tertia regulis. Verbi gratia: Pono tibi istam:

> Tu curris.

Qua admissa, propono tibi istam, et concedis[69] eam bene respondendo. Et tu scis eam esse falsam.

⟨II⟩ Secunda conclusio est ista. Non est inconveniens infra tempus obligationis concedere aliquam propositionem esse veram et necessariam et tamen negare ipsam vel[70] e converso.

Verbi gratia: Pono tibi istam:

> 'Deus est' et 'Homo est asinus' convertuntur.

---

[66] proponantur]proponuntur M
[67] illativus]formaliter deductivus E
[68] tu]*om*.M
[69] concedis]concedes M
[70] vel]et E

Every human being is running,
You are a human being

and

You are not running.

Therefore from one the opposite of the other can be inferred, and as a result from these premises it can be inferred that you are running.

⟨4.03⟩ Third argument: it follows from this view that nothing either follows from or is inconsistent with the *positum* and a proposition which has been granted, or the opposite of a correctly denied proposition. This is obvious because both the *positum* and the previously granted proposition are proposed successively, without any intermediary conjunction. Now if something were to be inconsistent with these propositions, its opposite would follow from them, which is not granted by those holding this view.

The inadequacy of this view will become even more apparent when I dissolve the special objections which are to be brought against Rule Twelve.

⟨*Section Four: Theses*⟩

The fourth section contains a number of theses.[1]

⟨I⟩ First thesis: The following inference is invalid:

You grant what you know to be false or you deny what you know to be true or uncertain, therefore you reply incorrectly.[2]

This thesis is obvious because of the second and third rules. For instance, I posit this to you:

You are running.

Once it has been admitted, I propose it to you, and when you grant it you reply correctly. Yet you know it to be false.

⟨II⟩ Second thesis: It is not awkward to grant some proposition to be true and necessary during the period of an *obligatio* and yet to deny it, or the reverse.[3]

For instance, I posit this to you:

'There is a God' and 'A human being is a donkey' are interchangeable.[4]

---

[1] Paul seems to be following Strode, op.cit., fols. 78va–79rb, in having a separate section for theses, though it should be noted that Strode included his rules under that heading. Some of Paul's theses appear as rules or as assumptions in other authors: see below.

[2] This is Strode's first thesis, op.cit., 78^{va-vb}.

[3] This is Marsilius's fourth thesis for *impositio*, op.cit., fol. 80^v; and is also Buser's fourth thesis for *impositio*, op.cit., fols. 74vb–75ra. In both Marsilius and Buser the thesis is linked to an earlier discussion. Marsilius had given as corollaries to his first three assumptions the following rules, op.cit., fols. 73^v–74^v: (1) An inference whose premiss has terms of second intention and whose conclusion has terms of first intention is invalid. Thus, 'P is true, therefore P' does not hold, nor does 'P is not true, therefore not P'. (2) An inference whose premiss has terms of first intention and whose conclusion has terms of second intention is invalid. Thus, 'P, therefore P is true' does not hold; nor does 'Not P, therefore P is not true'. Buser gave the same rules as corollaries of his first two assumptions: op.cit., fol. 73^{ra-rb}. The reason for these rules had to do with the belief that a *propositio* was an occurrent sentence, whether written or spoken, with a conventional meaning which could be altered. (These remarks were not taken to apply to mental *propositiones* which, although equally occurrent sentences, enjoyed natural, and hence unalterable, meaning.) In 'P is true' the *propositio* is being mentioned rather than used, and there is no guarantee that the set of written or spoken signs to which one's attention is drawn will continue to signify a particular state of affairs. As a result it is possible that 'God exists' is a false *propositio* even though it is granted that God does in fact exist; and it is equally possible that 'A human

Qua admissa, propono tibi illam:
> 'Deus est' est vera et necessaria.

Concedendum est, quia verum (220^{va}M) et impertinens. Deinde propono tibi istam[71]:
> 'Homo est asinus' est vera et necessaria.

Concedendum est quia sequitur ex posito et concesso. Nam sequitur:
> 'Deus est' et 'Homo est asinus' convertuntur, et haec est vera et necessaria 'Deus est'; igitur haec est vera et necessaria 'Homo est asinus'.

Ultimo propono illam:
> Homo est asinus,

et patet quod neganda est, quia ante casum erat neganda, et iam non est sequens. Et sic patet prima pars conclusionis. Secunda pars[72] probatur. Nam cedat tempus obligationis et ponatur[73] idem quod prius. Quo admisso, propono istam:
> Haec est falsa et impossibilis: 'Homo est asinus'.

Concedenda est quia vera et impertinens. Deinde propono illam:
> Haec est falsa et impossibilis: 'Deus est'.

Concedenda est, quia sequens ex posito et concesso. Ultimo propono illam:
> Deus est.

Et patet quod concedenda est quia sequens. Sequitur enim[74] a quolibet ut patet. Et si negatur, cedat tempus obligationis, et probatur quod in tempore negasti simpliciter necessarium, igitur (180^{rb}E) male. Quare etc.

Ex ista conclusione sequitur istud corollarium: videlicet quod non est inconveniens infra tempus concedere aliquam consequentiam esse bonam et tamen negare ipsam et e contra.

Patet, nam concedere aliquam consequentiam esse bonam non est nisi concedere illationem consequentis ex antecedente esse necessariam. Modo sicut stat concedere[75] aliquam propositionem esse veram et necessariam, et tamen negare ipsam, et e converso, ita contingit in consequentia. Exemplum enim habetur in primo casu vel secundo. Nam facta impositione, fiat haec consequentia

---

[71] istam]haec *add*.E
[72] pars]*om*.M
[73] ponatur]ponitur E
[74] enim]aliquid *add*.E
[75] concedere]*om*.E

---

being is a donkey' is a true *propositio* even though it is granted that no human beings are in fact donkeys.

This sharp separation between use and mention is of great importance for the type of *obligatio* commonly called *impositio*, which involved the imposing of new meaning on particular sets of sounds or symbols. Note the reference to *impositio*, p. 76, last line.

It will be noted that Buser and Marsilius, like other medieval logicians, would reject Tarski's adequacy condition for truth, as exemplified in '"Snow is white" is true if and only if snow is white'. The medieval position on this point is very close to that taken by Casimir Lewy in *Meaning and Modality* (Cambridge: Cambridge University Press, 1976). He argues that neither 'The English sentence "Snow is white" means that snow is white (and nothing else)' nor 'The English sentence "Snow is white" is true ≡ snow is white' is logically necessary, and he bases his arguments on the logical possibility that any set of English words might have had a different

When this has been admitted, I propose this to you:

'There is a God' is true and necessary.

This should be granted, because it is true and irrelevant. Then I propose this to you:

'A human being is a donkey' is true and necessary.

This should be granted because it follows from the *positum* and a proposition which has been granted. This is a valid inference:

'There is a God' and 'A human being is a donkey' are interchangeable, and 'There is a God' is true and necessary; therefore 'A human being is a donkey' is true and necessary.

Finally I propose this:

A human being is a donkey.

It is obvious that it should be denied, because it should have been denied before the case was stated, and it does not follow at the moment. Thus the first clause of the thesis is clear. Now I will prove the second clause. Let the period of the *obligatio* come to an end, and let the same proposition as before be posited. When it has been admitted, I propose this:

'A human being is a donkey' is false and impossible.

This should be granted because it is true and irrelevant. Then I propose this:

'There is a God' is false and impossible.

This should be granted because it follows from the *positum* and a proposition which has been granted. Finally I propose this:

There is a God.

It is obvious that this should be granted because it follows. Indeed, as is clear, it follows from any proposition whatsoever. And if it is denied, let the period of the *obligatio* come to an end, and I will prove that you have denied a simple necessary proposition during the period of the *obligatio*, which means that you have replied incorrectly. Therefore etc.

From this thesis a corollary follows, namely that it is not awkward to grant during the period of the *obligatio* that some inference is valid and yet to reject it; and the reverse.[5]

This is obvious, because to grant an inference to be valid is simply to grant the necessity of the link between the premiss and the conclusion. But just as it is consistent to grant that some proposition is true and necessary while denying it, and the converse, so it can happen with an inference. An example can be drawn from either the first or the second case above. After the *impositio* has been carried out, let this inference be formulated:

---

meaning (p. 11, pp. 19–20. I have chosen the formulations given in note 2 on p. 19 in order to prevent confusion between medieval and modern uses of the word 'proposition'.). He concludes (p. 21) that it is only the necessary proposition 'That snow is white is true ≡ snow is white' which 'gives an adequacy condition for what Tarski calls the "classical" (i.e. the correspondence) conception of truth'.

[4] This example is standard. See Albert, op.cit., fol. 47ra; fol. 47va. See below, Part 2, chapter 1, against rule 5, sophism 1.

[5] This corollary is Marsilius's fifth thesis for *impositio*, op.cit., fol. 80^v; and also Buser's fifth thesis for *impositio*, op.cit., fol. 75ra.

> Deus est, igitur homo est asinus;

et patet quod neganda est, quia ante casum fuisset negata, etiam in casu non est sequens. Et si dicitur:

> Illa consequentia est bona et necesssaria,

concedatur quia sequens ex casu. Si enim illae duae convertuntur, sequitur quod illa consequentia sit[76] bona.

⟨III⟩ Tertia conclusion est ista: Concedens in casu se male respondere non male, sed bene respondet; ita quod[77] non est inconveniens concedere in casu se male respondere.

Probatur, nam ista

> Tu male respondes

est possibilis, igitur potest esse positum obligatum, aut sequens, aut sequens ex aliquo posito obligato et concesso; et cum omne positum obligatum aut sequens ex aliquo tali sit concedendum, sequitur quod aliquando ista:

> Tu male respondes

infra tempus obligationis est a te concedenda. Non enim debet reputari[78] inconveniens quod aliquis infra tempus concedit[79] se male respondere; sed inconveniens esset vel ignominiosum, si alicui extra tempus probaretur quod infra tempus male respondisset[80]. Etiam ad metam ducitur, qui[81] non obligatus concedit se male respondere. Conclusio sic declaratur. Et pono tibi istam:

> Tu concedis duo contradictoria inter se contradicentia et scienter.

Qua admissa, quia possibilis, propono

> Tu male respondes.

Concedenda est, quia sequens ex posito obligato. Tamen[82] non possum probare extra tempus quod infra tempus male respondisti, quia infra tempus concessisti solum sequens ex posito obligato, igitur tunc bene respondebas.

Contra istam conclusionem arguitur sic. Omnis disputatio temptativa fit ad illum finem ut probetur respondentem male respondere; sed habito fine sive cessantibus[83] quae sunt ad finem, cessat disputatio; igitur cum fatetur respondens se male respondere, cessare debet disputatio.

---

[76] sit]est E
[77] quod]om.E
[78] reputari]repugnari M
[79] concedit]concedat M
[80] respondisset]respondisti E
[81] qui]quia E
[82] Tamen]cum E
[83] cessantibus]cessante M

There is a God, therefore a human being is a donkey.

It is obvious that it should be rejected because it would have been rejected before the case was stated, and also because it does not follow by the terms of the case. And if someone says:

This inference is valid and necessary,

this can be granted, for it does follow from the statement of the case. If indeed the two propositions were interchangeable, it would follow that the above inference was valid.

⟨III⟩ Third thesis: Someone who, according to the terms of the case, grants that he replies incorrectly does not reply incorrectly, but correctly. Thus it is not awkward, given the terms of the case, to grant that one replies incorrectly.[6]

This can be proved, for

You reply incorrectly

is a possible proposition. Hence it can be a *positum obligatum*, or it can follow ⟨from the *positum obligatum*⟩, or it can follow from some *positum obligatum* together with a previously granted proposition. Since every *positum obligatum* and what follows from it should be granted, it follows that

You reply incorrectly

should sometimes be granted by you during the period of the *obligatio*. It should not be thought of as awkward if someone grants that he replies incorrectly during the period ⟨of an *obligatio*⟩; but it would be awkward or even disgraceful if one could prove to someone outside the period ⟨of an *obligatio*⟩ that he had replied incorrectly during the period. Indeed ⟨the opponent⟩ reaches his goal if he can make ⟨the respondent⟩ grant that he replies incorrectly when he is not obligated to do so. The thesis can be explained like this. I posit this to you:

You grant two contradictories which are mutually contradictory, and you do this knowingly.[7]

When this has been admitted, because it is possible, I propose:

You reply incorrectly.

This should be granted because it follows from the *positum obligatum*. However, I cannot prove outside the period that you replied incorrectly during the period, for during the period you only granted what followed from the *positum obligatum*, therefore you replied correctly during the period.

An argument against the thesis: Every disputation which is designed to test ⟨logical skills⟩ moves towards the goal of proving the respondent to reply incorrectly. But when the goal is reached, or when the means for reaching the goal have disappeared, the disputation comes to an end. Therefore, when the respondent confesses that he replies incorrectly, the disputation should come to an end.

---

[6] This is Marsilius's sixth thesis for *impositio*, op.cit., fol. 80ᵛ; it is also Buser's sixth thesis for *impositio*, op.cit., fol. 75ʳᵃ. It is Strode's second general thesis, op.cit., fol. 78ᵛᵇ.

[7] Marsilius, op.cit., fol. 76ᵛ, gave as rule 13 that the rules themselves were contingent, and hence there was no difficulty in admitting such *posita* as 'You grant two contradictories.' Buser, op.cit., fol. 74ʳᵃ, gave this as rule 10.

Huic dicitur negando consequentiam, quia[84] cum respondens fatetur, id est concedit, se male respondere, hoc non est pro vero sed pro sequente. Si tamen fateatur sic respondens extra tempus obligationis, tunc est probatum respondentem male respondere, et ideo tunc cessaret disputatio.(220^{vb}M) Opponens ergo praetendit unum istorum, videlicet aut[85] quod respondens infra tempus concedat se male respondere, et hoc non sit sequens; aut quod dicat aliqua propter quae extra tempus probatur[86] quod in tempore male respondebat. Quare etc.

⟨IV⟩ Quarta conclusio[87] est ista. Durante tempore obligationis non est certificanda quaecumque quaestio.

Probatur nam sit rei veritas quod solus Sortes loquatur, tunc pono tibi istam:

> Nullus Sortes loquitur.

Qua posita et admissa propono tibi istam:

> Aliquis homo loquitur.

Concedenda est quia vera et impertinens. Quod sit vera patet per suppositionem; quod autem sit impertinens patet quia non sequitur nec repugnat[88]. Deinde cum tu concedis istam

> Aliquis homo loquitur,

quaero quis est ille, et patet quod nullus adsignandus est, quia si dicitur quod Sortes est ille qui loquitur, conceditur repugnans posito. Si autem dicitur quod Plato, conceditur falsum et impertinens, et ita de quolibet alio. Igitur etc.

Confirmatur hoc in exemplo clariori: Pono tibi istam:

> Haec[89] est necessaria: 'Homo est asinus'.

Admittenda est quia possibilis. Qua admissa, propono tibi illam:

> Homo est asinus.

Neganda est ut patet, et si dicitur quare negas eam, dicas 'Quia[90] mihi placet. Extra tempus dicam causam'. Si enim diceres 'Quia[91] est impossibilis per se', tu concederes[92] repugnans posito. Ubi tamen opponens omnino vellet scire causam, dicas

---

[84] quia]quod E
[85] aut]*om*.E
[86] probatur]probat E
[87] conclusio]regula E
[88] repugnat]repugnaret M
[89] Haec . . . asinus]'Homo est asinus' est necessaria E
[90] Quia]quod   M
[91] Quia]quod   E
[92] concederes]impossibile et *add*.M

I reply to this by rejecting the inference. When the respondent confesses, that is, grants, that he replies incorrectly he does this not because it is true, but because it follows. However, if the respondent were to make his confession outside the period of the *obligatio*, then it would have been proved that he did reply incorrectly, and the disputation should then come to an end. The opponent therefore alleges one of two things, either that the respondent does grant that he replies incorrectly during the period of the *obligatio* when this does not follow, or that he says something on account of which one could prove outside the period that he did reply incorrectly during the period. Therefore etc.

⟨IV⟩ Fourth thesis: During the period of the *obligatio* one should not give a straight answer to every question.[8]

Proof: let it be true that Socrates alone is speaking. Then I posit this to you:

   No Socrates is speaking.

When this has been posited and admitted, I propose this to you:

   Some human being is speaking.

This should be granted because it is true and irrelevant. That it is true is clear from the *suppositio*; that it is irrelevant is clear because it neither follows nor is inconsistent. Then, when you grant this:

   Some human being is speaking,

I ask who he is. It is obvious that no one can be picked out. If one says that Socrates is the person who is speaking, one will grant a proposition which is inconsistent with the *positum*. If one says that Plato is the person, one will grant a proposition which is false and irrelevant; and the same applies to any other candidate. Therefore etc.

This argument can be supported by a clearer example. I posit this to you:

   'A human being is a donkey' is necessary.

This should be admitted, because it is possible. When it has been admitted, I propose this to you:

   A human being is a donkey.

This should be denied, as is obvious; and if it is asked why you deny it, you should say 'Because I want to. I will tell you the reason outside the period'. If however you were to say 'Because it is impossible *per se*', you would grant a proposition which is inconsistent with the *positum*. But where the opponent persists in wanting to know your reason, you should say

---

[8] This thesis, that not all questions need be given a straight answer, has an obvious function given the rules that possible *posita* should be admitted and that irrelevant truths should also be admitted. The thesis appears as a rule in Burley, op.cit., 3.35; and Albert, op.cit., fol. 47vb (with the word 'non' omitted.) It is rule 12 in Marsilius, op.cit., fol. 76^r; and rule 9 in Buser, op.cit., fols. 73vb–74ra. See Part 2, chapter 1, against rule 7, sophism 3 for further discussion.

Nego eam quia ante casum ipsam negassem, et iam non est sequens ex aliquo obligato vel concesso. Quare etc.

⟨V⟩ Quinta conclusio est ista: Eadem propositio infra idem tempus obligationis in uno loco proposita est pertinens et in alio loco proposita est impertinens.

Verbi[93] gratia: Pono tibi illam:

Aliquis homo est Parisius.

Qua admissa, si propono tibi istam primo:

Tu es homo,

et secundario istam:

Aliquis homo est Parisius et tu es homo,

patet quod haec copulativa est pertinens, quia sequitur ex posito et concesso. Ubi vero copulativa ista immediate post positum proponeretur, impertinens esset. (180^{va}E) Ex quo sequitur quod in respondendo per hanc artem est ordo maxime attendendus. Nam in casibus similibus ad propositiones omnino similes, propter hoc quod diversis ordinibus proponuntur[94], diversae dandae sunt responsiones. Verbi gratia: Ponatur illa:

Omnis homo currit.

Qua admissa, proponatur ista:

Tu es homo.

Concedenda est, quia impertinens scita esse vera. Si deinde proponatur

Tu curris,

concedenda est quia sequens ex posito obligato cum bene concesso. Sed si cedat tempus prioris obligationis, et ponatur casus de novo, et mutetur ordo ita quod immediate post positum obligatum proponatur illa:

Tu curris,

patet quod neganda est quia falsa et impertinens. Deinde si proponatur ista[95]:

Tu es homo,

neganda est quia repugnat posito et opposito bene negati, cum eius oppositum sequatur[96] ex eisdem. Sequitur enim:

---

[93] Verbi gratia]*om.*E
[94] proponuntur]proponatur M
[95] ista]*om.*M
[96] sequatur]sequitur E

I deny it because I would have denied it before the case was stated, and it does not now follow from any *obligatum* or previously granted proposition. Therefore etc.

⟨V⟩ Fifth thesis: One and the same proposition during the period of one *obligatio* may be relevant when it is proposed in one place but irrelevant when it is proposed in another place.[9]

For instance, I posit this to you:

Some human being is in Paris.

When this has been admitted, if I first propose this to you:

You are a human being

and second this:

Some human being is in Paris and you are a human being,

it is clear that the conjunction is relevant, because it follows from the *positum* and a previously granted proposition. But if this conjunction were proposed immediately after the *positum*, it would be irrelevant. From this it follows that the art ⟨of *obligatio*⟩ requires one to pay close attention to the order of propositions when one is replying.[10] Different replies have to be given to propositions which are altogether alike and which are put in like cases, just because they have been proposed in a different order. For instance, let this be posited:

Every human being is running.

When this has been admitted, let this be proposed:

You are a human being.

It should be granted because it is irrelevant and known to be true. If

You are running

is the next to be proposed, it should be granted because it follows from the *positum obligatum* together with a correctly granted proposition. But if the period of the first *obligatio* comes to an end, and the case is put again, and the order is changed so that

You are running

is proposed immediately after the *positum obligatum*, then it is clear that it should be denied because it is false and irrelevant. Then if

You are a human being

is proposed, it should be denied because it is inconsistent with the *positum* and the opposite of a correctly denied proposition, for its opposite can be inferred from these. This is a valid inference:

---

[9] This is a common rule, but was rejected by Swyneshed, since in his view relevance was a function only of a proposition's relation to the original *positum*. Albert of Saxony has this thesis both as his fifth rule, op.cit., fol. 47va and as the first corollary of his definitions, op.cit., fol. 47ra. The second corollary is that a proposition proposed in one place may be granted, and when proposed in another place, may be denied: cf. p. 82, line 14 ff. The third corollary is a rejection of Swyneshed's position. Albert's second corollary is found in Burley, op.cit., 3.34; Ockham, op.cit., p. 738; John of Holland, op.cit., fol. 102^{r-v}; Peter of Candia, op.cit., fol. 66va; Strode, op.cit., fol. 79^{ra-rb}. Albert's first and second corollaries were combined in his rule 7 by Marsilius, op.cit., fol. 75^{r}; and in his rule 5 by Buser, op.cit., fol. 73va. See also Peter of Mantua, op.cit., sig.G iii^{va}.

[10] The slogan "Est ordo maxime attendendus" is found in Burley, op.cit., 3.34; Ockham, op.cit., p. 738; Peter of Candia, op.cit., fol. 66va. It is Strode's fourth thesis, op.cit., fol. 79^{ra-rb}.

Omnis homo currit, tu non curris, igitur tu non es homo.

Ecce quomodo propositiones illae quae in priori casu concedebantur[97] in secundo negantur et hoc ratione ordinis proponendi et postponendi. Quare[98] etc.

⟨VI⟩ Sexta conclusio est ista: dum positum possibile[99] repugnaret[1] positioni et fiat admissio et obligatio, positum propositum est concedendum et positio proposita debet negari.

Hoc patet per vim obligationis, nam in tempore obligationis non tenetur respondens concedere vel negare aliquid virtute obligationis nisi quod concedendum vel negandum limitat obligatio. Sed obligatio consurgens ex positione et admissione non limitat concedere vel negare (221^{ra}M) positionem aut admissionem; sed solum obligatum positum et admissum. Igitur ratione obligationis est concedendum positum, quodcumque sit illud, et negandum repugnans eidem, sive fuerit positio seu quaevis alia propositio[2].

Ex ista conclusione sequitur quod insufficienter scribunt dicentes quod omne positum et admissum propositum non repugnans positioni est concedendum. Nam si velit[3] aliquis negare positum cum proponitur quia repugnans positioni, ad quod ergo servit quod admisit prius quod non fuit positio seu[4] positum.

Et si negetur[5] talis casus ubi positum repugnat positioni, pari ratione sunt omnes tales casus negandi:

 Tu non es,

vel

 Omnis homo bibit, tacet, vel dormit.

Et sic non admittitur cuiuslibet consequentiae non bonae oppositum consequentis stare cum antecedente, ut

 Tu es, igitur ego sum.

Immo tales casus sunt negandi, cum pono tibi quod taceam vel cum[6] ego[7] sedens hic pono tibi quod omnis homo currit[8] vel quod omnis homo est Romae. Videatur igitur finis huius artis, et constabit quod[9] talis responsio fuga dici poterit miserorum, qui huius artis nesciunt principia neque finem. Quo namque[10] iure admittens quod nihil est sibi positum, quod sit A, ⟨tenetur⟩

---

[97] concedebantur]et *add*.M
[98] Quare]diversi E
[99] possibile]*om*.M
[1] repugnaret]repugnat E
[2] propositio]positio M
[3] velit]vellet E
[4] seu]sed M
[5] negetur]negatur E
[6] cum]*om*.E
[7] ego]sum *add*.E
[8] currit]currat E
[9] quod]*om*.M
[10] namque]nam E

Every human being is running, you are not running; therefore you are not a human being.

You can see how those propositions which were to be granted in the first case are denied in the second, and this by virtue of the order in which one proposition is proposed before or after another. Therefore etc.

⟨VI⟩ Sixth thesis: When a *positum* which is a possible proposition is inconsistent with the *positio*, provided that the *admissio* and *obligatio* are completed, the *positum* should be granted when it is proposed, and the *positio* should be denied when it is proposed.[11]

This is obvious from the force of the *obligatio*, for during the period of an *obligatio* the respondent does not have to grant or deny anything by virtue of the *obligatio* unless the *obligatio* limits him to granting or denying it. But an *obligatio* which arises from the *positio* and the *admissio* does not limit one with respect to granting or denying the *positio* or *admissio*. The only limitation concerns the *obligatum, positum*, and *admissum*. Therefore by virtue of the *obligatio* the *positum* should be granted, no matter what it is, and anything inconsistent with it should be denied, whether it is the *positio*, or any other proposition.[12]

From this thesis it follows that the views of those who wrote that every *positum* and *admissum* which is proposed and which is not inconsistent with the *positio* should be granted, are inadequate. For if someone wants to deny the *positum* when it is proposed because it is inconsistent with the *positio*, what point was there in his admitting something which now turns out not to have been a proper *positio* or *positum*?

And if one denies some case in which the *positum* is inconsistent with the *positio*, by parity of reasoning one should deny all cases like this:

You do not exist,[13]

or

Every human being is drinking, or silent, or asleep.

As a result one would not be able to admit that every invalid inference is such that the opposite of the conclusion is consistent with the premiss, e.g.

You exist, therefore I exist.

Indeed, cases like this would have to be denied, as when I posit to you that I am silent, or when while sitting down here I posit to you that every human being is running or that every human being is in Rome. One can see how this would finish the art ⟨of *obligatio*⟩; and it has been established that such a reply could be called the escape route of wretches who know neither the principles nor the goal of this art. For by what right could the one who admits that

---

[11] This thesis and the reasons for it are found in Strode, thesis 3, op.cit., fols. 78vb–79ra. Marsilius had noted in his *descriptiones* that 'obligatio non obligat ad sustinendum obligationem sed obligatum tantum', and drew the conclusion that propositions which were relevant to the *obligatio* alone, the *admissio* alone, or to both together, without also being relevant to the *obligatum*, need not be taken into consideration: Marsilius, op.cit., fol. 72^v. For similar remarks, see Buser in his discussion of the sophism 'Tu non es', along with two other sophisms: Buser, op.cit., fol. 76rb.

[12] There were a number of authors who disagreed with Strode and Paul on this issue. These authors adopted one of three positions: (1) A *positum* which is inconsistent with the *obligatio* or

concedere quod A est sibi positum, aut quod aliquid est sibi positum, cum sit expresse repugnans in rei veritate; licet infra tempus non convenienter adsignetur[11] ista causa, sed cessante tempore obligationis.

Et si dicatur quod rei veritas est quod A est sibi positum, non tamen sequitur illud esse concedendum quia stat illud bene negari per quartam regulam. Sicut ego sedens et admittens istam

    Ego curro,

negarem in illo casu istam:

    Tu sedes

propositam, non obstante quod sit vera. Non enim reputo turpius vel absurdius verum contingens cum repugnaret[12] negare, quam falsum contingens dum est sequens concedere; quare non est mirandum si ex obligato falso concesso sequantur[13] falsa quam plura concedenda vel sibi repugnant[14] multa vera neganda.

⟨VII⟩ Septima conclusio est ista: Nulla[15] propositio de terminis autentice impositis ad significandum a se et suis similibus condistincta[16] potest per solam positionem aut impositionem fieri aliqualis qualis iam non est vel fuit.

Volo dicere quod nulla talis propositio

    Homo est animal,

vel

    Tu curris,

potest esse falsa vel impossibilis ex sola nova positione aut impositione. Similiter nec aliqua talis

    Homo est asinus,

potest esse vera vel necessaria ex sola positione vel impositione aut quovis modo terminorum variatione. Patet, nam quacumque positione facta de novo vel impositione adhuc manet prima impositio, quia tua adventicia impositio non debet autenticam destruere. Igitur dato quod poneres vel imponeres istam

    Homo est animal

---

[11] adsignetur]adsignatur E
[12] repugnaret]repugnat E
[13] sequantur]sequatur M
[14] repugnant]repugnent M
[15] Nulla]nam E
[16] condistincta]condistinctim E

---

the *admissio* or both together, should not be admitted. Albert, op.cit., fol. 49[rb], wrote: 'Possibile licet falsum non repugnans obligationi nec admissioni nec his simul est admittendum'. (2) A *positum* which is inconsistent with the *positio* should be admitted but denied: see the discussion of the sophism 'Tu non es' in Billingham, op.cit., fol. 90[v], *Lat.misc.e 79*, fol. 19[ra–rb], and *Lib.Soph. Oxon.*, sig.C v[v]. However, they did not appeal to this principle in their discussion of 'Nihil est tibi positum', which they granted: Billingham, op.cit., fols. 90[v]–91[r], *Lat.misc.e 79*, fol. 19[rb]. *Lib.Soph.Oxon.*, sig.C v[v], says the *positum* should be denied in this sophism, but the text makes sense only if 'deny' is replaced by 'grant', as can be seen if one compares the text with Corpus Christi College Cambridge MS 378, fol. 49[v]. (3) A *positum* which is inconsistent with the *positio* should be admitted, but treated as irrelevant. Swyneshed's first rule, op.cit., p. 265, §62, was 'Omne positum sine obligatione ad hoc pertinente non repugnans positioni in tempore positionis est concedendum.' In §64 he explained 'quod positum non repugnans positioni est ex quo non sequitur oppositum positionis', and he used the example 'Nihil est tibi positum': cf. Martinus, op.cit., fol. 129[v] ('Nulla obligatio tibi fit'); Lavenham, op.cit., pp. 228–229, §6, §8. Swyneshed also said, op.cit., p. 265, §64: 'Si tamen positum repugnat positioni respondendum est ad illud sicut ad impertinens.' See also Martinus, loc.cit.; Lavenham, op.cit., p. 229, §8. Fland, op.cit., p. 47, §23, described this rule as 'nova', though Martinus treated it as a common

nothing is posited to him, which is A, ⟨be forced⟩ to grant that A is posited to him, or that something is posited to him, when this is clearly inconsistent, given the truth of the matter; even though the reason ⟨for the inconsistency⟩ cannot appropriately be given during the period of the *obligatio*, but only when it has come to an end.

And if someone says that the truth of the matter is that A is posited to him, it does not follow that this should be granted, for by the fourth rule it is consistent that it should be correctly denied. In the same way when I am sitting down but admit

I am running,

I should, given this case, deny

You are sitting down

when it is proposed ⟨to me⟩, even though it is true. For I do not think it is more disgraceful or more absurd to deny a contingent truth when it is inconsistent than to grant a contingent falsehood when it follows. Hence one should not be amazed if a great many falsehoods which should be granted follow from a false *obligatum* which has been granted, or if many truths which should be denied are inconsistent with it.

⟨VII⟩ Seventh thesis: No proposition whose terms have been authentically endowed with the power to signify things which are distinct from the terms themselves or other similar terms, can acquire characteristics which it does not now have, and never did have, by virtue of a *positio* or an *impositio* alone.[14]

I mean to say that no proposition of this sort:

A human being is an animal

or

You are running

can become false or impossible just because of a new *positio* or *impositio*. Similarly no proposition of this sort:

A human being is a donkey

can become true or necessary just because of a *positio* or an *impositio* or any means of producing variation in the terms. This is obvious, because no matter what new *positio* or *impositio* is produced, the first *impositio* remains, because your adventitious *impositio* ought not to destroy the authentic one. Therefore, even if you posit or imposit this:

A human being is an animal

---

rule. Certainly it does not seem to have any link with Swyneshed's peculiar rules for conjunctions and disjunctions. Albert acknowledged Swyneshed's rule as an alternative, op.cit., fol. 49rb, and pointed out that this would involve a revision of his own rule. Instead of placing a restriction on the *posita* which were to be admitted, the restriction was placed on the *posita* which were to be granted. He said 'Et tunc regula iam posita potest poni universaliter, scilicet "Omne positum possibile licet falsum est admittendum".'

[13] 'Tu non es' was a popular sophism, as was 'Nihil est tibi positum'. For discussion of both, see Part 2, chapter 1, against rule 4, sophism 1. The examples in this section were taken from Strode and I have corrected the text on p. 84, last line, in accordance with Strode's text.

[14] Swyneshed gave the following rule, op.cit., p. 254, §21: 'Propter impositionem alicujus propositionis ad illam non est responsio varianda.' See also Lavenham, op.cit., pp. 235–236,

significare adaequate hominem esse asinum et[17] illam
> Homo est asinus

adaequate significare hominem esse animal, non sequitur tamen in rei veritate propter tuam positionem et meam admissionem primam esse impossibilem et secundam necessariam. Sed[18] bene sequitur quod obligor ad sustinendum primam esse impossibilem et secundam necessariam. Unde non sequitur:
> Pono quod illa sit vera 'Homo est asinus', igitur illa est vera 'Homo est asinus'.

Immo nec sequitur[19]:
> Pono quod illa sic significet, igitur illa sic significat[20].

Aliter enim facta impositione (180^{vb}E) ista
> Homo est asinus

esset concedenda, quia tunc significaret adaequate hominem esse animal quod est falsum.

⟨VIII⟩ Octava conclusio: Quaelibet propositio de terminis non habentibus firmam et certam significationem potest per solam positionem aut impositionem esse aliqualis qualis iam non est vel fuit.

Pro cuius declaratione notandum quod terminorum quidam habent firmam significationem ex prima institutione[21] sicut illi termini 'homo', 'animal', 'deus', 'ens' et huiusmodi; quidam autem indifferentem, sicut pronomina demonstrativa et nomina materialia (221^{rb}M) videlicet A, B, C; semper loquendo de significatione quae potest dirigi ad distincta significata ipsorum signorum vel consimilium.

De terminis primo modo[22] sumptis procedit alia[23] conclusio. De aliis vero[24] terminis procedit haec conclusio. Nam haec est falsa:
> Hoc est homo,

demonstrando asinum; et per solam impositionem de novo fiet[25] vera ponendo[26] quod per ly .hoc. demonstretur[27] homo. Similiter haec est falsa:
> A est B

dato quod extrema materialiter supponant; et per solam impositionem fieret[28]

---

[17] et . . . animal]*om*.E
[18] Sed]quia M
[19] sequitur]quod *add*.E
[20] significat]significet E
[21] ex . . . institutione]*om*.M
[22] modo]*om*.M
[23] alia]illa E
[24] vero]autem E
[25] de novo fiet]novam fieret E
[26] ponendo]*om*.M
[27] demonstretur]demonstratur E
[28] fieret]fiet M

---

§22; Fland, op.cit., p. 55, §73; Martinus, op.cit., fols. 129^v–130^r; *Lib.Soph.Cant.*, sig.C ii^v; *Lib.Soph.Oxon.*, sig.C viii^r; Strode, op.cit., fol. 89vb; Peter of Mantua, sig.G ii^{va}. In Bodleian MS *Lat.misc.e 79*, fol. 22vb, we find: 'Alia regula est ista: quod semper propter novam impositionem non est responsio varianda ad propositionem in se, scilicet quando imponitur nova significatio, sed tunc debet mutare quando proponitur ista est vera vel falsa.' In other words 'P is true' is to be treated differently from P. The reason for this was hinted at by Swyneshed, loc.cit., §34, §35, §36, but was made quite clear by Marsilius, op.cit., fol. 78^v (for a less truncated version see the printed edition, op.cit., sig.B i^{vb}); and by Buser, op.cit., fol. 74rb. They gave as a rule 'Omne impositum est impertinens suae impositioni', and Buser wrote: ' . . . Non enim sequitur "Impono quod 'Homo est asinus' significat deum esse, ergo homo est asinus", nec sibi repugnat de forma, prout elici potest ex primo corollario suppositionis prius datae.' (For the

to signify adequately that a human being is a donkey; and this:

> A human being is a donkey

to signify adequately that a human being is an animal, it does not follow that in truth the first is impossible and the second necessary, just because of your *positio* and my *admissio*. But it does follow that I am obligated to uphold the first as impossible and the second as necessary. Hence this:

> I posit that 'A human being is a donkey' is true; therefore 'A human being is a donkey' is true[15]

is an invalid inference; as indeed is this:

> I posit that it signifies in such and such a way; therefore it does signify in such and such a way.

Otherwise when the *impositio* had been carried out

> A human being is a donkey

would have to be granted, because it would have come to signify adequately that a human being was an animal, which it does not.

⟨VIII⟩ Eighth thesis: Any proposition whose terms do not enjoy a fixed and certain signification can acquire characteristics which it does not now have and never did have, by virtue of a *positio* or *impositio* alone.

In order to explain this, one should note that some terms have a fixed signification by virtue of a primary institution. Such terms include 'human being', 'animal', 'God', 'being' and so on. Other terms have a variable signification. Such terms include demonstrative pronouns and material names such as A, B, C.[16] In these remarks I am speaking only of the signification which draws one's attention to things which are distinct from the signs themselves, or their equiforms.

My other thesis applies to terms of the first sort. The present thesis applies to terms of the second sort. This is false:

> This is a human being

when a donkey is indicated; but it could become true solely by virtue of a new *impositio* if one posited that 'this' indicated a human being. In the same way

> A is B

is false, given that the end-terms have material *suppositio*; yet it could

---

corollary referred to, see this section note 3.) See also Strode, op.cit., fol. 89vb.

It seems that Buridan rejected the usual rule: John Buridan, *Sophismata*, edited by T.K. Scott (Stuttgart-Bad Cannstatt: Frommann Holzboog, 1977) p. 105; quoted in translation by Spade in *CH*, p. 340. Richard Brinkley also explicitly rejected the rule, as appears from a passage quoted by Spade in *CH*, p. 339, note 29.

[15] Strode's example, op.cit., fol. 89vb is more colourful: 'Nam qualitercumque ponatur vel varietur significatio talis propositionis "Tu curris", non sequitur propter hoc ut movearis vel quiescas plus quam si comburatur talis propositio.'

[16] The distinction between different kinds of terms has been taken from Strode, op.cit., fol. 89vb, though Strode makes a sharper distinction between pronouns which 'sunt instituta significare quicquid placuerit per ea demonstrare vel inferre', and A, B, C, which 'non sunt imposita ad aliquid significandum saltem autentice.' Strode's rule, op.cit., fol. 90ra, is 'Nec est varianda responsio nisi fiat impositio respectu termini qui non prius autentice primarie significavit, ut ad tales: Hoc est verum 'A est B.' Ad quas, cum proponitur sine demonstratione vel impositione tali, dicatur quod non intelligo illam. Cum tamen facit impositionem, poteris talem concedere vel negare prout tibi videtur faciendum.' (corrected from MS fol. 44vb).

vera, dato quod ponam ly .A. significare adaequate hominem et ly .B. animal. Unde facta hac impositione, ita est illa concedenda et dicenda esse vera:

    A est B,

sicut illa

    Homo est animal,

et non sequitur:

    Ante impositionem illa fuit impossibilis, igitur modo est neganda.

Non valet argumentum, quia iam non est impossibilis sed necessaria propter mutationem significationis. Unde si ponatur quod illa

    A est B

significet adaequate hominem esse animal, et proponatur

    A est B,

concedenda est. Et si dicitur

    Ipsa est falsa et impertinens,

concedo[29] quod est impertinens sed nego quod sit falsa. Et si dicitur

    Cedat tempus,

admitto, et cum[30] proponitur[31]

    A est B,

nego eam, si supponunt termini materialiter, et concedo quod est falsa[32]. Non tamen fuit falsa in tempore obligationis, quia in eodem tempore mutavit[33] significationem propter impositionem novam.

Et si contra haec dicta allegaretur aliquod dictum meum, dicatur illud intelligendum esse de terminis et propositionibus habentibus firmam et certam significationem.

Ex his ergo patet quod in casu isto ita concedenda est ista:

    A est homo

et illa:

    B est animal

sicut illa:

---

[29] concedo]concedendo M
[30] cum]*om*.M
[31] proponitur]proponatur M
[32] falsa]et *add*.M
[33] mutavit]mutant E

It should be noted that a word's *significatio* includes its power to make something known. This is why Paul adds that he is not concerned with the kind of *significatio* which makes the words themselves known. A word could also be thought of as making known its utterer, its utterer's concepts, and the things referred to by the utterer.

The use of the phrase 'nomina materialia' is of some interest. In *Logica Magna* I. 2, fol. 16vb Paul explains that such non-complex terms as A and B always have material *suppositio* unless they receive a new *impositio*, and one may assume that 'materialia' is used to express this fact. In the absence of a new *impositio*, 'A est B' can only mean 'The sign "A" is identical to the sign "B"', which is false.

Geach has pointed out to me that Paul's use of *impositio* for A and B is not uniform. Sometimes A and B are used as abbreviations, to stand in for other expressions (e.g. p. 88, line 2 from bottom, ff.) and sometimes they are used as names, to stand for propositions (e.g. p. 96, line 8 ff.)

become true solely by virtue of a new *impositio*, if I posited that the expression 'A' adequately signified a human being and the expression 'B' an animal. Hence if such an *impositio* were carried out

    A is B

would have to be granted and said to be true just as much as

    A human being is an animal.

And this does not follow:

    Before the *impositio* that proposition was impossible; therefore it should now be denied.

The argument is not valid because the proposition is not impossible now. Instead it is necessary, because of the change in its signification. Hence if someone posits that

    A is B

adequately signifies that a human being is an animal, and then proposes

    A is B,

it should be granted. And if someone says

    That proposition is false and irrelevant,

I grant that it is irrelevant but I deny that it is false. And if someone says

    Let the period come to an end,

I admit this; and when this is proposed:

    A is B,

I deny it if the terms have material *suppositio*, and I grant that it is false. However, it was not false during the period of the *obligatio*, for during that period its signification was changed because of the new *impositio*.

And if you try to use my own words against me, it must be pointed out that what I said earlier had to do with terms and propositions which enjoy a fixed and certain signification.

From these remarks it follows that in the case stated above

    A is a human being

should be granted; and so should

    B is an animal;

just as much as these propositions

Homo est homo

aut³⁴ illa:

Animal est animal,

et hoc propter causam dictam. Quare etc.

Ex praedicta conclusione sequuntur quaedam corollaria communiter concessa.

⟨1⟩ Primum est:

A est aliquid et tamen nihil est A.

Patet quod si A imponeretur ad significandum tantum quantum haec oratio 'omnis homo', tunc sicut³⁵ haec esset concedenda:

Omnis homo est aliquid,

ita illa:

A est aliquid,

et sicut concedenda esset ista:

Nihil est omnis homo,

ita et ista:

Nihil est A.

⟨2⟩ Secundum corollarium:

A est B et tamen nullum B est A.

Patet dato quod³⁶ A imponatur³⁷ ad significandum tantum quantum haec oratio 'omnis homo' et B tantum quantum ly . homo..

⟨3⟩ Tertium corollarium:

A et B convertuntur et tamen nec A est B nec B est A.

Patet dato quod A imponatur ad significandum tantum quantum haec oratio 'omnis homo' et B similiter.

⟨4⟩ Quartum corollarium:

A est B et tamen B existente, impossibile est A esse.

Patet quia si A imponeretur³⁸ ad significandum tantum quantum haec oratio 'quilibet hominum', B tantum quantum haec oratio 'solus unus homo'. Et³⁹ tunc illa esset concedenda:

A est B,

sicut illa:

Quilibet hominum est solus unus homo;

---

³⁴ aut]et E
³⁵ sicut]sic E
³⁶ quod]haec *add.*E
³⁷ imponatur]imponeretur E
³⁸ imponeretur]imponetur M
³⁹ Et]*om.* M

A human being is a human being

and

An animal is an animal.

This is so for the reason given above. Therefore etc.

From the aforesaid thesis certain corollaries follow which are commonly granted.[17]

⟨1⟩ First corollary:

A is something and yet there is nothing which is A.

This is obvious, for if A were imposed to be tantamount in signification to the phrase 'every human being', then just as this ought to be granted:

Every human being is something,

so should this:

A is something;

and just as this would have to be granted:

There is nothing which is every human being,

so should this:

There is nothing which is A.

⟨2⟩ Second corollary:

A is B and yet no B is A.

This is obvious given that A is imposed to be tantamount in signification to the phrase 'every human being' and B tantamount to the expression '(a) human being'.

⟨3⟩ Third corollary:

A and B are interchangeable, yet A is not B, nor is B A.

This is obvious given that A is imposed to be tantamount in signification to the phrase 'every human being' and B is similarly imposed.

⟨4⟩ Fourth corollary:

A is B, yet if B exists it is impossible for A to exist.

This is obvious if A is imposed to be tantamount in signification to the phrase 'each of ⟨several⟩ human beings' and B is imposed to be tantamount in signification to the phrase 'just one human being'. In this case

A is B

would have to be granted, as would

Each of ⟨several⟩ human beings is just one human being.

---

[17] Corollary 6 seems to be Paul's own. The others are found in Albert, op.cit., fol. 48^{rb-va}; Marsilius, op.cit., fol. 78^v; and Buser, op.cit., fol. 74^{rb-va}. The sophisms depend on the fact that A and B look as if they play the role of simple subjects and predicates, whereas by imposition syncategorematic terms are added. As medieval logicians well knew, syncategorematic terms cannot be switched around without a radical alteration in the structure of the sentence: see E.J. Ashworth, 'Mental language and the unity of propositions: A semantic problem discussed by early sixteenth century logicians', *Franciscan Studies*, 41 (1981), 61–96.

et tamen si⁴⁰ B est⁴¹, impossibile est A esse, sicut si solus unus homo est, impossibile est quod quilibet hominum sit.

⟨5⟩ Quintum corollarium:

A videt B et tamen B non videtur ab A.

Patet⁴², dato⁴³ quod A convertatur cum ly .omnis homo. et B cum ly .homo, et cum hoc ponatur quod quilibet homo videat seipsum et nullum alium; quo posito, sequitur corollarium.

⟨6⟩ Sextum corollarium:

A differt a⁴⁴ B et tamen ⟨non⟩⁴⁵ B differt ab A.

Patet⁴⁶ dato quod⁴⁷ A convertatur cum ly .homo. et B cum ly .omnis homo. .

Oppositum huius conclusionis atque corollariorum tenet unus magister, dicens quod admissa impositione negandum est A esse B, et concedendum est nullum B esse A quia ista:

A est B,

negaretur extra tempus obligationis, et nunc non est sequens, igitur neganda. Consequentia tenet⁴⁸ per unam regulam. Quod autem non sit sequens probatur⁴⁹, quia non sequitur:

Imponatur A ad significandum tantum quantum haec oratio 'omnis homo' et B tantum quantum ly .homo., igitur A est B.

Et ita consequenter dicit in aliis⁵⁰ corollariis, negando quodlibet⁵¹ illorum affirmativorum, quia semper⁵² negasset extra tempus obligationis, et quamlibet talem concedit esse veram.

Sed haec responsio insufficienter procedit; ut patet ex dictis⁵³. Nam (221ᵛᵃM) pono⁵⁴ tibi illam⁵⁵:

Hoc est homo (181ʳᵃE)

et certum est quod tu quaeres quid demonstretur⁵⁶ per ly .hoc. . Tunc dico sic:

Pono quod demonstretur⁵⁷ asinus.

Et patet quod negabis eam, quia nescis⁵⁸ quomodo aliter respondebis⁵⁹. Concessa igitur illa, arguo contra te per argumentum proprium

⁴⁰ si]*om*.E
⁴¹ est]*om*.E
⁴² Patet] et *add*. E
⁴³ dato]*om*.M
⁴⁴ a]ab M
⁴⁵ non] nullum M,E *correxi*
⁴⁶ Patet]et *add*.E
⁴⁷ quod]ly *add*.M
⁴⁸ tenet]patet dicit E
⁴⁹ probatur]probat   E
⁵⁰ in aliis]etiam de omnibus aliis   E
⁵¹ quodlibet illorum affirmativorum]quamlibet illarum affirmativarum   E
⁵² semper]sic E
⁵³ dictis]praedictis E
⁵⁴ pono]propono   E
⁵⁵ illam]*om*.M
⁵⁶ demonstretur]demonstratur   E
⁵⁷ demonstretur]demonstratur   E
⁵⁸ nescis]nescio   E
⁵⁹ respondebis]respondes   M

Yet if B exists, it is impossible for A to exist; just as if there were only one human being in existence, it would be impossible for each of ⟨several⟩ human beings to exist.

⟨5⟩ Fifth corollary:

> A sees B and yet B is not seen by A.

This is obvious given that A is interchangeable with the expression 'every human being' and B with the expression 'a human being'. One also has to posit that each human being sees himself and no one else. If this is posited, the corollary follows.

⟨6⟩ Sixth corollary:

> A differs from B, but it is not the case that B differs from A.[18]

This is obvious, given that A is interchangeable with the expression 'a human being' and B with the expression 'every human being'.

There is one master who holds the opposite of this thesis and its corollaries.[19] He says that when the *impositio* has been admitted one should deny that A is B and grant that no A is B because this

> A is B

would be denied outside the period of the *obligatio*, and it does not follow now; hence it should be denied. The inference holds because of a rule. That the proposition does not follow is proved on the grounds that this is an invalid inference:

> Let A be imposited to be tantamount in signification to this phrase 'every human being' and B tantamount to the expression 'a human being'; therefore A is B.[20]

He argues in the same way about the other corollaries, in each case denying the affirmative claims because they would always have been denied outside the period of the *obligatio*, while at the same time granting them to be true.

But this reply is inadequate, as is obvious from what has been said. I posit this to you:

> This is a human being.[21]

It is certain that you will ask what is indicated by the word 'this'. I answer:

> I posit that a donkey is indicated.

It is obvious that you will deny ⟨the first proposition⟩, because you will not know how else you could reply. Once these things have been granted, I can argue against you by an argument of his own:

---

[18] I have emended the text to read 'non' rather than 'nullum', since 'nullum omnis homo' does not make sense. Probably the scribe was misled by the analogy with Corollary 2 (where 'nullum' is neuter to agree with B rather than with 'homo'.)

The point of Corollary 6 can be understood if one considers the doctrine of *exponibilia* as it was applied to sentences containing 'differt'. 'A differs from B' was expounded as 'A exists and B exists and A is not B' (see *Logica Parva*, p. 99, *Logica Magna* I. 3, fol. 31va). Given the doctrine of *suppositio*, it turns out that the third exponent of the first sentence, 'Homo non est omnis homo', is true, because no individual human being is identical to every human being taken together, and the third exponent of the second sentence, 'Omnis homo non est homo', is false, because every human being is in fact identical to some human being or other. As Geach pointed out to me, the use of 'differ' in ordinary English seems to be the reverse: 'Every human being differs from a human being [sc. some human being or other]' is true, and 'A human being differs from every human being' is false.

Illa propositio ante positionem[60] fuit a te dubitanda, ut patet, et iam non est sequens, igitur iam est[61] a te dubitanda.

Patet quod ista consequentia non valet et per consequens nec illa istius magistri.

Item si ponatur[62] ut prius quod continue ante hoc[63] demonstrabatur[64] asinus per ly .hoc. et nunc[65] demonstretur homo, patet quod continue ante hoc fuit neganda et modo est concedenda. Et hoc propter solam positionem[66] et mutationem significationis. Et ita dicatur de A et B.

Secundo arguitur sic. Et pono quod A sit illa:

Deus est.

Admittenda est, nam eam admittunt communiter[67] disputantes. Qua posita et admissa, propono tibi:

A est verum.

Et patet iuxta modum respondendi omnium logicorum quod concedendum est A esse verum. Sed probo quod non per argumentum illud. Nam ante positionem[68] fuit illa:

A est verum

neganda a te vel non intellecta, sed modo non sequitur ex posito, quia non sequitur:

A est illa 'Deus est', igitur A est verum.

Igitur iam in tempore est a te neganda, vel non intellecta[69]. Patet quod ipse negaret consequentiam et sic solveret proprium[70] argumentum.

Item iste magister plane contradicit sibi. Nam in capitulo de impositione, imponit quod A significet tantum praecise sicut una illarum:

Rex sedet

et

Nullus rex sedet,

et lateat te[71] quae illarum sit vera. Qua posita[72] et admissa immediate proponit

Tu scis A esse verum.

Ad quam respondet concedendo; et tamen patet quod ante casum ipsam negasset, et iam non sequitur ex impositione nec ex imposito.

---

[60] positionem]impositionem E
[61] est]*om*.E
[62] ponatur]proponatur E
[63] hoc]continue *add*.E
[64] demonstrabatur]demonstrabitur E
[65] nunc]tunc E
[66] positionem et mutationem]*transp*.E
[67] communiter]consequenter E
[68] positionem]impositionem E
[69] intellecta]intelligenda M
[70] proprium]*om*.E
[71] te]*om*.E
[72] posita]proposita E

---

[19] These arguments are found in Buser, op.cit., fol. 74[rb–va]; and in Marsilius, op.cit., fols. 78[v]–79[v]. Buser gave his arguments concurrently with the sophisms, but Marsilius listed the sophisms first. I assume that Paul means Buser when he speaks of 'unus magister'.

[20] As Buser explains, it is invalid to argue: 'A is B' is true, therefore A is B.

[21] Buser, op.cit., fol. 75[rb], used 'Hoc est homo' as an example. If one is pointing to an ass, would it be true that 'human being' signifies a braying creature, he asks? There may also be an echo of a discussion in Strode, op.cit., fol. 91[rb–va]; and in William Heytesbury, *Casus Obligationis* in Oxford, Bodleian Library MS *Canon.Class.Lat.* 278, fol. 70[ra–rb].

That proposition should have been doubted by you before the *positio*, as is clear, and it does not follow in the present circumstances, so it should be doubted by you now.

It is clear that this inference does not hold, and as a result neither does the argument of that master.

Likewise if one posits, as above, that before the present circumstances a donkey kept on being indicated by the word 'this', whereas a human being is now indicated, it is clear that the proposition should always have been denied before the present circumstances, but should be granted now. This is just because of the *positio* and the change in signification. The same applies to both A and B.

Second argument: I posit that A is this:

There is a God.

This should be admitted, for disputants commonly admit it. When it has been posited and admitted, I propose to you:

A is true.[22]

It is clear that one should grant that A is true in accordance with the method of reply adopted by all logicians. But I can prove that this is not so, by using his arguments. Before the *positio*

A is true

should either have been denied by you or you should have said that you did not understand it; but it does not follow from the *positum* in the present circumstances, since this is an invalid argument:

A is the proposition 'There is a God', therefore A is true.

So the proposition should be denied by you in the present circumstances, or you should say that you do not understand it. It is clear that he would deny the inference, and so he would destroy his own argument.

Likewise this master thoroughly contradicts himself. In his chapter on *impositio* he imposits that A signifies in exactly the same way as one of the following:

A king is sitting down

and

No king is sitting down.

It is hidden from you which of the two is true.[23] When this has been posited and admitted, he immediately proposes

You know that A is true.

He replies to this by granting it; and yet it is obvious that before the case was stated he would have denied it; nor, in the present circumstances, does it follow either from the *impositio* or from the *impositum*.

---

[22] This is a very popular sophism: see below, Part 2, chapter 1, against rule 1, sophism 4. Marsilius discussed it, op.cit., fol. 83^{r-v}; but it does not appear in Buser. One of my reasons for thinking that Paul uses Buser rather than Marsilius is that he seems to be inquiring into what his source would have said, if he had been confronted with this sophism.

[23] This is another popular sophism. It was discussed by Heytesbury, op.cit., fol. 70ra; Albert of Saxony, op.cit., fol. 49ra; Marsilius, op.cit., fol. 83^v; Buser, op.cit., fol. 75vb; and Peter of Candia, op.cit., fols. 68va–69ra. Paul himself discusses the sophism in *Logica Magna Part I*

Deinde facit aliam[73] impositionem dicens:

Sit quod A significet alteram istarum 'Deus est' et 'Homo est asinus', te sciente; et sit A in rei veritate illa 'Deus est', sed hoc lateat te.

Tunc proponit:

A est verum.

Ad quam respondet dubie, et tamen patet quod ante impositionem ipsam negasset, quia sibi significasset talem litteram A esse veram propositionem. Et nunc in casu non sequitur ex imposito nec ex[74] impositione ut manifeste apparet. Igitur etc.

Non igitur in istis terminis non habentibus firmam significationem sed continue mutabilem per[75] mutationem novae impositionis est respondendum sicut in aliis habentibus fixam et determinatam significationem. Sed recte respondendum est sicut ad alias propositiones significantes ex impositione prima et autentica; unde ex sola prima[76] impositione conceditur illa:

Aliquis homo est animal

et dicitur quod est vera, non faciendo difficultatem ibi[77] inter 'concedere illam' et 'concedere esse veram', sed utraque adseritur. Et tamen patet quod illa non sequitur ex prima impositione nec ex primo imposito qua imponebatur[78] illos terminos sic significare. Primo ita in proposito respondeatur ad propositiones de A et B in nostra impositione ac si esset impositio prima facta. Et nisi hoc sit verum, nescio quomodo magni logici, philosophi ac[79] geometrae atque theologi vere loquantur in suis casibus et suppositionibus, qui modum consimilem habent loquendi. Quare etc.

---

[73] aliam]illam M
[74] ex]om.E
[75] per]ad M
[76] prima]om.M
[77] ibi]om.M
[78] imponebatur]imponebam E
[79] ac]om.E

Fascicule 7 [Tractatus de Scire et Dubitare], edited with an English translation and notes by Patricia Clarke (Oxford: published for the British Academy by the Oxford University Press, 1981) pp. 27–29, 35–63. His initial statement of the sophism follows that given by Heytesbury and Peter of Candia. His first reply (p. 35 ff.) is Peter of Candia's second; his second reply (p. 45 ff.) is Peter of Candia's first; and his fourth reply (p. 49 ff.) is Peter of Candia's third.

Then he produces another *impositio* by saying:

Let A signify one of the two propositions 'There is a God' and 'A human being is a donkey'. You know this. Let A in fact signify 'There is a God'. This is hidden from you.[24]

Then he proposes:

A is true.

He replies to this with uncertainty; and yet it is clear that before the *impositio* he would have denied it, because it would then have signified to him that the letter 'A' was a true proposition. And given the case as stated, the proposition does not now follow from the *impositum* or from the *impositio* as is more than clear. Therefore etc.

Therefore in the case of a change made by a new *impositio*, one should not make the same kind of reply when dealing with those terms which lack a fixed signification and are continuously variable as when one is dealing with those terms which have a settled and determinate signification. The correct reply will be like the reply made to those other propositions which signify by virtue of a primary and authentic *impositio*. Thus by virtue of the primary *impositio* alone this proposition

Some human being is an animal

is granted; and it is said to be true, provided that one makes no difficulty about the difference between 'to grant it' and 'to grant it to be true', but asserts both. Yet it is clear that this proposition does not follow from the first *impositio* or from the first *impositum* in which the terms were endowed with their signification. So in the first proposal above one should reply to the propositions concerning A and B by treating our *impositio* as if it were the very first *impositio*. Unless this were the case, I really do not see how the great logicians, philosophers, geometers and theologians who have adopted a similar way of talking, would be able to speak truly in the cases and assumptions they put before us. Therefore etc.

---

[24] This is another popular sophism: see Buser, op.cit., fol. 75vb. For other sources see Swyneshed, op.cit., pp. 268–269, §81; Albert, op.cit., fol. 49ra; Marsilius, op.cit., fols. 83^v–84^r; Strode, op.cit., fol. 92rb; Peter of Candia, op.cit., fols. 67vb–68va. There is a discussion of Heytesbury's position in Stump, 'Roger Swyneshed', pp. 153–63, in the section 'William Heytesbury's *Regulae*'. Paul himself discusses the sophism in *Logica Magna Part I Fascicule 7*, pp. 3–5, 9–15.

⟨PARS SECUNDA: DE POSITIONE⟩

⟨Capitulum Primum: Contra Regulas⟩

Contra regulas tertii articuli intendo arguere et argumenta contra[1] easdem[2] dissolvere ut[3] eisdem fides firmius debeat adhiberi.

⟨Contra Regulam Primam⟩

Prima ergo regula ponit quod omne possibile aut per accidens impossibile scitum ab aliquo esse tale eidem positum est admittendum.

⟨1⟩ Contra istam regulam (221^{vb}M) arguitur primo sic: Et pono tibi omne possibile[4].

⟨1.1⟩ Si negatur[5] casus, habetur oppositum istius regulae.

⟨1.2⟩ Item omne possibile est a te admittendum. Sed nihil pono tibi nisi possibile, igitur nihil tibi pono nisi a te admittendum. Igitur quod tibi pono est a te[6] admittendum et illud negas, ergo male respondes.

⟨1.3⟩ Confirmatur sic. Quodlibet a me tibi positum est a te negandum; sed omne possibile est a me tibi positum, ergo omne possibile est a te negandum. Et per consequens nullum tale est a[7] te concedendum vel admittendum.

⟨1.4⟩ Ideo si admittitur casus, propono tibi illam:

Tu es homo.

Et patet quod est concedenda, quia posita et admissa, cum sit possibilis. Deinde propono tibi illam:

Tu non es homo.

Vel concedis vel negas. Si concedis, cedat tempus obligationis et deducitur quod eodem modo respondisti ad contradictoria, ergo male. Si negas, iterum cedat tempus obligationis et sequitur quod tu negasti (181^{rb}E) tibi positum obligatum, quia tibi ponebatur et admisisti omne possibile, et ista fuit

---

[1] contra]*om*.E
[2] easdem]eadem   E
[3] ut]et   M
[4] possibile]et *add*.E
[5] negatur]negetur E
[6] a te]*om*.M
[7] a . . . vel]*om*.M

⟨PART TWO: CONCERNING *POSITIO*⟩

⟨Chapter One: Against the Rules⟩
I now plan to produce arguments against the rules which were given in section three, and then to destroy these arguments so that our faith in the rules will be strengthened.
⟨Against Rule One⟩
The first rule posits that every possible or *per accidens* impossible proposition known by someone to be such should be admitted when posited to him.[1]
⟨1⟩ First argument against rule one: I posit to you every possible proposition.[2]

⟨1.1⟩ If the case is denied, then we obtain the opposite of the rule.

⟨1.2⟩ Again, every possible proposition should be admitted by you. But I do not posit anything to you other than what is possible; therefore I do not posit anything to you other than what should be admitted by you. Therefore what I posit to you should be admitted by you. But you deny it; therefore you reply incorrectly.

⟨1.3⟩ A supporting argument: whatever is posited to you by me should be denied by you; but every possible proposition is posited to you by me; therefore every possible proposition should be denied by you. As a result no such proposition should be granted or admitted by you.

⟨1.4⟩ However, if the case is admitted, I propose this to you:
　You are a human being.
It is clear that it should be granted since, being possible, it has been posited and admitted. Then I propose this to you:
　You are not a human being.
Either you grant this or you deny it. If you grant it, let the period of the *obligatio* come to an end. It will be shown that you have replied in the same way to contradictory propositions; therefore, you have replied incorrectly. If you deny it, let the period of the *obligatio* again come to an end. It follows that you have denied the *positum obligatum* which was put to you, since every possible proposition was posited to you and admitted by you. This was a

---

[1] All but the first of the seven sophisms in this section have to do with *impositio*, which Paul obviously regarded as part of *positio*. All the sophisms are found in previous authors, but except where noted, Paul does not follow his sources closely.
[2] This first sophism is taken from Strode, op.cit., fol. 80[rb–vb], who used it against the same rule. Cf. Peter of Mantua, op.cit., sig.G iii[ra–rb]. Paul omits some of Strode's arguments, but in 1.2, 1.4, 1R and 1.2R he follows Strode closely.

possibilis, igitur ista erat tibi posita et a te admissa, et per consequens concedenda.

⟨1R⟩ Respondetur nec negando nec concedendo casum, quia non est negandum omne possibile nec[8] concedendum omne possibile, sed non admittendo, ac si diceretur:

    Non admitto omne[9] possibile;
sicut si quis poneret utramque[10]

    Rex sedet

et

    Nullus rex sedet,

non debes respondere concedendo nec negando, quia tunc concederes vel negares duo contradictoria, sed debes non admittere. Et ita in proposito non admittendum est omne possibile, quia ponendo omne possibile ponis contradictoria et incompossibilia.

⟨1.1R⟩ Et tunc ad argumentum cum concluditur

    Igitur regula falsa,

non valet argumentum, quia regula non ponit quod admittendum sit omne possibile positum, sed ponit quod omne possibile positum est admittendum. Ubi apparet magna[11] differentia, eo quod tibi[12] ponitur ut in sensu composito; regula[13] vero conceditur ut in sensu diviso, et iste est intellectus regulae.

⟨1.2R⟩ Ad aliud argumentum nego minorem, quod[14] nihil posuisti nisi possibile, quia posuisti incompossibilia ut dictum est. Et si dicitur

    Pono tibi omnia compossibilia,

non admitto, quia iterum ponis incompossibilia. Nam ponendo omnia compossibilia, ponis[15] illa duo

    Tu es homo

et

    Tu curris,

quae[16] sunt compossibilia, et illa similiter:

    Tu non es homo

---

[8] nec . . . possibile] *om*.M
[9] omne] quodlibet M
[10] utramque] utrumque M
[11] magna] magis E
[12] tibi] regula M
[13] regula] prima M
[14] quod] quia M, E *correxi*
[15] ponis] pono E
[16] quae] *om*.E

possible proposition; therefore it was posited to you and admitted by you, and as a result it should have been granted.

⟨1R⟩ I reply not by denying or by granting the case, since one should not deny every possible proposition, nor should one grant every possible proposition. Instead, I do not admit the case. It is as if I were to say:

I do not admit every possible proposition.

In the same way, if someone were to posit both of these

A king is sitting down

and

No king is sitting down,

you should not reply by granting or by denying, because then you would grant or deny two contradictories, but you ought not to admit the case. And so in the proposed case, every possible proposition should not be admitted because in positing every possible proposition you posit contradictory and incompatible propositions.

⟨1.1R⟩ Now ⟨one can say that⟩ the argument whose conclusion is:

Therefore the rule is false

does not hold, because the rule does not posit that one should admit every possible *positum*. Instead it posits that every possible *positum* is to be admitted. The big difference here is that the version posited to you was taken as if in the composite sense; but the rule is granted as if in the divided sense[3] and this is the correct understanding of the rule.

⟨1.2R⟩ ⟨In reply⟩ to the other argument I deny the minor premiss, that you have posited nothing other than what is possible, for you have posited incompatible propositions, as was said above. And if you say

I posit all compatible propositions to you,

I do not admit it, because once more you are positing incompatible propositions. In positing all compatible propositions, you posit these two:

You are a human being

and

You are running,

which are compatible. Similarly you posit these

You are not a human being

---

[3] In the composite sense all possible propositions would be taken together, as in a conjunction. In the divided sense they are taken one at a time.

et

> Tu non curris

quae sunt etiam[17] compossibilia. Sed admissis illis compossibilibus, necessarie admittis haec incompossibilia:

> Tu es homo

et

> Tu non es homo;
> Tu curris

et

> Tu non curris.

⟨1.3R⟩ Ad confirmationem nego maiorem, quod quodlibet a te mihi positum sit a me negandum, quia ponendo omne possibile ponis illam:

> Ego sum homo,

et haec non est a me neganda. Quare etc.

⟨2⟩ Secundo contra regulam arguitur sic:

> A convertitur cum illo termino 'asinus' in propositione vera et cum illo termino 'homo' in propositione falsa et cum illo[18] disiuncto 'homo vel non homo' in propositione dubia[19].

Est possibile, et tamen non est admittendum, igitur[20] regula falsa.

Consequentia tenet cum maiori; et minorem probo. Quia si illud est admittendum, admitte ergo illud a me positum. Tunc propono tibi istam:

> Homo est A.

Vel concedis vel negas vel dubitas. Si concedis et bene respondes[21], tunc talis propositio est vera, et per consequens ly .A. convertitur cum ly .asinus. . Ergo concedendo hominem esse A, concedis hominem esse asinum. Si negas et bene respondes, tunc talis est falsa:

> Homo est A,

et per consequens ly .A. convertitur cum ly .homo. . Et si sic, haec est falsa:

> Homo est homo.

---

[17] etiam]entia M
[18] illo]hoc E
[19] dubia]et *add.* E
[20] igitur]illa *add.* E
[21] respondes]respondis M

and
> You are not running,

which are also compatible. But once these compatible propositions have been admitted, you must necessarily admit these incompatible ⟨pairs⟩:
> You are a human being

and
> You are not a human being;
> You are running

and
> You are not running.

⟨1.3R⟩ Reply to the supporting argument: I deny the major premiss, that everything posited by you to me should be denied by me, because in positing every possible proposition you posit this:
> I am a human being.

This should not be denied by me. Therefore etc.

⟨2⟩ Second argument against rule one:
> A is interchangeable with the term 'donkey' in a true proposition, and with the term 'human being' in a false proposition, and with this disjunctive phrase 'a human being or not a human being' in an uncertain proposition.[4]

This is possible, but it should not be admitted; therefore the rule is false.

The inference and the major premiss both hold; and I can prove the minor premiss. If the case ought to be admitted, then admit my *positum*. Then I propose this to you:
> A human being is an A.

Either you grant this or you deny it or you doubt it. If you grant it and you are replying correctly, then the proposition in question is true, and as a result the expression 'A' is interchangeable with the expression 'donkey'. Thus in granting that a human being is an A, you are granting that a human being is a donkey. If you deny it, and you are replying correctly, then this is false:
> A human being is an A.

As a result, the expression A is interchangeable with the expression 'human being'. And if this is so,
> A human being is a human being

---

[4] This sophism, like the next, illustrates the case in which a simple term is given the meaning of another simple term: see Albert, op.cit., fol. 48va. Along with 'Nihil est tibi positum' and '"Homo est asinus" et "Deus est" convertuntur', this is one of the most popular sophisms discussed in treatises on *obligationes*. It is found in Burley, op.cit., 1.03, 1.04; Swyneshed, op.cit., pp. 259–261, §§39–46; Lavenham, op.cit., pp. 236–238, §§24–27; Fland, op.cit., pp. 56–58, §§75–86; Albert, op.cit., fol. 48va; John of Holland, op.cit., fol. 103^{r-v}; Marsilius, op.cit., fols. 82^v–83^r; Buser, op.cit., fol. 75^{va-vb}; Strode, op.cit., fol. 91^{va-vb}; Buridan, op.cit., p. 110; *Copulata*, fols. xci^v–xcii^r.

Paul admits the *positum*. This was not the inevitable move. Burley and Albert had refused to

Si dubitas istam, igitur ly .A. convertitur cum hoc[22] disiuncto 'homo vel non homo', et tunc haec esset a te[23] dubitanda:

Homo est homo vel non homo,

quod est falsum, quia est necessaria.

Respondetur admittendo positum illud; et cum proponitur

Homo est A,

dicitur primo non intelligendo eam, quia non est certificatio aliqua facta de sua significatione. Positum est[24] (222^{ra}M) ipsam significare, sed[25] in confuso, quare suum significatum est mihi[26] ignotum. Ideo non respondeatur affirmative, negative, nec dubitative quousque non fuerit facta distincta[27] certificatio de significato[28] illius termini 'A'.

Secundo modo potest responderi concedendo quod homo est A. Quo concesso, non sequitur:

Ista est a te concedenda et bene respondes concedendo eam, igitur ipsa est vera,

nam posita illa et a te admissa

Tu es Romae,

tunc propono illam:

Tu es Romae;

et patet quod est a te concedenda et concedendo eam bene respondes, quia posita obligata, et tamen non sequitur quod sit vera. Ita non sequitur:

Illa est a te neganda et negas eam bene respondendo, igitur ipsa est falsa.

Patet de ista

Tu non es Romae,

quae vera est et tamen neganda quia repugnat posito.

Tertio modo respondetur negando illam:

Homo est A

quia ante casum negabatur. Et in casu isto non est certificatio[29] eius[30] significati[31], igitur adhuc est neganda, et conceditur quod ipsa est falsa. Et cum dicitur[32]

[22] hoc]illo M
[23] a te]*om*.E
[24] est]enim *add*.E
[25] sed]*om*.E
[26] mihi]*om*.E
[27] distincta]dicta E
[28] significato . . . 'A']isto termino 'A' E
[29] certificatio]certificata E
[30] eius]*om*.M
[31] significati]significatio E
[32] dicitur] igitur *add*.E

---

admit the *positum*, because 'ponat significatum vocis dependere ex veritate propositionis': Burley, op.cit., 1.04; cf. Albert, loc.cit. A similar position was held by Buridan who rejected the case as impossible 'quia propositio praesupponit terminorum significationem. Prius enim oportet terminos esse impositos ad significandum quam aliqua propositio ab eis formetur.' The anonymous *Tractatus obligatoriorum* reported in its discussion of the sophism that Buridan and Marsilius were opposed on this point, since Marsilius believed that 'omne ponibile si ponatur est admittendum': *Copulata*, fol. xcii^r. Another way of rejecting the case was reported by John of Holland, who attributed the following argument to 'Thomas Manlevolt, vir subtilis'. The case leads to a contradiction. Every proposition is either true and false, so A must signify either a human being or a donkey; yet in an uncertain proposition it is said to signify the equivalent of any being, which contradicts the first claims. John remarked that this contradiction could be avoided by adding the phrase 'scita esse vera/falsa/dubia' (as Strode was to do), and he himself preferred Burley's solution. Cf. Buser, op.cit., fol. 76vb.

is false. If you doubt it, then the expression 'A' is interchangeable with the disjunctive phrase 'a human being or not a human being', and then you would have to doubt:

A human being is a human being or not a human being.

But it must be false ⟨that you should doubt it⟩, since the proposition is necessary.

I reply by granting the *positum*; and when

A human being is an A

is proposed, my first reaction is to say that I do not understand it, because no account has been given of its signification.[5] It has been posited that it does signify, but in a confused way, because its significate is unknown to me. Hence one cannot reply affirmatively, negatively, or with uncertainty, until some clear account of the significate of that term 'A' has been given.

One can reply in a second way by granting that a human being is an A.[6] Though this has been granted, the inference

This should be granted by you, and you reply correctly when you grant it, therefore it is true

is invalid. Suppose that

You are in Rome

has been posited and admitted by you, and that I then propose

You are in Rome.

It is clear that it should be granted by you, and that in granting it you reply correctly, for it is the *positum obligatum*. Yet it does not follow that it is true. In the same way the inference

This should be denied by you, and you reply correctly when you deny it, therefore it is false

is invalid, as is clear from the example

You are not in Rome

which is true, and yet should be denied because it is inconsistent with the *positum*.

One can reply in a third way by denying this:[7]

A human being is an A

on the grounds that it was denied before the case was stated. The case gives no account of the relevant significate, so the proposition should still be denied, and one should grant that it is false. When someone says

---

[5] This first argument is found in Strode, op.cit., fol. 91vb. 'Respondetur admittendo casum, et cum proponitur aliqua talis "Tu es A" vel "Tu non es A" vel "Homo est A", dicatur quod non intelligo illam; nam non facta impositione, non foret aliqua intelligibilis a me.'

[6] I have not found this mode in any other sources. It relies on the distinction between use and mention.

[7] The third mode is from Buser's solution, op.cit., fol. 75^{va-vb}. Marsilius, op.cit., fol. 83^r mentioned as alternative solutions that the case was impossible, and that such *impositiones* should not be admitted. For versions of the third mode, see also Swyneshed, op.cit., p. 260, §40; Lavenham, op.cit., p. 237, §27; Fland, op.cit., p. 57, §81. Once more Paul is relying on the distinction between use and mention. If the mentioned sentence is false, then it cannot be used to express a necessary truth, and must have acquired some other meaning.

Illa est falsa 'Homo est homo',

concedo[33] quod est falsa. Non tamen neganda sed continue concedenda est, et dicendum est ipsam esse falsam iuxta declarationem secundae[34] conclusionis.

Et si arguitur sic:

Ista 'Homo est homo' est falsa et ista significat adaequate hominem esse hominem, igitur hominem esse hominem est falsum, et per consequens negandum,

dicitur negando minorem quia repugnat duobus concessis. Sequitur enim:

Homo est homo et haec est falsa 'Homo est homo', igitur non significat adaequate[35] hominem esse hominem.

Quare etc[36].

⟨3⟩ Tertio contra eandem regulam[37] arguitur sic.

A significare omne quod non est A est possibile et non admittendum. Igitur etc.

Consequentia patet[38] cum maiori nam[39] ille terminus 'homo' significat omne illud[40] quod non est iste terminus 'homo', et ille terminus 'animal', similiter, igitur a pari possibile est quod ly .A. significet omne quod non est A. Posset enim esse quod aliquis terminus esset A, et nullum suum significatum, saltim a se distinctum, esset A. Minorem probo. Nam si illud est admittendum, admittatur ergo a te. Tunc quaero an tu es A an tu non es A. Si tu es A, et A significat omne quod non est A, igitur tu non es A. Si tu non (181^{va}E) es A, et A significat omne quod non est A, igitur tu es A.

Ad istud potest responderi primo non intelligendo aliquam[41] illarum

Tu es A,

Tu non es A,

propter causam dictam superius.

Aliter dicitur concedendo quod tu non es A, et non sequitur:

Tu non es A et A significat omne quod non est A, igitur tu es A,

quia non sequitur illa affirmativa ex illis quarum una est affirmativa et alia negativa. Immo nec sequitur cum constantia negativae, sicut non sequitur:

---

[33] concedo]concedendo M
[34] secundae]regulae E
[35] adaequate]om.E
[36] Quare etc.]om.E
[37] regulam]om.E
[38] patet]tenet E
[39] nam]quia E
[40] illud]om.M
[41] aliquam]aliqua E

This is false: 'A human being is a human being',

I grant that it is false. However, one should not deny it [sc. 'A human being is a human being'] but rather keep on granting it. One should also say that it is false, in accordance with the explanation of the second thesis.

If someone argues like this:

'A human being is a human being' is false, and this proposition adequately signifies that a human being is a human being, therefore it is false that a human being is a human being and as a result it should be denied,

I reply by denying the minor premiss, because it is inconsistent with two propositions which have been granted. This is a valid inference:

A human being is a human being, and 'A human being is a human being' is false; therefore it does not adequately signify that a human being is a human being.

Therefore etc.

⟨3⟩ Third argument against rule one:

For A to signify everything which is not an A is possible,[8] but it should not be admitted. Therefore etc.

The inference is obvious, as is the major premiss. This term 'human being' signifies everything which is not the term 'human being' and the same is true of the term 'animal'; so by parity ⟨of reasoning⟩ it is possible that the term 'A' does signify everything which is not an A. It could be the case that some term is ⟨the term⟩ A, and that none of its significates, at least, those which are distinct from the term, is ⟨the term⟩ A. I prove the minor premiss like this. If the case ought to be admitted, then let it be admitted by you. Now I ask whether you are an A or whether you are not an A. If you are an A, and A signifies everything which is not an A, then you are not an A. If you are not an A, and A signifies everything which is not an A, then you are an A.

To this one can reply first by saying that one does not understand any of these:

You are an A,

You are not an A,

for the reason given above.

One can reply in another way by granting that you are not an A. But the inference:

You are not an A, and A signifies everything which is not an A, therefore you are an A

is not valid because the affirmative conclusion does not follow from those two premisses of which one is affirmative and the other negative. It would remain invalid even if one were to add an existential premiss,[9] just as this inference is invalid:

---

[8] This sophism is found in Burley, op.cit., 1.10, 1.11; Albert, op.cit., fol. 48ᵛᵃ; and Marsilius, op.cit., fol. 83ʳ. Albert refused to accept the *impositio*. Marsilius accepted it, and granted 'You are not A'. He then accepted the inference 'This is true "You are not A", therefore A signifies you', but denied the further inference 'A signifies you, therefore you are A' (text corrected from E, sig.B vʳᵇ) on the grounds that it involved an illicit move from a premiss with

Tu es et tu non es ille terminus 'homo' et ille terminus 'homo' significat omne illud[42] quod non est iste terminus 'homo', igitur tu es iste terminus 'homo'. Non est ergo inconveniens quod A significet omne illud[43] quod non est A, sed inconveniens foret quod A esset omne quod non est A, quia tunc idem esset A et non esset A.

⟨4⟩ Quarto contra eandem regulam arguitur sic. A converti cum illa propositione 'Deus est' est possibile, ut patet, et non admittendum. Probo. Quia si sic, admitte ergo eam, et quaero utrum A sit verum vel falsum. Si verum, contra: A non est propositio cum non habeat subiectum nec praedicatum nec copulam, igitur A non est verum. Si dicitur quod est falsum vel dubium, contra: A convertitur cum vero et necessario ut ponit casus, igitur etc.

Respondetur admittendo positum; et concedo quod A est verum. Et cum dicitur quod[44] A non est propositio, nego; et ad argumentum

> A non habet subiectum nec praedicatum nec copulam, igitur non est propositio,

neganda est consequentia. Nam saepissime dictum est quod secunda pars illius copulativae

> Omnis homo est animal et e converso,

est propositio quae non habet huiusmodi nominatas[45] partes. Si tamen proponitur antecedens illius consequentiae[46], debet dubitari quia stat quod habeat illas partes et quod non habeat. Unde cum casu stat quod A sit ista (222^{rb}M) propositio

> Prima causa est ens,

quae convertitur cum ista

> Deus est.

Quo dato, patet[47] quod A habet partes sicut ista:

> Prima causa est ens

sic arguendo:

> Haec propositio habet[48] tales partes et ista propositio est A, igitur A habet tales partes.

---

[42] illud] *om*. M
[43] illud] *om*. M
[44] quod] *om*. M
[45] nominatas] denominatas E
[46] consequentiae] consequentia E
[47] patet] *om*. M
[48] habet] *om*. M

---

terms of second intention to a conclusion with terms of first intention. Paul's discussion owes little to these three sources.

⁹ *Constantia* is an existential premiss introduced to ensure the validity of certain inferences. This move was necessary given the standard assumption that affirmative propositions with non-referring subjects were false, and that negative propositions with non-referring subjects were true.

You exist, and you are not the term 'human being' and this term 'human being' signifies everything which is not the term 'human being'; therefore you are the term 'human being'.

Hence there is no awkwardness ⟨in saying⟩ that A signifies everything which is not an A. It would be awkward if ⟨one were to say⟩ that A is everything which is not an A, for then one and the same thing would be an A and would not be an A.

⟨4⟩ Fourth argument against rule one: it is possible for A to be interchangeable with the proposition 'There is a God',[10] as is obvious, but it should not be admitted. Proof: if it should be admitted, then admit it. I ask whether A is true or false. If the answer is 'True', then one can argue against it like this: A is not a proposition because it does not have a subject, predicate, or copula; therefore A is not true. If the answer is that it is false or uncertain, one can argue against it like this: A is interchangeable with a necessary truth, as the case states; therefore etc.

I reply by admitting the *positum*, and I grant that A is true. I deny the claim that A is not a proposition. ⟨In reply⟩ to the argument

> A does not have a subject, predicate or copula; therefore it is not a proposition,

⟨I say that⟩ the inference should be rejected. It is often pointed out that the second clause of the conjunction

> Every human being is an animal and the converse

is a proposition which does not have the parts mentioned above. If, however, the premiss of that inference is proposed, one must doubt it because it is consistent both that it should have those parts and that it should not. It is consistent with the stated case that A should be this proposition

> The first cause is a being,

which is interchangeable with this:

> There is a God.

In this case, it is clear that A has parts, just as

> The first cause is a being

has parts, by appeal to the following argument:

> This proposition has such parts, and this proposition is A; therefore A has such parts.

---

[10] This sophism illustrates the case in which a simple term is given the meaning of a complex: see Albert, op.cit., fol. 48va. For earlier discussions of this sophism, see Albert, op.cit., fol. 48^{va-vb}; Fland, op.cit., p. 54, §§66–67; Marsilius, op.cit., fol. 83^{r-v}. Cf. Buridan, op.cit., pp. 107–108.

Stat etiam quod illa[49] simplex vox 'A' convertatur cum ista propositione
> Deus est.

Quo dato, concedendum est A non habere praedicatum et huiusmodi modo quo dictum est.

⟨5⟩ Quinto contra regulam arguo sic.
> Et pono quod tu sis A si primum tibi propositum sit falsum, et quod tu non sis A si primum tibi propositum sit verum.

Isto posito patet quod positum est possibile, et tamen non est admittendum. Quia[50] si sic, admittatur ergo, et propono:
> Tu es A.

Et[51] si dicitur quod tu es A, et quod ista est vera
> Tu es A,

sequitur quod tu[52] non es A, quia
> Tu es A

est primum propositum tibi. Si autem dicitur quod tu non es A et[53] quod ista est[54] falsa
> Tu es A,

et cum illa sit primum propositum tibi, sequitur quod primum propositum tibi est falsum, et per consequens tu es A.

Consequentia patet ex casu.

Ad istud potest tripliciter responderi: Primo modo negando casum eo quod includit duas[55] conditionales quarum quaelibet est falsa, et per consequens impossibilis simpliciter.

Secundo modo admisso casu, volendo quod ly .si. non teneatur consequentialiter, sed solum conditionaliter sub quadam conditione sicut communiter solet loqui, respondetur sicut prius non intelligendo aliquam istarum:
> Tu es A;
> Tu non es A,

ex quo non est adsignata distincta significatio.

Tertio modo dicitur, et hoc[56] est maxime sustinendum[57], cum proponitur

---

[49] illa . . . 'A']ista simpliciter 'A' vox E
[50] Quia]*om.* E
[51] Et]*om.* M
[52] tu]*om.* E
[53] et]*om.* E
[54] est]sit E
[55] duas]regulas M
[56] hoc]haec E
[57] sustinendum]sustinenda E

It is also consistent that the simple utterance 'A' should be interchangeable with the proposition
   There is a God.
In this case, one must grant that A does not have a predicate and so forth in the manner described.

⟨5⟩ Fifth argument against rule one:
   I posit that you are an A if the first proposition proposed to you is false, and that you are not an A if the first proposition proposed to you is true.[11]

When this has been posited it is clear that the *positum* is possible; yet it should not be admitted. If it ought to be admitted, then let it be admitted. I propose:
   You are an A.
If it is said that you are an A, and that
   You are an A
is true, it follows that you are not an A, because
   You are an A
is the first proposition proposed to you. But if it is said that you are not an A, and that
   You are an A
is false, since that is the first proposition proposed to you, it follows that the first proposition proposed to you is false, and as a result you are an A. The inference is obvious from the stated case.

One can reply to this argument in three ways. The first way is to deny the stated case because it includes two conditionals each of which is false and, as a result, simply impossible.[12]

The second way is to admit the stated case, while stipulating that 'if' should not be taken inferentially ⟨as signalling a formal conditional statement⟩ but conditionally, as signalling the presence of some condition, in accordance with the common manner of speaking. Then one can go on to reply as above by saying that one does not understand any of these
   You are an A,
   You are not an A,
on the grounds that no distinct signification has been assigned ⟨to A⟩.

The third way, and the one which should be most strongly supported, is to reply, when

---

[11] This sophism and the next illustrate dependent *impositio*, in which a condition has to be met: see Albert, op.cit., fol. 48vb. This sophism is found in Burley op.cit., 1.17, 1.18; Albert, op.cit., fol. 48vb; Marsilius, op.cit., fols. 84^{v}–85^{r}; and Buser, op.cit., fol. 75va.

[12] Albert, following Burley, argued that the *impositio* 'Let A be your name' should be admitted only if consistent with the sentence first proposed. The reason that Paul gives for denying the case is based on the standard belief that all true conditionals are necessary and all false conditionals are impossible.

>   Tu es A,
>
> negando illam quia negassem eam ante obligationem, et nunc non est facta certificatio de sua significatione. Et cum dicitur
>
>   Illa est falsa,
>
> concedo[58]. Deinde[59] cum subiungitur
>
>   Illa est primum propositum tibi,
>
> negatur, quia repugnat posito et[60] uni concesso et opposito bene negati. Nam sequitur:
>
> >   Tu es A si primum propositum tibi sit falsum, sed tu non es A, et illa 'Tu es
> >   A' est falsa, igitur illa non est primum propositum tibi,
>
> quod est oppositum illius.
>
>   Si autem mutetur ordo proponendi ita quod statim post positum proponatur illa
>
>   Tu es A,
>
> qua negata, proponitur
>
>   Ipsa est primum propositum tibi,
>
> concedatur, quia verum et impertinens. Deinde ultimo
>
>   Ipsa est falsa,
>
> negatur. Nam ipsam esse veram sequitur ex posito cum uno concesso et opposito bene negati, ita quod bene sequitur:
>
> >   Tu non es A si primum tibi propositum est verum, sed tu non es A et ista
> >   'Tu es A' est primum propositum tibi, ergo ipsa est vera.
>
> Si enim ipsa[61] esset falsa et primum propositum tibi, tu esses A, quod repugnat uni concesso.
>
> ⟨6⟩ Sexto contra regulam arguo[62] sic.
>
>   Pono quod A sit primum instans (181vb E) in quo proponetur tibi falsum. Hoc positum est possibile ut patet, et tamen[63] non est[64] admittendum. Quia si sic, admittatur ergo, et propono tibi
>
>   A est.
>
> Concedenda est, quia vera et impertinens. Deinde propono tibi

---

[58] concedo]concedendo M
[59] Deinde]et E
[60] et]om. M
[61] ipsa]om. E
[62] arguo]arguitur E
[63] tamen]om. M
[64] est]om. M

You are an A

is proposed, by denying it because I would have denied it before the period of the *obligatio*, and because no account of its signification has now been given.[13] And when

It is false

is stated, I grant it. Then when

It is the first proposition proposed to you

is added, I deny it because it is inconsistent with the *positum* together with a previously granted proposition and the opposite of a correctly denied proposition. This is a valid inference:

You are an A if the first proposition proposed to you is false, but you are not an A and the proposition 'You are an A' is false; therefore that proposition is not the one first proposed to you.

⟨The conclusion⟩ here is the opposite of the above statement.

But if the order of proposing is changed so that

You are an A

is proposed immediately after the *positum* and, when it has been denied,

This proposition is the first proposed to you

is proposed, then I grant it because it is true and irrelevant. Then finally:

This proposition is false

⟨is proposed and⟩ I deny it. That the proposition is true follows from the *positum* together with a previously granted proposition and the opposite of a correctly denied proposition. This is a valid inference:

You are not an A if the first proposition proposed to you is true, but you are not an A and 'You are an A' is the first proposition proposed to you, therefore it is true.

If indeed it were false and were the first proposition proposed to you, you would be an A, which is inconsistent with a proposition granted above.

⟨6⟩ Sixth argument against rule one:

I posit that A is the first moment in which something false is proposed to you.[14]

This *positum* is possible, as is obvious; yet it should not be admitted. If it ought to be admitted, then let it be admitted. I propose to you:

A exists.

This should be granted because it is true and irrelevant. Then I propose to you:

---

[13] Marsilius and Buser both denied 'Tu es A'. Buser wrote: 'Quando proponitur ista "Tu es A", nego casum, quia est impertinens quam extra tempus negarem. Ulterius concedo quod primum mihi positum est falsum et quod A est nomen tuum, sed nego istam consequentiam: "A est nomen tuum, ergo tu es A" quia antecedens est de terminis secundae intentionis et consequens est de terminis primae intentionis, et talem consequentiam non oportet valere. . . .' Paul did not follow his sources closely.

[14] This sophism comes from Burley, op.cit., 1.19, 1.20; and Albert, op.cit., fol. 48vb. They both argued that the *impositio* should be admitted only if it was consistent with the first sentence proposed.

Hoc est falsum 'A est'.

Si concedis, igitur A non est. Si negas vel dubitas, contra: Tu negas vel dubitas sequens ex posito et concesso, igitur male. Nam sequitur:

> A est primum instans in quo proponetur tibi falsum, et A est, igitur A esse est falsum.

Respondetur admittendo positum, et cum proponitur

> A est,

concedo[65]. Et cum dicitur:

> Hoc est falsum 'A est',

nego. Et cum dicitur:

> Tu negas sequens etc.,

nego. Nam non sequitur:

> A est primum instans in quo proponitur tibi falsum, et A est, igitur 'A est' est falsum.

Non valet argumentum quia stat cum toto antecedente quod aliud falsum quod non est ista

> A est

proponatur. Et si proponitur (222^{va}M) ultimo illa:

> Nihil proponitur nisi A ⟨est⟩

negatur tamquam repugnans. Nam sequitur:

> A est primum instans in quo proponitur falsum et A est et[66] non est ista falsa 'A est', ergo aliud proponitur ab A ⟨est⟩.

Ubi tamen mutaretur ordo ita quod concessa illa

> A est,

proponeretur:

> Nihil proponitur nisi illa 'A est',

concedatur tamquam vera et impertinens. Deinde si proponitur:

> Ista est falsa 'A est',

concedo[67] tamquam sequens. Nam sequitur:

> A est primum instans in quo proponitur falsum, sed A est, igitur in A

---

[65] concedo]concedendo M
[66] et . . . nisi illa 'A est']*om*.M
[67] concedo]concedendo M

'A exists' is false.

If you grant it, then A does not exist. If you deny it or doubt it, then I argue against you: you deny or doubt something which follows from the *positum* and a previously granted proposition, therefore you reply incorrectly. This is a valid inference:

> A is the first moment in which something false is proposed to you, and A exists, therefore it is false that A exists.

I reply by granting the *positum*, and when you propose

> A exists,

I grant it. And when you say

> 'A exists' is false,

I deny it. And when you say

> You deny what follows etc.,

I deny it. This is not a valid inference:

> A is the first moment in which something false is posited to you, and A exists, therefore 'A exists' is false.

The argument is not valid because it is consistent with the premisses that some other falsehood which is not this:

> A exists

might be proposed. And if you finally propose this:

> Nothing except 'A ⟨exists⟩' is proposed,

I deny it as inconsistent. This is a valid inference:

> A is the first moment in which something false is proposed, and A exists, and ⟨the falsehood⟩ is not this falsehood 'A exists', therefore something other than 'A ⟨exists⟩' is proposed.

But where the order is changed so that when

> A exists

has been granted,

> Nothing other than 'A exists' is proposed

is proposed, it is granted as true and irrelevant. Then if you propose

> 'A exists' is false,

I grant it as following. This is a valid inference:

> A is the first moment in which something false is proposed, but A exists, therefore something false is proposed at A. But nothing other than 'A

proponitur falsum. Sed non proponitur nisi illa 'A est', igitur ipsa est falsa. Ulterius cum proponitur

A non est,

nego quia non sequitur:

Ista est falsa 'A est', igitur A non est,

sicut[68] non sequitur:

Haec est falsa 'Tu es', igitur tu non es.

⟨7⟩ Septimo contra eandem regulam arguitur sic.

Et pono quod ly .hominem est. convertatur cum illa 'Deus est'.

Hoc positum est possibile, ut patet, et non admittendum; igitur etc. Minorem probo. Quia si sic, admittatur ergo, et propono tibi

Hominem est.

Si concedis vel negas vel dubitas, contra: ante tempus non fuit[69] illa concedenda nec neganda nec dubitanda propter sui incongruitatem, et iam est impertinens ut patet, et est de terminis notis, ergo nunc non est concedenda, neganda nec[70] dubitanda. Quod si conceditur: contra:

Ipsa est propositio, ergo concedenda, neganda, vel dubitanda.

Antecedens[71] patet quia convertitur cum illa

Deus est.

Respondetur admittendo positum; et cum proponitur

Hominem est,

non respondeo ad illam[72] affirmative nec negative nec dubitative. Et cum dicitur

Ipsa est propositio,

nego, quia falsum et impertinens. Contra:

Convertitur cum illa 'Deus est'.

Concedo, et nego quod illa

Deus est

sit propositio tamquam repugnans. Sequitur enim:

Ly .hominem est. non est propositio, sed ly .hominem est. convertitur

---

[68] sicut]sic M
[69] fuit]erat E
[70] nec]vel E
[71] Antecedens]consequentia E
[72] illam]nec *add.*E

exists' is proposed; therefore that proposition is false.
Further when
> A does not exist

is proposed, I deny it because this does not follow:
> 'A exists' is false, therefore A does not exist,

any more than this follows:
> 'You exist' is false; therefore you do not exist.

⟨7⟩ Seventh argument against rule one:
> I posit that the expression 'a human being to be' is interchangeable with 'There is a God'.[15]

This *positum* is possible, as is obvious, and it should not be admitted. Therefore etc. I prove the minor premiss like this. If it ought to be admitted, then let it be admitted. I propose to you:
> A human being to be.

If you grant it or deny it or doubt it, I argue against you: before the period ⟨of the *obligatio*⟩ that phrase ought not to have been granted or denied or doubted because of its grammatical failings. It is irrelevant now, as is obvious, and all the terms in it are known. Therefore it should not now be granted or denied or doubted. If you grant this, then I argue against you:
> That phrase is a proposition; therefore it should be granted, denied, or doubted.

The premiss is obvious because the phrase is interchangeable with
> There is a God.

I reply by granting the *positum* and when
> A human being to be

is proposed, I do not reply to it either affirmatively or negatively or with uncertainty. And when you say
> That phrase is a proposition,

I deny it, for it is false and irrelevant. When you argue against this by saying
> It is interchangeable with 'There is a God'

I grant this, and I deny that
> There is a God

is a proposition, for this is inconsistent. This is a valid inference:
> The expression 'A human being to be' is not a proposition, but the

---

[15] This sophism illustrates the case in which an ungrammatical complex is given the meaning of another complex: see Albert, op.cit., fol. 48vb. The sophism is found in Albert, op.cit., fols. 48vb–49ra, in this precise form. Slightly different examples are found in Swyneshed, op.cit., pp. 262–263, §§53–54; Marsilius, op.cit., fol. 82^r–v; Strode, op.cit., fol. 90va–vb.

cum illa 'Deus est', igitur nec ista 'Deus est' est propositio[73].
Si tamen mutaretur ordo sic quod statim post istam
>Hominem est

ad quam non est responsum, proponeretur
>Haec est propositio 'Deus est',

concederem quia verum et impertinens. Deinde:
>Haec est propositio 'Hominem est'.

Concederem quia est sequens. Ulterius:
>'Hominem est' est concedendum, negandum vel dubitandum.

Concedo[74] etiam quia sequens.

Et si dicitur 'Pro qua parte?', proponantur partes divisim, et negentur quaecumque sint illae duae primo[75] propositae, et tertia concedatur quia sequitur ex uno concesso et oppositis bene negatorum. Ita quod si primo proponatur ista
>'Hominem est' est concedendum,

negetur[76] quia falsa et impertinens. Deinde
>'Hominem est' est negandum,

negetur propter eandem causam. Tunc tertio:
>'Hominem est' est dubitandum.

Concedatur quia sequitur:
>'Hominem est' est concedendum, negandum, vel dubitandum; sed non concedendum nec negandum; igitur dubitandum.

Et si dicitur contra:
>Ista 'Deus est' est concedenda, igitur et ista 'Hominem est',

negetur antecedens tamquam repugnans, nam sequitur:
>Istae duae convertuntur, et ista 'Hominem est' est dubitanda, igitur et ista 'Deus est'.

Verumtamen quotienscumque proponitur ista
>Deus est,

concedatur; et ad illam

---

[73] propositio]igitur *add*.E
[74] Concedo]concedendo M
[75] primo]primae M
[76] negetur]negatur E

expression 'A human being to be' is interchangeable with 'There is a God'; therefore 'There is a God' is not a proposition either.

However, if the order is changed so that immediately after

    A human being to be,

to which there is no reply,

    'There is a God' is a proposition

is proposed, then I will grant it because it is true and irrelevant. Then:

    'A human being to be' is a proposition.

I shall grant this because it follows. Further I will also grant:

    'A human being to be' should be granted, denied, or doubted,

because it follows.

And if you ask 'On account of which clause?', the clauses should be proposed separately, and whichever are the first two to be proposed should be denied. The third should be granted because it follows from one previously granted proposition and the opposites of correctly denied propositions. Thus if

    'A human being to be' should be granted

is proposed first, it should be denied because it is false and irrelevant. Then

    'A human being to be' should be denied

should be denied for the same reason. Then thirdly:

    'A human being to be' should be doubted.

This ought to be granted because the following is a valid inference:

    'A human being to be' should be granted, denied or doubted; but it ought not to be granted or denied; therefore it should be doubted.

If

    'There is a God' should be granted; therefore 'A human being to be' ⟨ought to be granted⟩ as well

is offered as a contrary argument, the premiss should be denied as inconsistent, because the following inference is valid:

    These two propositions are interchangeable, and 'A human being to be' should be doubted; therefore 'There is a God' ⟨ought to be doubted⟩ as well.

Nevertheless:

    There is a God

should be granted however often it is proposed. And when

> Hominem est

absolute positam non respondeatur concedendo, negando nec[77] dubitando.
 Eodem modo respondendum est cum ponitur quod

> Deus est

et

> Deum esse

convertuntur[78]. Qua admissa, semper concedatur illa

> Deus est,

et ad illam

> Deum esse,

non respondeatur concedendo, negando, nec dubitando. Et si proponitur

> Haec 'Deus est' est propositio vera et necessaria,

concedatur tamquam verum et impertinens. Deinde:

> '⟨Deum⟩[79] esse' est propositio vera et necessaria.

Concedatur quia sequens. Ulterius:

> '⟨Deum⟩[80] esse' est concedendum.

Concedo[81] quia sequens. Quare etc.

> Et[82] sic est finis huius capituli.
>
> Stude bene et fortiter quia necessarium est. (222vb M)

⟨*Contra Regulam Secundam*⟩

Secunda regula fuit ista. Omne positum obligatum sub forma positi[83] in tempore obligationis propositum[84] scitum esse tale est continue ab eodem concedendum.

⟨1⟩ Contra istam regulam arguitur sic.

> Et pono tibi illam propositionem de qua cogito.

Si admittitur, proponatur ista

> Homo est asinus.

Si negatur, arguitur sic.

---

[77] nec]vel E
[78] convertuntur]convertantur M
[79] Deum]hominem M,E. *correxi*
[80] Deum]hominem M,E, *correxi*
[81] Concedo]concedendo M
[82] Et . . .necessarium est]*om.*E
[83] forma positi]formaliter ponenti E
[84] propositum]*om.*M

> A human being to be

is posited unconditionally, no one should reply to it by granting, denying or doubting.

The same sort of reply should be given when it is posited that
> There is a God

and
> A God to be

are interchangeable.[16] When the *positum* has been admitted, one should always grant
> There is a God

and no one should reply to
> A God to be

by granting, denying or doubting it. And if someone proposes
> 'There is a God' is a true and necessary proposition

this should be granted as true and irrelevant. Then:
> '⟨A God⟩ to be' is a true and necessary proposition

is granted, since it follows. Further
> '⟨A God⟩ to be' should be granted.

I grant this because it follows. Therefore etc.

And so this chapter ends.

Study diligently, for this is really necessary.

⟨*Against Rule Two*⟩

The second rule was this: Every *positum obligatum* which is proposed in the form of the *positum* during the period of the *obligatio* and is known to be such ⟨by someone⟩ should always be granted by that person.

⟨1⟩ First argument against rule two:
> I posit to you the proposition I am thinking about.[17]

If you admit this, let
> A human being is a donkey

be proposed. If you deny it, then I argue thus:

---

[16] This example is found in Swyneshed, op.cit., pp. 263–264, §§56–57; Albert, op.cit., fol. 49ra; Marsilius, op.cit., fol. 82^v; Fland, pp. 53–54, §64.

[17] This sophism is found in Strode, op.cit., fols. 80vb–81ra. Cf. Peter of Mantua, op.cit., sig.G iii^{ra}. Paul's discussion follows Strode's fairly closely.

Ista est tibi posita et admissa, igitur positum obligatum est a te negandum.

Consequentia tenet. Antecedens est tibi dubium, igitur consequens non est a te negandum; et per consequens oppositum regulae.

Si dicitur quod non admisisti illam, contra:

Admisisti istam quam cogitavi, sed solum istam cogitavi, igitur admisisti illam.

Ista consequentia est bona scita a te esse bona, cuius antecedens, ut prius, est a te dubitandum; igitur non consequens[85] est a[86] ⟨te⟩ negandum, et negas, ergo male.

Si negatur casus, contra:

Ista quam cogito est illa 'Tu curris', igitur illa est a te admittenda.

Consequentia scitur esse bona, et[87] antecedens est tibi dubium, igitur consequens non est a te negandum.

Item si primo modo dubitetur casus, contra: Nihil quod non intelligis habes dubitare, sed non intelligis casum tibi positum, quia nihil nec aliqualiter intelligis per illum, cum non scis quae propositio sit vel qualis, ergo non habes istum casum dubitare. Antecedens probatur. Tu non dubitas sic esse vel sic, quocumque demonstrato, nisi primitus naturaliter comprehendas et moveatur intellectus per sic esse vel sic; sed oportet intellectum sic moveri et inde considerare a quo movetur, et sic intelligere. Igitur non dubitas sic vel sic nisi intelligas sic, quod fuit probandum.

Forte respondebitur ad casum non concedendo[88], negando nec dubitando illum, sed quaereretur[89] quae est ista propositio quam cogitas. Si ergo sic quaeritur, pono quod scias quae est illa, et quod ista sit contingens ad utrumlibet.

Si admittatur ideo propositio de qua cogito, proponatur eadem. Si negatur vel dubitatur, hoc vadit contra regulam. Si conceditur, propono:

Tu non es homo.

Si negatur, cedat tempus et arguitur sic:

Infra tempus concessisti propositionem tibi propositam[90] de qua cogitavi, sed solum de illa 'Tu non es homo' cogitavi; igitur infra tempus concessisti istam.

---

[85] consequens]non *add*.E
[86] est a]*om*.M
[87] et]*om*.M
[88] concedendo]concedo E
[89] quaereretur]quaeritur E
[90] propositam]positam E

> This proposition is posited to you and admitted by you; therefore there is a *positum obligatum* which ought to be denied by you.

The inference holds. The premiss is uncertain in your view, therefore the conclusion ought not to be denied by you, and as a result we obtain the opposite of the rule.

If you argue that you have not admitted that proposition, I argue against you like this:

> You admitted the proposition which I was thinking about, but this was the only proposition which I was thinking about, so you admitted it.

This inference is valid and known by you to be such. Its premiss, as before, should be doubted by you; therefore it is not the case that the conclusion should be denied by ⟨you⟩.[18] But you do deny it, so you reply incorrectly.

If you deny the stated case, then I argue against your denial:

> What I am thinking about is the proposition 'You are running'; therefore this should be granted by you.

The inference is known to be valid, and the premiss is uncertain in your view; therefore the conclusion ought not to be denied by you.

Likewise, if the stated case is doubted to begin with, then I argue against you like this: You should not doubt anything which you do not understand, but you do not understand the case which was posited to you. You do not understand anything or in any way by means of it, because you do not know what the proposition is or of what sort it is. Hence you should not doubt the case. Proof of the premiss: you do not doubt whether things are like this or like that, whatever it is that is indicated, unless you begin with some natural comprehension, and unless your mind is affected by things being like this or like that. There is a necessary progression from the mind's being affected to your consideration of the causes and hence to your understanding of them. Therefore you do not doubt whether things are like this or like that unless you understand what it is for them to be like that; and this is what had to be proved.

Perhaps you will reply to the case not by granting, denying or doubting it, but by asking what proposition is it that you are thinking about. If you do ask this question, I posit that you know what the proposition is, and that it is contingent in the full sense.

If, then, the proposition which I am thinking about is admitted as the *positum*, let it be proposed. If you deny it or doubt it, you are going against the rule. If you grant it, than I propose:

> You are not a human being.

If you deny it, let the period come to an end and I will argue like this:

> During the period you granted the proposition proposed to you, which was the one I was thinking about; but I was only thinking about 'You are not a human being', therefore you granted this proposition during the period of the *obligatio*.

---

[18] Here Paul gives a rule for *dubitatio*. Few treatises on *obligationes* gave such rules. For one example, see Burley, op.cit., 5.04: '. . . consequens ad dubitatum, si sit verum est conceden-

Haec consequentia est scita a te esse bona cuius antecedens nunc est a te dubitandum, igitur consequens non est a te negandum, nec etiam concedendum, quia infra tempus negasti eam. Igitur consequens est a te dubitandum. Tunc arguo sic:

>Infra tempus obligationis negasti istam 'Tu non es homo' et infra idem tempus concessisti eam, igitur male respondisti.

Illa consequentia scitur a te esse bona cuius antecedens est a te dubitandum, igitur consequens non est a te negandum. Quare etc.

Ad hoc[91] respondetur breviter tam ad primum casum quam ad secundum non admittendo aliquem illorum. Nam primus non est admittendus, quia ex mihi dubio tu cogitas propositionem impossibilem.

Ad secundum dico quod casus est possibilis, videlicet quod sciam quae est ista quam cogitas et quod ista sit contingens ad utrumlibet. Ideo[92] ista quam cogitas est admittenda, quia potest certificari de ipsa. Non tamen admittam eam[93] quousque non fuero certificatus quae sit ista. Et haec est[94] intentio regulae primae.

Verumtamen non esset inconveniens, admisso casu gratia disputationis, extra tempus obligationis dubitari[95] an in tempore concessit duo contradictoria vel quod negavit positum et an male respondebat, quia in rei veritate admisso casu continue dum respondeo dubito an bene respondeam et an concedam pertinens aut[96] impertinens. Quare etc.

⟨2⟩ Secundo contra regulam arguitur sic.

>Et pono tibi alterum illorum quae scis invicem contradicere, scilicet[97] 'Rex sedet' et 'Nullus rex sedet.'

⟨2.1.1⟩ Si non admittitur, quia non sit[98] mentio specialis de aliquo illorum, sicut nec admittendum (223ra M) est si dicatur

>Pono tibi aliquam propositionem,

contra: tunc pari ratione non admittentur[99] tales[1] casus

>Pono quod scias unam illarum vel quod A sit altera illarum;

nec foret admittendum si poneretur[2] quod aliquis homo currit, quia non sit limitatio de isto vel de illo.

---

[91] hoc]haec E
[92] Ideo]igitur E
[93] eam]casum E
[94] est] sit E
[95] dubitari]divisive E
[96] aut]an E
[97] scilicet]videlicet E
[98] sit]fuit E
[99] admittentur]admitteretur E
[1] tales]talis E
[2] poneretur]proponeretur M

---

dum. Sed si consequens ad dubitatum sit falsum, ad illud respondendum est dubie, quia non debet concedi, cum sit falsum, nec negari, quia, negato consequente, oportet negare antecedens, et ita oporteret negare dubitatum.' Cf.Ockham, op.cit., p. 742; Marsilius, op.cit., fols. 99^v–101^r. A more likely source for the discussion of such rules is in treatises on inference. Paul himself gave this rule in *Logica Magna* II.9, fol. 147ra (rule 10).

This inference is known by you to be valid. Its premiss should be doubted by you at this point; therefore the conclusion should not be denied by you. Nor should it be granted, because you denied it during the period ⟨of the *obligatio*⟩. Therefore the conclusion should be doubted by you. Then I argue like this:

> During the period of the *obligatio* you denied 'You are not a human being', but you granted it during the same period; therefore you replied incorrectly.

This inference is known by you to be valid and its premiss should be doubted by you; therefore the conclusion should not be denied by you. Therefore etc.

To this I reply briefly, ⟨and I deal with⟩ both the first and the second case, by not admitting either of them. The first should not be admitted because by virtue of my uncertain premiss you are thinking about an impossible proposition.

To the second I say that the case is possible, namely that I should know what proposition it is that you are thinking about and that it is contingent in the full sense. The proposition which you are thinking about should be admitted, because one can give an account of it. However, I will not admit it until I have been satisfied as to what it is. And this is the intention of the first rule.

Nevertheless, it would not be awkward, having admitted the case for the sake of the disputation, to doubt outside the period of the *obligatio* whether someone granted two contradictories during the period, or whether he denied the *positum*, or whether he replied incorrectly. As a matter of fact, after the case has been admitted, I am always uncertain as I reply whether I am replying correctly or whether I am granting something relevant or irrelevant. Therefore etc.

⟨2⟩ Second argument against rule two:

> I posit to you one of these propositions which you know to be mutually contradictory, namely 'A king is sitting down' and 'No king is sitting down'.[19]

⟨2.1.1⟩ If you do not admit the case, because no special mention is made of either proposition, just as you would not admit the case if I said

> I posit to you some proposition or other,

then I argue against you like this: By parity of reasoning such cases as

> I posit that you know one of these or that A is one of these

would not be admitted. Nor would one be able to admit the case if it were posited that some human being was running, since there would be no restriction to this person or that person.

---

[19] This sophism and nearly all of the subsequent discussion comes directly from Strode, op.cit., fol. 82^{ra-va}. The passages not found in Strode are p. 130, line 14 – p. 132, line 2 and p. 132, line 6 from bottom – p. 136, line 9.

⟨2.1.2⟩ Item, sit rei veritas quod nulla propositio falsa sit, et pono tibi omnem propositionem. Talis casus est admittendus (182rbE) igitur a fortiori est admittendum cum pono tibi particulariter aliquam propositionem.

⟨2.2⟩ Admisso ergo primo casu, propono positum obligatum. Si negas, habeo intentum contra regulam. Si concedis³, propono tibi istam
    Rex sedet.
Si concedatur vel negetur⁴, cedat tempus, et constat te⁵ concessisse vel negasse infra tempus obligationis propositionem tibi dubiam. Nec scivisti an sequebatur vel repugnavit tibi posito obligato⁶, igitur nulla de causa fuit ista concedenda a te nec neganda.

⟨2.3⟩ Si autem cum proponitur primo
    Rex sedet,
dubitetur, proponatur ista:
    Nullus rex sedet.
Si conceditur vel negatur, cedat tempus obligationis⁷ et arguitur quod male respondetur quia dubitato uno contradictoriorum⁸ reliquum propositum debet dubitari. Ideo forte dubitatur illa
    Nullus rex sedet.
Sed contra: Cedat tempus. Infra tempus utramque illarum dubitasti et concessisti alteram istarum, quia quam admisisti, igitur pro eodem tempore concessisti aliquam propositionem quam dubitasti, et eodem modo quam negasti, ut si proponatur infra tempus oppositum positi. Et per hunc modum videtur posse concludi quod concessisti aliquam propositionem, quia alteram illarum; et tamen nullam illarum concessisti nec admisisti, et sic a te concedebatur et a me ponebatur⁹ aliqua propositio sed ista nec fuit a me posita nec a te concessa.

⟨2.3R1⟩ Ad istud argumentum solet responderi quod dubitatis illis
    Rex sedet
et
    Nullus rex sedet,

---

³ Si concedis ... istam]*om*.M
⁴ negetur]negatur E
⁵ te] *om.* M
⁶ obligato]*om*.M
⁷ obligationis]*om*.M
⁸ contradictoriorum]contrariorum E
⁹ ponebatur]proponebatur M

⟨2.1.2⟩ Likewise, let it be true that no false proposition does in fact exist. I posit to you every proposition. Such a case should be admitted; therefore *a fortiori* any case should be admitted in which I posit some proposition in particular to you.

⟨2.2⟩ So when the first case has been admitted, I propose the *positum obligatum*. If you deny this, I have made my point against the rule. If you grant it, I propose this to you:

A king is sitting down.

If you grant or deny it, let the period come to an end. It is agreed that during the period of the *obligatio* you have granted or denied a proposition which you were uncertain about. Nor did you know whether it followed from or was inconsistent with the *positum obligatum* which had been put to you, so there was no reason for it to be granted or denied by you.

⟨2.3⟩ However, if

A king is sitting down

is doubted when it is first proposed, then let

No king is sitting down

be proposed. If you grant or deny this, let the period of the *obligatio* come to an end, and I will argue that you reply incorrectly because if one contradictory is doubted the other should be doubted when it is proposed. But perhaps you do doubt

No king is sitting down.

Then I will argue against you like this: let the period come to an end. During the period you doubted each of these, but you granted one of them, because you admitted it. Therefore, during the same period you granted a proposition which you doubted, and, in the same way, ⟨you doubted⟩ one which you denied, e.g. if the opposite of the *positum* was proposed during the period.[20] In this manner it seems that one can prove that you did grant a proposition, because you granted one of them, and yet neither of them did you grant or admit. Thus there was granted by you and posited by me some proposition, even though it was not posited by me or granted by you.

⟨2.3R1⟩ It is usual to reply to this argument that when

A king is sitting down

and

No king is sitting down

---

[20] In my translation of this passage, I take it that the phrase 'quam negasti' has a parallel function to the phrase 'quam admisisti' rather than to 'quam dubitasti'.

Much of the argument in 2.3 and the two replies to it rests on an analogy between such intentional verbs as 'promise' and the obligational verbs 'grant', 'doubt', and so on. For discussion and references, see E.J. Ashworth, '"I promise you a horse": a second problem of meaning and reference in late fifteenth and early sixteenth century logic', *Vivarium*, 14 (1976), 62–79. For Paul's views, see *Logica Magna* I.2, fol. 20vb, fol. 28vb, fol. 29^{rb-vb}.

In order to understand the argument, one must first notice that two separate issues are raised: (i) Can one say 'I grant (or deny) a proposition which I doubt'? (ii) Can one say 'I grant (or deny) a proposition but there is no proposition which I grant (or deny)'? On the face of it, the case as stated would license one to make both claims. In agreeing to admit one or other of the pair 'A, not-A' the respondent seems ipso facto to grant one or other of the pair; in denying the opposite of the *positum*, the respondent seems ipso facto to deny one or other of the pair (since

non oportet concedere extra tempus obligationis quod concessi[10] propositionem quam dubitavi. Et tunc ad argumentum

Quamlibet illarum dubitasti et concessisti alteram istarum, igitur concessisti alteram illarum quam dubitasti,

negatur consequentia, sicut non sequitur:

Promitto tibi denarium et omnem denarium promitto Sorti, igitur promitto tibi denarium quem promitto Sorti.

Etiam non sequitur:

Volo dare tibi equum meum et omnem equum volo Sorti dare, igitur volo dare tibi equum quem volo dare Sorti.

Et[11] dicitur consequenter quod ly .concedo[12]., .nego., .admitto., et huiusmodi[13] faciunt diversitatem inter sensum compositum et sensum[14] divisum sicut isti termini .significo., .impono., et huiusmodi.

⟨2.3R1O⟩ Haec responsio est apparens sed non est similitudo formae ad formam. Licet enim non sequatur[15]

Promitto tibi denarium et omnem denarium promitto Sorti, igitur promitto tibi denarium quem promitto Sorti[16],

tamen bene sequitur:

Promitto tibi[17] unum istorum duorum denariorum et quemlibet istorum duorum denariorum promitto Sorti, igitur promitto tibi denarium quem promitto Sorti.

Non enim bene videtur imaginabile[18] oppositum consequentis cum antecedente et ita in proposito sequitur:

Concessisti alteram istarum et quamlibet istarum dubitasti, igitur concessisti alteram illarum quam dubitasti.

Item est mirabile quod ponatur eadem vis in illis verbis 'promitto', 'concedo', et 'admitto' ita quod sicut conceditur

Promitto tibi denarium et tamen nullum denarium tibi promitto,

ita possit concedi quod admitto aliquam propositionem, et tamen[19] nullam

---

[10] concessi]concessisti E
[11] Et]si *add*.M
[12] concedo]concedendo M
[13] et huiusmodi]*om*.M
[14] sensum]*om*.M
[15] sequatur]sequitur E
[16] Sorti]sed *add*.E
[17] tibi]*om*.E
[18] imaginabile]*om*.M
[19] tamen]*om*.M

---

the opposite of A is not-A and the opposite of not-A is equivalent to A); yet neither A nor not-A has in fact been posited, admitted or granted as such. Furthermore when both A and not-A are proposed, each is doubted.

Paul denies that the second claim can be made: see the end of 2.3R1O and the end of 2.3R2. The claim derives its plausibility from Heytesbury's argument that 'I promise you a penny' and 'There is no penny which I promise you' can both be true since there is no penny of which it is true to say 'This is the penny I promise you'. Paul rejects the analogy between 'promise' and 'grant' or 'deny' which would license the second claim (although he does seem to allow the drawing of an analogy in some contexts).

He treats the first claim, 'It is legitimate to say "I grant (or deny) a proposition which I doubt",' in two different ways. In 2.3R1, he argues that the conclusion 'You granted one of these which you doubted' cannot be inferred from the premiss 'Each of these you doubted and you

have been doubted, one ought not to grant outside the period that one has granted a proposition which one doubted. When faced with the argument:

> Each of these you doubted and you granted one of these; therefore you granted one of these which you doubted,

I reject the inference, just as I reject

> I promise you a penny and every penny I promise to Socrates; therefore I promise you a penny which I promise to Socrates.

Nor is this inference valid:

> I want to give you my horse and every horse I want to give to Socrates; therefore I want to give you a horse which I want to give to Socrates.

As a result one can say that the verbs 'grant', 'deny', 'admit', and the like produce a distinction between the composite and the divided sense in the same way as the terms 'signify', 'imposit' and so on.

⟨2.3R1O⟩ This reply is plausible, but there is no formal likeness ⟨between the relevant arguments⟩. Even if this is not a valid inference:

> I promise you a penny and every penny I promise Socrates; therefore I promise you a penny which I promise Socrates,

the following inference is valid:

> I promise you one of these two pennies, and each of these two pennies I promise Socrates; therefore I promise you a penny which I promise Socrates.

It does not seem possible to imagine that both the opposite of the conclusion and the premiss ⟨are true⟩ together. In the case proposed above, this inference is also valid:

> You granted one of these and each of these you doubted; therefore you granted one of these which you doubted.

Moreover, it is amazing that someone would endow the verbs 'promise', 'grant', and 'admit' with the same force, so that just as one grants

> I promise you a penny and yet there is no penny which I promise you,

one could also grant that I admit some proposition, and yet there is no

---

granted one of these'. In 2.3R2 he accepts the inference, but argues that it is innocuous on the grounds that one cannot infer the further conclusion 'You granted a proposition and the same one you doubted'. One should pay careful attention to the way in which the premisses are formulated. In 'I promise you a penny' (cf. 'You granted one of these') 'penny' comes after the verb and it has merely confused *suppositio* which is immobile, so one cannot replace 'penny' with a disjunction of singular terms. In 'Every penny I promise to Socrates' 'penny' comes before the verb, it is distributed, and one can carry out a suppositional descent to 'This penny I promise to Socrates and this penny I promise to Socrates, and so on'. However, one cannot infer 'I promise this penny to Socrates and I promise this penny to Socrates and so on'; nor can one infer that I owe Socrates every penny there is. Paul's argument seems to be that just as the unspecified penny which I promise you is bound to be identical to one or other of the actual or possible pennies which might be used to fulfil my promise to Socrates, so the unspecified proposition which I grant is bound to be identical to one or other of the propositions which I doubt. But one cannot go on to infer that I granted some individual proposition and, at the same time, subjected that proposition to doubt, any more than one can infer that I picked out some individual penny as being the one I promised you, and at the same time, promised it to Socrates.

Whether one can in fact grant an unspecified proposition in the way that one can promise an unspecified penny is the problem touched on in 2.1.1R and 2.1.2R.

propositionem admitto, et quod concedo aliquam propositionem et tamen[20] nullam propositionem concedo; et ita 'nego', 'dubito', et huiusmodi.

Haec tamen responsio non est multum improbabilis licet non bene sonat[21] quis consequenter diceret ut prius etc.

⟨2.1.1R⟩ Propterea debet dari alia responsio, videlicet cum ponis alterum illorum vel aliquam propositionem, quaeratur quae sit ista; et si dicatur

    Lateat te,

e converso respondeatur

    Lateat te an admitto istam.

Et si dicas:

    Pono quod scias quam pono,

similiter

    Volo quod scias an admitto istam,

et sic continue eodem modo quo tibi ponit, eodem modo (223^{rb}M) sibi admittas quousque devenerit[22] ad determinatam propositionem, et tunc respondeas iuxta regulas adsignatas.

Et tunc ad obiectionem[23] de causa diversitatis, quare non admitto alterum istorum cum mihi ponitur et tamen admitto quod A sit alterum istorum aut quod sciam alterum istorum vel quod homo currit, quia in istis casibus bene nosco quae propositio est[24] mihi posita et quae sibi sequitur vel repugnat[25]; in ista vero positione[26] non.

⟨2.1.2R⟩ Ad aliam confirmationem cum supponitur quod nulla propositio sit falsa, et ponitur omnis[27] propositio, non admittitur; non quia aliquod mihi positum sit impossibile, sed quia non (182^{va}E) debeo admittere mihi ignotum nec illud quod nescio esse mihi positum.

Et nota quod si opponens esset nimis importunus dicens hanc responsionem esse fugam, revertere ad priorem et[28] respondeas sicut ibi responsum est; vel admisso casu dubitas[29] quamlibet illarum

    Rex sedet

et

    Nullus rex sedet.

---

[20] tamen] om.M
[21] sonat]sonet E
[22] devenerit]deveniunt E
[23] obiectionem]obiectum E
[24] propositio est]sunt E
[25] repugnat]repugnant E
[26] positione]propositione E
[27] omnis]casus E
[28] et]om.E
[29] dubitas]dubites E

proposition which I admit; or that I grant some proposition, and yet there is no proposition which I grant; with similar examples for 'deny', 'doubt', and so forth.

However, this reply should not be rejected too harshly, even though anyone who would make the above comments in accordance with the view does not sound convincing.

⟨2.1.1R⟩ For this reason one should give another reply. When you posit one of these, or when you posit some proposition or other, you should be asked what proposition it is. If you reply

    It is hidden from you,

one can turn this around and reply

    It is hidden from you whether I admit it.

If you say

    I posit that you know what I posit,

one can reply

    I want it to be the case that you know whether I admit it.

Thus one can keep on admitting propositions in the same way that they are posited until one arrives at some determinate proposition. Then one can start to reply in accordance with the rules which have been given.

Now I can reply to the objection about the distinction I drew between various cases. The reason I do not admit one of these when it is posited to me, and yet I admit that A is one of these, or that I know one of these, or that some human being or other is running is that in the latter cases I have a good idea of what proposition is posited to me, and what follows from or is inconsistent with it. This is just not true of the first *positio*.

⟨2.1.2R⟩ I reply to the other supporting argument, when it was assumed that no proposition was false, and every proposition was posited, by not admitting it. I do this not because anything posited to me is impossible, but because I ought not to admit anything which is unknown to me, or anything which I do not know to have been posited to me.

Note that if the opponent is very persistent in claiming that this reply is just an evasion, you can revert to the first solution, and reply in accordance with the reply given there. Or, once you have admitted the case, you can doubt each of these:

    A king is sitting down

and

    No king is sitting down.

⟨2.3R2⟩ Et tunc ad argumentum quod fit extra tempus obligationis:

> Tu concessisti alteram[30] illarum et quamlibet illarum dubitasti, igitur concessisti alteram istarum quam dubitasti,

concedatur[31] consequentia et consequens, sicut etiam concederetur[32] quod si promitto tibi denarium et quemlibet denarium promitto Sorti quod promitto tibi denarium quem promitto Sorti. Nam ita ly .quem. stat confuse tantum sicut ly .denarium., et tunc non sequitur iuxta doctrinam alias traditam:

> Promitto tibi denarium quem promitto Sorti, igitur promitto tibi denarium et illum promitto Sorti;
>
> Concessisti propositionem quam dubitasti, igitur concessisti propositionem et illam dubitasti,

nec relativum stans confuse tantum habet resolvi sicut saepissime est supra exemplariter[33] demonstratum.

Et si arguatur:

> Tu concessisti propositionem quam dubitasti, igitur male respondebas,

non valet argumentum. Sicut non sequitur:

> Promitto tibi denarium quem tibi non promitto, igitur false promitto[34],

aut

> idem promitto[35] et non promitto[36],

quae bene sequeretur[37] hic[38] si aliquem denarium promitterem quem non promitterem; ita in proposito non valet consequentia, sed deberet pro antecedente sumi quod aliquam propositionem concessisti quam dubitasti, quod negabo sic respondendo et volendo cum priori responsione quod ly .concedo[39]. et .admitto[40]. et huiusmodi habeant[41] vim confundendi[42] confuse tantum et faciendi sophisma sicut ly .promitto., .volo., .significo., et huiusmodi.

Item est advertendum quod licet alias concesserim talia gerundia vel participia 'admittendum', 'concedendum', 'negandum'[43], 'dubitandum' et huiusmodi facere sophisma ⟨secundum⟩ compositionem aut divisionem, non

---

[30] alteram illarum]alterum illorum M
[31] concedatur]conceditur E
[32] concederetur]concedentur E
[33] exemplariter]om.E
[34] promitto]promittis M,E, *correxi*
[35] promitto]promittis M,E, *correxi*
[36] promitto]promittis M,E, *correxi*
[37] sequeretur]sequerentur E
[38] hic]haec M
[39] .concedo.]concedendo M
[40] et. admitto.]promitto E
[41] habeant]habet E
[42] confundendi]concedendi E
[43] negandum]et *add*.E

⟨2.3R2⟩ Then one can reply to the argument which was stated outside the period of the *obligatio*, i.e.

> You granted one of these and each of these you doubted; therefore you granted one of these which you doubted,

by granting the inference and the conclusion, just as one would grant that if I promise you a penny and every penny I promise Socrates, then I promise you a penny which I promise Socrates. This is because the word 'which' has merely confused *suppositio* just as the word 'penny' does, and so in accordance with the theory discussed elsewhere one cannot validly argue:

> I promise you a penny which I promise Socrates; therefore I promise you a penny and the same one I promise Socrates;
>
> You granted a proposition which you doubted; therefore you granted a proposition and the same one you doubted.

Nor should the relative term which has merely confused *suppositio* be any further resolved, as I have frequently shown above by means of examples.

And if someone were to argue

> You granted a proposition which you doubted; therefore you replied incorrectly,

the argument would not be valid. Just as

> I promise you a penny which to you I do not promise; therefore I make a false promise,

or

> ... the same thing I promise and do not promise

is an invalid inference, though it would be valid if ⟨the premiss read⟩ 'There is a penny I promise which I do not promise', so in the proposed case the inference is invalid. One should take the premiss as asserting that there is some proposition I granted which I doubted. But then I will deny the premiss, and in accordance with the first reply I will take it that such words as 'grant' and 'admit' have the same power to produce merely confused *suppositio* and to produce sophisms as do 'promise', 'wish', 'signify' and the like.

It is important to note that although I would otherwise grant that such gerunds or participles as 'to be admitted', 'to be granted', 'to be denied', 'to be doubted', and the like do produce sophisms concerning composite and

tamen concessi talia verba 'admitto', 'concedo', 'nego' et huiusmodi. Concessi enim quod a te neganda vel concedenda[44] est altera istarum

    Rex sedet

et

    Nullus rex sedet;

et quod nulla istarum est a te concedenda nec aliqua istarum est a te neganda, sed quaelibet dubitanda. Numquam tamen concessi quod[45] nego aut concedo aliquam propositionem, et tamen nullam concedo vel nego. Quare etc.

⟨3⟩ Tertio contra regulam arguitur sic.

    Sint tantum tres propositiones categoricae verae scilicet A, B, C, sic quod A sit unum[46] illorum tibi dubiorum 'Rex sedet' et 'Nullus rex sedet' quod scias esse tibi dubium. Deinde pono copulativam factam ⟨ex A, B, C⟩ significantem ut eius partes praetendunt.

    Si negatur casus, contra:

        Tota copulativa tibi posita est vera per suppositum, igitur illa est possibilis, igitur illa copulativa[47] est admittenda.

Dicitur forte negando antecedens, quia cum ponitur in casu quod A sit alterum istorum, sequitur quod istae propositiones sunt

    Rex sedet

et

    Nullus rex sedet,

et per consequens contradictoria sunt, igitur non (223^{va}M) omnes propositiones sunt verae et sic casus implicat.

    Contra: stat quod utraque illarum praecise significet deum esse, et per consequens utraque esset vera. Nec illae essent contradictoria, igitur non si istae propositiones sunt, contradictoria sunt.

    Item, casus non debet negari propter hoc quod A est tibi dubium per casum, et tamen scis A esse verum, quia illud non est inconveniens sicut in prima parte fuit ostensum.

---

[44] concedenda est]dubitanda esset E
[45] quod]et E
[46] unum]verum E
[47] copulativa]*om.*E

divided senses, I have not granted that this holds of such verbs as 'admit', 'grant', 'deny', and the like. I have indeed granted that you should regard as to be denied or granted each of these propositions

A king is sitting down

and

No king is sitting down,

and ⟨I have granted that⟩ neither of these propositions is to be granted by you or to be denied by you, but each is to be doubted. However, I have never granted this: I deny or grant some proposition and yet there is no proposition I grant or deny. Therefore etc.

⟨3⟩ Third argument against rule two:

Let there exist only three true categorical propositions, namely, A, B, and C, such that A is one of these propositions 'A king is sitting down' and 'No king is sitting down', which you take to be uncertain, and know that you do. Then I posit a conjunction formulated ⟨from A, B, and C⟩, which signifies in accordance with its clauses.[21]

If you reject the case, then I argue against you like this:

By the *suppositum*, the whole conjunction posited to you is true;

therefore it is possible, therefore the conjunction should be admitted. Perhaps someone will reply by denying the premiss, because when the case posits that A is one of these, it follows that these propositions do exist, namely:

A king is sitting down

and

No king is sitting down.

As a result contradictories exist, therefore not all the propositions ⟨making up the conjunction⟩ are in fact true, and so the stated case contradicts itself.

An argument against this: it is consistent ⟨with the case⟩ that each of these propositions should signify that there is a God, and as a result each could be true. Nor would they be contradictories, so it does not follow that if these propositions exist, some contradictories exist.

Likewise, the case ought not to be rejected on the grounds that, given the stated case you are uncertain about A, yet you also know A to be true, since this is not an awkward situation as was shown in the first part.

---

[21] This sophism comes from Strode, who presented it as strengthening the case made in the second sophism above: Strode, op.cit., fol. 82^{va-vb}. Paul does not follow Strode's arguments closely.

Si ergo admittitur casus, proponatur copulativa ista. Si negatur, habeo oppositum regulae. Si concedatur, contra: et propono A, qua concessa quia sequitur ex posito, proponitur B et C. Quibus concessis quia sequuntur ex copulativa posita cum sint partes eius, cedat tempus obligationis et arguo sic:

> Infra tempus illa mutuo contradicebant, scilicet 'Rex sedet' et 'Nullus rex sedet' et utramque[48] illarum concessisti, ergo male.

Consequentia patet[49] et maior et[50] rei veritas; et[51] minorem probo, nam[52] concessisti A, B, C, sed quaelibet istarum fuit A vel B vel C. Igitur concessisti quamlibet istarum.

Respondetur admittendo[53] casum suppositum, sed nego positum, nec admitto positionem ponentem illam copulativam ex A, B, C, quia talis copulativa includit contradictoria, videlicet

> Rex sedet

et

> Nullus rex (182^{vb}E) sedet.

Quas licet admitterem esse veras, sicut argumentum est, esse possibile, negarem tamen[54] casum, qui est[55] copulativa facta ex illis. Et[56] licet admitterem hanc esse veram scilicet

> Homo est asinus,

quandocumque ponitur mihi quod homo est asinus, nego casum.

Sed forte hic aliqualiter instatur:

> Pono quod ista sit vera 'Homo est asinus.'

Qua posita et admissa, propono tibi[57]:

> Illa est possibilis.

Concedendum quia sequens. Deinde propono:

> Ista 'Homo est asinus' est admittenda.

Si conceditur tamquam sequens iuxta significationem primae regulae, pono tibi istam:

> Homo est asinus,

et sequitur quod tu habes admittere eam.

---

[48] utramque]utrumque M
[49] patet]tenet E
[50] et]est E
[51] et]sed M
[52] nam]quia E
[53] admittendo]totum add.E
[54] tamen]tantum M
[55] est]esset ex M
[56] Et]om.M
[57] tibi] om.E

If therefore the case is admitted, let the conjunction be proposed. If you deny it, I have proved the opposite of the rule. If you grant it, I argue against you like this: I propose A, which is granted because it follows from the *positum*. Then I propose B and C. When these have been granted because, as clauses of the posited conjunction, they follow from it, let the period of the *obligatio* come to an end. Now I argue:

> During the period these propositions, 'A king is sitting down' and 'No king is sitting down', were mutually contradictory, but you granted each of them; therefore you replied incorrectly.

The inference is obvious, as is the major premiss, and the truth of the matter. Proof of the minor premiss: You granted A, B, and C, but each of the propositions in question was A or B or C, therefore you granted each of them.

I reply by admitting the assumed case, but I deny the *positum*. Nor do I admit the *positio* which posits the conjunction formulated from A, B, and C, for this conjunction includes contradictories, namely

> A king is sitting down

and

> No king is sitting down.

Although I might admit the possibility that these propositions are true, as the argument states, I will however reject the case, which is the conjunction made out of them. ⟨Similarly⟩, although I might admit that this

> A human being is a donkey

is true, whenever it is posited to me that a human being is a donkey I will reject the case.

But perhaps someone will insist on the following point:

> I posit that this is true: 'A human being is a donkey'.

When this has been posited and admitted, I propose to you:

> The above proposition is possible.

This should be granted because it follows. Then I propose:

> 'A human being is a donkey' should be admitted.

If this is granted as following in accordance with the meaning of rule one, I posit this to you:

> A human being is a donkey,

and it follows that you must admit it.

Dicitur admittendo positum et ultimo concedo quod ista est a me admittenda, non tamquam verum[58] sed tamquam sequens. Numquam tamen admittam eam mihi positam, nec hoc est inconveniens, quia sicut in posterum[59] apparebit[60] infra tempus obligationis concedam aliquam propositionem esse a me concedendam ut[61] istam

Homo est asinus

vel aliquam aliam impossibilem, et tamen quotienscumque mihi fuerit proposita, ipsam negabo.

⟨4⟩ Quarto contra regulam arguitur sic.

Sint A B C omnes categoricae verae ita quod A sit illa 'Rex sedet' vel ista 'Nullus rex sedet', sic quod scias A esse hanc vel hanc, sic quod hanc vel hanc scias esse A, et tibi positam obligatam.

Iste casus non implicat istas duas propositiones esse

Rex sedet

et

Nullus rex sedet,

sicut nec iste si ponatur quod A sit hoc sedens vel hoc non sedens, demonstrando regem. Quo admisso cum[62] copulativa facta ex A, B, C sit vera, pono tibi illam cum toto casu praecedente. Qua admissa, proponitur[63] eadem. Si negatur, habeo contra regulam. Si conceditur, propono A; et debet concedi, quia sequens[64]. Qua concessa, proponitur:

Rex sedet.

Qua dubitata, quia de facto nec scitur an sit vera nec falsa nec sequens nec repugnans, propono istam:

Nullus rex sedet.

Qua dubitata quia dubitatur oppositum eius, arguitur sic.

Omne scitum a te esse tibi positum obligatum est a te concedendum, sed hoc vel hoc est scitum a te esse tibi positum obligatum per casum, ergo hoc vel hoc est a te concedendum,

per primum 'hoc' demonstrando istam

---

[58] verum]vera E
[59] posterum]primo E
[60] apparebit]subiectum *add.* E
[61] ut]aut E
[62] sic]ita E
[63] cum]quia M
[64] proponitur]proponatur E
[65] quia sequens]*om.* E

I reply by admitting the *positum*, and finally I grant that this proposition should be admitted by me, not as true, but as following. However, I will never admit it when it is posited to me; nor is this awkward, for, as will be seen below, during the period of an *obligatio* I may grant that some proposition such as

> A human being is a donkey

or some other impossible proposition, should be granted by me; yet I will deny it however many times it is proposed to me.

⟨4⟩ Fourth argument against rule two:

> Let A, B, and C be all the true categorical propositions. Let A be either 'A king is sitting down' or 'No king is sitting down' so that you know A to be this or this, and this or this you know to be A and to be the *positum obligatum* which was put to you.

This case does not involve the claim that these two propositions exist, namely

> A king is sitting down

or

> No king is sitting down,

any more than this case would, if it were posited that A is either this sitting person or this non-sitting person, indicating a king. When the case has been admitted, because the conjunction formulated from A, B, and C is true, I posit the conjunction to you along with the entire preceding case. When it has been admitted, I propose it. If you deny it, I have made my point against the rule. If you grant it, I propose A. You ought to grant it, because it follows. When you have granted it, I propose:

> A king is sitting down.

When this has been doubted, because in fact you do not know whether it is true or false, following or inconsistent, I propose this:

> No king is sitting down.

When it has been doubted on the grounds that its opposite has been doubted, I argue like this:

> Everything which you know to be the *positum obligatum* should be granted by you, but by the stated case this or this is known by you to be the *positum obligatum*; therefore this or this should be granted by you.

Here the first 'this' indicates

Rex sedet,

et per secundum istam[66]:

Nullus rex sedet.

Etiam cedat tempus et arguitur sic:

Infra tempus concessisti[67] A, igitur infra tempus concessisti[68] alterum illorum.

Consequens falsum, quia nullum (223^{vb}M) illorum infra tempus concessisti[69], ut patet inductive.

Respondetur admittendo primum casum et non admittendo secundum, nisi magis limitetur mihi quae propositio sit A, quae B, et quae C, propter causam datam in responsione ad secundum argumentum.

Verumtamen potest aliter responderi admittendo positum[70] et cum proponitur A, conceditur quia positum obligatum scitum esse tale. Et cum proponitur aliqua istarum

Rex sedet,

Nullus rex sedet,

quaeratur quae est tibi posita. Quod si noluerit[71] opponens determinare, non ulterius respondeas. Et si dixerit:

Tu scis A esse istam vel istam tibi positam obligatam, igitur non expedit quod tu quaeras,

nego argumentum quia cum toto antecedente nescio quae illarum[72] est A, nec scio quae illarum est mihi posita. Et ubi adsignetur certa illarum, concedatur illa et negetur[73] alia tamquam repugnans.

Haec responsio solvit obligationem secundam et multas[74] alias ubi nescitur quid[75] sit positum, facta positione et admissione.

Tertio modo potest responderi admittendo positum; et concedo A. Et cum proponitur aliqua illarum

Rex sedet,

Nullus rex sedet,

dubitetur. Et tunc ad argumentum:

---

[66] istam]hoc M
[67] concessisti]concedenti E
[68] concessisti]concedenti E
[69] concessisti]concedenti E
[70] positum]casum E
[71] noluerit]negabunt M
[72] illarum]*om*.E
[73] negetur]negatur E
[74] multas]respondeas E
[75] quid]quod E

> A king is sitting down

and the second 'this' indicates

> No king is sitting down.

One can also let the period of the *obligatio* come to an end and argue like this:

> During the period you granted A, therefore during the period you granted one of these.

The conclusion is false, because you granted neither of them during the period, as is obvious by induction.

I reply by admitting the first case and not admitting the second unless it is made more clear to me which proposition is A, which B, and which C, for the reason given in the reply to the second argument.

Nevertheless, one can reply in another way by admitting the *positum*. When A is proposed, one can grant it because it is the *positum obligatum* and is known to be such. And when one of these is posited:

> A king is sitting down,
> No king is sitting down,

one may ask which is the *positum*. If the opponent does not want to settle this, you should not make any further reply. And if he says

> You know that A is this or this *positum obligatum*; therefore it is not useful to inquire further,

I reject the argument because, as the premisses stand, I do not know which of the propositions is A; nor do I know which of them is posited to me. When one of them has been identified, then it can be granted and the other can be denied as inconsistent.

This reply resolves the second *obligatio* and many others in which one does not know what the *positum* is, even after the *positio* and *admissio* have been completed.

One can reply in a third way by admitting the *positum*. Then I grant A. When one of these is proposed:

> A king is sitting down,
> No king is sitting down,

it may be doubted. When one is faced with the argument

> Omne scitum a te esse tibi positum obligatum est a te concedendum, sed hoc vel hoc est scitum a te esse tibi positum obligatum, igitur hoc vel hoc est a te concedendum,

concedatur consequentia et consequens. Numquam tamen concedam aliquam illarum mihi propositam,[76] sicut in exemplo: Pono tibi illam[77]

> Alterum illorum est concedendum a te.

Qua admissa, propono illam

> Rex sedet,

et patet quod habet dubitari. Deinde istam:

> Nullus rex sedet;

et eadem est responsio sibi danda. Deinde propono:

> Hoc vel hoc est concedendum a te.

Concedendum est tamquam sequens ex posito. Et si dicitur ex quo hoc vel hoc est concedendum a te, 'Quid[78] est illud?' dico quod proponas partes divisim in hoc (183^{ra}E) secundo exemplo. Et[79] patebit negando primam et concedendo[80] secundam tamquam sequentem ex concesso et opposito bene negati. Sed in priori argumento quacumque parte proposita, dubitetur talis

> Hoc est concedendum a me,

quia semper dubitatur[81] an sibi demonstretur positum obligatum.

Ad aliud argumentum quod fit extra tempus obligationis:

> Infra tempus concessisti[82] A, igitur infra tempus concessisti[83] alterum illorum,

concedo consequentiam et consequens, et nego quod nullum illorum concessi infra tempus. Immo[84] unum istorum concessi, sed nescio quid[85] est illud.

Et si arguitur sic:

> Alterum istorum concessisti et utrumque illorum dubitasti, igitur idem concessisti et dubitasti infra tempus obligationis,

concedo[86] consequentiam et consequens. Et si infertur

> Igitur male respondisti,

nego consequentiam, quia non scienter concessi et dubitavi idem quod

---

[76] propositam]positam E
[77] illam]*om.*E
[78] Quid]quod E
[79] Et]*om.*M
[80] concedendo]concedo E
[81] dubitatur]dubitetur   E
[82] concessisti]concedenti E
[83] concessisti]concedenti   E
[84] Immo]*om.*M
[85] quid]quod E
[86] concedo]concedendo   M

> Everything which you know to be the *positum obligatum* should be granted by you, but this or this is known by you to be the *positum obligatum*, therefore this or this should be granted by you,

both the inference and the conclusion may be granted. However, I will never grant any of these which is proposed to me, just as in this example: I posit this to you

> One of these should be granted by you.

When this has been admitted, I propose:

> A king is sitting down

and it is clear that it ought to be doubted. Then this:

> No king is sitting down.

The same reply should be given to this. Then I propose:

> This or this should be granted by you.

This should be granted as following from the *positum*. And if someone asks 'Which is it?', on the grounds that this or this should be granted by you, I say that in this second example you should propose the clauses separately. Then the answer should become clear through the denial of the first clause and the granting of the second, because it follows from a previously granted proposition together with the opposite of a correctly denied proposition. But in the first argument, no matter which clause has been proposed, this proposition

> This should be granted by me

will be doubted, because one can always doubt whether the *positum obligatum* has been indicated to him.

To the other argument which is stated outside the period of the *obligatio*, i.e.

> During the period you granted A; therefore during the period you granted one of these,

I grant the inference and the conclusion, and I deny that you granted neither of them within the period. On the contrary, you did grant one of them, but I do not know which it is.

And if someone argues like this

> You granted one of them and you doubted both of them; therefore you granted and doubted the same proposition during the period of one *obligatio*,

I grant the inference and the conclusion. And if it is inferred

> Therefore you replied incorrectly,

I reject the inference, because you did not knowingly grant and doubt the

oporteret⁸⁷ secundum quod regulae sonant. Quamlibet enim istarum dubitavi scienter sed unam earundem concessi inscienter.

Propterea cum quaeritur quam istarum concessisti, nescio. Haec etiam respondeo: vadit ad secundam obligationem, et ad quamcumque consimilem multas pono responsiones ut cui una non placet alteram eligat⁸⁸ etc.

⟨*Contra Regulam Tertiam*⟩

Tertia regula fuit ista. Omne sequens ex posito obligato scitum esse tale est in tempore obligationis concedendum.

⟨1⟩ Contra istam regulam arguitur sic:

> Et pono tibi istam quae sit A: 'Nullum tibi positum est a te concedendum', et hoc est tibi positum, (demonstrato A).

⟨1.1⟩ Si non admittitur casus, contra:

> Positum est possibile et non admittitur, igitur male.

Antecedens probatur. Nam possibile est quod ponam⁸⁹ tibi istam possibilem

> Nullum tibi positum est a te concedendum.

Quo dato, sequitur quod aliquid est tibi positum; sed non aliud quam illud, demonstrato A, ut suppono, igitur hoc est tibi positum, demonstrato A.

⟨1.2⟩ Admisso ergo casu (224ʳᵃM) propono tibi A. Si negas et bene respondes, habeo intentum contra regulam. Si concedis, contra⁹⁰: probo quod A non est a te⁹¹ concedendum.

> Nam nullum positum est a te concedendum, sed⁹² hoc est positum, demonstrato A, igitur A non est a te concedendum.

Antecedens est concedendum, quia positum, igitur et consequens. Tunc ultra:

> A non est a te concedendum et A est sequens ex posito cum sit altera pars eius, igitur non omne sequens ex posito est concedendum,

quod est iterum⁹³ contra regulam.

⟨1.2R⟩ Respondetur admittendo positum et cum proponitur A, concedatur. Et tunc⁹⁴ ad argumentum concedo consequentiam et consequens, videlicet

---

⁸⁷ oporteret]oportet E
⁸⁸ eligat etc]obligat E
⁸⁹ ponam]pono E
⁹⁰ contra]*om.*E
⁹¹ a te]*om.*E
⁹² sed . . . Tunc ultra: A non est a te concedendum]*om.* M
⁹³ iterum]verum   E
⁹⁴ tunc]*om.*E

same proposition as would be required by the meaning of the rules. You knowingly doubted each of the propositions, but you granted one of them in ignorance.

Hence when someone asks which of them you granted, ⟨I say that⟩ I do not know. I also make this reply: Go back to the second *obligatio*. To any similar *obligatio* I will offer a large number of replies, so that if a person does not like one, he can choose another.

⟨Against Rule Three⟩
The third rule was this: Everything which follows from the *positum obligatum* and which is known to do so should be granted during the period of the *obligatio*.

⟨1⟩ First argument against rule three:
   I posit to you the following proposition, which is A: 'Nothing posited to you ought to be granted by you'; and this is posited to you (indicating A).

⟨1.1⟩ If you do not admit the case, I argue against you:
   The *positum* is possible and you do not admit it; therefore you reply incorrectly.

Proof of the premiss: it is possible for me to posit this possible proposition to you:
   Nothing posited to you ought to be granted by you.

Given this, it follows that some proposition is posited to you; but on my assumption, that proposition can only be this (indicating A); therefore this (indicating A) is posited to you.

⟨1.2⟩ When, therefore, the case has been admitted, I propose A to you. If you deny it and are thereby replying correctly, I have made my point against the rule. If you grant it I argue against you by proving that you ought not to grant A:
   Nothing posited ⟨to you⟩ ought to be granted by you, but this is posited to you (indicating A), therefore A ought not to be granted by you.

The premiss should be granted, because it is the *positum*; therefore the conclusion should also be granted. I continue:
   A ought not to be granted by you, and A follows from the *positum* since it is one of its clauses; therefore not every proposition which follows from the *positum* should be granted.

This too goes against the rule.

⟨1.2R⟩ I reply by admitting the *positum*. When A is proposed, I grant it. With respect to the ⟨first⟩ argument, I grant both the inference and the conclusion, i.e. that A ought not to be granted by me. Then when it is argued

quod A non est concedendum a me. Et tunc ultra cum arguitur

    A non est concedendum a te et A est sequens ex posito, igitur etc.,
nego minorem quia repugnat. Sequitur enim:

    A non est concedendum a te, igitur A non est sequens ex posito,
semper intelligendo de posito obligato. ⟨Et tunc ultra cum arguitur⟩

    A est pars copulativae positae, igitur sequens ex posito,
nego antecedens tamquam repugnans, si intelligitur de copulativa negativa.

⟨1.1R⟩ Puto tamen quod[95] si poneretur ly .obligatum. cum .posito., quod casus non esset admittendus, quia includit[96] opposita. Sequitur:

    Hoc est tibi positum obligatum, igitur hoc[97] positum obligatum est a te
    concedendum, igitur aliquod tibi positum est a te concedendum,
quod est contradictorium alterius partis, videlicet

    Nullum tibi positum est[98] a te concedendum.

Et tunc ad rationem dico quod si poneres mihi istam et admitterem, non sequeretur aliquod esse positum obligatum sed potius sequeretur[99] oppositum ex illo admisso. Quare etc.

⟨2⟩ Secundo contra regulam arguitur sic. Ex ista regula sequitur quod infra tempus obligationis[1] duo contradictoria sunt concedenda, igitur regula non bene posita. Antecedens probatur. Et pono tibi illam:

    Tu es Romae et oppositum cuiuslibet talis est a te concedendum.
Copulativa illa est possibilis, nam stat quod[2] tu sis Romae et quod haec

    Tu non es Romae
sit tibi posita et a te admissa, sicut iam de facto tu es homo et tamen[3]

    Tu non est homo
tibi[4] ponitur et a te admittitur. Quo posito et admisso, illud est a te concedendum. Admisso ergo casu proponatur[5]

    Oppositum cuiuslibet talis est concedendum.
Illa[6] est altera pars copulativae, igitur concedenda. Deinde

    Tu es Romae.
Haec est formaliter sequens ex posito obligato. Sequitur enim

---

[95] quod]*om*.M
[96] includit]claudit E
[97] hoc]*om*.E
[98] est . . . positum]*om*.M
[99] sequeretur]sequitur E
[1] obligationis]*om*.E
[2] quod]*om*.E
[3] tamen]*om*.E
[4] tibi]*om*.E
[5] proponatur]proponitur E
[6] Illa . . .]*om*.M

> A ought not to be granted by you, and A follows from the *positum*; therefore etc.,

I deny the minor premiss because it is inconsistent. This inference is valid:

> A ought not to be granted by you; therefore A does not follow from the *positum*.

Here I take '*positum*' to mean '*positum obligatum*'. ⟨In reply to the argument contained in the minor premiss⟩

> A is a clause of the posited conjunction; therefore it does follow from the *positum*,

I deny the premiss as inconsistent, provided that one means a negated conjunction here.

⟨1.1R⟩ However, I do think that if one were to add the word '*obligatum*' to the word '*positum*', the case could not be admitted because it would include opposed propositions. This inference is valid:

> This is the *positum obligatum* which was put to you, therefore you should grant this *positum obligatum*; therefore some proposition which was posited to you should be granted by you.

But this conclusion is the contradictory of the other clause, namely

> Nothing posited to you ought to be granted by you.

And so to the initial argument for admitting the case, I say that if you were to posit the proposition to me, and I were to admit it, it would not follow that something was the *positum obligatum*. On the contrary, the opposite of this would follow from the *admissum*. Therefore etc.

⟨2⟩ Second argument against rule three: From the rule one can infer that two contradictories ought to be granted during the period of an *obligatio*; therefore the rule was not correctly stated. Proof of the premiss: I posit this to you:

> You are in Rome and you ought to grant the opposite of any such proposition.

This conjunction is possible, for it is consistent that you should be in Rome and that

> You are not in Rome

should be posited to you and admitted by you, just as ⟨it is consistent⟩ that you should be a human being, as indeed you are, and yet

> You are not a human being

is posited to you and admitted by you. When the above has been posited and admitted, it should be granted by you. Now that the case has been admitted, let this be proposed:

> You ought to grant the opposite of any such proposition.

This is the other clause of the conjunction; therefore it should be granted. Then:

> You are in Rome.

This follows from the *positum obligatum* by a formal inference, for this:

> Tu es Romae et oppositum cuiuslibet talis est concedendum[7], igitur tu es Romae

a copulativa ad alteram partem. Et tamen (183rbE) illa

> Tu es Romae

non est a te concedenda, igitur non omne sequens ex posito obligato est concedendum. Antecedens probatur, quia si illa sit concedenda et eius contradictorium est concedendum, ergo contradictoria sibi invicem sunt concedenda, quod fuit deducendum.

Respondetur admittendo positum, et cum proponitur aliqua istarum

> Tu es Romae

aut

> 'Tu non es Romae' est a te concedendum

concedo[8] quamlibet istarum et nego quod illa

> Tu es Romae

sit a me concedenda. Et nego tamquam repugnans quod

> Tu es Romae

sit sequens. Sequitur enim:

> 'Tu es Romae' non est a te concedendum, igitur non est sequens ex posito obligato.

Si tamen hoc ponatur cum posito quod ipsa sit sequens ex posito tunc[9] admitto totum positum; et nego adhuc quod

> Tu es Romae

est concedendum; et tunc ad argumentum

> Illa est sequens ex posito, igitur concedenda,

nego consequentiam, quia oportet addere quod sit sequens ex posito admisso vel[10] obligato, et hoc est repugnans. Nam si ista

> Tu es Romae

est sequens ex posito obligato, ipsa est concedenda; et oppositum cuiuslibet talis est concedendum, igitur contradictoria invicem sunt concedenda quod non oportet concedere[11].

---

[7] . . . . concedendum]*om*.M
[8] concedo]concedendo M
[9] tunc . . . posito]*om*.E
[10] vel]*om*.E
[11] oportet concedere]debet concedi E

> You are in Rome and you ought to grant the opposite of any such proposition; therefore you are in Rome

is a valid inference from a conjunction to one of its clauses. Nonetheless,

> You are in Rome

ought not to be granted by you; therefore not everything which follows from the *positum obligatum* should be granted. Proof of the premiss: if the above proposition ought to be granted, and if its contradictory ought also to be granted, then one ought to grant two mutually contradictory propositions, as was to be proved.

I reply by admitting the *positum*. When one of these

> You are in Rome

or

> 'You are not in Rome' ought to be granted by you

is proposed, I grant each of them; and I deny that this

> You are in Rome

ought to be granted by me. And I deny as inconsistent that

> You are in Rome

follows. This is a valid inference:

> 'You are in Rome' ought not to be granted by you; therefore it does not follow from the *positum obligatum*.

If, however, one were to add to the *positum* that the proposition did follow from the *positum*, then I would admit the entire *positum*. I would still deny that

> You are in Rome

should be granted. ⟨In reply⟩ to the argument

> This does follow from the *positum*; therefore it should be granted,

I reject the inference; for one ought to add that it follows from the *positum admissum* or *obligatum*, and this is inconsistent. If

> You are in Rome

does follow from the *positum obligatum*, it should be granted; but the opposite of any such proposition should also be granted; therefore two mutually contradictory propositions should both be granted, which one ought not to grant.

⟨3⟩ Tertio contra regulam arguitur sic. Et pono tibi illam:

    Tu curris et 'Tu non curris' est a te concedendum.

Casus est possibilis quia[12] possibile est quod tu curras et quod illa

    Tu non curris

sit tibi posita et a te[13] admissa et consequenter a te concedenda.

    Admisso ergo casu propono tibi istam:

    'Tu non curris' est a te concedenda.

Si conceditur quia sequens, propono tibi illam:

    Tu curris.

Si concedis, contra:

    'Tu curris' est a te concedendum et 'Tu non curris' est a te concedendum,

    igitur duo contradictoria sunt a te concedenda. (224^{rb}M)

    Item propono tibi illam:

    Tu non curris.

Si concedis, concedis repugnans uni concesso, igitur male. Si negas, aut igitur quia falsa et impertinens aut quia repugnans, sed qualitercumque dicatur, sequitur quod ista

    Tu non curris,

est a te concedenda, et per consequens non est a te neganda[14], quod est oppositum unius concessi. Et sic habeo dupliciter quod non quodlibet sequens ex posito est a te concedendum quia nec illa

    Tu curris

nec illa

    Tu non curris

est a te concedendum.

    Respondetur admittendo positum et cum proponitur aliqua illarum

    'Tu non curris' est a te concedendum

    Tu curris,

concedo[15] quamlibet istarum. Et tunc ad argumentum:

    'Tu curris' est a te concedendum et 'Tu non curris' est a te concedendum,

---

[12] quia]et E
[13] a te]*om*.M
[14] neganda]concedenda M
[15] concedo]concedendo M

⟨3⟩ Third argument against rule three: I posit this to you:

You are running and 'You are not running' should be granted by you.[22]

The case is possible because it is possible that you should be running and that

You are not running

should be posited to you and admitted by you and, as a result, ought to be granted by you.

When the case has been admitted, I propose this to you:

'You are not running' should be granted by you.

If you grant this because it follows, I propose this to you:

You are running.

If you grant this, I argue against you:

'You are running' should be granted by you, and 'You are not running' should be granted by you; therefore two contradictories should both be granted by you.

Likewise I propose this to you:

You are not running.

If you grant it, you grant a proposition which is inconsistent with a previously granted proposition; therefore you reply incorrectly. If you deny it, this must be either because it is false and irrelevant or because it is inconsistent; but whatever you say, it follows that

You are not running

should be granted by you, and as a result ought not to be denied by you, which is the opposite of something that has been granted. And thus I have two ways of proving that not everything which follows from the *positum* should be granted by you, because neither this

You are running

nor this

You are not running

ought to be granted by you.

I reply by admitting the *positum* and when either of these:

'You are not running' should be granted by you,

You are running,

is proposed, I grant each of them. Then ⟨in reply⟩ to the argument:

'You are running' should be granted by you and 'You are not running'

---

[22] Strode discusses this example in his section on conjunctions: see Strode, op.cit., fol. 88rb–va. The manuscript text (MS fols. 43vb–44ra) is clearer, partly because 'est a te concedendum' has been omitted from the statement of the sophism in the printed edition. Paul's discussion is more elaborate than Strode's.

ergo duo contradictoria sunt simul concedenda,
non valet argumentum. Verumtamen non concessi quod illa
> Tu curris

sit a me concedenda, sed concessi eam. Ubi ergo immediate post concessionem eius proponatur[16]
> Ista est a te concedenda,

concedo quia verum et impertinens. Deinde si proponitur
> Ista sunt duo contradictoria,

nego tamquam repugnans. Sequitur:
> Quaelibet istarum est a me concedenda, igitur illa non sunt contradictoria.

Item si immediate post concessionem illius
> Tu curris

proponatur[17]
> Illa sunt duo contradictoria 'Tu curris' et 'Tu non curris',

concedendum est quia verum et impertinens. Deinde
> 'Tu curris' est a te concedendum

negatur[18] tamquam repugnans. Sequitur enim
> 'Tu non curris' est a te concedendum et 'Tu non curris' et 'Tu curris' sunt duo[19] contradictoria, ergo 'Tu curris' non est a te concedendum.

Item si immediate post concessionem illius
> Tu curris

proponatur ista copulativa:
> 'Tu curris' est a te concedenda et illa sunt contradictoria,

demonstratis prioribus, negetur[20] haec copulativa. Et si quaeritur pro qua parte, non adsignetur[21] aliqua quousque non fuerint ambae propositae. Quibus propositis, semper concedatur prima pars, quia vera et impertinens; et secunda negatur quia repugnans uni concesso et opposito bene negati illius copulativae. Nam sequitur
> 'Tu curris' non est a te concedendum vel ista non sunt contradictoria, sed
> 'Tu curris' est a te concedendum, igitur ista non sunt contradictoria.

---

[16] proponatur]postponatur E
[17] proponatur]postponatur E
[18] negatur]nego E
[19] duo]*om.* E
[20] negetur]negatur E
[21] adsignetur]adsignatur E

should be granted by you, therefore two contradictories should both be granted by you,

⟨I say that⟩ the argument is not valid. In fact, I did not grant that

You are running,

should be granted by me; I simply granted it. But where

This should be granted by you

is proposed immediately after I have granted the above, I grant it because it is true and irrelevant. Then if

These are two contradictories

is proposed, I deny it as inconsistent. This is a valid inference:

Each of these should be granted by me; therefore they are not contradictories.

Likewise if immediately after I have granted

You are running,

this is proposed:

'You are running' and 'You are not running' are two contradictories,

it should be granted because it is true and irrelevant. Then:

'You are running' should be granted by you

is denied as inconsistent. This is a valid inference:

'You are not running' should be granted by you, and 'You are not running' and 'You are running' are two contradictories; therefore 'You are running' ought not to be granted by you.

Likewise if immediately after I have granted

You are running

this conjunction is proposed:

'You are running' should be granted by you and these are contradictories,

indicating the above pair of propositions, I deny the conjunction. And if you ask on account of which clause, I shall not tell you which until both have been proposed. When they have been proposed, I shall always grant the first clause, because it is true and irrelevant, and deny the second, because it is inconsistent with a previously granted proposition and the opposite of the conjunction which has been correctly denied. This is a valid inference:

Either 'You are running' ought not to be granted by you or these are not contradictories, but 'You are running' should be granted by you; therefore these are not contradictories.

Similiter sequitur:

> 'Tu curris' non est a te concedendum vel illa non sunt contradictoria, sed illa sunt contradictoria, igitur 'Tu curris' non est a te concedendum.

Patet quaelibet istarum a disiunctiva ad alteram partem cum destructione unius[22] etc.

Ad confirmationem cum proponitur

> Tu non curris,

nego eam. Numquam tamen concedo[23] quod sit neganda, quia repugnat. Sequitur enim

> 'Tu non curris' est a te concedendum, igitur non est a te negandum.

Et cum dicitur

> Tu negas eam,

concedo[24]. Et cum dicitur

> Aut igitur quia falsa et impertinens aut quia repugnans

dico quod nec sic nec sic, quia repugnat utrumque istorum. Et si quaeritur quare negas eam, dico quod non quaelibet (183^{va}E) quaestio est certificanda iuxta doctrinam quartae conclusionis, sed post tempus obligationis dicam causam quare, quia repugnavit uni concesso videlicet illi

> Tu curris.

Et si arguitur contra responsiones istas, probando quod tu concedis contradictoria, nam cedat tempus obligationis et propono:

> Tu concessisti[25] duo contradictoria, videlicet '"Tu curris" est a te concedendum' et '"Tu non curris" est[26] a te concedendum.'

Dico quod istae non sunt contradictoria sed propositiones affirmativae possibiles. Quare etc.

⟨4⟩ Quarto arguitur sic. Et pono quod

> Illa copulativa sit tibi posita obligata 'Aliquid sequitur (224^{va}M) ex posito et nullum sequens ex posito[27] est concedendum.'

Casus est possibilis. Nam ista copulativa est possibilis:

---

[22] unius etc.]*om*.M
[23] concedo]concedendo M
[24] concedo]concedendo M
[25] concessisti]concedenti E
[26] est]*om*.E
[27] posito]proposito M

Similarly this is a valid inference:
> Either 'You are running' ought not to be granted by you, or these are not contradictories, but these are contradictories; therefore 'You are running' ought not to be granted by you.

Both of these inferences are obvious because they go from a disjunction with the negation of one clause to the assertion of the other.

Reply to the supporting argument: When
> You are not running

is proposed, I deny it. But I never grant that it ought to be denied, because this is inconsistent. This is a valid inference:
> 'You are not running' should be granted by you; therefore it ought not to be denied by you.

And when someone says
> You do deny it,

I grant this. And when someone says
> ... either because it is false and irrelevant or because it is inconsistent

I say that neither is the case, because each clause is inconsistent. And if someone asks why you do deny it, I say that not every question should be given a straight answer according to the teaching of the fourth thesis; but I will give my answer after the period of the *obligatio*, i.e. that ⟨the disjunction⟩ was inconsistent with a previously granted proposition, namely
> You are running.

If someone argues against these replies, trying to prove that you do grant contradictories, then let the period of the *obligatio* come to an end. I propose:
> You granted two contradictories, namely '"You are running" should be granted by you' and '"You are not running" should be granted by you'.

I state that these are not contradictories, but affirmative possible propositions. Therefore etc.

⟨4⟩ Fourth argument against rule three: I posit that
> This conjunction is the *positum obligatum*: 'Something follows from the *positum* and nothing which follows from the *positum* should be granted'.

The case is possible. This conjunction is possible:

Aliquid sequitur ex posito et nullum sequens ex posito est concedendum, igitur potest esse posita obligata.

Admisso igitur casu, propono tibi illam[28]:

Aliquid sequitur ex posito.

Concedenda est, quia sequens. Deinde propono tibi istam:

Nullum sequens ex posito est concedendum.

Concedenda est similiter propter eandem causam. Deinde propono tibi:

Non omne sequens ex posito est concedendum.

Vel concedis vel negas[29]. Si concedis, habeo intentum. Si negas, contra:

Tu negas sequens ex concesso vel concessis, igitur male.

Respondetur admittendo positum, et cum proponitur:

Aliquid sequitur ex posito,

concedendo ipsam[30], non quia sequens sed quia vera et impertinens. Deinde cum proponitur:

Nullum sequens ex posito est concedendum,

negatur quia falsum et impertinens. Immo nego istam copulativam:

Aliquid sequitur ex posito et nullum sequens ex posito est a te concedendum,

quia est falsa et non sequens, quia non sequitur:

Ista copulativa est tibi posita obligata 'Aliquid sequitur ex posito et nullum sequens ex posito est concedendum', igitur aliquid sequitur ex posito et nullum sequens ex posito est concedendum.

Et si arguitur[31] contra:

Ista copulativa est posita obligata, igitur concedenda,

conceditur conclusio: repugnat enim quod sit neganda. Tamen quotienscumque proponitur, ipsam[32] nego quia falsa et impertinens. Et si arguitur:

Ista est a te concedenda et tu negas eam, igitur male respondes,

concedo consequentiam et nego antecedens, quia est copulativa falsa et impertinens. Et si quaeritur pro qua parte, dico quod pro secunda parte, quia repugnat concesso et opposito bene negati. Sequitur enim:

---

[28] illam] *om*. E
[29] negas] neges E
[30] ipsam] illam E
[31] arguitur] arguatur M
[32] ipsam] eam E

> Something follows from the *positum* and nothing which follows from the *positum* should be granted;

therefore it could be a *positum obligatum*.

Having therefore admitted the case, I propose this to you:

> Something follows from the *positum*.

This should be granted, because it follows. Then I propose this to you:

> Nothing which follows from the *positum* should be granted.

This should also be granted for the same reason. Then I propose to you:

> Not everything which follows from the *positum* should be granted.

Either you grant this or you deny it. If you grant it, I have made my point. If you deny it, I argue against you:

> You deny what follows from a previously granted proposition (or propositions); therefore you reply incorrectly.

I reply by admitting the *positum* and when

> Something follows from the *positum*

is proposed, I grant it, not because it follows but because it is true and irrelevant. Then when

> Nothing which follows from the *positum* should be granted

is proposed, it is denied because it is false and irrelevant. Indeed, I deny this conjunction:

> Something follows from the *positum* and nothing which follows from the *positum* should be granted by you

because it is false and does not follow. This inference is invalid:

> This conjunction, 'Something follows from the *positum* and nothing which follows from the *positum* should be granted' is the *positum obligatum*; therefore something follows from the *positum* and nothing which follows from the *positum* should be granted.

And if someone argues against this ⟨by saying⟩

> This conjunction is the *positum obligatum*; therefore it should be granted,

the conclusion is granted, for it is inconsistent that it should be denied. But however often the ⟨conjunction⟩ is proposed, I deny it because it is false and irrelevant. And if someone argues

> This should be granted by you and you deny it; therefore you reply incorrectly,

I grant the inference and I deny the premiss, because it is a false and irrelevant conjunction. And if you ask on account of which clause, I say on account of the second clause, because it is inconsistent with a previously granted proposition and the opposite of a correctly denied proposition. This is a valid inference:

Ista non est a te concedenda vel tu non[33] negas eam, sed ista est a te concedenda, igitur tu non negas eam.

Ubi bene advertas quod feci duas negationes. Prima dirigebatur ad totam copulativam, secunda ad istam categoricam

Tu negas eam.

Et hoc dico propter aliquos qui dicunt quod non est nisi[34] una negatio et exspectant quod proponantur partes ac si quaelibet primo loco proposita esset neganda, quod non est verum ex quo concessa est una pars copulativae et negatur ista copulativa. Caveat[35] bene respondens ne neget istam partem antequam neget[36] copulativam, quia tunc negaret verum et impertinens et per consequens male responderet[37].

⟨5⟩ Quinto contra regulam arguitur sic. Et pono tibi illam:

A est aliqua propositio posita obligata et sit A ista 'Nulla propositio est tibi posita.'

Qua admissa, propono tibi illam:

Aliqua propositio est tibi ⟨posita⟩ obligata,

quae[38] sit B. Vel igitur concedis vel negas. Si negas, contra:

Tu negas sequens ex posito, igitur male.

Antecedens patet, nam sequitur:

A est aliqua[39] propositio tibi posita obligata[40], ergo aliqua propositio est tibi posita obligata.

Si concedis, arguo sic:

B non est a te concedendum et[41] B sequitur ex posito obligato, igitur intentum.

Consequentia patet cum minori, et maiorem probo. Nam B est oppositum A, sed A est a te concedendum cum sit obligatum per casum; igitur B est a te negandum.

Ad istud argumentum respondetur ut prius admittendo positum, et cum proponitur B, concedo tamquam sequens et nego A. Non enim sequitur

A est aliqua propositio mihi posita, igitur nulla propositio est mihi posita.

---

[33] non]*om*. E
[34] nisi]ibi E
[35] Caveat]tamen E
[36] neget]istam *add*.E
[37] responderet]respondetur M
[38] quae]*om*.M
[39] aliqua propositio]*om*.E
[40] obligata]*om*.M
[41] et . . .concedendum]*om*.E

> Either this should not be granted by you or you do not deny it, but this should be granted by you; therefore you do not deny it.

Here you notice that I have produced two denials. The first was applied to the entire conjunction, the second to this categorical proposition:

> You deny it.

I make these remarks on account of some people who say that there is only one denial and wait for the clauses to be proposed, as if whichever is proposed in the first place should be denied. This is not the case, because one clause of the conjunction has been granted and the whole conjunction is denied. The respondent should take great care lest he deny this clause before he denies the conjunction, for then he would deny a true and irrelevant proposition and as a result would reply incorrectly.

⟨5⟩ Fifth argument against rule three. I posit this to you:

> A is some proposition which is put to you as the *positum obligatum*, and let A be this: 'No proposition is posited to you'.

When this has been admitted, I propose this to you:

> Some proposition is put to you as the ⟨*positum*⟩ *obligatum*.

Let this be B. Either you grant it or you deny it. If you deny it, I argue against you:

> You deny something which follows from the *positum*; therefore you reply incorrectly.

The premiss is obvious, for this is a valid inference:

> A is some proposition which is put to you as the *positum obligatum*; therefore some proposition is put to you as the *positum obligatum*.

If you grant it, I argue thus:

> B ought not to be granted by you, and B follows from the *positum obligatum*; therefore I have made my point.

The inference is obvious, as is the minor premiss. Proof of the major premiss: B is the opposite of A, but A should be granted by you since according to the case it is the *obligatum*; therefore B should be denied by you.

I reply to this argument by admitting the *positum*, as above. When B is proposed I grant it as following, and I deny A. This is an invalid inference:

> A is some proposition which is posited to me; therefore no proposition is posited to me.

A, ergo, quia est falsum non sequens, debet negari quandocumque proponitur. Et cum (224^{vb}M) dicitur

A est obligatum positum, igitur A est concedendum,

concedo[42] consequentiam et consequens, et nego quod A sit a me negandum. Propterea admisso[43] quod B sit oppositum A, proposito B, concedo ipsum et nego ipsum esse concedendum, quia tunc duo contradictoria essent concedenda. Et si arguitur sic:

A est repugnans, ergo negandum,

concedo consequentiam et nego antecedens quia licet in rei veritate ita sit quod A est repugnans, non tamen habeo concedere quod sit repugnans quia oppositum sequitur sic arguendo:

A est (183^{vb}E) concedendum, igitur non est[44] repugnans.

Modo consimili est respondendum ad illam communem obligationem[45]. Pono tibi istam:

'Nihil est tibi positum' ⟨est tibi positum⟩ et admissum.

Qua admisso, conceditur[46] illa:

Aliquid est tibi positum,

et negatur illa

Nihil est tibi positum,

quia repugnans. Et si proponitur

'Nihil est tibi positum' est a te concedendum,

concedo[47]. Deinde si proponitur:

Illa sunt contradictoria 'Aliquid est tibi positum' et 'Nihil est tibi positum',

concedo quia verum et impertinens. Ulterius si proponitur[48] illa

'Aliquid est tibi positum' est a te concedenda,

nego quia repugnans duobus concessis. Si tamen in principio proponeretur haec

'Aliquid[49] est tibi positum' est a te concedenda,

et posterius illa

Haec sunt contradictoria,

---

[42] concedo]concedendo M
[43] admisso]concesso E
[44] est]*om.*M
[45] communem obligationem]conclusionem obligatam E
[46] conceditur]concedatur M
[47] concedo]concedendo M
[48] proponitur]proponatur E
[49] Aliquid]nihil M,E. *Corr.M*² *in marg.*

A, therefore, should be denied whenever it is proposed, for it is a false proposition which does not follow. And when someone says

A is the *positum obligatum*; therefore A should be granted,

I grant the inference and the conclusion, and I deny that A ought to be denied by me. Therefore, when it has been admitted that B is the opposite of A and B has been proposed, I grant it; and I deny that it should be granted, because otherwise two contradictories would have to be granted. If someone argues like this:

A is inconsistent; therefore A should be denied,

I grant the inference and I deny the premiss. Although the truth of the matter is that A is inconsistent, I do not have to grant that A is inconsistent, because the opposite is proved by this argument:

A should be granted; therefore A is not inconsistent.

One ought to reply in a similar way to this common *obligatio*: I posit this to you:

'Nothing is posited to you' is ⟨posited to you⟩ and admitted ⟨by you⟩.[23]

When this has been admitted, let this be granted:

Something is posited to you;

and let

Nothing is posited to you

be denied, because it is inconsistent. And if

'Nothing is posited to you' should be granted by you

is proposed, I grant it. Then if:

'Something is posited to you' and 'Nothing is posited to you' are contradictories

is proposed, I grant it because it is true and irrelevant. Further if

'Something is posited to you' should be granted by you

is proposed, I deny it because it is inconsistent with the two previously granted propositions. If however

'Something is posited to you' should be granted by you

were proposed at the beginning, and next this:

These are contradictories,

---

[23] I have restored the text in accordance with Strode's discussion: Strode, op.cit., fol. 87^{rb-va}. Paul gives the essence of the solution Strode offered in his last paragraph. For the genuinely common version of this sophism see below: against rule 4, sophism 1.

concederem primum et negarem secundum tamquam repugnans ut dictum est.

⟨6⟩ Sexto contra regulam arguitur sic. Et pono tibi illam

>Tu negas necessarium simpliciter.

Qua posita et admissa, propono tibi[50] istam:

>Tu male respondes.

Si negas, contra:

>Tu negas sequens ex posito, ergo male.

Si concedis, arguo quod illud non est concedendum et illud est sequens ex posito obligato, igitur etc. Consequentia patet cum minori et maiorem probo. Nam tu concedis sequens ex posito, igitur bene respondes, et per consequens tu[51] non male respondes, quod[52] est oppositum illius concessi et sequenti ex posito.

Ad hoc solet responderi admittendo positum et negando illam

>Tu bene respondes,

et concedendo illam:

>Tu male respondes

tamquam sequens ex posito. Et ad argumentum:

>Tu concedis sequens ex posito, igitur bene respondes,

negatur antecedens quia repugnat. Sequitur enim, ut dicitur:

>Tu male respondes, igitur non concedis sequens ex posito,

et ita negetur[53] quaelibet propositio ex qua infertur bene respondere.

Haec responsio non[54] videtur mihi vera quia non sequitur:

>Tu male respondes, igitur tu non bene respondes,

ita quod ista stant simul

>Tu bene respondes

et

>Tu male respondes.

Et facio hanc consequentiam:

>Tu concedis necessarium et negas necessarium, igitur bene respondes et male respondes.

---

[50] tibi]*om*.M
[51] tu]*om*.M
[52] quod . . . sequens ex posito] tamquam sequentem et nego illam tu bene respondes. M
[53] negetur]negatur E
[54] non]*om*.E

I would grant the first and deny the second as inconsistent, as has been said.

⟨6⟩ Sixth argument against rule three: I posit this to you:

You deny a proposition which is simply necessary.

When this has been posited and admitted, I propose this to you:

You reply incorrectly.[24]

If you deny this, I argue against you:

You deny a proposition which follows from the *positum*; therefore you reply incorrectly.

If you grant it, I argue that it ought not to be granted and that it follows from the *positum obligatum*; therefore etc. The inference is obvious, as is the minor premiss. Proof of the major premiss: You grant a proposition which follows from the *positum*, therefore you reply correctly and as a result you do not reply incorrectly. But ⟨this conclusion⟩ is the opposite of the previously granted proposition, which does follow from the *positum*.

People usually reply to this by admitting the *positum*, denying

You reply correctly,

and granting

You reply incorrectly

as following from the *positum*. ⟨In reply⟩ to the argument

You grant a proposition which follows from the *positum*; therefore you reply correctly

the premiss is denied because it is inconsistent. For this:

You reply incorrectly, therefore you do not grant a proposition which follows from the *positum*

is a valid inference, as is claimed; and in this way every proposition from which one infers that one has replied correctly can be denied.

This reply does not seem true to me. The following is an invalid inference:

You reply incorrectly; therefore you do not reply correctly

because the propositions

You reply correctly

and

You reply incorrectly

are mutually consistent. I construct this inference:

You grant a necessary proposition and you deny a necessary proposition; therefore you reply correctly and you reply incorrectly.

---

[24] See Peter of Candia, op.cit., fol. 67rb. It is Peter of Candia's solution that Paul first describes (p. 164, lines 13–21) and then attacks.

Consequentia est bona et[55] antecedens est possibile, igitur et consequens.

Item non videtur mihi quod illa consequentia sit bona:

    Tu male respondes, igitur tu non concedis sequens ex posito,

quia oppositum consequentis stat cum antecedente. Probatur. Et pono quod A et B sequantur ex tibi posito obligato et quod tu concedas A et neges B. Quo posito, patet quod tu male respondes et tamen concedis sequens ex posito obligato.

Ideo aliter respondetur admittendo positum[56]. Et cum proponitur

    Tu male respondes,

concedo. Et quando[57] dicitur

    Tu concedis sequens ex posito obligato

concedo, quia verum et impertinens. Deinde:

    Tu bene respondes.

Concedo, quia sequens. Deinde cum arguitur

    Tu male respondes, igitur non bene respondes,

nego consequentiam.

Sed forte arguitur sic:

    Tu male respondes et non respondes nisi ad unum, igitur tu[58] non bene respondes.

Nego minorem tamquam repugnantem. Sequitur enim:

    Tu male respondes et bene respondes, igitur ad plura respondes quam[59] ad unum.

Item si in principio post concessionem illius

    Tu male respondes

proponatur illa:

    Tu non respondes nisi ad unum,

concedatur[60] quia verum et impertinens. Deinde:

    Tu bene respondes.

Negatur[61] quia repugnans duobus concessis. Sequitur[62] enim:

    Tu male respondes et tu non respondes nisi ad unum, igitur tu non bene respondes.

---

[55] et]*om.* M
[56] positum]casum E
[57] Et quando dicitur]deinde E
[58] tu]*om.*M
[59] quam]et E
[60] concedatur]conceditur E
[61] Negatur]negetur E
[62] Sequitur . . .]*om.*M

The inference is valid and the premiss is possible; therefore the conclusion is also possible.

Again, this inference does not seem valid to me, i.e.
> You reply incorrectly; therefore you do not grant a proposition which follows from the *positum*.

The opposite of the conclusion is consistent with the premiss. Proof: I posit that both A and B follow from the *positum obligatum* which was put to you, and that you grant A but deny B. When this has been posited it is clear that you reply incorrectly even though you do grant a proposition which follows from the *positum obligatum*.

Thus another reply must be given. The *positum* is admitted. When
> You reply incorrectly

is proposed, I grant it. And when it is said
> You grant something which follows from the *positum obligatum*,

I grant it because it is true and irrelevant. Then:
> You reply correctly.

I grant it, because it follows. Then when it is argued:
> You reply incorrectly; therefore you do not reply correctly,

I reject the inference.

But perhaps someone will argue like this:
> You reply incorrectly, and you reply only to one proposition; therefore you do not reply correctly.

I deny the minor premiss as inconsistent. This is a valid inference:
> You reply incorrectly and you reply correctly; therefore you reply to more than one proposition.

Likewise if in the beginning, after
> You reply incorrectly

had been granted,
> You reply only to one proposition

had been proposed, it must be granted as true and irrelevant. Then:
> You reply correctly

must be denied because it is inconsistent with the two previously granted propositions. This is a valid inference:
> You reply incorrectly and you reply only to one proposition; therefore you do not reply correctly.

Et si arguitur contra:

Tu concedis⁶³ sequens ex posito obligato aut verum impertinens, igitur bene respondes,

negatur antecedens pro qualibet eius⁶⁴ parte⁶⁵ quia repugnat opposito illius negati

Tu bene (225ʳᵃM) respondes

ut satis liquet.

⟨7⟩ Septimo arguitur sic. Et pono tibi istam:

Tu concedis istam 'Homo est asinus.'

Quo admisso, propono tibi illam:

Tu concedis impossibile.

Et arguo sic.

Illa sequitur ex posito obligato et non concedenda est, igitur oppositum regulae.

Consequentia patet⁶⁶ cum maiori, quia sequitur:

Tu concedis istam 'Homo est asinus', igitur tu concedis impossibile.

Sed quod non sit a te concedenda probatur, quia est falsa et non sequens, igitur neganda. Prima pars patet et secundam probo, quia non sequitur:

Tu concedis istam 'Homo est asinus', igitur tu concedis impossibile,

quia stat quod tu⁶⁷ concedis eam et quod⁶⁸ ipsa sit necessaria et ad nullam⁶⁹ aliam respondeas.

Ideo respondetur admittendo positum et negando (184ʳᵃE) istam:

Tu concedis impossibile,

quia falsa est et impertinens. Et ad argumentum nego consequentiam, sed oportet addere in minori quod ista

Homo est asinus

sit impossibilis, quod si admittitur⁷⁰ negatur tamquam repugnans etc.

---

⁶³ ... concedis]*om*.M
⁶⁴ eius]*om*.E
⁶⁵ parte]etc.*add*.E
⁶⁶ patet]tenet E
⁶⁷ tu]dum E
⁶⁸ et quod]*om*.E
⁶⁹ nullam]unam E
⁷⁰ admittitur]additur E

If someone argues against this by saying:

> You grant a proposition which either follows from the *positum obligatum* or is true and irrelevant; therefore you reply correctly,

the premiss must be denied on account of each of its clauses because, as is sufficiently obvious, each is inconsistent with the opposite of this proposition:

> You reply correctly,

which was denied.

⟨7⟩ Seventh argument against rule three: I posit this to you:

> You grant this: 'A human being is a donkey'.[25]

When this has been admitted, I propose this to you:

> You grant an impossible proposition.

And I argue thus:

> This proposition follows from the *positum obligatum*, but it ought not to be granted; therefore the opposite of the rule holds.

The inference is obvious, as is the major premiss, because this is a valid inference:

> You grant 'A human being is a donkey'; therefore you grant an impossible proposition.

But the proof that the proposition ought not to be granted by you is that it is false and it does not follow, therefore it should be denied. The first clause is obvious, and I can prove the second because

> You grant 'A human being is a donkey'; therefore you grant an impossible proposition

is an invalid inference. It is consistent for you to grant that proposition and for it to be necessary, and for you to reply to no other proposition.[26]

Thus one should reply by admitting the *positum* and by denying

> You grant an impossible proposition,

because it is false and irrelevant. ⟨In reply⟩ to this argument, I reject the inference. One ought to add to the minor premiss the claim that

> A human being is a donkey

is an impossible proposition. But if this is admitted, it will be denied as inconsistent.

---

[25] Cf. Strode, op.cit., fol. 87^{ra-rb}. Strode sets up an interesting case in which the respondent has to reply 'sicut asinus, si sciret loqui', and the opponent then posits 'Tu es asinus'. If the respondent grants this, is he granting an impossible proposition or not? Cf. also Peter of Candia, op.cit., fol. 67rb: 'Ponitur ista propositio "Tu concedis impossibile". Qua admissa propono tibi istam: "Homo est asinus".' In his discussion he makes the point: 'Aliud est haec propositio "Homo est asinus" et aliud est "Tu concedis istam 'Homo est asinus'".'

[26] It could be necessary because the quoted sentence could have acquired another meaning.

⟨*Contra Regulam Quartam*⟩

Quarta regula fuit ista. Omne posito obligato repugnans scitum esse tale in tempore obligationis est negandum.

⟨1⟩ Contra istam regulam arguitur sic. Et pono tibi istam:

    Nihil est tibi positum.

Qua admissa, quia[71] possibilis, propono tibi istam:

    Aliquid est tibi positum.

Si concedis et bene respondes, igitur intentum quod repugnans[72] posito obligato scitum esse tale est concedendum. Si negas, contra:

    Ego posui tibi istam 'Nihil est tibi positum', sed[73] ista 'Nihil est tibi positum' est aliquid, igitur aliquid est tibi positum.

⟨1.1⟩ Confirmatur hoc idem tripliciter, et primo sic. Pono tibi istam:

    Tu nihil admittis.

Qua admissa quia est[74] possibilis, propono tibi istam:

    Aliquid admittis.

Si concedis, concedis repugnans posito obligato et bene respondes, igitur intentum. Si negas, contra:

    Tu admittis istam 'Nihil admittis'[75], sed[76] ista est aliquid, ergo aliquid admittis.

Nec etiam habes dubitare, ut patet.

⟨1.2⟩ Confirmatur secundo sic. Et[77] pono tibi illam:

    Tu non es.

Qua admissa quia possibilis, propono tibi istam[78]:

    Tu admittis aliquid.

Si negas vel dubitas, contra:

    Ego posui tibi illam 'Tu non es', et tu admittis eam et ipsa est aliquid, ergo aliquid admittis.

Si concedis, propono tibi istam

    Tu es.

Si concedis et bene respondes[79], habeo intentum. Si negas, tu negas sequens ex

---

[71] quia possibilis] *om.* E
[72] repugnans] repugnat E
[73] sed] et E
[74] est] *om.* M
[75] Nihil admittis] *om.* E
[76] sed] et E
[77] Et] *om.* E
[78] istam] *om.* M
[79] respondes] respondis M

⟨*Against Rule Four*⟩

Rule four was this: Everything which is inconsistent with the *positum obligatum* and is known to be such should be denied during the period of the *obligatio*.

⟨1⟩ First argument against rule four. I posit this to you:
  Nothing is posited to you.[27]
When this has been admitted because it is possible, I propose this to you:
  Something is posited to you.
If you grant it and thereby reply correctly, I have made my point that a proposition which is inconsistent with the *positum obligatum* and is known to be such should be granted. If you deny it, I argue against you:
  I have posited 'Nothing is posited to you' to you, but 'Nothing is posited to you' is something; therefore something is posited to you.

⟨1.1⟩ First of three supporting arguments. I posit this to you:
  You admit nothing.
When this has been admitted because it is possible, I propose this to you:
  You admit something.
If you grant it, you grant a proposition which is inconsistent with the *positum obligatum*, yet you reply correctly; therefore I have made my point. If you deny it, I argue against you:
  You admit 'You admit nothing', but this is something; therefore you admit something.
Nor should you doubt it, as is obvious.

⟨1.2⟩ Second supporting argument. I posit this to you:
  You do not exist.[28]
When this has been admitted because it is possible, I propose this to you:
  You admit something.
If you deny or doubt it, I argue against you:
  I posited 'You do not exist' to you and you admit it and it is something; therefore you admit something.
If you grant it, I propose this to you:
  You exist.
If you grant it and thereby reply correctly, I have made my point. If you deny it, you deny a proposition following from a previously granted

---

[27] This sophism was discussed by Burley, op.cit., 3.17, 3.19; Ockham, op.cit., p. 737; Swyneshed, op.cit., p. 256, §28, p. 265, §62, §64, p. 271, §§91–92; Lavenham, op.cit., pp. 234–235, §19; Albert, op.cit., fol. 49rb; Marsilius, op.cit., fol. 85^{r-v}; Buser, op.cit., fol. 76^{ra-rb}; John of Holland, op.cit., fol. 104^r; Strode, op.cit., fols. 78vb–79ra; Peter of Candia, op.cit., fol. 67ra. For the context of much of the discussion, see references in Part 1, section 4, note 12. See also Spade in *CH*, p. 340.

The statement of the sophism and the three subsidiary sophisms come from Albert. Buser and Marsilius omitted the first of the subsidiary sophisms.

[28] 'Tu non es' was a popular sophism. It was approached in three different ways. (1) The *positum* is not to be admitted. Albert, op.cit., fol. 49rb, gave this as his main solution, saying that the *positum* was inconsistent with its *admissio*. (2) The *positum* is to be admitted, because it is possible, but it should be denied. This solution is found in Billingham, op.cit., fol. 90^v; and he was followed by *Lat.misc.e 79*, fol. 19^{ra-rb}., and *Lib.Soph.Oxon.*, sig. C v^v. It was explained that the rule that any possible *positum* should be granted applied only when the *positum* was not

concesso, igitur male. Antecedens patet[80], nam sequitur:
    Tu admittis ipsam[81] 'Tu non es', igitur tu[82] es.
⟨1.3⟩ Confirmatur tertio sic[83]. Et pono tibi illam:
    Tu non es obligatus.
Qua admissa, propono tibi illam:
    Tu es obligatus.
Quam[84] si concedis, habeo propositum. Si negas, contra:
    Ego posui tibi istam 'Tu non es obligatus', et tu admisisti eam, igitur tu es obligatus.
    Ad haec[85] multae solent dari responsiones.
    Prima non admittit aliquam propositionem factam propter repugnantiam positi ad positionem vel admissionem. Dicit enim quod in prima positione positum repugnat positioni, in secunda repugnat admissioni, in tertia et in quarta repugnat positioni[86] et admissioni tam simul quam divisim.
    Haec positio est fuga miserorum secundum quod ostendit conclusio et non mirum quia[87] nesciat quid sit obligatio, quid obligatum, ad quid[88] obligatio obliget. Quis enim sciens naturam obligationis diceret ipsam obligare ad concedendum positionem vel admissionem[89] nisi inquantum positio vel admissio esset quid[90] obligatum. Quare etc.
    Secunda responsio admittit quamlibet illarum positionum. Et tunc ad primum cum proponitur
    Aliquid est tibi positum,
negat[91]; et cum dicitur
    Posui tibi illam 'Nihil est tibi positum' et ipsa est aliquid, igitur aliquid est tibi positum,
concedit consequentiam et maiorem sed negat[92] (225[rb]M) minorem dicens quod nulla propositio est aliquid.
    Haec responsio in hoc quod negat minorem est miserior fuga quam prima, quia in arte haec[93] disputatoria sumitur ly .aliquid. communiter pro quolibet

---

[80] patet]probatur E
[81] ipsam]illam E
[82] tu]non add.M,E
[83] sic]om.M
[84] Quam]om.E
[85] haec]omnia add.E
[86] positioni]om.E
[87] quia]quod E
[88] quid]quod E
[89] vel admissionem]om.M
[90] quid]om.E
[91] negat]negant M,E, *correxi*
[92] negat minorem]negatur minor E
[93] haec]om.E

---

inconsistent with the *positio*. *Lib.Soph.Oxon.* added that from every *positio* there follows the existence of three things: he who posits, he to whom something is posited, and the *positum* itself. To deny the existence of one of these three things produces inconsistency. (3) The *positum* is to be admitted and granted: see Buser, op.cit., fol. 76[ra–rb]; Marsilius, op.cit., fol. 85[r–v]; and Strode, fol. 83[va]. One should now go on to deny that one grants anything. As Strode pointed out, one must grant what follows from the *positum* and deny what is inconsistent, op.cit., fol. 83[va]. He added that if you were asked why you had granted 'You do not exist', 'dicatur quod non est causa danda. . . . sicut si quaeris quare est quod tu non es Papa, vel cardinalis, vel asinus, vel aliquid aliud, non est causa danda. . . .'

proposition; therefore you reply incorrectly. The premiss is obvious, for this is a valid inference:

You admit 'You do not exist'; therefore you exist.

⟨1.3⟩ Third supporting argument. I posit this to you:

You are not obligated.

When this has been admitted, I propose this to you:

You are obligated.

If you grant this, I have made my point. If you deny it, I argue against you:

I posited 'You are not obligated' to you, and you admitted it; therefore you are obligated.

Various replies are usually given to these arguments.

First reply: none of the propositions put forward is admitted because there is an inconsistency between the *positum* and the *positio* or the *admissio*.[29] The view holds that in the first *positio* the *positum* is inconsistent with the *positio*, in the second it is inconsistent with the *admissio*, and in the third and fourth it is inconsistent with the *positio* and *admissio* whether taken alone or together.

This view is the escape route of wretches as thesis ⟨six⟩ showed, and one should not be surprised, because they are ignorant of what an *obligatio* is, what an *obligatum* is, and what an *obligatio* obligates one to. Who indeed who knows the nature of an *obligatio* would say that he was obligated to grant a *positio* or an *admissio* except insofar as the *positio* or the *admissio* was something obligated. Therefore etc.

Second reply: each *positio* is admitted. In the first when

Something is posited to you

is proposed, they deny it; and when

I posited 'Nothing is posited to you' and it is something; therefore something is posited to you

is stated, they grant the inference and the major premiss and deny the minor premiss, saying that no proposition is something.[30]

Inasmuch as this reply denies the minor premiss it is an even more wretched escape route than the first reply. In this disputatory art the word 'something' is normally taken to refer to anything which exhibits some kind of

---

The third solution raised the problem of whether one can deny one's own actions. As Wyclif explained in his discussion of the similar sophism 'Tu es mortuus', op.cit., p. 71, cf. Ockham, op.cit., p. 736, it does not follow from the denial of 'You grant something' that you are denying your own actions, for if you are dead, you cannot act by replying, granting or denying. Nonetheless, Wyclif did allow the denial of one's own acts in certain circumstances: '... respondens debet aliquando negare proprium actum si repugnat casui', op.cit., pp. 72–73; and John of Holland gave this as a rule, op.cit., fol. 105[r]. Thus, John said, one could grant both 'Tu non es' and 'Tu non respondes'.

[29] This first reply was given by Albert of Saxony and others: see Part 1, section 4, note 12. Marsilius said 'hae responsiones sunt frivolae', op.cit., fol. 85[r], and Buser, in a phrase echoed by Paul, said 'Istae responsiones sunt fugae miserorum', op.cit., fol. 76[ra].

[30] This was given as a possible alternative by Marsilius, op.cit., fol. 85[v]; and Buser, op.cit., fol. 76[ra]. Cf. Strode, op.cit., fol. 87[va].

quod habet aliqualem unionem, sive proprie dictam sive improprie dictam quemadmodum est unio aggregationis. Item in hoc quod concedit maiorem, concedit repugnans opposito bene negati, igitur male.

Tertia responsio admittit haec omnia et semper concedit oppositum positi, videlicet

    Aliquid est tibi positum,

    Tu[94] es,

    Tu es obligatus,

et huiusmodi. Et cum dicitur

    Tu concedis duo contradictoria,

negat et ita putans consequenter respondere negat illa esse contradictoria.

Haec responsio leviter decipitur in hoc. Nam cedat tempus obligationis, et arguo quod concessisti duo contradictoria videlicet

    Aliquid est tibi positum

et

    Nihil est tibi positum,

et per consequens male respondebas.

Item cum proponebatur tibi

    Ista sunt contradictoria,

et negasti, tu negasti[95] verum non repugnans, ut patet. Igitur etc.

⟨1R⟩ Ideo est aliter respondendum ad principale. Admitto positum et cum proponitur

    Aliquid est tibi positum,

nego eam. Et tunc ad argumentum:

    Ego posui tibi illam 'Nihil est tibi positum', igitur aliquid est tibi positum,

nego antecedens tamquam repugnans posito obligato. Non enim stant illa simul

    Nihil est tibi positum

et

    Posui tibi illam 'Nihil est tibi positum.'

---

[94] Tu es]*om*.E
[95] tu negasti]*om*.M

union, whether properly or improperly so-called, insofar as it is a union of aggregation. Inasmuch as this reply grants the major premiss, it grants a proposition inconsistent with a correctly denied proposition; therefore the reply is incorrect.

Third reply: all these things are admitted, and the opposite of the *positum* is always granted, namely

> Something is posited to you,
> You exist,
> You are obligated,

and so forth. And when it is claimed

> You grant two contradictories,

the reply denies this, and then, thinking to abide by the consequences, it also denies that they were contradictories.[31]

This reply is somewhat misled over the last point. Let the period of the *obligatio* come to an end. I argue that you have granted two contradictories, namely

> Something is posited to you

and

> Nothing is posited to you;

and as a result you replied incorrectly.

Likewise when

> These are contradictories

was proposed to you and you denied it, you denied a true proposition which was not inconsistent, as is obvious. Therefore etc.

⟨1R⟩ Therefore one should reply to the main argument in another way.[32] I admit the *positum* and when

> Something is posited to you

is proposed, I deny it. And then ⟨in reply⟩ to the argument:

> I posited 'Nothing is posited to you' to you; therefore something is posited to you,

I deny the premiss as inconsistent with the *positum obligatum*. These propositions

> Nothing is posited to you

and

> I posited 'Nothing is posited to you' to you

---

[31] This reply is found in Peter of Candia, op.cit., fol. 67ra, who explained that it rested on the doctrine that a part cannot supposit for the whole of which it is a part. The propositions 'Nihil est tibi positum' and 'Aliquid est tibi positum' must therefore have different referents and cannot be contradictories. Peter did not relate this answer to the other sophisms. Cf. Ockham, op.cit., p. 732.

[32] The essence of this reply and the subsequent replies is found in Marsilius, op.cit., fols. 85v–86r, and Buser, op.cit., fol. 76ra. See also Peter of Candia, op.cit., fol. 67ra.

Et si arguitur sic:

> Positio repugnat tibi posito, igitur aliquid est tibi positum, (184^{rb}E) nego antecedens tamquam repugnans. Contra:
>> Tu negas istam 'Aliquid est tibi positum' et istam similiter, 'Posui tibi illam "Nihil est tibi positum"', et non nisi quia repugnans dicitur.

Concessa prima parte, nego secundam[96]. Et si quaeritur causa quare ego nego, hanc quaestionem nolo determinare quousque ab hac obligatione non fuero deliberatus.

⟨1.1R⟩ Ad primam confirmationem patet responsio admittendo positum et concedendo ipsum. Et cum proponitur eius oppositum aut aliquod antecedens ad eius oppositum, semper negetur[97]; et si quaeritur causa, non detur alia nisi quia placet mihi.

⟨1.2R⟩ Ad secundam confirmationem admisso casu concedo[98] istam:

> Tu non es.

Et nego istam:

> Tu es.

Et nego quod aliquid admittatur, aut aliquid concedam vel negem aut[99] dubitem, aut quod respondeam bene vel male; quia haec omnia antecedunt ad oppositum positi obligati.

⟨1.3R⟩ Ad tertiam confirmationem admisso casu, nego quod sim obligatus. Et cum dicitur:

> Posui tibi illam 'Tu non es obligatus' et eam admisisti, igitur tu es obligatus,

ad bonum intellectum negatur antecedens quia repugnans, sicut dictum est. Et notanter dicitur 'ad bonum intellectum', quia iuxta superius dicta non valet argumentum, quia non semper ex qualibet positione et admissione sequitur obligatio. Ideo deberet in antecedente addi illa particula 'sine conditione impediente obligationem'. Quae autem sit illa conditio, patet in primo articulo.

⟨2⟩ Secundo contra regulam arguo sic. Et pono tibi illam copulativam:

> Tu es Romae et omne repugnans huic propositioni 'Tu es Romae' est a te[1] concedendum.

---

[96] secundam]antecedentis *add*.E
[97] negetur]negatur E
[98] concedo]concedendo M
[99] aut]vel E
[1] a te]*om*.E

are not consistent. And if someone argues like this
> The *positio* is inconsistent with the *positum*; therefore something is posited to you,

I deny the premiss as inconsistent. ⟨Someone may argue⟩ against me:
> You deny 'Something is posited to you' and you also deny 'I posited "Nothing is posited to you" to you', and this could only be because they are inconsistent.

When the first clause has been granted, I deny the second. And if you ask the reason why I deny it, I express my unwillingness to answer the question until I have been released from this *obligatio*.

⟨1.1R⟩ Reply to the first supporting argument. It is clear that one replies by admitting the *positum* and then granting it. When its opposite, or some premiss from which the opposite can be inferred is proposed, it should always be denied. If someone asks the reason for this, the only reason they will be given is that I wanted to make that reply.

⟨1.2R⟩ Reply to the second supporting argument. When the case has been admitted I grant
> You do not exist

and I deny
> You exist.

I deny that something is admitted, or that I grant or deny or doubt something, or that I reply correctly or incorrectly, because all these things serve as premisses from which the opposite of the *positum obligatum* can be inferred.

⟨1.3R⟩ Reply to the third supporting argument. When the case has been granted I deny that I am obligated. And when
> I posited 'You are not obligated' to you and you admitted it; therefore you are obligated

is stated, the premiss, when correctly understood, is to be denied because it is inconsistent, as has been said. It should be noted that I say 'when correctly understood', for in accordance with what has been stated above the argument is invalid, because an *obligatio* does not always arise from any *positio* and *admissio*. Thus one should add the phrase 'without a condition which impedes the *obligatio*' to the premiss. What such a condition might be is made clear in the first section.

⟨2⟩ Second argument against rule four. I posit this conjunction to you:
> You are in Rome and everything inconsistent with the proposition 'You are in Rome' should be granted by you.

Deinde propono:

    Ista copulativa est posita obligata.

Vera et impertinens, igitur concedenda. Deinde:

    Utraque pars copulativae est posita ⟨obligata⟩.

Sequens, igitur concedendum[2]. Deinde:

    'Tu es Romae' est altera pars copulativae.

Vera et impertinens, igitur (225^{va}M) concedenda. Quibus concessis arguitur sic:

    'Tu es Romae' est[3] positum obligatum et omne repugnans huic propositioni[4] 'Tu es Romae' est concedendum, igitur[5] omne repugnans posito obligato est concedendum, et per consequens non omne repugnans est negandum.

Ad istud respondetur admittendo positum et conceditur quod[6] ista copulativa est posita obligata. Deinde[7] cum proponitur

    Utraque pars copulativae est posita obligata,

nego quia falsum et impertinens. Unde dico quod sola ista copulativa est posita[8] obligata, et nulla eius pars, non obstante quod quaelibet sit sequens ex posito obligato. Unde si ponerem istam

    Tu es Romae,

haec

    Tu es Romae,

esset posita et admissa et[9] esset obligata, et non ista

    Tu es,

licet[10] sit sequens.

Ubi tamen placeret opponenti quod quotienscumque poneretur copulativa poneretur utraque eius pars et ita obligaretur quaelibet illarum, esset aliter respondendum. Conceditur ergo totum quousque proponitur

    'Tu es Romae' est altera pars huius copulativae,

quae neganda est quia repugnans. Sequitur enim,

---

[2] concedendum]neganda E
[3] est]tibi *add*.M
[4] propositioni]*om*.M
[5] igitur . . . negandum]et per consequens non omne repugnans est negandum E
[6] quod]*om*.M
[7] Deinde]*om*.M
[8] posita]et *add*.M
[9] et]*om*.M
[10] licet]*om*.M

Then I propose
> This conjunction is the *positum obligatum*.

This is true and irrelevant; therefore it should be granted. Then:
> Each clause of the conjunction is a *positum ⟨obligatum⟩*.

This follows, therefore it should be granted. Then:
> 'You are in Rome' is one clause of the conjunction.

This is true and irrelevant; therefore it should be granted. When these propositions have been granted, the argument goes like this:

> 'You are in Rome' is a *positum obligatum* and everything inconsistent with this proposition 'You are in Rome' should be granted, therefore everything which is inconsistent with the *positum obligatum* should be granted, and as a result not every inconsistent proposition ought to be denied.

I reply to this by admitting the *positum*. I grant that this conjunction is the *positum obligatum*. Then when
> Each clause of the conjunction is a *positum obligatum*

is proposed, I deny it because it is false and irrelevant. Hence I say that only the conjunction is the *positum obligatum*, and not either of its clauses, notwithstanding that each of them does follow from the *positum obligatum*. Hence if I were to posit
> You are in Rome,

this:
> You are in Rome

would be the *positum* and *admissum* and it would be the *obligatum* and this:
> You exist

would not, even though it does follow.

However, if the opponent were to agree that whenever the conjunction was posited each of its clauses would also be posited and each would thereby have an obligating force, one would have to reply in another way. Everything is to be granted as above until
> 'You are in Rome' is one clause of the conjunction

is proposed. This should be denied because it is inconsistent. This is a valid inference:

Utraque pars illius[11] copulativae est posita obligata, sed omne repugnans huic 'Tu es Romae' est a te[12] concedendum, igitur haec 'Tu es Romae' non est altera pars illius[13] copulativae.

⟨3⟩ Tertio contra eandem regulam arguitur sic. Et pono tibi illam:

Omnis homo est Romae.

Qua posita et admissa, propono tibi haec:

'Homo non est Romae' est a te concedenda.

Si negas vel dubitas, contra:

Tu[14] negas vel dubitas verum et impertinens scitum esse tale, igitur male.

Antecedens patet, nam quod sit verum manifestum est. Quod autem[15] sit impertinens probatur, quia non sequitur nec repugnat. Si autem conceditur illa[16], arguitur sic.

'Homo non est Romae' est a te concedendum, sed 'Homo non est Romae' est repugnans posito obligato, ergo aliquod repugnans posito obligato est a te concedendum, et per consequens non omne repugnans est negandum.

Respondetur admittendo positum et concedendo illam

'Homo non est Romae' est a te concedendum.

Et tunc ad argumentum nego minorem tamquam repugnantem. Sequitur enim

'Homo non est Romae' est a te concedendum, igitur 'Homo non est Romae' non est repugnans posito obligato.

⟨4⟩ Quarto contra regulam arguitur[17] sic. Et pono tibi illam:

Nihil est repugnans posito.

Quo posito et admisso, propono tibi istam:

Aliquid est repugnans posito.

Si concedis et bene respondes, igitur intentum. Si negas, contra:

Illa est vera et impertinens, igitur concedenda.

Quod sit vera patet, sed quod sit impertinens probatur nam (184^{va}E) nihil est repugnans posito, et ipsa est, igitur est impertinens.

Respondetur admittendo positum, et nego quod illa sit impertinens. Et ad

---

[11] illius]*om*.E
[12] a te]*om*.E
[13] illius]eius E
[14] Tu]*om*.M
[15] autem]*om*.E
[16] illa]*om*.E
[17] arguitur]*om*.M

Each clause of this conjunction is a *positum obligatum* but everything inconsistent with 'You are in Rome' should be granted by you; therefore 'You are in Rome' is not a clause of this conjunction.

⟨3⟩ Third argument against rule four. I posit this to you:

Every human being is in Rome.

When this has been posited and admitted, I propose this to you

'A human being is not in Rome' should be granted by you.

If you deny or doubt it, I argue against you:

You deny or doubt a proposition which is true and irrelevant and is known to be such; therefore you reply incorrectly.

The premiss is clear, for it is obvious that the proposition is true, and that it is irrelevant can be proved because it neither follows nor is inconsistent. But if you grant the proposition, I argue like this:

'A human being is not in Rome' should be granted by you, but 'A human being is not in Rome' is inconsistent with the *positum obligatum*; therefore something inconsistent with the *positum obligatum* should be granted by you, and as a result not every inconsistent proposition should be denied.

I reply by admitting the *positum* and by granting

'A human being is not in Rome' should be granted by you.

⟨In my reply⟩ to the argument I deny the minor premiss as inconsistent. This is a valid inference:

'A human being is not in Rome' should be granted by you; therefore 'A human being is not in Rome' is not inconsistent with the *positum obligatum*.[33]

⟨4⟩ Fourth argument against rule four. I posit this to you:

Nothing is inconsistent with the *positum*.

When this has been posited and admitted, I propose this to you:

Something is inconsistent with the *positum*.

If you grant this and thereby reply correctly, I have made my point. If you deny it, I argue against you:

This is true and irrelevant; therefore it should be granted.

That it is true is obvious. I prove that it is irrelevant because nothing is inconsistent with the *positum*, but this proposition exists; therefore it is irrelevant.

I reply by admitting the *positum*, and I deny that the proposition is

---

[33] As usual, one must remember Paul's distinction between sentences which are used and sentences which are mentioned. Because the sentence 'Homo non est Romae' is mentioned, he can conclude that it (whatever it now means) is not inconsistent with the *positum*. If the sentence were used, he would of course have to deny it.

argumentum nego consequentiam. Stat enim quod sit sequens ex posito, ideo si proponitur

> Ipsa est sequens ex posito,

concedatur[18] tamquam sequens. Sequitur enim:

> Nihil est repugnans posito, et ipsa est vera et non est[19] impertinens, igitur est sequens.

Et si concluditur[20]

> igitur est concedenda,

conceditur consequentia et consequens. Numquam tamen concedam ipsam mihi propositam.

Item si post negationem illius

> Aliquid est repugnans posito

proponeretur ista copulativa:

> Haec est vera et non repugnans posito,

nego eam quia falsa et impertinens. Et si quaeritur pro qua parte, dicitur quod pro prima, quia oppositum sequitur ex uno concesso et opposito bene negati. Sequitur enim:

> Illa non est vera vel[21] est repugnans posito, sed non est repugnans posito per positum, igitur ipsa non est vera.

Item si post negationem illius

> Aliquid est repugnans posito,

non proponeretur aliqua (225^{vb}M) copulativa sed solum partes divisim, et primo[22]

> Haec est vera,

concedendum, quia verum non repugnans. Deinde

> Ipsa non est repugnans,

iterum conceditur quia sequens ex posito obligato. Ultimo

> Ista est a te concedenda,

conceditur tamquam sequens ex his ultimo concessis. Quare etc.

---

[18] concedatur]conceditur E
[19] est]*om*.E
[20] concluditur]concludatur M
[21] vel]nihil E
[22] primo]copulativae *add*.E

irrelevant. ⟨In my reply⟩ to the argument I reject the inference. It is consistent for the proposition to follow from the *positum*, so that if someone proposes
   It follows from the *positum*,
this must be granted as following. This inference:
   Nothing is inconsistent with the *positum*, and this proposition is true but it is not irrelevant; therefore it follows,
is valid. And if someone draws the conclusion:
   Therefore it should be granted,
I grant the inference and the conclusion. However, I will never grant the proposition when it is proposed to me.

Likewise if after the denial of
   Something is inconsistent with the *positum*,
this conjunction
   This is true and it is not inconsistent with the *positum*,
were proposed, I would deny it because it is false and irrelevant. And if someone asks on account of which clause, I say on account of the first, because its opposite follows from a previously granted proposition together with the opposite of a correctly denied proposition. This is a valid inference:
   Either this is not true or it is inconsistent with the *positum*, but by virtue of the *positum* it is not inconsistent with the *positum*; therefore it is not true.

Likewise if after the denial of this
   Something is inconsistent with the *positum*,
no conjunction were proposed, but only its clauses separately, with
   This is true
in first place, then it should be granted because it is true and not inconsistent. Then
   This is not inconsistent
is once more to be granted because it follows from the *positum obligatum*. Finally
   This should be granted by you
is granted because it follows from the propositions which have just been granted. Therefore etc.

⟨5⟩ Quinto contra regulam arguitur sic.

    Sit rei veritas quod tu sis albus, et pono tibi illam 'Tu es niger' quae praecise maneat tibi posita donec proponatur tibi[23] aliquod a te negandum, et non ultra sis obligatus ad istam.

Qua posita et admissa, propono tibi istam:

    Tu es albus.

Si concedis et bene respondes, igitur intentum. Patet consequentia nam ista repugnat posito, ut patet, et adhuc manet tempus obligationis quod probatur sic. Nam tempus obligationis durat per casum donec proponatur aliquod negandum a te, sed adhuc non proponebatur tibi[24] aliquod negandum a te, igitur adhuc tempus obligationis durat.

    Si negatur ideo cum primo proponitur illa:

    Tu es albus,

contra:

    Tu negas verum non obligatus, igitur male respondes.

Consequentia tenet et probatur antecedens, nam obligatio non durat nisi donec proponatur aliquod negandum a te, sed cum cito proponebatur haec[25]:

    Tu es albus,

proponebatur aliquod[26] a te negandum, quia aliter non negasses illam vel saltem male respondisti negando quod non fuit a te negandum, igitur cum tibi proponebatur ista

    Tu es albus,

tu[27] non eras obligatus ad eandem nec etiam fuisti[28] ad aliquid aliud obligatus, ut suppono. Igitur tunc non eras obligatus, quod fuit probandum.

    Respondetur admittendo casum, et cum proponitur illa

    Tu es albus,

concedo[29] eam et nego quod sim obligatus. Et cum dicitur

    Non proponebatur aliquod negandum a te,

nego. Immo dico quod ista

    Tu es albus

---

[23] tibi]*om.*E
[24] tibi]*om.*E
[25] haec]ista E
[26] aliquod]aliquid E
[27] tu]*om.*M
[28] etiam fuisti]tu eras E
[29] concedo]concedendo M

⟨5⟩ Fifth argument against rule four:

Let it be true in fact that you are white. I posit 'You are black' to you on the understanding that it will remain the *positum* just until something which should be denied by you is proposed to you, and after that you will not be obligated by it.[34]

When this has been posited and admitted, I propose this to you:

You are white.

If you grant it and thereby reply correctly, I have made my point. The inference is obvious, for the proposition is inconsistent with the *positum*, as is clear, and the period of the *obligatio* is still in force, as can be proved thus. By virtue of the case the period of the *obligatio* lasts until something which should be denied by you is proposed, but thus far nothing which should be denied by you has been proposed to you; therefore thus far the period of the *obligatio* is still in force.

If you deny

You are white

when it is first proposed, I argue against you like this:

You deny a true proposition without being obligated to do so; therefore you reply incorrectly.

The inference holds. The premiss can be proved, for the *obligatio* only lasts until something which you should deny is proposed, but as soon as

You are white

was proposed, something which you should deny was proposed, because otherwise you would not have denied it or at least you would have replied incorrectly by denying something which ought not to have been denied by you. Therefore when

You are white

was proposed to you, you were not obligated in relation to it nor were you obligated in relation to anything else, given my assumption. Therefore you were not obligated then, which is what had to be proved.

I reply by admitting the case. When

You are white

is proposed, I admit it and I deny that I am obligated. And when it is said

Nothing which you should have denied was proposed

I deny it. On the contrary, I say that

You are white

---

[34] This is a standard sophism. It deals with *positio cadens*, a form of *positio dependens*. It is found in Burley, op.cit., 3.164–3.165; Albert, op.cit., fol. 51rb; Marsilius, op.cit., fols. 96^v–97^r; Buser, op.cit., fol. 77vb; and Strode, op.cit., fols. 83vb–84ra. Strode uses the examples 'Tu curris' and 'Tu sedes', but otherwise Paul follows Strode's arguments exactly. See Part 1, section 1, note 28 for reference to the distinction which Albert, following Burley, made between the inclusive and exclusive senses of 'donec'.

cum proponebatur mihi fuit neganda vel saltem dum fuit in propositione.
Et si arguitur:
>Ista tunc fuit neganda a te et concessisti istam, igitur concessisti negandum a te, igitur male respondes,

dicitur primo negando primam consequentiam. Sicut non sequitur
>Vidisti istum et iste fuit episcopus, igitur vidisti episcopum,

sed bene sequitur quod episcopum vidisti, ita in proposito non sequitur quod concessisti a te negandum, sed quod a te negandum concessisti.

Secundo dicitur negando secundam consequentiam, quia licet concesserim negandum a me, tamen illud non erat negandum a me pro tempore adaequato vel instanti quo concessi illud, sed pro tempore ante responsionem meam.

⟨6⟩ Sexto arguitur sic. Et pono tibi illam:
>Tu non es obligatus.

Qua admissa
>Cedat tempus obligationis.

Si non admittis, sequitur quod aeternaliter eris obligatus, quia non videtur quare plus semel sit admittendum quam[30] semper. Si admittis, admittis repugnans posito. Sed[31] omne admissum[32] est concedendum, igitur repugnans posito est concedendum. Consequentia patet cum minori, et maiorem probo. Nam sequitur:
>Tu non es obligatus, igitur non cedit[33] tempus obligationis.

Dicitur quod sicut ly .pono. est signum obligationis, ita ly .cedat. est signum obligationis. Quare cum dicitur:
>Cedat tempus obligationis[34],

admitto et nego quod admitto repugnans[35] posito obligato, quia iam non sum obligatus. Nec sequitur:
>Tu non es obligatus, igitur non cedit[36] tempus obligationis,

unde in fine admissionis de obligatione cedit[37] tempus obligationis et tunc non sum obligatus.

⟨7⟩ Septimo arguitur sic. Et pono quod

---

[30] quam]et non E
[31] sed]si E
[32] admissum]admittendum E
[33] cedit]cedat   E
[34] obligationis]om.E
[35] repugnans]repugnat E
[36] cedit]cedat E
[37] cedit]cedat E

should have been denied when it was proposed to me or at least while it was being proposed.[35]

And if someone argues
> This should have been denied by you then and you granted it; therefore you granted what should have been denied by you; therefore you reply incorrectly

I say first that I reject the first inference. Just as this
> I saw him and he was a bishop; therefore I saw a bishop

is an invalid inference, though one can validly infer that a bishop I saw,[36] so in the present case it does not follow that you granted what should have been denied by you, though ⟨one can infer that⟩ what should have been denied by you, you granted.

I say secondly that I reject the second inference, because although I might have granted what should have been denied by me, it did not count as what should have been denied by me at the exact time or moment when I granted it. It counted as such only during the period before my reply.[37]

⟨6⟩ Sixth argument against rule four. I posit this to you:
> You are not obligated.

When this has been admitted, ⟨I propose⟩:
> Let the period of the *obligatio* come to an end.

If you do not admit this it follows that you will be obligated eternally, since there seems no good reason why ⟨your initial⟩ *admissio* should happen just once rather than always. If you do admit the proposition, you admit a proposition which is inconsistent with the *positum*. But every *admissum* should be granted; therefore a proposition inconsistent with the *positum* should be granted. The inference is obvious, as is the minor premiss. Proof of the major premiss: this inference
> You are not obligated; therefore the period of the *obligatio* does not come to an end

is valid. One can say that just as the word 'posit' is a mark of an *obligatio*, so the phrase 'come to an end' is a mark of an *obligatio*. Hence when it is said
> Let the period of the *obligatio* come to an end,

I admit it, and I deny that I admit something which is inconsistent with the *positum obligatum* because I am not obligated now. Nor is this a valid inference:
> You are not obligated, therefore the period of the *obligatio* does not come to an end.

Hence, as the *admissio* of the above *obligatio* comes to an end, so does the period of the *obligatio*, and then I am not obligated.

⟨7⟩ Seventh argument against rule four. I posit that:

---

[35] Strode, op.cit., fol. 84[ra], writes 'vel saltem cum incepit illa proponi.' The sophism hinges on the difference between ceasing to be obligated when 'Tu es albus' begins to be uttered, and ceasing to be obligated only when it has been uttered.

[36] 'Vidisti episcopum' is true if I saw the bishop and recognized him as such at the time I saw him, whereas 'Episcopum vidisti' is true if I saw the man who is now bishop, whether I knew this or not, and whether he held the position at the time I saw him or not. As Strode explained,

Quodcumque istorum contradictoriorum 'Rex sedet' et[38] 'Nullus rex sedet' tibi primo propono[39], sit tibi positum et admissum.

Isto posito et admisso arguitur sic.

Utrumque istorum, si primo loco proponitur, est a te concedendum, et alterum istorum est repugnans (226^{ra}M) posito, igitur repugnans posito est a te concedendum.

Consequentia patet (184^{vb}E) cum maiori et minorem probo. Nam utrumque istorum si primo loco proponitur est alteri repugnans, sed alterum istorum primo loco proponitur, igitur alterum illorum est repugnans posito.

Respondetur admittendo positum primum quod est quaedam suppositio et positio simul ad futurum positum.

Ad argumentum igitur concedo consequentiam, et nego minorem, videlicet quod alterum istorum est repugnans posito. Nam nullum istorum est propositum, ut patet: quomodo ergo aliquod istorum est repugnans posito? Ex quo patet quod altera minor est falsa, videlicet

Alterum istorum primo loco proponitur.

Si tamen post admissionem proponeretur ista:

Rex sedet,

concederem ipsam[40] sustinendo ipsam esse positam; et alteram videlicet

Nullus rex sedet,

negarem tamquam repugnantem. Et si negativa primo loco[41] proponeretur, dicerem ipsam esse positam et concedendam; alteram vero affirmativam adsererem esse repugnantem et negandam.

Et si arguitur:

Primo proposita ista 'Rex sedet', isto modo haec 'Nullus rex sedet' si primo proponeretur esset concedenda, sed hoc est repugnans posito obligato, igitur repugnans posito obligato est[42] concedendum.

Non valet argumentum, sed debet concludi:

Igitur repugnans posito si primo loco proponeretur esset concedendum,

[38] et]om.M
[39] propono]proponitur E
[40] ipsam]istam E
[41] loco]om.M
[42] est]esset E

---

op.cit., fol. 84ra, I could have seen a man four years before he became Pope and the sentence 'Papam vidisti' would still be true. These claims were justified by the theory of *appellatio*, whereby certain verbs such as 'see' were said to 'appellate' the form of their objects if the object came after the verb, but not if the object came before. It should be noted that the word '*appellatio*' was not used in this way before the fourteenth century, and that the theory of *appellatio* found in Peter of Spain and others has nothing to do with the theory I have just described.

For a fuller account of late fourteenth century doctrines of *appellatio*, see E.P. Bos, 'Peter of Mantua's Tract on *Appellatio* and his Interpretation of Immanent Forms' in *English Logic in Italy in the 14th and 15th Centuries*, edited by Alfonso Maierù (Napoli: Bibliopolis, 1982), pp. 231–252.

[37] Strode explains, loc.cit.: 'illud fuit negandum solum pro primo instanti suae prolationis, sed concessisti illam postquam erat integre prolata'.

Whichever of these contradictories 'A king is sitting down' and 'No king is sitting down' I first propose to you is the *positum* and *admissum*.

When this has been posited and admitted, I argue thus:

Each of these, if it is proposed in the first place, should be granted by you, and one of these is inconsistent with the *positum*; therefore a proposition which is inconsistent with the *positum* should be granted by you.

The inference is obvious, as is the major premiss. Proof of the minor premiss: each of these, if it is proposed in the first place, is inconsistent with the other, but one of these is proposed in the first place, therefore one of these is inconsistent with the *positum*.

I reply by admitting the first *positum* which is at once a *suppositio* and a *positio* with respect to a future *positum*.

⟨In reply⟩ to the argument, therefore, I grant the inference, and I deny the minor premiss, namely that one of these is inconsistent with the *positum*. Neither of these has been proposed, as is clear: how then can one of them be inconsistent with the *positum*? From this it is clear that the other minor premiss is false, namely

One of these is proposed in the first place.

If, however, after the *admissio*

A king is sitting down

were proposed, I would grant it by upholding it as the *positum*, and the other, namely

No king is sitting down,

I would deny as inconsistent. And if the negative were proposed in the first place, I would say that it was the *positum* and should be granted. Then I would claim that the other affirmative proposition was inconsistent and should be denied.

Someone might argue as follows:

Let 'A king is sitting down' be proposed first. In the same way, if 'No king is sitting down' were proposed first it ⟨too⟩ should be granted. But this ⟨second proposition⟩ is inconsistent with the *positum obligatum*. Therefore a proposition inconsistent with the *positum obligatum* should be granted.

This argument is not valid. The conclusion ought to be:

Therefore a proposition which is ⟨now⟩ inconsistent with the *positum*, if it were proposed in the first place, should be granted,

et hoc est verum. Et si ex hoc concluditur quod si primo loco proponeretur repugnans posito, illud esset concedendum, non valet argumentum. Arguitur enim a propositione de conditionato extremo ad propositionem conditionalem. Unde non sequitur

> Album si esset, esset animal; igitur si album esset, esset animal.

Consequens est falsum, ut patet, et antecedens probo, nam hoc, si hoc[43] esset, esset animal, demonstrato Antichristo, et hoc est album vel potest esse album, igitur etc. Et sic non procedit.

⟨8⟩ Octavo arguitur sic. Et pono tibi illam:

> Nulla propositio est tibi dubia[44].

Quo posito et admisso, propono[45] illam

> Rex sedet.

Si respondes aliter quam dubitando, cedat tempus, et probo[46] quod concessisti vel[47] negasti tibi dubium non sequens nec repugnans posito[48] obligato, igitur male. Si dubitatur, propono tibi

> Haec est tibi dubia.

Si conceditur et bene respondes, igitur intentum. Patet consequentia, nam sequitur:

> Haec est tibi dubia, igitur aliqua propositio est tibi dubia,

quod est oppositum positi. Si negas, contra:

> Ante casum fuit tibi dubia et ex casu non sequitur istam esse concedendam nec negandam, igitur adhuc est tibi dubia.

Probo consequentiam, quia si illa non foret tibi dubia ipsa esset a te concedenda vel neganda, sed nullum illorum sequitur ex casu, igitur etc.

Respondetur admittendo positum et cum proponitur

> Rex sedet,

dubito istam; et nego quod ista sit mihi dubia tamquam repugnans. Et tunc ad argumentum nego consequentiam, sicut non sequitur:

> Ante casum concessisti istam 'Tu curris' et ex casu non sequitur ipsam esse concedendam nec negandam, igitur adhuc concedis eam.

---

[43] hoc]*om*.E
[44] tibi dubia]dubitanda M
[45] propono]pono E
[46] probo]propono E
[47] vel]*om*.M
[48] posito]*om*.E

and this is true. And if someone draws the conclusion that if a proposition inconsistent with the *positum* were proposed in the first place, it should be granted, the argument is invalid. The argument moves from a proposition with a conditional end-clause to a conditional proposition. Thus this is an invalid inference:

> A white thing if it were to exist would be an animal, therefore if a white thing were to exist, it would be an animal.

The conclusion is false, as is obvious; and I prove the premiss thus: this, indicating Antichrist, if it were to exist would be an animal, and this is a white thing or it could be a white thing, therefore etc. And so the argument does not work.

⟨8⟩ Eighth argument against rule four. I posit this to you:

> No proposition is uncertain to you.

When this has been posited and admitted, I propose this:

> A king is sitting down.

If you reply other than by doubting, let the period come to an end, and I will prove that you granted or denied something which was uncertain to you and which was neither following from nor inconsistent with the *positum obligatum*. Therefore you replied incorrectly. If you do doubt the proposition, I propose this to you:

> This proposition is uncertain to you.

If you grant it and thereby reply correctly, I have made my point. The inference is clear, for

> This proposition is uncertain to you; therefore some proposition is uncertain to you

is a valid inference. ⟨The conclusion⟩ is the opposite of the *positum*. If you deny it, I will argue against you:

> Before the case was stated the proposition was uncertain to you, and it does not follow from the case that it ought to be granted or denied; therefore it is still uncertain to you.

I prove the inference, because if it were not uncertain to you it would have to be granted or denied by you, but neither of these follows from the case; therefore etc.

I reply by admitting the *positum* and when

> A king is sitting down

is proposed, I doubt it; and I deny that it is uncertain to me, as inconsistent.[38] ⟨In my reply⟩ to the argument I reject the inference, just as this is not a valid inference

> Before the case was stated you granted 'You are running' and it does not follow from the case that it ought to be granted or denied, therefore you still grant it.

---

[38] This sophism hinges on the usual distinction between mention and use. When 'Rex sedet' is proposed, Paul replies by holding it to be uncertain; but when '"Rex sedet" est tibi dubia' is proposed, Paul replies by denying it, for the quoted sentence may have changed its meaning.

Dato quod poneretur suum oppositum
> Tu non curris,

patet quod[49] consequentia non valet. Verumtamen concedo quod ista
> Rex sedet

est a me dubitanda. Et si arguitur sic:
> Ista est a te dubitanda et est impertinens, igitur est tibi dubia,

nego minorem tamquam repugnantem. Sequitur enim
> Illa est a te dubitanda et non est tibi dubia, igitur non est impertinens.

Sed si poneretur quod nulla propositio esset a te dubitanda, qua admissa, proponeretur illa
> Rex sedet.

Qua concessa, arguitur sic:
> Illa est tibi dubia et impertinens, igitur dubitanda.

Nego antecedens, et si dicitur 'Pro qua parte?', proponantur partes et prima concessa, quaecumque sit, illa secunda negetur[50] quia (226^{rb}M) repugnat uni concesso et opposito bene negati. Et hoc[51] universaliter sustineatur quando copulativa est impertinens cuius quaelibet pars est contingens et nulla necessaria est, intelligendo[52] 'necessario' simpliciter. Notanter dico 'cuius quaelibet pars est contingens', quia si una esset necessaria et alia contingens, negata copulativa contingens debet negari[53] et non necessaria. Dico etiam notanter 'cuius nulla pars est concessa'[54], quia si una pars esset concessa, non oportet exspectare quod proponerentur, sicut alias dixi, sed statim negare aliam[55] non concessam. Verbi gratia, si in isto casu statim proponatur post positum:
> Haec est tibi dubia 'Rex sedet',

concedatur quia verum et impertinens. Deinde si argueretur sic:
> Haec est tibi dubia et impertinens, ergo dubitanda,

concedo[56] consequentiam et nego antecedens. Pro qua parte? Pro secunda parte, quia repugnat sicut est ostensum, et in sequentibus melius ostendetur. (185^{ra}E)

---

[49] quod] om. M
[50] negetur] negatur E
[51] hoc] haec M
[52] intelligendo] de add. E
[53] negari] vocari E
[54] concessa] contingens E
[55] negare aliam] negarem illam M
[56] concedo] concedendo M

If one grants that its opposite
>   You are not running

is posited, it is obvious that the inference does not hold. However, I do grant that
>   A king is sitting down

should be doubted by me. And if someone argues
>   This should be doubted by you and it is irrelevant; therefore it is uncertain to you,

I deny the minor premiss as inconsistent. This is a valid inference:
>   This should be doubted by you and it is not uncertain to you; therefore it is not irrelevant.

But if it is posited that no proposition is to be doubted by you, then when this has been admitted let this be proposed:
>   A king is sitting down.

When this has been granted, it is argued thus:
>   This is uncertain to you and irrelevant; therefore it should be doubted.

I deny the premiss, and if someone says 'On account of which clause?' the clauses should be proposed and the first having been granted, whichever it is, the second is to be denied because it is inconsistent with a previously granted proposition and the opposite of a correctly denied proposition. And this ⟨method⟩ is to be adopted without exception when dealing with an irrelevant conjunction of which each clause is contingent and neither is necessary, meaning by that 'simply necessary'. It is to be noted that I say 'of which each clause is contingent' for if one were necessary and the other contingent, when the conjunction had been denied the contingent proposition would have to be denied and not the necessary proposition. It should also be noted that I say 'of which neither part has been granted', for if one clause had been granted one would not need to wait for both to be proposed, as I said at another time, but one could at once deny the clause which had not been granted. For instance, if in the present case
>   'A king is sitting down' is uncertain to you

were proposed immediately after the *positum*, it would be granted because it is true and irrelevant. Then if one were to argue thus:
>   This is uncertain to you and irrelevant; therefore it should be doubted,

I would grant the inference and deny the premiss. On account of which clause? On account of the second clause because it is inconsistent as has been shown, and as will be even better shown in what follows.

⟨*Contra Regulam Quintam*⟩

Altera regula, videlicet quinta in ordine, fuit ista. Omne sequens ex posito obligato et bene concesso vel bene concessis scitum esse tale infra tempus obligationis est ab eodem concedendum.

⟨1⟩ Contra istam regulam multipliciter arguitur et primo sic. Et pono tibi istam:

'Deus est' et 'Homo est asinus' convertuntur.

Quo posito et admisso quia possibile, propono tibi istam:

Deus est.

Si respondes aliter quam concedendo[57], sequitur quod tu[58] negas vel dubitas necessarium simpliciter[59] scitum a te esse tale, igitur male. Si concedis, propono tibi istam:

Homo est asinus.

Si concedis vel dubitas, contra:

Tu[60] concedis vel dubitas impossibile per se scitum a[61] te esse tale, igitur male.

Si negas sicut neganda est, arguitur sic.

Haec propositio 'Homo est asinus' est a te neganda et sequitur ex posito et concesso, igitur aliquod sequens ex posito et concesso est a te negandum, et per consequens non omne sequens est concedendum.

Antecedens principale probatur, nam sequitur:

'Deus est' et 'Homo est asinus' convertuntur, sed deus est, igitur homo est asinus.

Patet consequentia a simili quia bene sequitur:

'Homo currit' et 'Risibile currit' convertuntur, sed homo currit, ergo risibile currit.

Dimissis multis sophisticationibus quae hanc obligationem[62] non solvunt sed fugiunt, admitto casum; et cum proponitur

Deus est,

concedo. Deinde:

Homo est asinus.

---

[57] concedendo]concedo E
[58] tu]*om*.E
[59] simpliciter]*om*.M
[60] Tu]*om*.E
[61] a te]*om*.E
[62] obligationem]*om*.E

⟨Against Rule Five⟩

The fifth rule was this: Everything which follows from the *positum obligatum* together with a correctly granted proposition (or propositions) and is known ⟨by someone⟩ to follow should be granted by that person during the period of the *obligatio*.

There are many arguments against this rule.

⟨1⟩ First argument against rule five. I posit this to you:

'There is a God' and 'A human being is a donkey' are interchangeable.[39]

When this has been posited and admitted because it is possible, I propose this to you:

There is a God.

If you reply other than by granting it, it follows that you deny or doubt a proposition which is simply necessary and known by you to be such; therefore you reply incorrectly. If you grant it, I propose this to you:

A human being is a donkey.

If you grant or doubt it, I argue against you:

You grant or doubt a proposition which is impossible *per se* and known by you to be such; therefore you reply incorrectly.

If you deny it, as it should be denied, then I argue:

This proposition 'A human being is a donkey' should be denied by you, and it follows from the *positum* and a proposition which has been granted; therefore something which follows from the *positum* and a proposition which has been granted should be denied by you, and as a result not everything which follows ought to be granted.

I can prove the main premiss, for this inference:

'There is a God' and 'A human being is a donkey' are interchangeable, but there is a God; therefore a human being is a donkey

is valid. The inference is clear on the basis of one similar to it, for this inference

'A human being is running' and 'A creature able to laugh is running' are interchangeable, but a human being is running; therefore a creature able to laugh is running,

is certainly valid.

Having abandoned many elaborate comments which evade this *obligatio* rather than dissolving it,[40] I admit the case. When

There is a God

is proposed, I grant it. Then

A human being is a donkey.

---

[39] This sophism was discussed in Part 1, section 4, thesis 2 (p. 74, last line). It is found in Albert, op.cit., fol. 47ra, 47va, 47vb; Swyneshed, op.cit., pp. 264–5, §§58–61; John of Holland, op.cit., fol. 102^v; Marsilius, op.cit., fols. 79^v–82^r; Buser, op.cit., fols. 74va–75va. It is usually classified as a sophism concerning the type of absolute *impositio* (absolute as opposed to dependent) in which a complex is given the meaning of another complex. Paul's arguments in the first part of the discussion seem to be new, presumably because he is focussing on rule 5.

[40] Marsilius and Buser are the only two authors I know who offer really elaborate arguments. Presumably Paul is referring to Buser.

Nego. Et tunc ad argumentum:

    Illa est a te neganda,

concedo quia verum et impertinens.

    Et est sequens ex posito[63] et uno concesso.

⟨Nego quia⟩ nego istam consequentiam:

    'Deus est' et 'Homo est asinus' convertuntur, sed deus est, igitur homo est asinus.

Et tunc ad similitudinem concedo secundam et non primam; causam non dico. Extra[64] tempus obligationis, si ergo cedit[65] tempus obligationis, dico quod infra tempus illae non convertebantur:

    Deus est

et

    Homo est asinus,

non obstante quod sic posuerim, sed illae de facto convertebantur

    Homo currit

et

    Risibile currit,

propterea una consequentia erat bona et alia non.

Contra istam responsionem pono casum de novo. Quo admisso, propono ut prius

    Deus est.

Qua concessa, propono

    Homo est asinus.

Si negatur, contra[66] arguitur multipliciter sic.

⟨1.1⟩ Illae[67] duae propositiones convertuntur 'Deus est' et 'Homo est asinus', sed prima est a te concedenda, igitur et secunda.

⟨1.2⟩ Secundo arguitur sic.

Et facio tibi istam consequentiam: 'Deus est, ergo homo est asinus.' Haec consequentia est bona et antecedens est concedendum a te, igitur et consequens.

---

[63] posito et]*om*.E
[64] non dico. Extra]autem dicam ex E
[65] cedit]cedat E
[66] contra]*om*.E
[67] Illae . . . propositiones]*om*.E

I deny it. ⟨In reply⟩ to the argument
> This ought to be denied by you,

I grant it, because it is true and irrelevant.
> And it follows from the *positum* and a proposition which has been granted.

⟨I deny this⟩, because I reject this inference:
> 'There is a God' and 'A human being is a donkey' are interchangeable, but there is a God; therefore a human being is a donkey.

When the appeal to similarity is made, I grant the second ⟨inference⟩ and reject the first. I give no reason. Outside the period of the *obligatio*, if it does come to an end, I say that within the period these propositions:
> There is a God

and
> A human being is a donkey

were not interchangeable, notwithstanding the fact that I posited ⟨their interchangeability⟩.[41] However, these propositions
> A human being is running

and
> A creature able to laugh is running

are in fact interchangeable. Therefore one inference was valid and the other not.

Against this reply I posit the case anew.[42] When it has been admitted, I propose as before
> There is a God.

When this has been granted, I propose
> A human being is a donkey.

If this is denied, I present a number of arguments against the denial.

⟨1.1⟩ ⟨First argument against⟩:
> These two propositions, 'There is a God' and 'A human being is a donkey' are interchangeable, but the first should be granted by you; therefore the second should also be granted.

⟨1.2⟩ Second argument against:
> I put this inference to you: 'There is a God, therefore a human being is a donkey'. This inference is valid; and the premiss should be granted by you; therefore the conclusion should also be granted.[43]

---

[41] Just as '"A human being is a donkey" is true' does not imply that human beings are donkeys, so '"A human being is a donkey" is interchangeable with "There is a God"' does not imply that we can interchange these sentences in use: see Part 1, section 4, note 3 and note 14. Strode, op.cit., fol. 90ra, argued that if one's replies were varied in accordance with new *impositio*, an infinite regress would be possible: ' . . . nam si propter impositionem talem foret responsio varianda, nullus haberet concedere vel negare aliquam propositionem sibi propositam, quantumcumque notam, nisi fieret impositio terminorum in principio; nec talem impositionem admittere deberet donec fiat impositio significationis respectu cuiuslibet partis, et sic nec alterius impositionis; et sic esse processus in infinitum, unde numquam convenirent opponens et respondens in terminorum significationibus.'

[42] Here Paul turns to the standard style of argument about the sophism.

[43] This argument is found in Buser, op.cit., fol. 74vb, as his first argument against the denial of 'Homo est asinus'. Cf. Strode, op.cit., fol. 90rb.

Quod autem ista consequentia (226^{va}M) sit bona patet[68], quia
> Deus est

et
> Homo est asinus

convertuntur per casum.

⟨1.3⟩ Tertio:
> Omne[69] necessarium simpliciter est concedendum, sed illa 'Homo est asinus' est necessarium simpliciter, igitur ipsa est concedenda.

Maior probatur, nam omne sequens ex posito obligato est concedendum, sed omne necessarium simpliciter[70] est sequens ex quolibet posito obligato, quia necessarium simpliciter sequitur a quolibet, igitur etc.

⟨1.4⟩ Quarto arguitur sic:
> Negando illam 'Homo est asinus', tu negas verum et impertinens, igitur male respondes.

Consequentia tenet[71] et antecedens probatur, nam[72] quod illa sit vera patet[73] quia convertitur cum vero. Sed quod sit impertinens probo[74], quia non sequitur nec repugnat. Quod non sequatur concessum est, quia non sequitur
> 'Deus est' et 'Homo est asinus' convertuntur, sed deus est, igitur homo est asinus.

Sed quod non sit repugnans, probo, quia convertitur cum uno concesso et concedendo[75], igitur non est repugnans.

⟨1.5⟩ Quinto arguitur sic. Cedat tempus obligationis et arguitur sic.
> Infra tempus haec consequentia fuit bona 'Deus est, igitur homo est asinus', et concessisti antecedens et negasti consequens, igitur male.

Quod autem illa consequentia fuit bona patet, quia illae propositiones adinvicem convertebantur, ut posuit casus.

⟨1.6⟩ Sexto arguitur sic.
> Negando istam 'Homo est asinus', tu negas sequens ex uno concesso, igitur male respondes.

---

[68] patet]probatur E
[69] Omne]*om*.E
[70] simpliciter]*om*.E
[71] tenet]patet E
[72] nam]*om*.E
[73] patet]*om*.E
[74] probo]probatur E
[75] concedendo]concedo M

The validity of this inference is obvious because
> There is a God

and
> A human being is a donkey

are interchangeable by virtue of the stated case.

⟨1.3⟩ Third argument against:
> Every proposition which is simply necessary should be granted, but 'A human being is a donkey' is simply necessary; therefore it should be granted.[44]

Proof of the major premiss: everything which follows from the *positum obligatum* should be granted, but every proposition which is simply necessary follows from any *positum obligatum*, because a proposition which is simply necessary follows from any proposition whatsoever. Therefore etc.

⟨1.4⟩ Fourth argument against:
> In denying 'A human being is a donkey' you deny a proposition which is true and irrelevant; therefore you reply incorrectly.[45]

The inference holds. Proof of the premiss: it is obvious that it is true, because it is interchangeable with a true proposition. I prove that it is irrelevant, because it neither follows nor is inconsistent. It has been granted that it does not follow, because the inference
> 'There is a God' and 'A human being is a donkey' are interchangeable, but there is a God; therefore a human being is a donkey,

is invalid. I prove that it is not inconsistent because it is interchangeable with a proposition which has been granted and ought to be granted. Therefore it is not inconsistent.

⟨1.5⟩ Fifth argument against: Let the period of the *obligatio* end and argue like this:
> During the period this inference, 'There is a God, therefore a human being is a donkey', was valid, and you granted the premiss and denied the conclusion; therefore you replied incorrectly.[46]

It is obvious that this inference was valid, because those propositions were mutually interchangeable, as the case posited.

⟨1.6⟩ Sixth argument against:
> In denying 'A human being is a donkey' you deny what follows from a previously granted proposition; therefore you reply incorrectly.[47]

---

[44] This argument is found in Buser as his third argument, op.cit., fol. 74vb.

[45] This is Buser's fourth argument: op.cit., fol. 74vb.

[46] This is a subordinate argument in Buser, appearing as part of his reply to his own second argument, op.cit., fol. 75ra.

[47] Cf. Strode, op.cit., fol. 90rb.

Consequentia tenet et antecedens probatur, nam ipsa sequitur ex illa concessa[76]
    Deus est,
cum adinvicem convertantur. Igitur etc.

  Ad haec respondetur:
  ⟨1.1R⟩ Ad primum dico sicut prius semper negando illam
    Homo est asinus.
Et tunc[77] ad argumentum
    Illae convertuntur et prima est a te concedenda, igitur et secunda,
hic dicit una responsio quod non valet argumentum[78]
    Illae duae[79] convertuntur et prima est a te concedenda[80], igitur et secunda.
  Contra istam responsionem arguitur sic.
    Sequitur 'Illae convertuntur', igitur ex his consequentia est bona, igitur est[81] necessaria simpliciter, sed omne necessarium simpliciter est concedendum, ut nunc probavi in deductione tertii argumenti, igitur ipsa[82] consequentia est a te concedenda.
Arguo tunc sic:
    Illa consequentia est a te concedenda et antecedens est concedendum a te, igitur et consequens.
Quare, si illae duae convertuntur, et una est (185^{rb}E) concedenda a te, altera similiter.

Ideo dico concedendo consequentiam et negando antecedens, istam copulativam videlicet:
    Illae convertuntur et prima est concedenda a te[83],
quia est una copulativa falsa et impertinens. Et si quaeritur pro qua parte, dico quod[84] pro secunda parte[85], quia repugnat uni concesso et opposito bene negati. Sequitur enim:
    Illae non[86] convertuntur vel prima non est concedendum, sed illae convertuntur per positum concessum, igitur prima non est a te concedenda.

---

[76] concessa] *om.* E
[77] tunc] *om.* E
[78] argumentum] sed bene sequitur *add* E
[79] duae] *om.* M
[80] concedenda] esse vera *add* E
[81] est] *om.* M
[82] ipsa] ista E
[83] a te] *om.* M
[84] quod] *om.* E
[85] parte] *om.* M
[86] non] duae E

The inference holds and I can prove the premiss. It follows from the previously granted proposition:
>There is a God,

since they are mutually interchangeable. Therefore etc.

Replies:

⟨1.1R⟩ Reply to the first argument. As I said before, one should always deny
>A human being is a donkey.

One reply to the argument
>They are interchangeable and the first should be granted by you; therefore the second should also be granted by you,

claims that the argument
>They are interchangeable and the first should be granted by you; therefore the second should also be granted by you,

is invalid.[48]

One can argue against this reply as follows:
>The conclusion does follow from the premiss 'They are interchangeable'; therefore the inference is valid; therefore it is ⟨equivalent to a conditional proposition which is⟩ simply necessary. But every proposition which is simply necessary should be granted, as I have already proved in the deduction of the third argument; therefore this inference should be granted by you.

I then argue like this:
>The inference should be granted by you, and the premiss should be granted by you; therefore the conclusion should also be granted by you.

Thus it follows that if those two propositions are interchangeable, and one ought to be granted by you, the other ought similarly to be granted.

I now reply by granting the inference and by denying the premiss, namely the conjunction
>They are interchangeable and the first should be granted by you,

for this is a false and irrelevant conjunction. And if you ask on account of which part, I say on account of the second part, because it is inconsistent with a previously granted proposition and the opposite of a correctly denied proposition. This is a valid inference:
>Either they are not interchangeable or the first ought not to be granted, but by virtue of the *positum* which was granted they are interchangeable; therefore the first ought not to be granted by you.

---

[48] Swyneshed, op.cit., p. 265, §61, said: 'Ad aliam formam conceditur hoc '"Homo est asinus" est neganda.'' Et conceditur quod "Deus est" convertitur cum illa et hoc bene scio. Et negatur consequentia: "igitur, illa est a te neganda".' In note 28, Spade writes 'The conclusion does not follow from the conceded conjuncts alone, although it would presumably follow from their conjunction.' That is, he suggests that Swyneshed's rejection of the inference has to do with his special rules for conjunction. Buser had another suggestion: he wrote, op.cit., fol. 74^{va-vb}: 'Nego consequentiam. Ad regulam dico "Negato uno convertibilium, oportet negare reliquum" non habet veritatem nisi sic intelligatur quod negato uno convertibilium esse verum, oportet negare reliquum esse verum. Et per opposita, concesso uno convertibilium esse verum, oportet concedere reliquum esse verum.'

Haec tamen responsio non debet opponentem prostrasse, quia dicat opponens

    Cedat tempus,

et iterum faciat eandem[87] obligationem, et immediate post negationem illius

    Homo est asinus,

arguatur[88] continue categorice et non hypothetice, videlicet: propono tibi istam

    Illae convertuntur.

Concedenda est quia positum. Deinde propono tibi istam:

    'Deus est' est concedenda.

Conceditur quia verum et impertinens. Deinde propono tibi[89]:

    Illa est a te[90] concedenda 'Homo est asinus.'

Si negas vel dubitas, male respondes, quia negas vel dubitas sequens ex posito et uno concesso. Sequitur enim

    Illae[91] convertuntur et prima est a te concedenda, igitur et secunda.

Conceditur breviter quod illa

    Homo est asinus

est a me concedenda. Nolo tamen concedere ipsam mihi propositam. Et si arguitur[92]

    Ista est a te concedenda et tu negas eam, igitur male respondes,

negetur[93] copulativa ut prius quia falsa et impertinens. Et si dicitur (226^{vb}M) 'Pro qua parte?' dicitur[94] pro secunda parte[95], quia repugnat uni concesso et opposito bene negati. Si tamen arguatur categorice, concedo[96] quod male respondeo[97] non tamquam verum sed tamquam sequens ex duobus concessis.

⟨1.2R⟩ Secunda ratio solvitur per ea quae sunt dicta in prima. Cum dicitur:

    Illa consequentia est bona et antecedens est concedendum a te, igitur et
        consequens

negatur illa copulativa quae est antecedens. Si tamen[98] arguatur categorice praecise concedo[99] quod consequens est a me concedendum, et sic ultra consequenter ut prima.

---

[87] eandem]*om*.M
[88] arguatur]arguitur E
[89] tibi]*om*.M
[90] a te]*om*.E
[91] Illae]duae *add*.E
[92] arguitur]arguatur E
[93] negetur]negatur E
[94] dicitur]*om*.M
[95] parte]*om*.M
[96] concedo]concedendo M
[97] respondeo]respondes E
[98] tamen]non E
[99] concedo]concedendo M

This reply should not have overthrown the opponent, because the opponent could say:

Let the period come to an end,

and then he could put forward the same *obligatio* again. Immediately after the denial of

A human being is a donkey,

he could keep on arguing by means of categorical rather than hypothetical propositions. That is, ⟨it could go like this⟩: I propose this to you:

They are interchangeable.

This should be granted, because it is the *positum*. Then I propose this to you:

'There is a God' should be granted.

This is granted because it is true and irrelevant. Then I propose to you:

'A human being is a donkey' should be granted by you.

If you deny or doubt it, you reply incorrectly, because you deny or doubt something which follows from the *positum* and a previously granted proposition. This is a valid inference:

They are interchangeable, and the first should be granted by you; therefore the second should also be granted by you.

In short, I grant that this

A human being is a donkey

should be granted by me. But I do not wish to grant it when it is proposed to me.[49] And if someone argues

This should be granted by you, and you deny it; therefore you reply incorrectly,[50]

I deny the conjunction as above because it is false and irrelevant. And if someone says 'On account of which clause?', I say on account of the second clause, because it is inconsistent with a previously granted proposition and the opposite of a correctly denied proposition. If, however, you present your arguments by means of categorical propositions, I grant that I reply incorrectly, not as true but as following from two previously granted propositions.

⟨1.2R⟩ Reply to the second argument. The reasoning here is unravelled by means of what was said in ⟨reply to⟩ the first ⟨argument⟩.[51] When it is said

This inference is valid and the premiss should be granted by you; therefore the conclusion should also be granted by you,

I deny the conjunction which serves as premiss. If, however, the argument is presented just by means of categorical propositions, I grant that the conclusion should be granted by me, and as a result I then proceed as I did above.

---

[49] Here we have the standard distinction between use and mention. Paul denies P while granting 'P is to be granted'.

[50] This argument and both replies are found in Buser, in his reply to his own third argument. He does not make the distinction between the molecular and the categorical approach. Buser, op.cit., fol. 75rb.

[51] Buser denied the inference, op.cit., fol. 75ra, having previously explained that since valid

⟨1.3R⟩ Ad tertium eodem modo dicatur[1] negando antecedens ut prius; et si dicitur 'Pro qua parte?' dicitur[2] pro secunda. Ulterius si quaeritur an illa sit falsa
    Homo est asinus,
conceditur tamquam verum et impertinens; deinde
    Ista est falsa 'Deus est',
conceditur tamquam sequens.

⟨1.4R⟩ Ad quartum nego quod illa
    Homo est asinus
sit vera; et cum dicitur
    Convertitur cum vero,
nego. Contra:
    Convertitur cum ista 'Deus est'[3] et ipsa est vera.
Nego tamquam repugnans. Item nego quod sit impertinens, et si proponitur
    Ipsa est sequens,
nego[4] intelligendo sequelam eodem[5] modo quo regulae loquuntur. Et si proponitur:
    Ipsa est repugnans,
concedo[6] quia per se impossibilis, et ita consequenter est dicendum de illa
    Deus est.
Quare etc.

⟨1.5R⟩ Ad quintum cum dicitur
    Cedat tempus obligationis,
admitto et nego quod infra tempus illa consequentia fuit bona. Immo nihil valuit, nec etiam illae duae convertebantur; et si dicitur quare ergo huiusmodi concessisti, dico quod eam[7] concessi propter positionem factam.

⟨1.6R⟩ Ad sextum cum dicitur
    Negando illam 'Homo[8] est asinus' tu negas sequens ex uno concesso, ergo male respondes,
concedo[9] consequentiam et consequens, nec hoc est inconveniens infra tempus dummodo sequetur[10].

---

    [1] dicatur]dicitur E
    [2] dicitur]*om*.M
    [3] est]concedo *add*.M
    [4] nego]negatur E
    [5] eodem]eo M
    [6] concedo]concedendo M
    [7] eam]*om*.E
    [8] Homo]tu E
    [9] concedo]concedendo M
    [10] sequetur]sequatur E

---

inferences were equivalent to necessary conditionals, they had to be treated in the same way within an obligational disputation as without, op.cit., fol. 74vb. That is, he appealed to the principle that the necessary is always to be granted, the impossible denied. He wrote 'Ista consequentia "Deus est, ergo homo est asinus" infra tempus obligationis non est concedenda. Probatur: quia talis non est sequens, ipsa non est concedenda nisi quia vera; et si esset bona, tunc etiam per praecedentem solutionem talis consequentia esset extra tempus concedenda, quod tamen nullus faceret.' Buser, op.cit., fol. 74vb.

⟨1.3R⟩ Reply to the third argument. This reply is like the second. I deny the premiss as I did above;[52] and if someone says 'On account of which clause?', I say on account of the second. Further, if someone asks whether

> A human being is a donkey

is false, I grant that it is, as true and irrelevant. Then:

> 'There is a God' is false

is granted as following.

⟨1.4R⟩ Reply to the fourth argument. I deny that

> A human being is a donkey

is true;[53] and when someone says

> It is interchangeable with a true proposition,

I deny it. If someone argues against this by saying

> It is interchangeable with 'There is a God', which is a true proposition,

I deny it as inconsistent. Likewise I deny that it is irrelevant; and if someone proposes

> It follows,

I deny this, meaning by 'follows' what is meant in the rules. And if someone proposes

> It is inconsistent,

I grant this because the proposition is impossible *per se*. As a result the same things have to be said of

> There is a God.

Therefore etc.

⟨1.5R⟩ Reply to the fifth argument. When it is said

> Let the period of the *obligatio* come to an end,

I admit this, and I deny that that inference was valid during the period of the *obligatio*.[54] On the contrary, it was worth nothing; nor were those two propositions interchangeable. If someone asks why I granted them in that way, I say that I granted them because of the *positio* which was put forward.

⟨1.6R⟩ Reply to the sixth argument. When it is said

> In denying 'A human being is a donkey' you deny what follows from a previously granted proposition; therefore you reply incorrectly,

I grant the inference and the conclusion;[55] nor is this awkward during the period of the *obligatio* so long as it does follow.

---

[52] Unlike Paul, Buser granted the premiss: op.cit., fol. 75rb.

[53] See Buser, op.cit., fol. 75rb.

[54] See Buser, op.cit., fol. 75ra.

[55] Paul did not classify 'Homo est asinus' as *pertinens sequens*: see below, p. 206, line 7. His argument here has to do with the consequences of accepting the premiss. See Part 1, section 4, thesis 3. Cf. Strode, op.cit., fol. 90ra: 'Si tamen ponatur iterum tibi "Deus est asinus", negatur casus ut prius, et cum proponitur "Tu negas eam", conceditur quia verum non repugnans. Deinde si concluditur "Tu male respondes", conceditur infra tempus, non quia verum sed quia sequens licet falsa.'

Potest igitur pro maiori evidentia sic procedi in obligatione ista. Pono tibi

'Deus est' et 'Homo est asinus' convertuntur.

Admitto. Propono tibi:

Deus est.

Concedo. Propono tibi:

Homo est asinus.

Nego. Propono tibi:

Haec est vera 'Deus est.'

Concedo[11]. Propono tibi[12]:

Haec est vera 'Homo est asinus.'

Concedo. Propono tibi:

Haec est a te concedenda 'Deus est.'

Concedo[13].

Haec[14] est a te concedenda 'Homo est asinus.'

Concedo.

Tu negas eam.

Concedo[15].

Tu[16] male respondes.

Concedo[17].

Item posset ordo mutari, nam statim post positum propono:

Haec est vera 'Homo est asinus.'

Nego quia falsum et impertinens. Propono[18]

Haec est vera 'Deus est.'

Nego quia repugnans posito et opposito bene negati. Propono[19]

Haec est a te concedenda 'Homo est asinus.'

Nego, quia falsum et impertinens.

Haec est a te concedenda 'Deus est.'

Nego, quia repugnans ut prius. Tunc sic:

Haec non est a te concedenda 'Deus est.'

---

[11] Concedo]concedendo M
[12] tibi]*om*.M
[13] Concedo]concedendo M
[14] Haec . . . Concedo]*om*.E
[15] Concedo]concedendo M
[16] tu]igitur M
[17] Concedo]concedendo M
[18] Propono]*om*.M
[19] Propono]*om*.M

One can clarify matters considerably by giving the following account of how to proceed with this *obligatio*:

I posit to you:
> 'There is a God' and 'A human being is a donkey' are interchangeable.

I admit this. I propose to you:
> There is a God.

I grant it. I propose to you:
> A human being is a donkey.

I deny it. I propose to you:
> 'There is a God' is true.

I grant it. I propose to you:
> 'A human being is a donkey' is true.

I grant it. I propose to you:
> 'There is a God' should be granted by you.

I grant it.
> 'A human being is a donkey' should be granted by you.

I grant it.
> You deny it.

I grant it.
> You reply incorrectly.

I grant it.

The order can be changed like this. Immediately after the *positum* I propose:
> 'A human being is a donkey' is true.

I deny it because it is false and irrelevant. I propose
> 'There is a God' is true.

I deny it because it is inconsistent with the *positum* and the opposite of a correctly denied proposition. I propose:
> 'A human being is a donkey' should be granted by you.

I deny it because it is false and irrelevant.
> 'There is a God' should be granted by you.

I deny it because it is inconsistent, as above. Then:
> 'There is a God' ought not to be granted by you.

Concedo.
> Et tu concedas[20] eam.

Concedo[21].
> Ergo male respondes.

⟨Concedo.⟩
> Sed forte arguitur quod[22] haec est vera
>> Deus est
>
> in hoc secundo ordine, nam deum esse est verum, et haec propositio
>> Deus[23] est,
>
> significat adaequate deum esse, igitur ipsa est vera. Nego minorem tamquam repugnantem. Sequitur enim[24]:
>> Ipsa non est vera et deum esse est verum, igitur ipsa non significat adaequate deum esse[25] etc.

Et ita dicatur de illa
> Homo est asinus

suo modo. Quare etc.

⟨2⟩ Secundo contra eandem regulam arguitur sic. Et pono tibi istam
> Omnis homo currit.

Qua posita et admissa, propono tibi illam
> Tu es homo.

Concedenda quia vera et impertinens. (185^{va}E) Deinde propono tibi
> Haec 'Tu curris' est a te concedenda.

Si concedis, contra:
> Tu concedis falsum non sequens, igitur male.

Antecedens patet[26], nam quod illa sit falsa patet, et quod non sequatur[27] probatur quia non sequitur
> Omnis homo currit et[28] tu es homo, igitur haec 'Tu curris' est a te concedenda.

Si autem negatur, arguitur sic:
> Haec 'Tu curris' non est a te concedenda, et ipsa est sequens ex posito et

---

[20] concedas]negas E
[21] Concedo]concedendo M
[22] quod]quia E
[23] Deus est]*om*.E
[24] enim]*om*.M
[25] esse]*om*.E
[26] patet]et *add*.E
[27] sequatur]sequitur E
[28] et]*om*.E

I grant it.
> And you grant it.

I grant it.
> Therefore you reply incorrectly.

⟨I grant it⟩.
> But perhaps someone will argue that
>> There is a God

is true in this second ordering, because it is true that there is a God, and this proposition
> There is a God

adequately signifies that there is a God; therefore the proposition is true. I deny the minor premiss as inconsistent, for this is a valid inference:
> The proposition is not true and it is true that there is a God; therefore this proposition does not adequately signify that there is a God.

With appropriate changes, the same can be said of
> A human being is a donkey.

Therefore etc.

⟨2⟩ Second argument against rule five. I posit this to you:
> Every human being is running.

When this has been posited and admitted, I propose this to you:
> You are a human being.

This should be granted because it is true and irrelevant. Then I propose to you:
> 'You are running' should be granted by you.

If you grant it, I argue against you:
> You grant a false proposition which does not follow; therefore you reply incorrectly.

The premiss is obvious. It is clear that the proposition is false. I prove that it does not follow because this inference is invalid:
> Every human being is running and you are a human being; therefore 'You are running' should be granted by you.

But if you deny it, I argue like this:
> 'You are running' ought not to be granted by you, and it follows from the *positum* and a previously granted proposition; therefore not everything

concesso, igitur non omne sequens ex posito obligato et concesso est a te concedendum.

Consequentia patet (227^{ra}M) cum maiori et minorem probo, quia bene sequitur in tertio primae:

Omnis homo currit, tu es homo, igitur tu curris.

Respondetur admittendo positum et concedendo istam

Tu es homo

et illa similiter, si proponeretur,

Tu curris,

primam quia est[29] impertinens, secundam quia sequens est. Tunc ultra quando proponitur[30]

Haec 'Tu curris' est a te concedenda,

nego quia falsum et impertinens. Tunc ad argumentum nego minorem tamquam repugnantem opposito bene negati. Sequitur enim

Illa non est a te concedenda, igitur non sequitur ex posito et concesso.

Item si immediate post concessionem illius

Tu es homo,

fuisset propositum

Haec 'Tu curris' sequitur ex posito et concesso,

concessissem illam tamquam veram et impertinentem, et consequenter concessissem quod illa

Tu curris

est a me concedenda tamquam sequentem[31]. Sequitur enim

'Tu curris' sequitur ex posito et concesso, igitur est concedenda.

Sed forte in priori ordine arguitur sic faciendo consequentiam hanc

Omnis homo currit, tu es homo, igitur tu curris.

Consequentia est bona et antecedens est concedendum a te, igitur et consequens.

Dico negando antecedens copulative[32] sumptum. Et si post hanc negationem dicatur 'Pro qua parte?' dico quod pro prima[33] videlicet quod illa

---

[29] est]*om*.E
[30] proponitur]ponitur E
[31] sequentem]sequens E
[32] copulative]collective E
[33] prima]secunda E

which follows from the *positum obligatum* and a previously granted
proposition should be granted by you.

The inference is obvious, as is the major premiss. Proof of the minor
premiss: this is a valid example of the third mood of a first figure syllogism:

Every human being is running, you are a human being; therefore you
are running.

I reply by granting the *positum* and granting

You are a human being

and similarly granting

You are running,

if it is proposed, the first because it is irrelevant, the second because it
follows. Then when

'You are running' should be granted by you

is proposed, I deny it because it is false and irrelevant. Then ⟨in reply⟩ to the
argument I deny the minor premiss as inconsistent with the opposite of a
correctly denied proposition. This is a valid inference:

This ought not to be granted by you; therefore it does not follow from
the *positum* and a previously granted proposition.

Likewise if immediately after you had granted

You are a human being,

this:

'You are running' follows from the *positum* and a previously granted
proposition

had been proposed, I would have granted it as true and irrelevant; and as a
result I would have granted that

You are running

should be granted by me as following. This is a valid inference:

'You are running' follows from the *positum* and a previously granted
proposition; therefore it should be granted.

But perhaps in ⟨relation to⟩ the first ordered sequence someone might
present an argument about this inference:

Every human being is running, you are a human being; therefore you
are running,

⟨saying that⟩ the ⟨above⟩ inference is valid and the premiss should be granted by
you; therefore the conclusion should be granted.

I reply by denying the above premiss when it is taken as a conjunction.
And if after my denial someone asks 'On account of which clause?', I say on

consequentia sit bona, quia repugnat eo modo quo pluries dictum est.

Si tamen antecedens mihi praecise categorice et divisim partibiliter proponatur, concedo[34] consequentiam et consequens, videlicet quod consequens illius consequentiae est a me concedendum. Sed tunc arguitur sic:

> Consequens illius consequentiae est a te concedendum, sed consequens illius consequentiae est haec 'Tu curris', igitur haec 'Tu curris' est a te concedenda, quod fuit negatum.

Dicitur negando minorem tamquam repugnantem uni concesso et opposito bene negati. Sequitur enim

> Haec[35] 'Tu curris' non est a te concedenda et consequens illius consequentiae est a te concedendum, igitur haec 'Tu curris' non est consequens illius consequentiae.

Et si dicitur 'Quid[36] est consequens illius consequentiae?' nolo hanc quaestionem determinare. Et si dicitur

> Cedat tempus,

admitto. Quid[37] fuit consequens illius consequentiae? Dico quod ista

> Tu curris.

Et quare non sic dixisti in tempore obligationis? Quia tunc ipsam esse[38] consequens illius repugnabat[39] ut dictum fuit[40].

⟨3⟩ Tertio contra regulam arguitur sic. Et pono tibi illam

> Quandocumque profertur propositio universalis, omne currens sit[41] asinus, et quandocumque profertur propositio singularis, tu sis currens.

Isto posito et admisso, propono tibi illam:

> Omne currens est asinus.

Si negatur, contra:

> Quandocumque profertur propositio universalis omne currens est asinus, sed nunc profertur[42] propositio universalis, igitur omne currens est asinus.

Si ergo conceditur illa[43] propono tibi[44] istam

---

[34] concedo]concedendo M
[35] Haec]om.E
[36] Quid]quod E
[37] Quid]quod E
[38] esse]etiam E
[39] repugnabat]repugnat E
[40] fuit]est E
[41] sit]est E
[42] profertur]illa add.E
[43] illa]om.E
[44] tibi istam]om.M

account of the first, namely that the ⟨above⟩ inference is valid, because ⟨this clause⟩ is inconsistent in the way which has frequently been stated.⁵⁶

However, if the premiss is proposed to me in the form of two separate categorical propositions, I grant the above inference and the conclusion, namely that the conclusion of the above inference should be granted by me. But then one can argue like this:

> The conclusion of the above inference should be granted by you, but 'You are running' is the conclusion of the above inference; therefore 'You are running' should be granted by you. But this was denied.

I reply by denying the minor premiss as inconsistent with a previously granted proposition and the opposite of a correctly denied proposition. This is a valid inference:

> 'You are running' ought not to be granted by you, and the conclusion of this inference should be granted by you; therefore 'You are running' is not the conclusion of this inference.

And if someone asks 'What is the conclusion of this inference?', I do not wish to settle the question. And if someone says

> Let the period come to an end,

I admit it. 'What was the conclusion of that inference?' I say that it was this:

> You are running.

And why did I not say that during the period of the *obligatio*? Because then ⟨the claim⟩ that it was the conclusion of the above inference was inconsistent, as has been said.

⟨3⟩ Third argument against rule five. I posit this to you:

> Whenever a universal proposition is put forward, every running thing is a donkey; and whenever a singular proposition is put forward, you are a running thing.⁵⁷

When this has been posited and admitted, I propose this to you:

> Every running thing is a donkey.

If you deny it, I argue against you:

> Whenever a universal proposition is put foward, every running thing is a donkey; but a universal proposition is now put forward; therefore every running thing is a donkey.

If you grant it, I propose this to you:

---

⁵⁶ It is permissible to grant an inference while denying 'This inference is valid': see Part 1, section 4, corollary to thesis 2 (p. 76).
⁵⁷ Strode, op.cit., fol. 88ᵛᵃ⁻ᵛᵇ, gives this sophism.

> Tu es currens.

Si negatur, arguitur⁴⁵ sic:

> Quandocumque proponitur propositio singularis tu es currens, sed nunc proponitur illa singularis, igitur tu es currens.

Si ergo conceditur⁴⁶, propono tibi istam:

> Tu es⁴⁷ asinus.

Si concedis eam, tu concedis per se impossibile, ergo male. Si negas eam et bene respondes, igitur est a te neganda et est sequens ex duobus concessis ex adiutorio positi, igitur non omne sequens ex posito et concesso vel concessis est concedendum. Antecedens patet, nam⁴⁸ bene sequitur:

> Omne currens est asinus, tu es currens, igitur tu es asinus.

Dicitur quod casus de virtute sermonis est impossibilis, nam ex prima parte sequitur quod omne currens est asinus et ex secunda sequitur quod tu sis currens, ex quibus sequitur quod tu sis asinus. Unde bene sequitur

> Quandocumque tu curris, tu disputas, igitur tu curris et tu⁴⁹ disputas.

Tamen ad bonum intellectum admittitur casus, ita quod ly .profertur. idem⁵⁰ significet sicut ly .profertur de futuro. . Et tunc cum proponitur

> Omne currens est asinus,

nego quia est falsa et⁵¹ (227ʳᵇM) non sequens. Et tunc ad argumentum nego minorem tamquam repugnantem. Sequitur enim

> Quandocumque profertur propositio universalis omne currens est asinus, sed nunc⁵² non omne currens est asinus, igitur nunc non profertur propositio universalis.

Et ita dicatur ad istam

> Tu es currens⁵³

negando⁵⁴ ipsam⁵⁵, et si arguitur ut prius, negando quod ista sit aliqua⁵⁶ singularis prolata, quia repugnat.

Verumtamen posset variari casus ita quod statim post admissionem proponatur ista

> Haec⁵⁷ 'Omne currens' est⁵⁸ universalis prolata.

---

⁴⁵ arguitur sic]contra E
⁴⁶ conceditur]concedatur M
⁴⁷ Tu es]Homo est M,E *correxi*
⁴⁸ nam]quia E
⁴⁹ tu]*om*.E
⁵⁰ idem . . . profertur]*om*.M, intelligatur add.M² *in marg.*
⁵¹ est falsa et]falsum E
⁵² nunc]*om*.M
⁵³ es currens]curris M
⁵⁴ negando]nego M
⁵⁵ ipsam]ut prius *add*.E
⁵⁶ aliqua]categorica M
⁵⁷ Haec]hic E
⁵⁸ est]etc *add*.E

You are a running thing.
If you deny it, I argue like this:
> Whenever a singular proposition is put foward, you are a running thing; but a singular proposition is now put forward; therefore you are a running thing.

If you grant it, I propose this to you:
> You are a donkey.

If you grant this, you grant a proposition which is impossible *per se*; therefore you reply incorrectly. If you deny it and thereby reply correctly, therefore it ought to be denied by you; and it follows from two previously granted propositions with the aid of the *positum*, therefore not everything which follows from the *positum* and a previously granted proposition or propositions ought to be granted. The premiss is obvious, because this is a perfectly valid inference:
> Every running thing is a donkey, you are a running thing; therefore you are a donkey.

I reply that the case is impossible by virtue of the way it was stated. From the first clause it follows that every running thing is a donkey, and from the second clause it follows that you are a running thing, and from these it follows that you are a donkey.[58] By the same kind of reasoning
> Whenever you run, you dispute; therefore you run and you dispute

is a valid inference.

However, the case can be admitted if one understands it correctly, so that the expression 'put forward' is taken as meaning the same as the expression 'put forward in the future'. And then when
> Every running thing is a donkey

is proposed, I deny it because it is false and does not follow. Then ⟨in my reply⟩ to the argument I deny the minor premiss as inconsistent. This is a valid inference:
> Whenever a universal proposition is put forward, every running thing is a donkey, but at the moment not every running thing is a donkey; therefore a universal proposition is not put forward at the moment.

In reply to this:
> You are running,

I deny it; and if someone argues as at first, I deny that it counts as a singular proposition which has been put forward, because this is inconsistent.

Nevertheless the case can be varied so that immediately after the *admissio* this is proposed:
> 'Every running thing ⟨is a donkey⟩' is a universal proposition which has been put forward.

---

[58] Strode's treatment hinges on the claim that in uttering the *positum* one is *ipso facto* uttering the universal and the singular proposition. Hence the point, made by Paul on p. 214, line 16 ff., about the sense of 'profertur'. Strode's conclusion was: 'Et melius potest dici negando casum cum ex prima parte sequitur maior, et ex secunda minor dicti syllogismi, nisi dicatur quod proferetur in tempore futuro, et tunc argumentum nihil probaret.'

Paul makes the additional point that the argument depends on the view that 'Whenever A, B' entails 'A and B', from which B can in turn be inferred.

Conceditur quia (185^{vb}E) verum et impertinens. Deinde

> Omne currens est asinus.

Conceditur tamquam sequens. Deinde si proponitur

> Haec est singularis prolata 'Tu es currens'

negatur tamquam repugnans. Sequitur enim

> Tu non es asinus et omne currens est asinus, igitur tu non es currens,

et ultra:

> igitur non profertur aliqua propositio singularis.

Contra hoc arguitur sic:

> Ista est propositio categorica ergo universalis, particularis, indefinita vel singularis. Sed non universalis nec particularis nec indefinita ut patet, quia non est maior ratio de una quam de alia, igitur est singularis.

Negatur minor, supposito gratia disputationis quod omnis categorica sit alicuius quantitatis. Et si dicitur 'Pro qua parte?' proponantur partes et videbitur. Propono ergo:

> Illa non est universalis.

Concedo[59], quia verum et impertinens. Propono

> Illa non est particularis.

Concedo[60] per idem. Ultimo:

> Illa non est indefinita.

Nego quia repugnans. Sequitur enim:

> Ista 'Tu es currens' est universalis, particularis, indefinita vel singularis, sed non est universalis nec particularis nec singularis, igitur est[61] indefinita.

Et ita consequenter dicatur si aliquis alius discursus fiat huic consimilis[62] vel aequalis.

⟨4⟩ Quarto contra regulam arguitur sic. Et pono tibi istam

> Omnis homo est Romae.

Qua admissa propono

> Haec propositio est impertinens 'Tu es Romae.'

---

[59] Concedo]concedendo M
[60] Concedo]concedendo M
[61] est]*om.*M
[62] consimilis]similis E

This is granted because it is true and irrelevant. Then:
> Every running thing is a donkey.

This is granted as following. Then, if
> 'You are a running thing' is a singular proposition which has been put forward

is proposed, it is denied as inconsistent. This is a valid inference:
> You are not a donkey and every running thing is a donkey; therefore you are not a running thing,

and further:
> Therefore no singular proposition has been put forward.

Some may argue against the above like this:
> This is a categorical proposition; therefore it is a universal, particular, indefinite or singular proposition. But it is not universal, particular or indefinite, as is obvious, because there is no more reason for it to be one than another; therefore it is a singular proposition.

I deny the minor premiss, assuming for the purpose of the disputation that every categorical proposition is of some quantity (i.e. is of one of the four types listed). And if someone says 'On account of which clause?', the clauses should be proposed, and we will see. Therefore I propose:
> This is not a universal proposition.

I grant this, because it is true and irrelevant. I propose
> This is not a particular proposition.

I grant this for the same reason. Finally
> This is not an indefinite proposition.

I deny this because it is inconsistent. This is a valid inference:
> 'You are running' is universal, particular, indefinite or singular, but it is not universal, particular or singular; therefore it is an indefinite proposition.

As a result one should make the same reply if someone puts forward another piece of discourse equiform with or equivalent to this one.

⟨4⟩ Fourth argument against rule five. I posit this to you:
> Every human being is in Rome.

When this has been admitted I propose
> 'You are in Rome' is an irrelevant proposition.[59]

---

[59] This sophism is found in Peter of Candia, op.cit., fol. 67vb.

Concedenda est nam ista
> Tu es Romae,

non sequitur nec repugnat ut patet, igitur est impertinens. Deinde propono
> Tu es homo.

Haec concedenda est quia vera et impertinens. Qua concessa, proponitur illa:
> Tu es Romae.

Si negas eam bene respondendo habeo intentum quod non omne sequens ex posito et concesso vel concessis est concedendum. Sequitur enim:
> Omnis homo est Romae, tu es homo, igitur tu es Romae.

Si concedis eam, contra: ipsa est impertinens, igitur non est[63] sequens; et est falsa, igitur neganda. Quare etc.

Ista ratione[64] volunt aliqui probare quod idem est concedendum et negandum infra tempus obligationis. Patet de tali
> 'Tu es Romae' est impertinens

quae debet concedi proposita immediate post positum, et debet[65] negari post concessionem illius
> Tu es homo.

Ad istam obligationem solet talis enuntiari responsio. Quando enim ponitur
> Omnis homo est Romae,

admittitur, et quando proponitur
> Haec est impertinens 'Tu es Romae',

conceditur. Et ulterius quando proponitur
> Tu es homo,

similiter conceditur cum sit vera et impertinens. Et ulterius quando[66] proponitur haec
> Tu es Romae,

conceditur, et[67] etiam quod est impertinens. Et cum arguitur:
> Ipsa est impertinens, ergo non sequens,

negatur consequentia, quia haec propositio
> Tu es Romae

---

[63] est]*om.* E
[64] Ista ratione]istam rationem M
[65] debet]*om.* M
[66] quando]cum E
[67] et]*om.* M

This should be granted because
> You are in Rome

neither follows nor is inconsistent, as is obvious; therefore it is irrelevant. Then I propose
> You are a human being.

This should be granted because it is true and irrelevant. When it has been granted, this is proposed:
> You are in Rome.

If you deny it and thereby reply correctly, I have made my point that not everything which follows from the *positum* and a previously granted proposition or propositions ought to be granted. This is a valid inference:
> Every human being is in Rome, you are a human being; therefore you are in Rome.

If you grant it, I argue against you: the proposition is irrelevant, therefore it does not follow; and it is false, therefore it should be denied. Therefore etc.

By this kind of reasoning some people want to prove that the same proposition should be both granted and denied during the period of an *obligatio*.[60] This is obvious from a proposition like this:
> 'You are in Rome' is irrelevant

which ought to be granted when it is proposed immediately after the *positum*, and ought to be denied ⟨when it is proposed⟩ after this
> You are a human being

has been granted.

A reply like the following is usually given to this *obligatio*. When
> Every human being is in Rome

is posited, it is admitted. When
> 'You are in Rome' is irrelevant

is proposed, it is granted. And further when
> You are a human being

is proposed, this similarly is granted since it is true and irrelevant. And further when
> You are in Rome

is proposed, it is granted, also on the grounds that it is irrelevant. And when it is argued:
> The proposition is irrelevant; therefore it does not follow,

the inference is rejected, because this proposition:
> You are in Rome

---

[60] Peter of Candia introduced the sophism with these words, loc.cit.,: 'Item notandum est secundum aliquos quod non est inconveniens aliquod in arte obligatoria prima concedere unam propositionem tamquam veram et impertinentem, et postea negare eam tamquam repugnantem.' He commented that this could look like accepting two contradictories, and as an alternative offered the solution which Paul dismisses (p. 220, line 5) as purely verbal. Peter of Candia liked both solutions: 'Circa praedictum sophisma de duabus rationibus elige quae tibi plus placet; quaelibet enim illarum per se sufficiens est.'

in principio proposita fuit impertinens posito. Nunc autem est impertinens[68] eidem et pertinens sibi et concesso simul, videlicet pertinens sequens. Stat enim bene quod eadem propositio sit impertinens et sequens respectu diversorum.

Haec responsio argumentum verbaliter solvit sed non percipit ipsius difficultatem. Pono enim casus ut prius. Quo admisso, propono tibi

Haec 'Tu es Romae' est falsa et non sequens.

Concedendum est, nam quod sit falsa (227^{va}M) patet et quod non sit sequens probatur quia[69] non sequitur:

Omnis homo est Romae, igitur tu es Romae.

Deinde propono illam:

Tu es homo.

Concedenda[70] est ut prius. Ultimo propono istam

Tu es Romae.

Si negas, habetur[71] intentum. Si concedis, contra:

Illa est falsa et non sequens, igitur non est a te concedenda.

Similiter:

Tu concedis falsum non sequens, igitur male respondes.

Ideo respondetur concedendo in principio quod illa est falsa et[72] non sequens

Tu es Romae.

Et tunc quando proponitur illa

Tu es homo,

concedo[73] eam, et istam[74] similiter

Tu es Romae.

Et tunc ad argumentum

Illa est falsa et[75] non sequens, igitur non est concedenda,

concedo consequentiam et consequens. Tamen quandocumque mihi proponetur[76] concedam eam. Et tunc quando arguitur

Tu concedis falsum et non sequens, igitur male respondes,

concedo consequentiam et consequens, modo quo in prioribus dictum est.

---

[68] impertinens]*om.*E
[69] quia]nam E
[70] Concedenda est]*om.*M
[71] habetur]habes M
[72] et]*om.*E
[73] concedo]concedendo M
[74] et istam]*om.*M
[75] et]*om.*E
[76] proponetur]proponeretur E

was irrelevant to the *positum* when it was proposed at the beginning. Now however it is irrelevant to the same ⟨*positum*⟩, but relevant to the *positum* and a previously granted proposition taken together, that is, it is relevant as following. It is quite consistent that the same proposition should be both irrelevant and following, when looked at from different angles.

This reply dissolves the argument at the verbal level, but it does not come to grips with the true difficulty. I posit the case as before. When it has been admitted, I propose to you:
> 'You are in Rome' is false and does not follow.

This should be granted. It is obvious that it ⟨sc. 'You are in Rome'⟩ is false; and I can prove that it does not follow because this is not a valid inference:
> Every human being is in Rome; therefore you are in Rome.

Then I propose this:
> You are a human being.

This should be granted as above. Finally I propose this:
> You are in Rome.

If you deny it, I have made my point. If you grant it, I argue against you:
> This is false and does not follow; therefore it ought not to be granted by you.

Similarly:
> You grant a false proposition which does not follow; therefore you reply incorrectly.

Thus one should reply by granting at the beginning that
> You are in Rome

is false and does not follow. Then when
> You are a human being

is proposed, I grant it; and similarly this:
> You are in Rome.

⟨In reply⟩ to the argument:
> This is false and does not follow; therefore it ought not to be granted,

I grant the inference and the conclusion. However, I shall grant ⟨the proposition⟩ whenever it is proposed to me. And then when it is argued:
> You grant a false proposition which does not follow; therefore you reply incorrectly,

I grant the inference and the conclusion, in the way which was explained above.

⟨*Contra Regulam Sextam*⟩

Sexta regula fuit ista. Omne repugnans posito obligato et concesso vel concessis scitum esse tale infra tempus obligationis est ab eodem negandum.

Contra istam regulam procedunt argumenta contra alteram regulam, facta mutatione aliquali.

⟨1⟩ Verumtamen specialiter[77] contra ipsam arguo sic. Et pono tibi istam:
Omnis homo currit.

Qua posita et admissa, propono tibi istam:
Tu es homo.

Concedenda est quia vera et impertinens. Deinde:
'Tu non curris' est a te concedenda.[78]

Si negatur vel dubitatur, contra:
Ipsa est vera et impertinens, igitur concedenda.

Tunc arguitur sic:
'Tu non curris' est a te concedendum, sed 'Tu non curris' repugnat posito et concesso, (186^{ra}E) igitur repugnans posito et[79] concesso est a te[80] concedendum.

Solutio huius potest patere ex aliis admittendo positum, et cum proponitur
Tu es homo,
conceditur. Deinde
'Tu non curris' est a te concedendum
conceditur similiter, quia verum et impertinens; et nego tamquam repugnans quod repugnat[81] posito et concesso. Et si arguitur sic:

Ista consequentia est bona 'Omnis homo currit, tu es homo, igitur tu curris', igitur[82] oppositum consequentis[83] repugnat antecedenti,
concedo[84] totum. Et tunc ultra:

Oppositum consequentis repugnat antecedenti, sed[85] oppositum consequentis est illa 'Tu non[86] curris', igitur ista 'Tu non[87] curris' repugnat antecedenti.

Concedo[88] totum, et si arguitur ultra:

---

[77] specialiter]aliqualiter M
[78] concedenda]concedendum M
[79] et]*om.*E
[80] a te]*om.*E
[81] repugnat]repugnet E
[82] igitur]et E
[83] consequentis]est igitur oppositum consequentis *add.*E
[84] concedo]concedendo M
[85] sed]si E
[86] non]*om.*M,E *Add.* M² *s.lin.*
[87] non]*om.* M,E. *Add.* M²*s.lin.*
[88] Concedo]concedendo M

⟨Against Rule Six⟩

The sixth rule was this: Every proposition which is inconsistent with the *positum obligatum* and a previously granted proposition (or propositions) and is known to be such ⟨by someone⟩ should be denied by that person during the period of the *obligatio*.

If one makes some changes, the arguments against the other rule will work against this one. Nevertheless, I will produce some special arguments against the rule.

⟨1⟩ ⟨First argument against rule six⟩. I posit this to you:

Every human being is running.

When this has been posited and admitted, I propose this to you:

You are a human being.

This should be granted because it is true and irrelevant. Then:

'You are not running' should be granted by you.

If this is denied or doubted, I argue against you:

This is true and irrelevant; therefore it should be granted.

Then I argue like this:

'You are not running' should be granted by you, but 'You are not running' is inconsistent with the *positum* and a previously granted proposition; therefore something inconsistent with the *positum* and a previously granted proposition should be granted by you.

The solution of this *obligatio* can be revealed ⟨by appeal to⟩ the others. One admits the *positum*. When

You are a human being

is proposed, it is granted. Then

'You are not running' should be granted by you

is similarly granted, because it is true and irrelevant. I deny as inconsistent ⟨the claim⟩ that it is inconsistent with the *positum* and a previously granted proposition. If someone argues like this:

This inference, 'Every human being is running, you are a human being; therefore you are running', is valid; therefore the opposite of the conclusion is inconsistent with the premiss,

I grant the entire ⟨argument⟩. And then further:

The opposite of the conclusion is inconsistent with the premiss, but the opposite of the conclusion is 'You are not running'; therefore 'You are not running' is inconsistent with the premiss.

I grant the entire ⟨argument⟩. And if you argue further:

Illa 'Tu non[89] curris' repugnat antecedenti, sed[90] antecedens est positum et concessum, igitur repugnat posito et concesso,

nego minorem tamquam repugnantem. Sequitur enim

'Tu non[91] curris' non repugnat posito et concesso et repugnat illi antecedenti, igitur illud antecedens non est positum et concessum.

Et si arguitur contra:

Illa 'Omnis homo currit' est posita et illa[92] 'Tu es homo' est concessa et repugnat istis, igitur repugnat posito et concesso,

nego illam copulativam, videlicet[93]

'Omnis homo currit' est posita et illa 'Tu es homo' est concessa.

Et si dicitur 'Pro qua parte?' proponantur partes. Propono ergo

'Omnis homo currit' est posita.

Concedo[94]. Propono

'Tu es homo' est concessa.

Nego quia repugnat posito[95] concesso et opposito bene negati. Sequitur enim:

'Omnis homo currit' non est posita vel ista 'Tu es homo' non est concessa, sed ista 'Omnis homo currit' est posita, igitur illa 'Tu es homo' non est concessa.

Et si dicitur

Aliqua propositio est concessa,

concedo[96]. Quae fuit illa? Dico quod stat quod A vel B. Haec quaestio non est pro nunc determinanda. Quare etc.

⟨2⟩ Secundo contra regulam arguitur sic. Et pono tibi[97] illam:

Omnis homo currit et omne repugnans aliquibus praemissis est a te[98] concedendum.

Casus est possibilis quia possibile est quod omnis homo sit currens et quod non (227^{vb}M) sit aliquis syllogismus nec aliqua consequentia praeter istam

Omne currens est asinus, omnis homo est currens, igitur omnis homo est asinus.

---

[89] non]om. M,E. Add. M^2 s.lin.
[90] sed]et E
[91] non]om.M,E. Add. M^2 s.lin.
[92] illa]ita E
[93] videlicet]om.E
[94] Concedo]concedendo M
[95] posito]om.E
[96] concedo]concedendo M
[97] tibi]om.E
[98] a te]om.M

'You are not running' is inconsistent with the premiss, but the premiss is ⟨a conjunction formulated from⟩ the *positum* and a previously granted proposition; therefore it is inconsistent with ⟨a conjunction formulated from⟩ the *positum* and a previously granted proposition,

I deny the minor premiss as inconsistent. This is a valid inference:

'You are not running' is not inconsistent with ⟨a conjunction formulated from⟩ the *positum* and a previously granted proposition, but it is inconsistent with that premiss; therefore that premiss is not ⟨a conjunction formulated from⟩ the *positum* and a previously granted proposition.

If someone argues against me:

'Every human being is running' is the *positum* and 'You are a human being' is a previously granted proposition and it is inconsistent with these; therefore it is inconsistent with ⟨a conjunction formulated from⟩ the *positum* and a previously granted proposition,

I deny that conjunction, namely

'Every human being is running' is the *positum* and 'You are a human being' is a previously granted proposition.

And if someone says 'On account of which clause?', let the clauses be proposed. Therefore I propose:

'Every human being is running' is the *positum*.

I grant it. I propose:

'You are a human being' is a previously granted proposition.

I deny it because it is inconsistent with the *positum*, which has been granted ⟨to be the *positum*⟩ and the opposite of a correctly denied proposition. This is a valid inference:

Either 'Every human being is running' is not the *positum* or 'You are a human being' is not a previously granted proposition, but 'Every human being is running' is the *positum*; therefore 'You are a human being' is not a previously granted proposition.

And if someone says

Some proposition is a previously granted proposition,

I grant this. Which proposition was it? I say that it might well be A or B. This question ought not to be settled now. Therefore etc.

⟨2⟩ Second argument against rule six. I posit this to you:

Every human being is running and everything inconsistent with some premisses should be granted by you.

The case is possible because it is possible that every human being should be running and that there should be no syllogism or inference except this one:

Every running thing is a donkey, every human being is running; therefore every human being is a donkey.

Et tunc omne repugnans illis praemissis simul sumptis esset concedendum a te, videlicet

> Homo non est asinus.

Admisso ergo casu, propono istam:

> Omnis homo currit.

Concedenda est quia sequens. Deinde:

> Tu es homo.

Concedenda est quia vera et impertinens. Deinde:

> Tu non curris.

Si concedis istam[99] et bene respondes, igitur intentum. Si negas vel dubitas, contra:

> Omne repugnans aliquibus praemissis est a te concedendum, sed haec 'Tu non curris' est repugnans aliquibus praemissis, igitur ipsa est a te concedenda et tu negas ipsam, igitur male.

Respondetur admittendo positum, et concedo totum quousque proponitur ista

> Tu non curris,

quam nego. Et tunc ad argumentum nego illam copulativam

> Omne repugnans aliquibus praemissis est a te concedendum et haec 'Tu non curris' est repugnans aliquibus praemissis.

Et si quaeritur pro qua parte, non detur prima quia ipsa est positum vel sequens ex posito, sed detur secunda, quia repugnat uni concesso et opposito bene negati. Si tamen partes illius copulativae proponerentur categorice et non in copulativa illas[1] concederem[2], consequenter loquendo, ambas et ultimo quod ista est a me concedenda

> Tu non curris.

Numquam[3] tamen concedam ipsam, et consequenter concedo quod male respondeo non tamquam verum sed tamquam sequens.

⟨3⟩ Tertio contra regulam arguitur sic. Pono tibi

> Omnis homo currit et pono[4] tibi 'Tu non curris'.

---

[99] istam] *om.* E
[1] illas] illam M
[2] concederem] concedendum E
[3] Numquam] tamquam E
[4] pono tibi] *om.* M

Then everything inconsistent with these premises taken together ought to be granted by you, namely

    A human being is not a donkey.

When the case has been admitted, I propose this:

    Every human being is running.

It should be granted because it follows. Then:

    You are a human being.

This should be granted because it is true and irrelevant. Then:

    You are not running.

If you grant this and thereby reply correctly, I have made my point. If you deny or doubt it, I argue against you:

    Everything inconsistent with some premises ought to be granted by you, but 'You are not running' is inconsistent with some premises; therefore it ought to be granted by you; and you deny it; therefore you reply incorrectly.

I reply by granting the *positum* and I grant the whole ⟨argument⟩ until

    You are not running

is proposed. I deny it. And then ⟨in reply⟩ to the argument, I deny this conjunction:

    Everything inconsistent with some premises ought to be granted by you, and 'You are not running' is inconsistent with some premises.

And if someone asks on account of which clause, one should not pick the first clause because it is either the *positum* or something following from the *positum*; but one should pick the second because it is inconsistent with a previously granted proposition and the opposite of a correctly denied proposition. However, if the clauses of this conjunction were proposed as separate categorical propositions and not as a conjunction, then speaking ⟨only⟩ of what follows, I would grant them both, and finally ⟨I would grant⟩ that

    You are not running

should be granted by me. However, I would never grant that proposition. Consequently, I would grant that I reply incorrectly, not as true but as following.

⟨3⟩ Third argument against rule six. I posit to you

    Every human being is running and I posit 'You are not running' to you.

Quo posito et admisso propono tibi illam[5]
>Tu es homo.

Si negas, contra:
>Tu negas verum et non repugnans, igitur male.

Antecedens probatur, nam quod sit vera patet et quod sit non repugnans probatur, quia non sequitur
>Omnis homo currit, et pono tibi 'Tu non curris', igitur tu non es homo.

Concessa igitur illa, propono tibi
>Tu non curris.

Si concedis et bene respondes[6], habeo intentum quia repugnat posito, videlicet
>Omnis homo currit,

et concesso, scilicet
>Tu es homo.

Si negas, contra:
>Tu negas tibi positum et a te admissum, igitur male respondes.

Antecedens probatur[7] eo quod posui tibi[8] illam
>Tu non curris,

et tu[9] eam admisisti.

Respondetur quaerendo an sint duae propositiones vel solum una. Si una praecise respondeatur ut responsum[10] est. Et cum ultimo proponitur
>Tu non curris,

nego eam et concedo quod est mihi posita, sed non admisi istam sed bene istam copulativam
>Omnis homo currit et pono tibi 'Tu non curris'.

Et dato adhuc quod[11] admiserim utramque partem copulativae, non tamen admisi istam
>Tu non curris,

sed istam:
>Pono tibi 'Tu non curris'

ex qua non sequitur quod tu (186rbE) non curris. Si autem placeat[12] opponenti

---

[5] illam]om.M
[6] respondes]respondis M
[7] probatur]om.M
[8] tibi]om.M
[9] tu]om.M
[10] responsum]ostensum E
[11] quod]om.M
[12] placeat]placet E

When this has been posited and admitted, I propose this to you:
> You are a human being.

If you deny it, I argue against you:
> You deny something true and not inconsistent; therefore you reply incorrectly.

The premiss can be proved, for it is obvious that it is true, and that it is not inconsistent can be proved because
> Every human being is running and I posit 'You are not running' to you; therefore you are not a human being

is an invalid inference. Thus when the proposition has been granted, I propose to you:
> You are not running.

If you grant it and thereby reply correctly, I have made my point because it is inconsistent with the *positum*, namely
> Every human being is running,

and a previously granted proposition, namely
> You are a human being.

If you deny it, I argue against you:
> You deny the *positum* which was put to you and was admitted by you; therefore you reply incorrectly.

The premiss is proved, in that I posited
> You are not running

to you, and you admitted it.

I reply by asking whether there are two propositions or only one. If there is just one, I will reply as I replied above. And when
> You are not running

is finally proposed, I deny it; and I grant that it was posited to me, but I did not admit it. Instead ⟨I admitted⟩ this conjunction
> Every human being is running and I posit 'You are not running' to you.

Even given that I admitted each clause of the conjunction, I still did not admit this:
> You are not running,

but this:
> I posit 'You are not running' to you,

from which one cannot validly infer that you are not running. However if the

quod duo sint casus et duae positiones, admitto utramque; et si proponitur

> Omnis homo currit,

concedo[13], quia positum et admissum. Deinde[14]

> Tu non curris,

concedo quia alterum positum et[15] admissum. Deinde

> Tu es homo.

Concedo. Contra:

> Repugnat duobus concessis ergo male respondes[16].

Antecedens patet, nam sequitur

> Omnis homo currit et tu non curris, igitur tu non es homo;

et patet quod quaelibet pars antecedentis est a te concessa. Dico quod licet repugnet[17] duobus concessis, non tamen duobus concessis in eadem obligatione; propterea non sequitur quod sit negandum.

Sed forte instatur cum periculo sic. Concessa ista

> Tu es homo,

propono tibi

> Tu curris.

Si negas, contra:

> Tu negas sequens ex duobus concessis, igitur male.

Antecedens patet[18], nam sequitur

> Omnis homo currit et[19] tu es homo, igitur tu curris.

Si concedis et prius[20] concessisti suum contradictorium igitur male. Consequentia patet quia contradictoria non (228^{ra}M) debent concedi infra tempus obligationis.

Ideo pro omnibus istis est breviter dicendum quod non est inconveniens concedere et negare eandem propositionem, et duo contradictoria similiter in eodem tempore obligationis, sed in duabus obligationibus[21], sicut possibile est eandem propositionem concedi et negari[22] a duobus bene respondendo, et similiter contradictoria ita ab uno in duabus obligationibus quia tunc tenet vicem duorum. Antecedens patet, nam pono tibi et Sorti illam

---

[13] concedo]concedendo M
[14] Deinde] pro altero casu *add*.E
[15] et]*om*.M
[16] respondes]negas M,E *correxi*
[17] repugnet]repugnat M
[18] patet]probatur E
[19] et]*om*.E
[20] prius concessisti]praesens concedenti E
[21] obligationibus]unde *add*.M
[22] negari]negandi E

opponent wants there to be two cases and two *positiones*, I admit each of them. If
>Every human being is running

is proposed, I grant it because it is the *positum* and *admissum*. Then:
>You are not running.

I grant this because it is the other *positum* and *admissum*. Then:
>You are a human being.

I grant it. Someone may argue against me:
>It is inconsistent with two previously granted propositions; therefore you reply incorrectly.

The premiss is obvious, for this is a valid inference:
>Every human being is running and you are not running; therefore you are not a human being.

It is clear that each clause of the premiss was granted by you. I reply that although ⟨the proposition⟩ is inconsistent with two previously granted propositions, they were not, however, granted in the same *obligatio*. Hence it does not follow that the proposition ought to be denied.

But perhaps someone will produce a tricky objection. When
>You are a human being

has been granted, I propose to you:
>You are running.

If you deny it, I argue against you:
>You deny what follows from two previously granted propositions; therefore you reply incorrectly.

The premiss is obvious, for
>Every human being is running and you are a human being; therefore you are running

is a valid inference. If you grant it and you previously granted its contradictory, then you reply incorrectly. The inference is obvious, because contradictories ought not to be granted during the period of an *obligatio*.

Thus one may reply briefly to all these ⟨remarks⟩ that it is not awkward to grant and deny the same proposition, and similarly ⟨to grant or deny⟩ two contradictories, during the same period of *obligatio* so long as there are two *obligationes*. So also it is possible for the same proposition to be granted and denied by two people who both reply correctly, and similarly for contradictories ⟨to be granted or denied⟩ by one person in two *obligationes*, for then he takes the place of two ⟨people⟩. The premiss is obvious. I posit

Omnis homo currit.

Qua admissa ab utroque, propono tibi soli

Tu es homo.

Habes eam concedere, quia vera et impertinens. Deinde ambobus propono illam[23]

Tu curris,

et patet quod tu concedis[24] eam bene respondendo quia sequitur ex duobus concessis. Sortes vero negabit eam, quia falsa et impertinens in sua obligatione cum sibi non fuerit[25] prius illa

Tu es homo

proposita.

Est tamen notandum quod admissa illa totali positione, quae est duae positiones quarum quaelibet habet propriam responsionem, continue dum aliquid proponitur quaeratur an illud proponetur[26] in prima vel in secunda positione. Et secundum convenientiam respondeatur, nam[27] aliter ex tibi dubio continue male respondes.

Unde facta admissione propono tibi:

Omnis homo currit.

Quaero in qua obligatione proponis[28], an in prima vel in secunda. Si in prima concedo[29] eam, quia positam obligatam. Si in secunda, nego eandem, quia falsa et impertinens. Et si dicitur

Propono tibi eam tam in prima quam in secunda,

concedo et nego eam. Concedo namque eam in prima, et nego eandem in secunda. Nec hoc est inconveniens, quia sic responderent[30] duo[31] quorum vices pro nunc[32] teneo et ita consequenter in aliis propositionibus propositis[33] dicatur.

Ex praedictis sequitur quod ex unica positione[34] possunt partialiter duae obligationes consurgere. Patet si duobus ponam[35] istam

Omnis homo currit,

quam ipsi admittunt[36]. Similiter ex unica[37] admissione duae[38] oriuntur

---

[23] illam]*om.*E
[24] concedis]concedes E
[25] fuerit]fiunt E
[26] proponetur]proponatur E
[27] nam]non E
[28] proponis]propositionis E
[29] concedo]concedendo M
[30] responderent]respondent M
[31] duo]*om.*E
[32] nunc]habeo vel *add.*E
[33] propositis]*om.*E
[34] positione]propositione E
[35] ponam]proponam E
[36] ipsi admittunt]ipsa admittant E
[37] unica]dicta E
[38] duae . . . admissione]*om.*E

Every human being is running

both to you and to Socrates. When each has admitted it, I propose

You are a human being

to you alone. You must grant it because it is true and irrelevant. Then I propose

You are running

to both of you. It is clear that you grant it and thereby reply correctly, because it follows from two previously granted propositions. Socrates, however, will deny it because it is false and irrelevant in his *obligatio*, since

You are a human being

was not proposed to him first.

However, one should note that when one has admitted the entire *positio*, which is really two *positiones*, each having its own special reply, when something is proposed one should always ask whether the proposition at issue is proposed in the first or the second *positio*. One may reply as seems appropriate, since otherwise you will keep on replying incorrectly because of a premiss which is uncertain to you.

Hence, when the *admissio* has been completed, I propose to you

Every human being is running.

I ask whether you are proposing this in the first or the second *obligatio*. If it is in the first, I grant the proposition, because it is the *positum obligatum*. If it is in the second, I deny the same proposition, because it is false and irrelevant. And if someone says

I propose it to you in both the first and the second *obligatio*,

I grant and deny this. I grant it in the first *positio* and I deny the same proposition in the second. Nor is this awkward, because the two people whose place I am now taking would reply in this way. As a result one should reply in the same way to the other propositions which have been proposed.

From what has been said it follows that two *obligationes* can partially arise from a unique *positio*. This is clear if I posit

Every human being is running

to two people, and they admit it. Similarly two *obligationes* can arise from a

obligationes. Patet in ista positione et unica admissione
   Admitto utrumque positum.
Verumtamen non esset hoc[39] possibile ex unica positione et unica admissione, nam in primo[40] est una positio et duae admissiones. In secundo vero sunt duae positiones et una admissio. Quare etc.

⟨*Contra Regulam Septimam*⟩
Regula septima fuit ista. Omne sequens ex posito obligato et opposito bene negati vel bene[41] negatorum scitum esse tale infra tempus obligationis est ab eodem concedendum.
⟨1⟩ Contra istam regulam arguitur sic[42]. Nam data veritate ipsius sequitur quod admisso quocumque contingente falso sit quodlibet aliud contingens falsum et impertinens concedendum. Probatur. Et pono tibi illam:
   Tu es Romae.
Qua posita et admissa propono
   Tu es Romae et baculus stat in angulo.
Et patet quod haec copulativa neganda est quia falsa non sequens. Deinde proponitur:
   Nullus baculus stat in angulo.
Si negas et bene respondes igitur intentum contra regulam. Patet consequentia, quia sequitur ex posito et opposito bene negati. Sequitur enim:
   Tu non es Romae vel nullus baculus stat in angulo, sed tu es Romae per positum, igitur nullus baculus stat in angulo.
Si[43] ergo conceditur illa
   Nullus baculus stat in angulo,
habeo conclusionem[44] principaliter probandam, quia sicut[45] illa, ita[46] et quaelibet alia deducitur[47] dummodo suum oppositum coniungatur copulative cum posito, quae copulativa[48] immediate post positum proponatur.

---

[39] hoc]haec M
[40] primo]prima E
[41] bene]*om*.E
[42] sic]*om*.M
[43] Si . . . angulo]et sic E
[44] conclusionem]consequentiam M
[45] sicut]deducitur *add*.M
[46] ita]*om*.M
[47] deducitur]*om*.M
[48] quae copulativa]*om*.M

unique *admissio*. This is obvious if one takes the above *positio* and a unique *admissio* which says

I admit each *positum*.

Nevertheless this would not be possible on the basis of a unique *positio* and a unique *admissio*. In the first ⟨example above⟩ there is one *positio* but two *admissiones*. In the second ⟨example⟩ there are two *positiones* and one *admissio*. Therefore etc.

⟨*Against Rule Seven*⟩

Rule seven was this: Everything following from a *positum obligatum* and the opposite of a correctly denied proposition (or propositions) and known to be such ⟨by someone⟩ should be granted by that person during the period of the *obligatio*.

⟨1⟩ First argument against rule seven. Given the truth of the rule, it follows that whenever any contingent falsehood has been admitted, any other contingent and irrelevant falsehood must be granted.[61] Proof: I posit this to you:

You are in Rome.

When this has been posited and admitted, I propose:

You are in Rome and a stick is standing in the corner.

It is obvious that this conjunction should be denied because it is false and does not follow. Then I propose:

No stick is standing in the corner.

If you deny it and thereby reply correctly, I have proved my point against the rule. The inference is obvious because ⟨the proposition⟩ follows from the *positum* and the opposite of a correctly denied proposition. This is a valid inference:

Either you are not in Rome or no stick is standing in the corner, but you are in Rome (by virtue of the *positum*); therefore no stick is standing in the corner.

If, therefore, you grant

No stick is standing in the corner,

I have now demonstrated the thesis that I was principally trying to prove. In the same way that this proposition was deduced, any other proposition can be deduced so long as its opposite is conjoined with the *positum* in a conjunction which is proposed immediately after the *positum*.

[61] This point was made by others. See Burley, op.cit., 3.61–3.63; John of Holland, op.cit., fol. 104^v; Peter of Mantua, op.cit., sig.G vi^{ra}; Strode, op.cit., fol. 84^{ra-rb}. Burley and John of Holland presented it in the form of a rule, though Strode, like Paul, presented it as a possible objection.

Respondetur: conclusionem[49] deductam concedo[50], videlicet quod posita et admissa illa

> Tu curris

vel

> Tu es Romae,

deducam quod tu es episcopus vel papa, dormiens aut vigilans, et[51] quicquid mihi placuerit, dummodo illud sit falsum contingens[52], verum aut necessarium (228^{rb}M) coniunctum cum posito falso eodem[53] modo (186^{va}E) quo dictum est.

Potest etiam idem falsum contingens deduci dummodo ponatur disiunctive cum opposito positi. Verbi gratia: Pono tibi istam:

> Tu curris.

Qua admissa[54], propono tibi

> Tu non curris vel baculus stat in angulo

aut aliquam talem

> Tu es episcopus, vel papa.

Pono disiunctive[55] cum[56] opposito positi. Concedenda est quia vera et impertinens. Deinde propono

> Baculus stat in angulo.

Oportet concedere quia sequitur ex posito et uno concesso. Sequitur enim

> Tu non curris vel baculus stat in angulo, sed tu curris per positum, ergo baculus stat in angulo.

⟨2⟩ Secundo contra regulam arguitur sic. Et pono tibi istam disiunctivam:

> Tu es Romae vel 'Tu es Romae' est concedendum.

Qua admissa, propono tibi

> 'Tu es Romae' est concedendum.

Neganda est[57] quia falsa et impertinens. Deinde propono tibi:

> Tu es Romae,

et patet quod est formaliter sequens ex posito et opposito bene negati; et tamen illa non est concedenda, igitur regula non est vera. Probo antecedens pro prima parte, nam bene sequitur

---

[49] Conclusionem]concedendo consequentiam M
[50] concedo]*om*.M
[51] et]aut E
[52] contingens]et *add*.E
[53] eodem]eo M
[54] Qua admissa]*om*.M
[55] disiunctive]disiunctiva M
[56] cum]*om*.M
[57] est]*om*.M

Reply: I grant the thesis that has been deduced, namely that if this
> You are running

or this
> You are in Rome,

is posited and admitted, I can deduce that you are a bishop or the Pope, asleep or awake, or anything I please, so long as it is a contingent falsehood, or a truth, or a necessary proposition joined with a false *positum* in the manner described.

One can also deduce the same contingent falsehood so long as it is disjoined with the opposite of the *positum*. For instance, I posit this to you:
> You are running.

When it has been admitted, I propose to you:
> You are not running or a stick is standing in the corner,

or some such proposition as
> You are a bishop, or the Pope.

I disjoin this with the opposite of the *positum*. ⟨The disjunction⟩ should be granted because it is true and irrelevant. Then I propose:
> A stick is standing in the corner.

One ought to grant this because it follows from the *positum* and a previously granted proposition. This is a valid inference:
> Either you are not running or a stick is standing in the corner, but you are running (by virtue of the *positum*); therefore a stick is standing in the corner.

⟨2⟩ Second argument against rule seven. I posit this disjunction to you:
> Either you are in Rome or 'You are in Rome' should be granted.[62]

When this has been admitted I propose to you:
> 'You are in Rome' should be granted.

This should be denied because it is false and irrelevant. Then I propose to you:
> You are in Rome.

It is obvious that it follows from the *positum* and the opposite of a correctly denied proposition by a formal inference, yet ⟨the proposition⟩ ought not to be granted; therefore the rule is not true. Proof of the first clause of the premiss: this is a valid inference:

---

[62] See Burley, op.cit., 3.21–3.22; Strode, op.cit., fol. 89ʳᵃ. Strode used the example 'Tu curris vel "Tu curris" est a te concedendum.' For an analysis of Burley's argument, see Stump in *CH*, pp. 323–7. Paul's discussion is closer to that of Strode.

Tu es Romae vel 'Tu[58] es Romae' est a te concedendum, sed 'Tu es Romae'
non est a te concedendum, igitur tu es Romae.

Secunda pars antecedentis probatur, nam[59] sequitur

Illa est a te concedenda 'Tu es Romae', igitur[60] 'Tu es Romae' est a te
concedendum,

quod prius negabatur.

Respondetur admittendo positum; et cum proponitur

'Tu es Romae' est concedendum,

nego. Deinde:

Tu es Romae.

Concedo. Et tunc[61] ad argumentum

Illa est formaliter sequens ex posito et[62] opposito bene negati et illa non est
concedenda, igitur oppositum regulae,

nego maiorem tamquam repugnantem. Sequitur enim

Illa non est concedenda, igitur non sequitur ex posito et opposito bene
negati.

Si dicatur

Cedat tempus obligationis,

habeo concedere quod ista fuit sequens, et ideo infra tempus concessi illam.

Item si proponeretur[63] alio[64] modo, ita quod immediate post positum
proponeretur illa

Tu es Romae,

negarem eam, quia falsa et impertinens. Deinde

'Tu es Romae' est a te concedendum,

concedo quia sequens ex posito et opposito bene negati.

Et si arguitur sic

'Tu es Romae' est a te concedendum et tu negas eam, igitur male respondes,

nego antecedens. Et si quaeritur pro qua parte, dico quod pro secunda. Si tamen
partes illae divisim categorice proponantur, concedo[65] quamlibet istarum, et
ultimate quod male respondeo tamquam sequens.

---

[58] Tu]non *add*.E
[59] nam]quia bene E
[60] igitur . . .Romae]*om*.E
[61] tunc]*om*.E
[62] et]ex *add*.M
[63] proponeretur]proponetur M
[64] alio modo]aliqua E
[65] concedo]concedendo M

Either you are in Rome or 'You are in Rome' should be granted by you, but 'You are in Rome' ought not to be granted by you; therefore you are in Rome.

Proof of the second clause of the premiss: this is a valid inference:

This ought to be granted by you: 'You are in Rome'; therefore 'You are in Rome' should be granted by you.

⟨The conclusion⟩ was denied above, ⟨so one can infer the negation of the premiss⟩.

I reply by admitting the *positum*; and when

'You are in Rome' should be granted,

is proposed, I deny it. Then:

You are in Rome.

I grant it.[63] Then ⟨in reply⟩ to the argument:

This follows from the *positum* and the opposite of a correctly denied proposition by a formal inference, yet it ought not to be granted; therefore the opposite of the rule holds,

I deny the major premiss as inconsistent. This is a valid inference:

This ought not to be granted; therefore it does not follow from the *positum* and the opposite of a correctly denied proposition.

If someone says

Let the period of the *obligatio* come to an end,

I have to grant that it did follow, and for that reason I did grant it during the period of the *obligatio*.

Likewise if it were proposed in another way, so that

You are in Rome

was proposed immediately after the *positum*, I would deny it because it is false and irrelevant. Then I grant

'You are in Rome' should be granted by you

because it follows from the *positum* and the opposite of a correctly denied proposition.

And if someone argues like this:

'You are in Rome' should be granted by you and you deny it; therefore you reply incorrectly;

I deny the premiss. And if someone asks on account of which clause, I say on account of the second. However, if these clauses were proposed separately as categorical propositions, I would grant each of them, and finally ⟨I would grant⟩ that I reply incorrectly as following.

---

[63] In her analysis of Burley's argument, Stump argues (in *CH*, pp. 325–6) that 'You are in Rome' and 'That you are in Rome is to be granted' are equivalent, because 'if the respondent must grant p, he must also grant that he must grant p', and the reverse. This is precisely what Paul, following Marsilius, Buser, and Strode, denied.

⟨3⟩ Tertio arguitur sic. Sit rei veritas quod Sortes et Plato et Cicero sint omnes homines et quilibet istorum sedeat. Isto supposito, pono tibi istam:

>Aliquis homo currit.

Qua admissa, propono

>Sortes currit.

Neganda est[66], quia falsa et impertinens. Deinde:

>Plato currit.

Iterum neganda propter eandem causam. Tertio proponitur

>Cicero currit,

et videtur quod etiam sit neganda quia non est[67] maior ratio quare negatur prima vel secunda et non tertia, ex quo rei veritas est quod nullus illorum currit. Si igitur neganda est, et tamen sequitur ex posito et oppositis bene negatorum, igitur oppositum regulae. Consequentia tenet et antecedens probatur. Nam bene sequitur

>Aliquis homo currit et nullus Sortes currit nec aliquis Plato currit, igitur Cicero currit.

Patet consequentia, quia ipsi sunt omnes homines.

Respondetur admittendo positum et suppositum, et quando proponitur aliqua illarum trium

>Sortes currit,
>
>Plato currit,
>
>Cicero[68] currit,

nego quamlibet istarum et nego quod ultima (228^{va}M) sequatur[69] ex posito et oppositis illis[70] bene negatis. Et tunc ad consequentiam illam factam nego eam, et ad probationem

>Isti sunt omnes homines,

nego[71], tamquam repugnantem posito et tribus oppositis bene negatis. Sequitur enim:

>Aliquis homo currit et nullus Sortes currit nec aliquis Plato currit nec aliquis Cicero currit, igitur isti non sunt omnes homines.

---

[66] est]*om*.M
[67] est]videtur E
[68] Cicero currit]*om*.M
[69] sequatur]sequitur E
[70] illis]*om*.E
[71] nego]casum *add*.E

⟨3⟩ Third argument against rule seven. Let it be true in fact that Socrates and Plato and Cicero are all the human beings there are, and that each of them is sitting down. When this has been assumed, I posit this to you:

    Some human being is running.

When this has been admitted, I propose

    Socrates is running.

This should be denied, because it is false and irrelevant. Then:

    Plato is running.

This should also be denied for the same reason. Third:

    Cicero is running

is proposed. It seems that this should also be denied, because there is no greater reason why the first or second should be denied, and not the third, because the fact of the matter is that none of them is running. Therefore if it ought to be denied, even though it follows from the *positum* and the opposites of correctly denied propositions, we obtain the opposite of the rule. The inference holds and the premiss can be proved, for this is a valid inference:

    Some human being is running and Socrates is not running nor is Plato running, therefore Cicero is running.

The inference is obvious, because these are all the human beings there are.

I reply by admitting the *positum* and the *suppositum*. When any of these three:

    Socrates is running,
    Plato is running,
    Cicero is running,

is proposed, I deny each of them; and I deny that the last does follow from the *positum* and the opposites of those correctly denied propositions. Then I reject the inference which was put forward, and I deny the proof:

    These are all the human beings there are,

as inconsistent with the *positum* and the three opposites of correctly denied propositions. This is a valid inference:

    Some human being is running and Socrates is not running, nor is Plato running, nor is Cicero running; therefore these are not all the human beings there are.

Si tamen in principio immediate post positum proponeretur illa

> Sortes, Plato et Cicero sunt omnes homines,

concederem eam tamquam veram et impertinentem. Tunc:

> Sortes currit.

Nego quia falsa et impertinens.

> Plato currit.

Nego quia[72] falsa similiter.

> Cicero currit.

Concedo quia sequens ex posito concesso et oppositis bene negatis. Sequitur enim:

> Aliquis homo currit[73], Sortes[74] Plato et Cicero sunt omnes homines, et nullus[75] Sortes currit nec aliquis Plato currit, igitur omnis[76] Cicero currit.

Quare etc.

Ex praedictis sequitur quosdam nimis sophistice procedere adserentes aliquam indefinitam vel particularem concedendam, et tamen quamlibet eius singularem[77] negandam. In casu enim praesenti cum conceditur

> Aliquis homo currit

et negatur quaelibet istarum

> Sortes currit,
>
> Plato currit[78],
>
> Cicero currit,

negatur consequenter quod isti sunt omnes homines et conceditur quod aliquis est homo qui non est aliquis istorum. (186^{vb}E)

Et si quaeritur quis est ille, non determinetur haec quaestio quia stat quod sit A vel B. Et cum conceditur quod illi sunt omnes homines, semper duae singulares primo propositae sunt negandae propter falsitatem et impertinentiam, et tertia est concedenda.

Per hunc modum haberent ipsi respondere ad propria sophismata quando ponunt

---

[72] quia . . . similiter] propter eandem causam E
[73] currit] et *add*. E
[74] Sortes] et *add*. E
[75] nullus] non M
[76] omnis] omne M *correxi*, omnis] *om*. E
[77] singularem] esse *add*. M² *s. lin.*
[78] currit] et *add*. E

However if at the beginning

> Socrates, Plato, and Cicero are all the human beings there are

were posited immediately after the *positum*, I would grant it as true and irrelevant. Then:

> Socrates is running.

I deny it because it is false and irrelevant.

> Plato is running.

I deny it similarly because it is false.

> Cicero is running.

I grant it because it follows from the *positum* together with a previously granted proposition and the opposites of correctly denied propositions. This is a valid inference:

> Some human being is running; Socrates, Plato, and Cicero are all the human beings there are; Socrates is not running, nor is Plato running; therefore Cicero is running.

Therefore etc.

From what has been said it follows that some people are excessively sophistical when they claim that some indefinite or particular proposition ought to be granted even though each of the corresponding singular propositions ought to be denied.[64] In the present case, when

> Some human being is running

is granted and each of these:

> Socrates is running,
> Plato is running,
> Cicero is running,

is denied, one consequently denies that these are all the human beings there are, and grants that there exists a human being who is not one of the above.

And if someone asks who he is, this question need not be settled, for it is consistent that he should be A or B. And when one does grant that these are all the men there are, then the two singular propositions which are proposed first should always be denied because they are false and irrelevant, and the third should be granted.

They ought to reply in this way to their own sophisms, when they posit:

---

[64] Paul is attacking Burley, op.cit., 3.36; Albert, op.cit., fol. 49vb and fol. 47vb; John of Holland, op.cit., fol. 105^r; Marsilius, op.cit., fol. 76^r; and Buser, op.cit., fol. 74ra.

Sit rei veritas quod non sint nisi tres homines in mundo, scilicet Sortes, Plato et Cicero, et quod solus Sortes loquatur[79].

Tunc ponunt istam:

    Sortes tacet.

Admitto[80] eam. Deinde:

    Aliquis homo loquitur.

Concedo, quia vera et impertinens. Deinde:

    Sortes loquitur.

Nego quia repugnat posito. Deinde:

    Plato loquitur.

Nego[81] quia falsa et impertinens. Deinde[82]

    Cicero loquitur.

Nego[83] propter eandem causam. Ulterius:

    Ista particularis est concedenda 'Aliquis homo loquitur' et quaelibet eius singularis neganda.

Nego, quia isti non sunt omnes homines ut dictum est, sed est unus qui non est aliquis illorum qui non datur determinate. Si tamen proponatur in principio

    Isti sunt omnes homines,

concedatur et ultimo negatis illis

    Sortes loquitur,

    Plato loquitur,

concedo[84] quod Cicero loquitur, cuius causa dicta est.

Isti enim latius loquuntur, dicentes quod non est inconveniens in arte obligatoria concedere universalem et negare quamlibet eius singularem. Verbi gratia, sit rei veritas quod non sint nisi tres homines in mundo, scilicet Sortes, Plato, et Cicero, quorum nullus currat. Tunc[85] ponunt istam:

    Omnis homo currit.

Admitto eam. Tunc proponunt[86]:

    Sortes currit.

Nego ipsam quia falsa et impertinens. Deinde:

---

[79] loquatur]loquitur E
[80] Admitto]admittunt E
[81] Nego]negatur E
[82] Deinde]ulterius M
[83] Nego]negatur E
[84] concedo]concedendo M
[85] Tunc]et E
[86] proponunt]proponit M

Let it be true in fact that there are only three human beings in the world,
i.e. Socrates, Plato, and Cicero, and that only Socrates is speaking.[65]

Then they posit this:

Socrates is silent.

I admit it. Then:

Some human being is speaking.

I grant it, because it is true and irrelevant. Then:

Socrates is speaking.

I deny it because it is inconsistent with the *positum*. Then:

Plato is speaking.

I deny it because it is false and irrelevant. Then:

Cicero is speaking.

I deny it for the same reason. Further

This particular proposition, 'Some human being is speaking', should be granted, and each corresponding singular proposition should be denied.

I deny it, for these are not all the human beings there are, as has been said. There exists a person who is not one of the above, but who has not been identified. However, if

These are all the human beings there are

is proposed at the beginning, I grant it; and finally when

Socrates is speaking,

Plato is speaking,

have been denied, I grant that Cicero is speaking for the reason given above.

Those people cast their net more widely, saying that in the art of *obligatio* it is not awkward to grant a universal proposition while denying each of the corresponding singular propositions.[66] For instance, let it be true in fact that there are only three human beings in the world, i.e. Socrates, Plato, and Cicero, and none of them is running. Then they posit this:

Every human being is running.

I admit it. Then they propose:

Socrates is running.

I deny it because it is false and irrelevant. Then:

---

[65] This sophism appears in Burley, op.cit., 3.36; Albert, op.cit., fol. 47vb and fol. 49vb. See above, Part 1, section 4, thesis 4 (p. 80).

[66] Paul is attacking Albert, op.cit., fol. 49vb; Marsilius, op.cit., fol. 76^{r-v}, fol. 88^{v}; Buser, op.cit., fol. 74ra.

Plato currit.

Nego ipsam propter eandem causam. Tertio:

Cicero currit.

Nego ipsam quia falsa et impertinens. Non tamen ex hoc sequitur conclusio proposita, quia dico consequenter quod isti non sunt omnes homines. Immo dico quod nullus istorum est homo, quia sequitur:

Omnis homo currit, nullus Sortes currit, nec aliquis Plato currit, nec aliquis Cicero currit, igitur nullus istorum (228^{vb}M) est homo.

Et si quaeritur quis ergo est iste qui currit, dico quod non determino hanc quaestionem. Si tamen in principio fuisset illa proposita:

Isti sunt omnes homines,

concessissem eam et illam similiter

Quilibet illorum currit,

illis tribus demonstratis.

Aliter dicunt alii admittendo positum et negando omnes singulares praeter ultimam propter hoc quia licet nulla illarum[87] sit sequens nec etiam ultima sit sequens ex posito, tamen est sequens ex posito et concesso. Nam stante quod non sint nisi tres homines Sortes, Plato et Cicero[88], sequitur

Omnis homo currit et Sortes non currit et Plato non currit, igitur Cicero currit.

Sed haec responsio est impossibilis sicut in *Suppositionibus* est ostensum. Nam haec stant simul

Omnis homo currit et tamen nec Sortes[89] nec Plato[90] nec Cicero currit, quia post mille annos erit quaelibet istarum vera sic adaequate significante[91] posito quod tunc erit ita quod omnis homo currit.

Item tunc haec consequentia esset bona

Nullus Cicero currit nec Plato currit nec Sortes currit, igitur non omnis[92] homo currit.

Patet consequentia arguendo ex opposito consequentis cum[93] una praemissarum ad oppositum alterius praemissae. Et quod ista consequentia non valet

---

[87] illarum]aliarum M
[88] Cicero]et *add*.E
[89] Sortes]currit *add*.E
[90] Plato]currit *add*.E
[91] significante]significando E
[92] non omnis]nullus E
[93] cum]ex E

Plato is running.

I deny it for the same reason. Third:

Cicero is running.

I deny it because it is false and irrelevant. However, the proposed conclusion does not follow from this for I conclude that these are not all the human beings there are.[67] Indeed, I say that none of them is a human being ⟨at all⟩ because this is a valid inference:

Every human being is running, Socrates is not running, nor is Plato running, nor is Cicero running; therefore none of them is a human being.

And if someone asks who it is that is running, I say that I will not settle the question. However, if

These are all the human beings there are,

had been proposed in the beginning I would have granted it, and similarly this:

Each of these is running,

indicating those three.

Some people reply in another way by admitting the *positum* and denying all the singular propositions except the last on the grounds that although none of them follows and not even the last follows from the *positum*, yet it does follow from the *positum* and a previously granted proposition.[68] Given that there are only three human beings, Socrates, Plato, and Cicero, this is a valid inference:

Every human being is running; and Socrates is not running and Plato is not running; therefore Cicero is running.

But this reply is impossible, as I showed in my section on *Suppositio*.[69] These propositions are mutually consistent:

Every human being is running and yet neither Socrates nor Plato nor Cicero is running,

because after a thousand years each of the clauses, adequately signifying as they now do, will be true, given that at that point every human being is running.

Again, ⟨on their view⟩ this inference would be valid:

Cicero is not running, nor is Plato running, nor is Socrates running; therefore not every human being is running.[70]

The inference is obvious (if one takes the first inference above) and argues from the opposite of the conclusion together with one of the premisses to the opposite of the other premiss. That the inference is invalid is sufficiently

---

[67] Buser, loc.cit. Cf. Strode, op.cit., fol. 82ra. We must remember that no universal affirmative proposition implied the corresponding singular proposition. If the proper name was non-referring, the premiss could be true when the conclusion was false.

[68] This passage comes almost verbatim from Albert, op.cit., fol. 49va: 'Aliter alii respondent admittendo positum et negando omnes singulares praeter ultimam. . . .'

[69] See *Logica Magna* I. 2, fols. 20vb–21ra.

[70] The premiss is true if none of the named individuals exists, since negative propositions with non-referring subjects are true, but the conclusion is false if all existent human beings are in fact running.

satis liquet intuenti hic. In loco allegato, diffusius declarata sunt, quare supersedeo pro praesenti etc.

⟨*Contra Regulam Octavam*⟩

Octava regula fuit ista. Omne repugnans posito obligato[94] et opposito bene negati vel bene negatorum scitum esse tale infra tempus obligationis est negandum.

Contra istam regulam vadunt argumenta contra regulam immediatam.

⟨1⟩ Verumtamen in speciali arguo sic. Et pono tibi illam:

Omnis homo currit.

Qua posita et admissa, propono tibi illam

Tu curris.

Neganda est quia falsa et impertinens. Deinde propono tibi illam[95]

'Tu es homo' est[96] a te concedendum.

Concedenda est quia vera et impertinens. Deinde propono tibi

Tu es homo.

Si concedis, et ipsa repugnat posito et opposito bene negati, igitur intentum. Antecedens patet, nam[97] bene sequitur

Omnis homo currit, tu non curris, igitur tu non es homo.

Si negas vel dubitas, contra:

Ipsa sequitur ex uno a te concesso, igitur male.

Antecedens probatur, nam sequitur

'Tu es homo' est a te concedendum, igitur tu es, et per consequens, tu es homo.

Respondetur admittendo positum et negando[98] istam:

Tu curris

et istam similiter:

'Tu es homo' est a te concedendum,

sumendo 'concedendum' nominaliter, quia repugnat posito et opposito bene negati. Sequitur enim

---

[94] obligato]*om.* E
[95] tibi illam]*om.* E
[96] est ... homo]*om.* M
[97] nam]quia E
[98] negando]nego M

clear to anyone who considers it. In the place I mentioned I have said more about these matters, so I will refrain from discussing them further at the moment.

⟨*Against Rule Eight*⟩
Rule eight was this: Everything which is inconsistent with the *positum obligatum* and the opposite of a correctly denied proposition (or propositions) and is known to be such should be denied during the period of the *obligatio*.

The arguments against the immediately preceding rule also work against this one. However, I will present some special arguments against it.
⟨1⟩ ⟨First argument against rule eight⟩: I posit this to you:
   Every human being is running.
When this has been posited and admitted, I propose this to you:
   You are running.
It should be denied because it is false and irrelevant. Then I propose this to you:
   'You are a human being' should be granted by you.
This should be granted because it is true and irrelevant. Then I propose this to you:
   You are a human being.
If you grant it, although it is inconsistent with the *positum* and the opposite of a correctly denied proposition, I have made my point. The premiss is obvious, for this is a valid inference:
   Every human being is running; you are not running; therefore you are not a human being.
If you deny or doubt it, I argue against you:
   It follows from a proposition which you granted; therefore you reply incorrectly.
The premiss can be proved, for this is a valid inference:
   'You are a human being' should be granted by you; therefore you exist, and consequently you are a human being.
 I reply by granting the *positum* and denying
   You are running.
I similarly deny this:
   'You are a human being' is to be granted by you,
taking 'is to be granted' in the nominal sense ⟨sc. 'should be granted'⟩ because it is inconsistent with the *positum* and the opposite of the correctly denied proposition. This is a valid inference:

Omnis homo currit, tu non curris, igitur tu non es homo

et ultra

igitur tu non es, igitur nihil est a te concedendum.

⟨2⟩ Secundo contra eandem regulam arguitur sic: (187ʳᵃE) Et pono tibi istam disiunctivam

Tu curris vel rex sedet.

Qua posita et admissa, propono illam

Nullus rex sedet.

Si aliter respondes quam dubitando, arguitur quod male, quia est tibi dubia et impertinens. Si ergo dubitas eam, sicut dubitanda est, propono illam

Tu curris.

Neganda est quia falsa et impertinens. Deinde propono secundo illam

Nullus rex sedet.

Si concedis eam vel negas, et prius dubitasti, igitur in eodem tempore idem dubitas et concedis vel negas, et per consequens male. Consequentia tenet per tertiam suppositionem ponentem quod omnes responsiones retorquendae sunt ad idem instans. Si autem[99] dubitas et bene respondes, igitur ista est a te[1] dubitanda et non neganda, et tamen repugnat posito et opposito bene negati et hoc bene scis, igitur etc. Antecedens probatur[2], nam sequitur

Tu curris vel rex sedet, sed tu non curris, igitur rex sedet.

Respondetur admittendo positum, et cum proponitur

Nullus rex sedet,

dubitatur; et illa negatur

Tu curris,

et cum iterum (229ʳᵃM) proponitur

Nullus rex sedet,

nego eam, et cum dicitur

Prius dubitasti eam et modo negas, igitur male,

non valet argumentum. Et ad[3] suppositionem, dico quod intelligit de responsionibus repugnantibus sicut sunt concedere et negare; de[4] aliis

---

[99] autem]ergo E

[1] a te]*om*.E

[2] probatur]patet E

[3] ad]secundam *add*.E

[4] de . . . negare]etc. E

Every human being is running, you are not running; therefore you are not a human being,

and further:

Therefore you do not exist; therefore there is nothing which should be granted by you.

⟨2⟩ Second argument against rule eight: I posit this disjunction to you:

Either you are running or a king is sitting down.[71]

When this has been posited and admitted, I propose:

No king is sitting down.

If you reply other than by doubting it, I argue that you reply incorrectly because it is uncertain to you and irrelevant. If therefore you doubt it, as it ought to be doubted, I propose this:

You are running.

This should be denied because it is false and irrelevant. Then I propose this for the second time:

No king is sitting down.

If you grant it or deny it, but you doubted it at first, then you doubt and grant or deny one and the same proposition during the same period, and as a result you answer incorrectly. The inference holds by virtue of the third assumption which maintains that all replies should be referred back to the same moment.[72] But if you doubt it and thereby reply correctly, then it ought to be doubted by you and it ought not to be denied. Yet it is inconsistent with the *positum* and the opposite of a correctly denied proposition, and you are well aware of this, therefore etc. The premiss is proved, for this is a valid inference:

Either you are running or a king is sitting down, but you are not running; therefore a king is sitting down.

I reply by admitting the *positum*, and when

No king is sitting down

is proposed I doubt it.

You are running

is denied, and when

No king is sitting down

is proposed again, I deny it. When it is said

First you doubted it and now you deny it; therefore you reply incorrectly,

⟨I reply that⟩ the argument is not valid. With respect to the assumption, I say that it should be understood as speaking of inconsistent ⟨pairs of⟩ replies such as granting and denying, but not of ⟨other pairs⟩ such as doubting and granting

---

[71] See Part 2, chapter 3, rule 5. Cf. Albert, op.cit., fol. 50vb. Strode has a lengthy discussion of the sophism, op.cit., fols. 84va–85ra.

[72] Strode makes this point. He then replies: 'Respondetur admittendo casum, et cum proponitur "Rex sedet" dicatur "Nescio an rex sedet vel non." Et si quaeratur an concedis, an dubitas, an negas illam, dicas "Proponas mihi quamlibet illarum sigillatim et tunc scies bene." Et si tunc proponitur "Tu concedis vel negas istam", negatur. Si tunc proponitur "Tu dubitas istam", concedo sumendo "dubitare" pro nescire vel hesitare an illa sit vera vel falsa. Non tamen

autem non, ut dubitare et concedere vel negare. Ideo conceditur consequenter quod aliqua propositio in uno loco[5] est dubitanda et in alio[6] loco concedenda, ut admisso casu priori proposita ista

    Rex sedet

dubitatur et ista negatur

    Tu curris.

Iterum proposita ista

    Rex sedet

conceditur, quia sequens ex posito cum[7] opposito bene negati, ut est ostensum.

⟨3⟩ Tertio contra regulam arguitur sic. Et pono tibi istam:

    'Tu curris' est a te concedendum[8].

Qua admissa propono tibi illam[9]:

    Utrumque istorum est a te concedendum,

demonstratis illis

    Tu curris

et

    Tu es homo.

Si concedis, tu concedis falsum et impertinens, igitur male respondes. Antecedens probatur, nam quod sit falsum patet, et[10] quod sit impertinens probatur ex hoc quia non sequitur nec repugnat, ut manifeste patet. Deinde propono tibi istam:

    Tu es homo.

Si negas vel dubitas, cedat tempus, et arguo quod infra tempus negasti vel dubitasti verum et impertinens scitum a te esse tale. Si concedis, propono tibi istam:

    'Tu es homo' est a te concedendum.

Si negas vel dubitas, contra:

    Illa est vera et impertinens 'Tu es homo', igitur est a te concedenda.

Si concedis et bene respondes[11], habeo oppositum regulae quia[12] haec

    'Tu es homo' est a te concedendum,

repugnat posito et opposito bene negati, cum suum oppositum sequatur. Probo, nam sequitur:

---

[5] in uno loco]om.M
[6] alio]aliquo E
[7] cum]et E
[8] concedendum]concedenda E
[9] illam]om.E
[10] et]sed E
[11] respondes]respondis M
[12] quia]quod M

---

dubito illam sumendo "dubitare" pro "dubie respondere".' Strode, op.cit., fol. 84^{va-vb}, corrected from MS, fol. 41rb. To the claim that the assumption was violated he replied 'non vario responsionem ad illam, quia primo non respondebam ad illam.'

or ⟨doubting and⟩ denying.[73] As a result I grant that some proposition should be doubted in one place but should be granted in another place. So when the first case has been admitted and

> A king is sitting down

has been proposed, it may be doubted, and

> You are running

may be denied. When

> A king is sitting down

is proposed again, it is granted because it follows from the *positum* and the opposite of a correctly denied proposition as was shown.

⟨3⟩ Third argument against rule eight: I posit this to you:

> 'You are running' should be granted by you.

When this has been admitted, I propose this to you:

> Each of these should be granted by you,

indicating these:

> You are running

and

> You are a human being.

If you grant this you grant a false and irrelevant proposition; therefore you reply incorrectly. Proof of the premiss: it is obvious that the proposition is false, and that it is irrelevant is proved because it neither follows nor is inconsistent, as is absolutely clear. Then I propose this to you:

> You are a human being.

If you deny or doubt it, let the period come to an end. I argue that during the period you denied or doubted a proposition which was true and irrelevant and known by you to be such. If you grant it, I propose this to you:

> 'You are a human being' should be granted by you.

If you deny or doubt it, I argue against you:

> 'You are a human being' is true and irrelevant; therefore it should be granted by you.

If you grant it, and thereby reply correctly, I have obtained the opposite of the rule because this,

> 'You are a human being' should be granted by you,

is inconsistent with the *positum* and the opposite of a correctly denied proposition, since its opposite follows ⟨from them⟩. Proof: this is a valid inference:

---

[73] Strode gives this as the common reply: op.cit., fols. 84vb–85ra. Cf. Part 2, chapter 3, note 3.

Non utrumque istorum est a te concedendum sed 'Tu curris' est a te concedendum, igitur 'Tu es homo' non est a te concedendum.

Respondetur admittendo positum. Et cum proponitur:

Utrumque istorum est a te concedendum,

nego.

Tu es homo.

Concedo.

'Tu es homo' est a te concedendum.

Nego.

'Tu es homo' est verum et impertinens.

Nego quia repugnat. Sequitur enim:

'Tu es homo' non est a te concedendum, igitur non est verum et impertinens.

Item si immediate post negationem illius:

Utrumque istorum est a te concedendum,

proponeretur illa

'Tu es homo' est vera et impertinens,

negatur etiam, quia statim sequeretur quod esset[13] a te concedendum, et tunc utrumque istorum esset a te concedendum quod est negatum.

Item si immediate post positum proponeretur ista

'Tu es homo' est a te concedendum,

deberet illa concedi quia vera et impertinens, et consequenter ista

Utrumque istorum est a te concedendum,

quia sequens.

Et si dicitur in principio 'Negasti quod ista sit vera et impertinens

Tu es homo:

Pro qua parte?', dico quod proponas partes et videbis. Si igitur primo proponitur ista

'Tu es homo' est vera,

conceditur. Deinde:

---

[13] esset]est E

It is not the case that each of these should be granted by you, but 'You are running' should be granted by you; therefore 'You are a human being' should not be granted by you.

I reply by admitting the *positum*. And when

Each of these should be granted by you

is proposed, I deny it.

You are a human being.

I grant it.

'You are a human being' should be granted by you.

I deny it.

'You are a human being' is true and irrelevant.

I deny it because it is inconsistent. This is a valid inference:

'You are a human being' should not be granted by you; therefore it is not true and irrelevant.

Likewise if immediately after the negation of

Each of these should be granted by you,

this

'You are a human being' is true and irrelevant

were to be proposed, it would be denied because it would immediately follow that it should be granted by you, and then each of these would have to be granted by you, which was denied.

Likewise if immediately after the *positum*

'You are a human being' should be granted by you

were to be proposed, one would have to grant it because it is true and irrelevant and as a result ⟨one would have to grant⟩

Each of these should be granted by you

because it follows.

If someone says at the beginning: 'You denied that this,

You are a human being,

was true and irrelevant: On account of which clause?', I say that you should propose the clauses and you will see. If therefore

'You are a human being' is true

is proposed first, it is granted. Then:

> 'Tu es homo' est impertinens.

Negatur quia repugnat concesso et opposito bene negati. Sequitur enim:

> 'Tu es homo' non est vera vel non est impertinens, sed est vera, igitur non est impertinens.

Similiter si primo loco proponeretur ista

> 'Tu es homo' est impertinens,

concederem et alteram negarem, videlicet

> 'Tu es homo' est verum

modo priori. Quare etc.

⟨4⟩ Quarto ad principale arguitur sic. Et pono tibi istam

> Tantum homo est asinus est tibi positum,

quae sit A. Qua admissa quia possibilis, propono tibi

> A est 'Homo est asinus.'

Neganda est quia falsa et impossibilis non sequens. Deinde propono tibi

> A est tibi positum.

Si concedis, habeo oppositum regulae quia repugnat posito et opposito bene negati, cum suum oppositum (229^{rb}M) sequatur[14] ex ipsis. Sequitur enim

> Tantum 'Homo est asinus' est tibi positum sed A non est 'Homo est asinus', igitur A non est tibi (187^{rb}E) positum,

sicut a simili bene sequitur

> Tantum homo currit, sed A non est homo, igitur A non currit.

Si vero negas illam

> A est tibi[15] positum,

contra: A est a te concedendum, quia concedis A bene respondendo. Sed non est a te concedendum quia verum et impertinens, ut patet, nec etiam quia sequens ex aliquo priori concesso vel negato, ut patet similiter, igitur quia tibi positum.

Dicendum est quod in positione ista A potest dupliciter teneri: aut exclusive et exponibiliter[16], aut de excluso extremo et officiabiliter ratione

---

[14] sequatur]sequitur E
[15] tibi]*om.*E
[16] exponibiliter]exponitur E

'You are a human being' is irrelevant.

This is denied because it is inconsistent with the *positum* and the opposite of a correctly denied proposition. This is a valid inference:

> Either 'You are a human being' is not true or it is not irrelevant, but it is true; therefore it is not irrelevant.

Similarly if this

> 'You are a human being' is irrelevant

were proposed in the first place, I would grant it, and I would deny the other, i.e.

> 'You are a human being' is true

in the above manner. Therefore etc.

⟨4⟩ Fourth argument against rule eight. I posit this to you:

> Only a human being is a donkey is posited to you,[74]

where this is A. When it has been admitted because it is possible, I propose to you:

> A is 'A human being is a donkey'.

This should be denied because it is a false and impossible proposition which does not follow. Then I propose to you:

> A is posited to you.

If you grant this, I have obtained the opposite of the rule, because it is inconsistent with the *positum* and the opposite of a correctly denied proposition, since its opposite follows from these. This is a valid inference:

> Only 'A human being is a donkey' is posited to you, but A is not 'A human being is a donkey'; therefore A is not posited to you,

just as the similar inference

> Only a human being is running, but A is not a human being; therefore A is not running

is clearly valid.

But if you deny

> A is posited to you,

I argue against you: A should be granted by you, because in granting A you would reply correctly. But it should not be granted by you on the grounds that it is true and irrelevant, as is obvious; nor should it be granted on the grounds that it follows from some previously granted or denied proposition, as is similarly obvious; therefore ⟨it should be granted⟩ on the grounds that it is posited to you.

One must say that in the above *positio* A can be taken in two ways, either as an exclusive proposition which should be expounded, or as a proposition with an exclusive end-clause, which should be taken as functionalizable by virtue

---

[74] There is no punctuation here because the sophism hinges on the absence of quotation marks in medieval Latin. The sophism is found in *Lat.misc.e* 79, fol. 20ra; *Lib.Soph.Oxon.*, sig.C vi^v (Tantum homo est leo est vobis positum). Cf. Marsilius, op.cit., fol. 88^{r-v}; and Buser, op.cit., fol. 76^{va-vb} (Tantum deum esse deum est tibi positum).

illius termini 'positum'. Si primo modo tenetur[17], oportet concedere quod

    Homo est asinus

est tibi positum et nihil aliud quam

    Homo est asinus

est tibi positum tamquam ex positione sequens, et[18] etiam quod omnis tibi positum est

    Homo est asinus

tamquam universaliter sequens. Et tunc cum proponitur

    A est 'Homo est asinus'

nego et consequenter quod A est tibi positum. Et tunc ad argumentum

    A est concedendum a te quia concedis ipsum bene respondendo,

concedo gratia disputationis; et nego quod A non sit concedendum a me tamquam verum et impertinens nec tamquam sequens, et tunc quaecumque pars primo proponatur concedo eam et alteram nego quia repugnat uni concesso et opposito bene negati modo[19] saepissime declarato.

    Item si statim post negationem illius

    A est tibi positum

fuisset proposita ista

    A est a te concedendum,

ita quod non fuisset pars illius causalis, negassem eam tamquam falsam et impertinentem.

    Si vero in positione sumitur positum[20] de excluso extremo, nego quod

    Homo est asinus

est tibi positum, et istam similiter[21]

    Nihil aliud quam 'Homo est asinus' est tibi positum

dicendo quod quaelibet illarum est falsa non sequens, cum positum non sit exclusiva sed propositio officiabilis[22] probabilis; et ita consequenter negetur[23] ista universalis:

    Omne tibi positum est 'Homo est asinus.'

Positum enim convertibiliter significat et adserit quod illa exclusiva

    Tantum homo est asinus

est tibi posita. Ulterius quando proponitur

---

[17] tenetur]*om*.E
[18] et . . . sequens]*om*.E
[19] modo]non E
[20] positum]falsum E
[21] similiter]et *add*. E
[22] officiabilis]officiatis E
[23] negetur]negatur E

of the term 'posited'. If it is taken in the first way, one ought to grant that
>   A human being is a donkey
>
is posited to you, and nothing other than
>   A human being is a donkey
>
is posited to you, as following from the *positio*; and also that everything posited to you is
>   A human being is a donkey,
>
as following universally.[75] Then when
>   A is 'A human being is a donkey'
>
is proposed, I deny it, and as a result ⟨I deny⟩ that A is posited to you. ⟨In reply⟩ to the argument
>   A should be granted by you because in granting it you would reply correctly,
>
I grant it for the sake of the disputation. I deny that either A ought not to be granted by me ⟨on the grounds that it is⟩ true and irrelevant or ⟨on the grounds that⟩ it follows. Then whichever of these clauses is proposed first, I grant it, and I deny the other because it is inconsistent with a previously granted proposition and the opposite of a correctly denied proposition in the way which has been frequently explained.

Likewise if immediately after the denial of
>   A is posited to you,
>
this had been proposed:
>   A should be granted by you
>
in such a way that it was not a clause of the above causal proposition, I would have denied it as false and irrelevant.

But if the *positio* puts forward the *positum* as having an exclusive end-clause, I deny that
>   A human being is a donkey
>
is posited to you and similarly I deny that
>   Nothing other than 'A human being is a donkey' is posited to you.
>
I say that each of these is a false proposition which does not follow, since the *positum* is not an exclusive proposition but an acceptable functionalizable proposition. Consequently, I deny the universal proposition
>   Everything posited to you is 'A human being is a donkey',
>
for the *positum* interchangeably signifies and claims that this exclusive proposition
>   Only a human being is a donkey
>
is posited to you. Further when

---

[75] 'Only A is B' was analyzed as 'A is B and nothing other than A is B.' It was also said to be equivalent to 'Every B is A.' For Paul's analysis, see *Logica Magna* I.4, fol. 34^{ra-vb}. For further discussion, see E.J. Ashworth, 'The doctrine of exponibilia in the fifteenth and sixteenth centuries', *Vivarium*, 11 (1973), 137–167.

A est 'Homo est asinus',

neganda est ut prius dictum.

A est tibi positum,

concedo quia verum et impertinens. Et tunc ad argumentum patet quod ista consequentia non valet

'Tantum homo est asinus' est tibi positum et A non est 'Homo est asinus' igitur A non est tibi positum,

et ad similitudinem dico quod non est similitudo nisi primo modo.

Forte concessa ista

A est tibi positum,

quis posset proponere

A est a te concedendum.

Neganda est ut prius quia falsa non sequens. Non enim sequitur

A est tibi positum, igitur A est a te concedendum,

immo nec si adderetur ly .admissum. ut pluries est ostensum. Sed oportet etiam addere ly .sine repugnantia. vel .sine contradictione. ad ortum obligationis, quo praecedente cum aliis concederetur quod[24] A est a te concedendum[25].

⟨*Contra Regulam Nonam*⟩

Nona regula fuit ista. Ad omne impertinens est respondendum secundum sui qualitatem.

⟨1⟩ Contra istam regulam arguitur sic. Et pono tibi istam

Tu es Romae.

Qua admissa et concessa propono

Tu es Romae in hoc instanti,

demonstrando instans (229va M) quod est praesens. Si concedis habeo intentum, quia ista est falsa et impertinens, cum non sequatur[26], nec repugnat ut patet intuenti. Stat enim quod tu sis Romae[27] et tamen[28] non sis Romae in hoc instanti, sicut stat quod aliquod instans sit et[29] quod hoc instans non sit. Si ergo negatur ista

Tu es Romae in hoc instanti,

contra:

---

[24] quod]omne *add*.E
[25] concedendum]etc. *add*.E
[26] sequatur]sequitur E
[27] Romae]*om*.M
[28] tamen]*om*.M
[29] et]*om*.M

A is 'A human being is a donkey'

is proposed, it should be denied, as was said above.

A is posited to you.

I grant this because it is true and irrelevant. And then ⟨in reply⟩ to the argument ⟨I say that⟩ it is obvious that this inference is not valid:

'Only a human being is a donkey' is posited to you and A is not 'A human being is a donkey'; therefore A is not posited to you.

To the ⟨supposedly⟩ similar argument, I say that there is no similarity unless ⟨the *positum* is interpreted⟩ in the first way.

Perhaps when

A is posited to you

has been granted, someone might want to propose

A should be granted by you.

This should be denied as before because it is a false proposition which does not follow. This:

A is posited to you; therefore A should be granted by you

is an invalid argument, unless one adds the words 'and admitted', as has been shown a number of times. But one ought also to add the words 'without inconsistency' or 'without a contradiction' in order for the *obligatio* to arise. If this has been done one can grant that A should be granted by you, along with the other propositions.

⟨*Against Rule Nine*⟩

Rule nine was this: One must reply to each irrelevant proposition in accordance with its status.

⟨1⟩ First argument against rule nine. I posit this to you:

You are in Rome.

When this has been admitted and granted I posit

You are in Rome at this moment,[76]

indicating the present moment. If you grant this I have made my point, for the proposition is false and irrelevant. It does not follow nor is it inconsistent, as is obvious to anyone who considers the matter. It is consistent that you should be in Rome and yet that you should not be in Rome at this moment, just as it is consistent that some moment should exist and that this moment should not exist. If, therefore, you deny

You are in Rome at this moment,

I argue against you:

---

[76] This sophism is found in *Lat.misc.e 79*, fol. 19^{va-vb}; *Lib.Soph.Oxon.*, sig.C vi^r; Strode, op.cit., fol. 88^{ra-rb}; and Peter of Candia, op.cit., fol. 66^{va-vb}. The two anonymous texts denied the second sentence. Their solution depended on the claim that you might be in Rome at the end of the hour, whereas 'hoc instans' refers to a particular point in time at the beginning of the hour which no longer exists. The reference of 'hoc' was taken to be fixed at the time of utterance, no matter what was being indicated, as will be seen in the subsequent discussion. The two anonymous texts also denied the claim that 'Omne quod est Romae est Romae in hoc instanti' for the same reason. Peter of Candia made the same moves, but did not give the same explanation, preferring to say that the inference on p. 262, lines 1–2 involved a major premiss in the composite sense and a conclusion in the divided sense. Strode remarked, op.cit., fol. 88rb, that although the inference 'Tu es Romae,

Omne quod est Romae est Romae in hoc instanti, sed tu es Romae, ergo tu es Romae in hoc instanti.

Si negatur maior stet oppositum, videlicet quod aliquid est Romae quod non est Romae in hoc instanti, et pari ratione tales esse possibiles:

Aliquid est Romae quod nunc non est alicubi.

Similiter quod

Aliquid currit quod nunc[30] non habet pedes

et[31] quod:

Iam aliquis homo est incipiens qui adhuc non est generatus,

quae non apparent possibiles, quia sequitur

Hoc currit et hoc nunc non habet pedes, igitur[32] hoc caret pedibus, et sic carens pedibus currit,

loquendo proprie de currere prout soli animali convenit. Similiter

Iste homo disputat qui[33] adhuc non est generatus[34], et fuit, igitur in aeternum fuit

quod est impossibile.

Ad istam obligationem solet[35] responderi ut prius et consequenter concedendo[36] omnes illas conclusiones de possibili. Et ad argumentum contra regulam, negatur consequentia quia oportet ad illud concludendum sumere quod illud nunc sit, quod tamen repugnat posito et opposito bene negati. Consimiliter negatur alia consequentia facta contra aliam conclusionem, quia ly .adhuc. et .ante hoc., demonstrando instans,

---

[30] nunc]*om*.M
[31] et. . generatus]etiam quod nunc homo disputat qui adhuc non est grammaticus E
[32] igitur . . . currit]ergo hoc currens pedibus currit E
[33] qui]et E
[34] generatus]grammaticus E
[35] solet]solent E
[36] concedendo]concedo E

---

igitur tu es Romae in hoc instanti quod est praesens' was materially valid, it was not formally so 'quia per imaginationem staret me esse Romae licet nullum instans vel tempus esse; nam si motus non esset, nec tempus esset.' (Text corrected from MS, fol. 43vb.)

The rather complicated treatment of this sophism hinges on the different interpretations which can be given of temporal indexicals such as 'now' and of phrases which employ the demonstrative 'this' to fix a temporal reference. Paul agreed with his opponents that the phrase 'this moment' refers to the original moment of utterance, and that the reference does not shift when the sentence containing the phrase is repeated after a lapse in time (unless the speaker's intentions have changed). He also agreed with his opponents that the temporal reference of a present-tense proposition without any further temporal indexicals embraced a certain period of time, such as the one hour mentioned in the Oxford treatises. This interpretation of present-tense propositions seems not to have been unusual: Jerónimo Pardo (d. 1502 or 1505) routinely postulated that the present time occupied one hour in his discussion of whether a contingent proposition could change its truth-value: see his *Medulla Dyalectices* (Parisius, 1505) fols. xviii^{vb}–xix^{vb}. Hence, although 'He is in Rome, therefore he is in Rome at this moment' has a true premiss and a true conclusion at the initial moment of utterance, it is possible for the facts to be as stated by the premiss without them being as stated by the conclusion, and the inference is accordingly invalid.

Paul's opponents went on to treat temporal indexicals, such as 'now' and 'today' as if their reference was also fixed by the original moment of utterance. They apparently believed that 'now' and 'today' would be interchangeable with the demonstrative phrases 'this moment' and 'this day' if one were to add the extra phrase 'which is present' in order to capture the temporal

Everything which is in Rome is in Rome at this moment, but you are in Rome; therefore you are in Rome at this moment.

If you deny the major premiss then its opposite is possible, namely that something should be in Rome which is not in Rome at this moment. By parity of reasoning these will also be possible propositions:[77]

Something is in Rome which now is not anywhere;

similarly:

Something is running which now has no feet

and

Some human being is already beginning who up to now has not been conceived.

None of these seems possible, for they would make this a valid inference:

This is running and this now has no feet; therefore this lacks feet, and thus something which lacks feet is running.

I take 'running' here in its proper sense as something done by animals. Similarly ⟨this would be valid⟩:

This human being is disputing who up to now has not been conceived, and he did exist; therefore he has existed throughout eternity,

which is impossible.

People are accustomed to reply to this *obligatio* as above, and as a result they grant all these theses about what is possible. ⟨In reply to⟩ the argument against the rule, the inference is rejected because in order for it to reach a conclusion one ought to assume that ⟨the moment⟩ exists now. This, however, is inconsistent with the *positum* and the opposite of a correctly denied proposition, ⟨i.e. 'You are in Rome at this moment'⟩. In the same way the other

---

indexicals' connotation of presentness. Paul rejected this interpretation and argued that even with the extra phrase, there was no interchangeability. 'The Now exists, therefore this moment which is present exists' is invalid because the temporal reference of the premiss shifts without any change in the speaker's intentions, thus making its equiforms always true, whereas the reference of 'this moment which is present' is fixed, thus making the conclusion become false as soon as the moment in question has passed. On the other hand, 'The Now exists, therefore (the) moment which is present exists' would be a valid inference, because the reference of '(the) moment' is no more fixed than is the reference of 'now'. As a result of his arguments, Paul is able to reject the original sophism while retaining a commonsense belief in the validity of 'You are in Rome, therefore you are now in Rome' (or 'therefore you are in Rome today').

Paul went on to argue that 'it will at some time be true that Antichrist exists today . . . yet Antichrist does not exist . . . today'. At first glance, these remarks seem at variance with the position taken by such modern logicians as A.N. Prior, who wrote '. . . in "It will be the case tomorrow that I am sitting down now", the word "now" indicates the time that it would indicate if it occurred in the principal clause – the time of utterance' (A.N. Prior, 'Now', *Noûs* 2 (1968), p. 104. See also A.N. Prior, 'Recent advances in tense logic', *The Monist*, 53 (1969), 325–339, for further discussion and a bibliography). However, Prior was specifically concerned with oblique contexts (such as the one quoted or, e.g. 'Henry believed that he would now be President', 'John said that Mary would be arriving now') whereas Paul is concerned with token-sentences of the type 'Antichrist exists today'. His point is that at least one token of this type will be true when uttered in the future, but that any token currently uttered is false. If his point were to be rephrased in idiomatic English, and with the oblique context retained, it would have to read 'It will at some time be true that Antichrist exists on that day, and it will also at the same time be true that Antichrist does not exist today' (where 'today' refers to the day of utterance).

[77] The examples come from Strode, op.cit., fol. 88ra.

aequivalent. Ideo sicut stat quod iste homo generabatur[37] qui non ante hoc instans generabatur[38], sic (187^{va}E) stat quod iste[39] aliquando vel prius generabatur qui adhuc non generabatur. Et consequenter conceditur quod stat aliquid esse Romae quod nec cras nec hodie nec heri est Romae. Aequivalent enim apud hanc responsionem 'hodie' et 'haec dies', praeter hoc quod 'hodie' connotat praesentiam diei demonstratae. Et consimiliter ly .nunc. et .hoc instans. connotando eius praesentiam ita quod ly .hodie. vel .nunc. non convertitur cum ly .haec dies. nisi cum tali connotatione, nam ly .hodie. valet tantum sicut .haec dies qui est praesens., et consimiliter ly .hodierna dies.. Et sicut[40] non sequitur

    Omnis dies erit praesens, ergo omnis dies erit hodierna dies,
nec sequitur

    Omnis dies erit praesens dies, igitur omnis dies erit dies qui est praesens.

Et similiter[41] negatur quod omnis dies post hodiernum diem erit cras vel crastina dies, quia isti termini 'cras' vel 'crastina dies' valent tantum sicut diceretur 'dies immediate sequens diem quae nunc est praesens'. Et si quaeratur an ly .hodierna dies. vel .crastina dies. sint termini communes vel termini[42] singulares, dicitur quod sunt termini communes. Non oportet tamen quod utrumque istorum sit de pluribus praedicabilis sicut nec iste terminus .sol., .deus., vel .caelum.. Et tamen convertuntur .deus. et .iste deus., et sicut non potest esse quod iste deus est et alius deus est, sic nec quod hodierna dies sit et quod alia dies sit hodierna. Et similiter[43] dicatur de crastina et hesterna[44]. Quare etc.

    Haec autem pulchre dicta sunt, sed iudicio meo non in toto continent veritatem. Arguo enim probando quod ly .hodie. vel .nunc. non convertuntur cum ly .isto die. vel .hoc instanti. et tali connotatione. Nam facio istam[45] consequentiam:

    Nunc est aut hodie est, igitur hoc instans praesens est vel haec dies quae est praesens est,

et demonstrato hanc diem quae est A et hoc instans praesens quod sit B. Nam post hanc septimanam erit ita quod hodie est et nunc est sicut praesentialiter ita (229^{vb}M) est, et tunc non erit ita quod haec dies est,

---

[37] generabatur]generabitur E
[38] generabatur]generabitur E
[39] iste]*om.*E
[40] sicut]sic E
[41] similiter]consimiliter M
[42] termini]*om.*M
[43] similiter]consimiliter M
[44] hesterna]hodierna E
[45] istam]talem E

inference put forward against the other thesis is rejected, because the expressions 'up to now' and 'before this' indicating ⟨some⟩ moment ⟨or other⟩, are equivalent. Thus just as it is possible that this human being was conceived who was not conceived before this moment ⟨whichever it was⟩, so it is possible that he was at some time or previously conceived who up to now ⟨whenever it was⟩, was not conceived. As a result one can grant that it is possible for something to be in Rome which is not in Rome tomorrow or today or yesterday. According to this reply, 'today' and 'this day' are equivalent, except that 'today' ⟨unlike 'this day'⟩ connotes the presence of the indicated day. The same applies to the expressions 'now' and 'this moment' ⟨for the former, unlike 'this moment'⟩ connotes its own presence. Hence the expression 'today' or the expression 'now' is not interchangeable with the expression 'this day' unless ⟨the latter⟩ has such a connotation, for the expression 'today' has the same force as 'this day which is present'. The same applies to the expression 'this very day'. Just as the inference

> Every day will be the present day; therefore every day will be this very day

is invalid, so is the inference:

> Every day will be the present day; therefore every day will be ⟨identical with⟩ the day which is present.

Similarly it is denied that every day which comes after this very day will be tomorrow or the morrow, because these terms 'tomorrow' or 'the morrow' have the same force as 'the day immediately following the day which is now present'. And if someone asks whether the expressions 'this very day' or 'the morrow' are common or singular terms, the answer is that they are common terms. However, it is not required that each of them should be predicable of many things at once, any more than this is required of such terms as 'sun,' 'God', or 'heaven'. Yet 'God' and 'this God' are interchangeable, and just as it is impossible for this God to exist and for another God to exist, so it is impossible for this very day to exist and for another day to be this very day. The same can be said of tomorrow and yesterday. Therefore etc.

These remarks are very attractive, but in my judgment they do not capture the full truth. In my argument I will prove that the expressions 'today' or 'now' are not interchangeable with 'this day' or 'this moment' along with the required connotation of the present. I construct this inference:

> The Now exists or today exists; therefore this present moment exists or this day which is present exists

indicating this day which is A, and the present moment, which is B. After this week it will be the case that today exists and that the Now exists, just as at present, but it will not then be the case that this day exists, indicating A, or

demonstrato A, nec hoc instans est, demonstrato B instanti quod nunc est. Igitur adinvicem huiusmodi non convertuntur.

Confirmatur, nam si iste terminus 'deus' successive de pluribus esset verificabilis ita quod sua supposita corrumpentur[46] et non essent aeterna, haec consequentia non valeret[47]

Deus est, igitur hic deus est,

quocumque demonstrato, nec[48] converterentur illa duo 'deus' et 'hic deus', sicut nec convertentur[49] illa duo, 'aliquis homo' et 'iste homo', dato quod ly .aliquis homo. numquam haberet nisi unum suppositum sed successive plura, sicut dicimus de istis terminis 'phoenix' et 'ista phoenix'. Modo patet quod non sequitur

Phoenix est, igitur ista phoenix est,

nec ista

Aliquis homo est, igitur iste homo est,

quacumque connotatione vel relatione addita, igitur nec illa consequentia est bona:

Nunc est, igitur hoc instans quod est praesens est,

⟨nec ista⟩

Hodie est aliquis homo, igitur haec[50] dies quae[51] est praesens est aliquis homo.

Consequentia patet quia licet isti termini 'nunc' et[52] 'hodie' numquam plura supposita habeant simul, tamen habeant successive per continuam desitionem et inceptionem talium suppositorum.

Confirmatur iterum, et adsigno aliquos dies huius hebdomadae futurae, videlicet A, B, C, D. Et patet quod quandocumque erit ita quod tu es in A die, erit ita quod tu es nunc, et quod tu es hodie; et ita quandocumque erit verum quod tu es in B, in C, vel[53] in D. Sed tunc non erit ita quod tu es in hoc die demonstrato quae modo praesens est, nec tunc erit ita quod tu es in hoc instanti, demonstrato instanti quod[54] praesentialiter existit. Igitur talis convertibilitas est fugienda.

---

[46] corrumpentur]corrumperentur E
[47] valeret]valent E
[48] nec . . .'hic deus']*om*.E
[49] convertentur]convertuntur E
[50] haec]iste M
[51] quae]quod M
[52] et]*om*.E
[53] vel]*om*.E
[54] quod]praesens *add*.M

that this moment exists, indicating the moment B which exists now. Therefore these kinds of expression are not mutually interchangeable.

A supporting argument: if the term 'god' were successively verifiable of many things in such a way that its referents passed away and were not eternal, this inference would be invalid:

There is a god, therefore this god exists,

whatever was indicated; nor would the two phrases 'god' and 'this god' be interchangeable any more than are the two phrases 'some human being' and 'this human being', given that the expression 'some human being' never has more than one referent ⟨at a time⟩ but has many in succession, just as we claim of the terms 'phoenix' and 'this phoenix'. It is obvious that the inference

There exists a phoenix; therefore this phoenix exists

is invalid, just as the inference

Some human being exists; therefore this human being exists

is invalid no matter what connotation or relation one adds. Therefore this inference

The Now exists; therefore this moment which is present exists

is invalid, ⟨as is⟩:

Today some human being exists; therefore some human being exists on this day which is present.

My inference is obvious because although these terms 'now' and 'today' never have several referents at once, they do have them successively through the continual ending and beginning of these referents.

Another supporting argument: I pick out several days from next week, namely A, B, C, and D. It is obvious that whenever it comes about that you exist on day A, it will be true that you exist now and that you exist today; and the same will be the case whenever it is true that you exist on day B, day C, or day D. But it will not be true then that you exist on this day, indicating the day which is now present, nor will it be true then that you exist in this moment, indicating the moment which currently exists. Therefore the interchangeability ⟨claimed by these people⟩ should be avoided.

Ideo est aliter dicendum, respondendo ad obligationem sicut in argumento respondetur quousque proponuntur istae conclusiones quas nego; et dico quod si aliquid est Romae, illud nunc est Romae vel alicubi, quia si aliquid est Romae, illud est Romae in instanti praesenti et in instanti quod est praesens. Similiter, si aliquid est Romae, illud est Romae hodie. Numquam tamen concedo[55] quod si aliquid est Romae, illud est Romae in hoc instanti praesenti vel in hac die quae est praesens, cum adaequatum significatum antecedentis et significatum adaequatum oppositi consequentis sint[56] compossibilia. Et ita non est admittendum quod aliquid currat quod nunc non habet[57] pedes, licet sit admittendum quod aliquid currit[58] quod in hoc instanti praesenti non habet pedes. Nec etiam est concedendum quod aliquis homo disputet qui adhuc non sit generatus[59], licet concedendum sit in casu quod aliquis homo disputat qui ante[60] hoc instans praesens non sit generatus[61]. Haec autem in[62] materia de incipit et desinit nota sunt[63], ideo horum[64] verificationes quaerens inveniat.

Ex his ergo patet quod ly .nunc. et .instans praesens. convertuntur, et[65] non ly .nunc. et .hoc instans praesens. .Similiter 'hodie' et 'dies praesens' convertuntur et non 'hodie' (187^{vb}E) et 'haec dies praesens'. Idem est dicendum de 'hodierna die' et de aliis terminis 'dies crastina' et 'hesterna' suo modo, unde 'dies hesterna'[66] aequivalet huic 'dies praeterita immediate diei quae est praesens'; 'dies crastina'[67] aequivalet huic 'dies futura immediata diei quae est praesens' et non 'huic diei quae est praesens', sicut potest patere ex dictis.

Ex quibus sequitur quod licet et aliquando[68] fuit ita quod Adam est hodie et fuit heri, sive erit cras, non tamen est verum quod Adam (230^{ra}M) fuit hodie aut heri, et ita aliquando[69] erit verum[70] quod Antichristus est hodie et fuit heri et erit cras, et tamen Antichristus non est nec[71] erit hodie heri aut cras iuxta aequivalentias talium terminorum. Sicut etiam alias concessi quod Antichristus numquam erit praesens nec umquam[72] erit in instanti praesenti nec umquam[73] erit hodierna die, licet aliquando erit ita quod est praesens et

---

[55] concedo]concedendo M
[56] sint]sunt E
[57] habet]habeat E
[58] currit]currat E
[59] sit generatus]est grammaticus E
[60] ante]tamen E
[61] generatus]grammaticus E
[62] in]om.M
[63] sunt]est M
[64] horum]eorum E
[65] et . . . praesens]om.M
[66] hesterna]crastina M,E, correxi
[67] crastina]hesterna M,E, correxi
[68] et aliquando]om.E
[69] aliquando]bene E
[70] verum]unum E
[71] nec erit]om.E
[72] umquam]numquam E
[73] umquam]numquam E

For this reason one must adopt another solution. I reply to the *obligatio* as it was replied in the above argument until those theses are proposed. I deny them, and I say that if something is in Rome, then that thing is now in Rome, or somewhere, for if something is in Rome, that thing is in Rome in the present moment and in the moment which is present. Similarly, if something is in Rome, that thing is in Rome today. But I never grant that if something is in Rome, that thing is in Rome in *this* present moment, or on *this* day which is present, since the adequate significate of the premiss and the adequate significate of the opposite of the conclusion are compossible. Thus one ought not to admit that something is running which now has no feet, although one should admit that something is running which in this present moment has no feet. Nor should one grant that some human being is disputing who up to now has not been conceived, although in the stated case it should be granted that some human being is disputing who before this present moment has not been conceived. All these things have been noted in the material on 'Begins' and 'Ceases', so anyone asking for verification of my remarks can find it there.[78]

From these remarks it is obvious that the expressions 'now' and 'the present moment' are interchangeable, but not the expressions 'now' and 'this present moment'. Similarly 'today' and 'the present day' are interchangeable, but 'today' and 'this present day' are not. The same should be said of 'this very day' and the other terms 'tomorrow' and 'yesterday' with appropriate changes. Hence 'yesterday' is equivalent to this: 'the day immediately past the day which is present'; and 'tomorrow' is equivalent to 'the day immediately in the future of the day which is present' but not to ' . . . this day which is present', as can be made clear from what has been said.

From these remarks it follows that although it once was the case that Adam exists today and did exist yesterday or will exist tomorrow, it is not however true that Adam did exist today or yesterday. Thus it will at some time be true that Antichrist exists today and did exist yesterday and will exist tomorrow, yet Antichrist does not exist nor will he exist today, yesterday or tomorrow, in accordance with the equivalences holding between such terms. In the same way I granted elsewhere that Antichrist will never exist at present and will never exist in the present moment and will never exist this very day, although at some time it will be the case that he exists at present and in the present

---

[78] See *Logica Magna* I.18. *De incipit et desinit.*

in instanti praesenti et hodierna die. Si enim erit in instanti praesenti ipse erit[74] in instanti quod est praesens[75], quod[76] est falsum, et consequentia tenet quia ly .praesens instans. et ly .instans quod est. convertuntur. Quare[77] etc.

Sed contra iam dicta probatur quod sequitur

Tu es Romae, igitur tu es Romae in hoc instanti quocumque demonstrato, nam ex opposito sequitur oppositum. Sequitur enim

Tu non es Romae in hoc instanti quocumque demonstrato, igitur[78] tu non es Romae in hoc[79] instanti isto demonstrato nec isto demonstrato, nec sic de singulis, igitur tu non es Romae in aliquo instanti et per consequens tu non es Romae.

Secundo:

Tu es Romae, igitur tu es Romae in aliquo instanti, igitur tu es Romae in instanti praesenti, igitur tu es Romae in instanti quod est praesens. Sed solum hoc instans est, demonstrando instans praesens. Igitur etc.

Tertio arguitur sic. Sit rei veritas quod Sortes sit Romae in A instanti quod sit praesens, et redeo[80] ad primam responsionem negantem quod tu es Romae in A instanti et bene es Romae in aliquo instanti. Propono tibi

Sortes est Romae in A instanti

et[81] patet quod concedenda est quia vera et impertinens. Tunc arguitur sic:

Sortes est Romae in A instanti, et tu es Romae in aliquo instanti, igitur tu es Romae in A instanti.

Patet consequentia quia aliter plura instantia essent. Consequens est[82] impossibile, quia duo[83] talia nec possunt esse continua nec contigua.

Ad primum dicitur negando penultimam consequentiam, sicut non sequitur:

Non sum hoc animal, demonstrato asino, nec demonstrato homine nec demonstrato quocumque alio animali, igitur non sum animal,

supposito quod per ly .hoc. in antecedente demonstretur[84] asinus.

Ad secundum concedo quod sum in instanti quod est praesens et nego quod solum hoc instans est praesens, tamquam repugnans.

---

[74] ipse erit]tempore currit E
[75] praesens]om.M
[76] quod . . . et]om.E
[77] Quare etc.]om.E
[78] igitur]et E
[79] hoc]isto M
[80] redeo]reddo E
[81] et]om.E
[82] est]esset M
[83] duo]secundo E
[84] demonstretur]demonstreretur M

moment and this very day. If he will exist in the present moment, he himself will exist in the moment which is present, and this ⟨conclusion⟩ is false. The inference holds because the expressions 'present moment' and 'moment which exists' are interchangeable. Therefore etc.

First argument against what has been said: one can prove that this inference
> You are in Rome; therefore you are in Rome at this moment (whichever is indicated)

is valid because the opposite ⟨of the premiss⟩ follows from the opposite ⟨of the conclusion⟩. This is a valid inference:
> You are not in Rome at this moment (whichever is indicated); therefore you are not in Rome at this moment (indicating this, but not this, nor any of these); therefore you are not in Rome at any moment, and as a result you are not in Rome.

Second argument against:
> You are in Rome; therefore you are in Rome at some moment; therefore you are in Rome at the present moment; therefore you are in Rome at the moment which is present. But only this moment exists (indicating the present moment). Therefore etc.

Third argument against: let it be true in fact that Socrates is in Rome at moment A, which is the present moment. ⟨Having re-stated the original *positum*,⟩ I go back to the first reply and deny that you are in Rome at moment A, though you are in Rome at some moment. I propose to you:
> Socrates is in Rome at moment A.

It is clear that it should be granted because it is true and irrelevant. Then I argue thus:
> Socrates is in Rome at moment A, and you are in Rome at some moment; therefore you are in Rome at moment A.

The inference is obvious because otherwise several moments would exist. But this conclusion is impossible, because two such things can exist neither continuously nor contiguously.

Reply to the first argument. I reject the last inference for the same reason as this inference is invalid:
> I am not this animal (indicating a donkey, but not indicating a human being, or any other animal); therefore I am not an animal,

assuming that the word 'this' in the premiss indicates a donkey.

Reply to the second. I grant that I exist in the moment which is present, and I deny that only this moment is present as inconsistent.

Ad tertium, admissa suppositione nego quod Sortes sit Romae in A instanti, propter repugnantiam vel deductionem ad impossibile[85]. Tamen bene concedo quod Sortes est in aliquo instanti Romae, sicut concedo quod tu es Romae in aliquo instanti: primum quia verum et impertinens, secundum quia sequens ex posito. Et si quaeritur, ex quo Sortes est Romae in aliquo instanti et tu similiter, in quo instanti, dico quod stat in A vel in B[86]. Non est haec[87] quaestio determinanda.

⟨2⟩ Secundo ad principale arguitur sic. Et pono tibi istam

    Omnis propositio est vera.

Qua admissa proponitur

    Haec est vera 'Homo est asinus.'

Si conceditur habeo intentum, cum ipsa sit falsa et impertinens. Quod sit falsa patet, et[88] quod sit impertinens probatur quia non sequitur nec repugnat. Nam non sequitur

    Omnis propositio est vera, igitur haec est vera 'Homo est asinus',

cum oppositum consequentis stet cum antecedente. Stat enim quod illa

    Deus est

sit omnis propositio vera. Quod autem non repugnet manifestum est.

  Si autem negatur, contra:

    Omnis propositio est vera sed[89] ista 'Homo est asinus' est propositio, igitur ipsa est vera.

Dicitur concedendo[90] consequentiam et negando minorem tamquam repugnantem posito et opposito bene negati. Nam bene sequitur

    Omnis propositio est vera, ista 'Homo est asinus' non est vera, igitur illa

    'Homo est asinus' non est propositio.

Si autem post positum proponeretur[91] ista

    'Homo est asinus' est propositio,

concedenda est quia vera et impertinens. Deinde si proponatur

    'Homo est asinus' est vera,

concedatur quia sequens ex posito et bene[92] concesso.

---

[85] impossibile]sed *add*.E
[86] B]quod *add*.E
[87] haec]hic E
[88] et]sed E
[89] sed]*om*.M
[90] concedendo]concedo E
[91] proponeretur]proponetur M
[92] bene]*om*.E

Reply to the third: when the *suppositio* has been admitted, I deny that Socrates is in Rome at moment A because it is inconsistent or implies an impossible proposition. However, I do grant that Socrates is in Rome at some moment, just as I grant that you are in Rome at some moment; the first because it is true and irrelevant, the second because it follows from the *positum*. And if someone asks, given that Socrates is in Rome at some moment and you likewise, at what moment this is, I say that it might be A or it might be B. This question does not have to be settled.

⟨2⟩ Second argument against rule nine. I posit this to you:
> Every proposition is true.

When this has been admitted, I propose:
> 'A human being is a donkey' is true.[79]

If it is granted I have made my point, since it is false and irrelevant. It is obvious that it is false. It can be proved that it is irrelevant because it neither follows nor is inconsistent. It does not follow because this inference:
> Every proposition is true; therefore 'A human being is a donkey' is true

is invalid, since the opposite of the conclusion is consistent with the antecedent. It is possible that
> There is a God

should be every true proposition.[80] That it is not inconsistent is obvious.

But if it is denied, one can argue against ⟨the denial⟩:
> Every proposition is true, but 'A human being is a donkey' is a proposition; therefore it is true.

I reply by granting the inference and denying the minor premiss as inconsistent with the *positum* and the opposite of a correctly denied proposition. This is a valid inference:
> Every proposition is true, but 'A human being is a donkey' is not true; therefore 'A human being is a donkey' is not a proposition.

However if
> 'A human being is a donkey' is a proposition

were proposed after the *positum*, it should be granted because it is true and irrelevant. Then if
> 'A human being is a donkey' is true

is proposed, it is granted because it follows from the *positum* and a correctly granted proposition.

---

[79] This sophism is in Peter of Candia, op.cit., fol. 66vb.

[80] Since a *propositio* was an occurrent sentence, in order to be true it had to exist. It was logically possible that 'Deus est' was the only existent *propositio*.

Et si arguitur:

'Homo est asinus' est propositio vera, igitur homo est asinus,

non valet argumentum, quia ex possibili non sequitur impossibile.

Contra unum negatum, videlicet quod illa

Homo est asinus,

sit propositio, arguitur sic. Et facio (230^{rb}M) illam consequentiam

Omnis propositio est vera, igitur haec 'Homo est asinus' est propositio vera.

Ista consequentia per te[93] non valet. Stet igitur[94] oppositum consequentis cum antecedente, et arguo sic.

Oppositum consequentis stat cum antecedente, igitur oppositum consequentis est, igitur consequens illius (188^{ra}E) consequentiae est. Sed omne consequens illius consequentiae est ista 'Homo est asinus', igitur 'Homo est asinus' est, igitur 'Homo est asinus' est propositio.

Respondetur quod quia secundus casus repugnat dictis in primo casu, unum istorum expedit facere, aut non admittere secundum casum, aut si admittitur cedit obligatio prima[95]. Et tunc in secundo casu possum concedere[96] quod ista

Homo est asinus

est propositio nec tunc repugnat alicui. Aut tertio potest dici sicut superius dicebatur, admittendo simul duos casus oppositos per duas positiones, et tunc non est inconveniens concedere et negare eandem propositionem in diversis casibus, sed in eodem esset inconveniens. Verumtamen[97] potest secundus casus admitti cum primo. Et cum dicitur

Oppositum consequentis istius consequentiae stat cum antecedente eiusdem,

concedo[98].

Igitur oppositum consequentis est.

Concedo[99].

Sed omne consequens illius est ista 'Homo est asinus', igitur 'Homo est asinus' est.

---

[93] per te]parte E
[94] Stet igitur]stat enim E
[95] prima]primi M
[96] concedere]admittere E
[97] Verumtamen]verum E
[98] concedo]concedendo M
[99] Concedo]concedendo M

If someone argues

> 'A human being is a donkey' is a true proposition; therefore a human being is a donkey,

his argument is invalid, because an impossible proposition does not follow from a possible proposition.[81]

One can argue against a proposition which was denied, namely that this

> A human being is a donkey

is a proposition, in the following manner. I construct this inference:

> Every proposition is true; therefore 'A human being is a donkey' is a true proposition.

According to you this inference is invalid. Let us assume that the opposite of the conclusion is consistent with the premiss. I argue like this:

> The opposite of the conclusion is consistent with the premiss; therefore the opposite of the conclusion exists; therefore the conclusion of that inference exists. But the only conclusion of that inference is 'A human being is a donkey'; therefore 'A human being is a donkey' exists; therefore 'A human being is a donkey' is a proposition.

I reply that because this second case is inconsistent with what was said in the first case, one must do one of two things: either one ought not to admit the second case, or, if it is admitted, one ought to let the first *obligatio* come to an end. Then in the second case I am able to grant that

> A human being is a donkey

is a proposition; nor will this be inconsistent with anything. A third possibility is that one could reply as was replied above, by admitting two opposite cases at once by means of two *positiones*. It is not awkward to grant and deny the same proposition in different cases, though it is awkward in one and the same case. Nevertheless the second case can be admitted along with the first. And when it is said

> The opposite of the conclusion of this inference is consistent with its premiss,

I grant it.

> Therefore the opposite of the conclusion exists.

I grant it.

> But the only conclusion of that inference is 'A human being is a donkey'; therefore 'A human being is a donkey' exists.

---

[81] Up to this point, at which Peter of Candia ended his discussion, Paul has reproduced Peter's text almost verbatim.

Nego antecedens tamquam repugnans. Sequitur enim:
> Illa[1] 'Homo est asinus' non est propositio, igitur non est consequens illius consequentiae.

⟨3⟩ Tertio arguitur sic contra regulam. Et pono tibi istam copulativam:
> Rex sedet et nulla obligatio tibi fit.

Deinde:
> Rex sedet.

Si conceditur[2],
> Et ista est tibi[3] dubia et impertinens, igitur oppositum regulae.

Antecedens probatur, nam quod sit dubia de se patet, sed quod sit impertinens probatur. Nam
> Nulla obligatio tibi fit, igitur illa[4] est impertinens,

accipiendo 'impertinens' pro omni eo quod non est sequens nec repugnans. Illa consequentia est bona; antecedens est concedendum a te, igitur et consequens. Si in principio[5] dubitatur[6] ista
> Rex sedet,

tunc:
> Cedat tempus. Tu dubitasti sequens ex posito infra tempus, igitur male respondisti.

Forte dicitur quod repugnat illam esse mihi dubiam. Contra: Et pono tibi istam copulativam
> Rex sedet et 'Rex sedet' est tibi dubium et nulla obligatio est tibi facta.

Deinde:
> Rex sedet.

Si conceditur, tunc
> 'Rex sedet' est tibi dubium et nulla obligatio tibi facta est, igitur concedis tibi dubium sine aliqua obligatione, et per consequens tu[7] male respondes.

Respondetur admittendo positum[8] et cum proponitur
> Rex sedet,

concedo[9]; et cum arguitur
> Ista est tibi dubia et impertinens, igitur etc.,

---

[1] Illa]propositio *add*.M
[2] conceditur]concedatur M
[3] tibi]*om*.M
[4] illa]*om*.E
[5] principio]primo E
[6] dubitatur]dubitetur M
[7] tu]*om*.E
[8] positum]casum E
[9] concedo]concedendo M

I deny the premiss as inconsistent. This is a valid inference:
'A human being is a donkey' is not a proposition; therefore it is not the conclusion of that inference.

⟨3⟩ Third argument against rule nine. I posit this conjunction to you:
A king is sitting down and no *obligatio* comes into existence for you.

Then:
A king is sitting down.

If you grant it ⟨one can argue⟩:
This is uncertain to you and irrelevant; therefore the opposite of the rule ⟨follows⟩.

Proof of the premiss: it is patently obvious that the proposition is uncertain; but I can prove that it is irrelevant, for:
No *obligatio* comes into existence for you; therefore that proposition is irrelevant,

taking 'irrelevant' for everything which neither follows nor is inconsistent. The inference is valid; the premiss should be granted by you; therefore the conclusion should also be granted by you. If in the beginning you doubt
A king is sitting down,

then
Let the period come to an end. You doubted a proposition which follows from the *positum* during the period; therefore you replied incorrectly.

Perhaps someone will say that it is inconsistent for it to be uncertain to me. I argue against this. I posit this conjunction to you:
A king is sitting down and 'A king is sitting down' is uncertain to you and no *obligatio* has come into existence for you.

Then:
A king is sitting down.

If it is granted, then:
'A king is sitting down' is uncertain to you and no *obligatio* has come into existence for you; therefore you grant what is uncertain to you without any obligation to do so, and as a result you reply incorrectly.

I reply by admitting the *positum*, and when
A king is sitting down

is proposed, I grant it. And when it is argued
This is uncertain to you and irrelevant; therefore etc.

nego antecedens. Pro qua parte? Pro prima[10] ex quo ⟨secunda⟩ sequitur ex secunda parte casus. Si tamen proponantur partes[11] illae categoricae divisim, concedo[12] quod ista non est a me concedenda; tamen concedam ipsam quotienscumque proponetur. Et si dicitur

> Tu concedis illam et illa non est a te concedenda sed dubitanda, igitur male respondes,

dico negando antecedens ut prius copulative propositum. Categorice autem concedo[13]. Ultimate ⟨concedo⟩ quod male respondeo, non quia verum sed quia sequens.

⟨4⟩ Quarto ad principale arguitur sic.

> Aliquod impertinens falsum est pertinens vel[14] sequens vel repugnans, sed omne sequens est concedendum et omne repugnans negandum, igitur non semper ad impertinens est respondendum secundum sui qualitatem.

Consequentia tenet et antecedens probatur. Et pono tibi illam:

> Omnis homo est Romae et quaelibet propositio est impertinens posito et[15] obligato.

Tunc propono tibi:

> Omnis homo est Romae,

quae sit A. Conceditur. Deinde:

> A est positum (230^{va}M) obligatum vel sequens.

Conceditur quia verum et impertinens. Deinde:

> A est a te concedendum.

Conceditur quia sequens. Tunc arguitur sic. Si nulla obligatio esset facta, A esset negandum quia falsum[16], et nunc est concedendum; igitur solum propter positum est concedendum. Sed nullum falsum est concedendum propter positum nisi sequens, igitur ista est sequens; sed omnis propositio est impertinens posito obligato, igitur propositio falsa impertinens est sequens. Quare etc.

Respondetur admittendo et concedendo quod A est positum obligatum vel sequens, et quod est concedendum. Sed nego quod A[17] sit falsum tamquam repugnans. Sequitur enim:

---

[10] prima]secunda   E
[11] partes]*om.*E
[12] concedo]concedendo M
[13] concedo]concedendo M
[14] vel]videlicet E
[15] et]*om.*M
[16] negandum quia falsum]falsum quia negandum   E
[17] A]*om.*E

I deny the premiss. On account of which clause? On account of the first, because ⟨the second, sc. '"A king is sitting down" is irrelevant'⟩ follows from the second clause of the case. However if those clauses were proposed to me as separate categorical propositions I would grant that it ⟨sc. 'A king is sitting down'⟩ ought not to be granted by me, but I would still grant it however often it was proposed. And if someone says:

> You grant it, and it ought not to be granted by you but doubted; therefore you reply incorrectly,

I reply by denying the premiss as before when it is proposed as a conjunction. But when it is proposed in the form of categorical propositions, I grant ⟨them⟩. Finally I grant that I reply incorrectly, not because it is true but because it follows.

⟨4⟩ Fourth argument against rule nine:

> Something irrelevant and false is relevant as following or as inconsistent, but everything which follows should be granted, and everything inconsistent should be denied; therefore one should not always reply to an irrelevant proposition in accordance with its status.

The inference holds and the premiss can be proved. I posit this to you:

> Every human being is in Rome and every proposition is irrelevant to the *positum* and *obligatum*.

Then I propose to you:

> Every human being is in Rome,

which is to be A. It is granted. Then:

> A is either the *positum obligatum* or it follows.

This is granted because it is true and irrelevant. Then:

> A should be granted by you.

This is granted because it follows. Then I argue like this: if no *obligatio* had been produced, A would have to be denied because it is false. It should now be granted, therefore it should be granted only on account of the *positum*. But no falsehood should be granted on account of the *positum* unless it follows; therefore this proposition follows. But every proposition is irrelevant to the *positum obligatum*; therefore an irrelevant and false proposition does follow. Therefore etc.

I reply by admitting ⟨the case⟩ and granting that A is either the *positum obligatum* or it follows, and that it should be granted. But I deny that A is false as inconsistent. This is a valid inference:

> A est concedendum et omnis propositio est impertinens obligato[18], igitur A est propositio vera.

Item, nego quod si nulla obligatio foret, ista esset neganda tamquam repugnans. Sequitur enim:

> A est concedendum et omnis propositio est impertinens posito obligato, igitur si nulla obligatio foret A esset concedendum, et per consequens non esset negandum.

Si tamen primo proponatur

> A est falsum,

conceditur tamquam verum et[19] impertinens. Deinde:

> A est positum obligatum aut[20] sequens vel concedendum.

Nego quodlibet ipsorum[21] tamquam repugnans, quia sequitur

> Quaelibet propositio est impertinens posito obligato et A est falsum, igitur est a te negandum, et per consequens non est[22] concedendum nec positum obligatum aut (188rbE) sequens.

⟨5⟩ Quinto principaliter arguitur contra regulam. Et pono tibi istam:

> Omnis propositio praeter istam 'Tu es Romae' est impertinens posito obligato,

quae sit C. Deinde:

> Tantum C est tibi positum obligatum.

Concedenda est, quia vera et impertinens. Deinde:

> Tu es Romae.

Vel est concedenda vel neganda. Si neganda, contra:

> Illa est falsa possibilis non impertinens nec repugnans, igitur sequens vel positum obligatum; et omne tale est concedendum, igitur haec est concedenda.

Si dicatur quod est concedenda, contra:

> Ista est falsa et non sequens, igitur neganda.

Antecedens patet quoniam non sequitur

> Omnis propositio praeter istam 'Tu es Romae' est impertinens posito

---

[18] obligato . . . impertinens]*om*.M
[19] et]*om*.E
[20] aut]autem E
[21] ipsorum]istorum E
[22] est]*om*.E

A should be granted and every proposition is irrelevant to the *obligatum*; therefore A is a true proposition.

Likewise I deny that if there were no *obligatio* ⟨A⟩ would have to be denied, as inconsistent. This is a valid inference:

A should be granted and every proposition is irrelevant to the *positum obligatum*; therefore ⟨even⟩ if there were no *obligatio* A ought to be granted, and consequently A ought not to be denied.

However, if

A is false

were proposed first, it would be granted as true and irrelevant. Then:

A is the *positum obligatum* or it follows or it should be granted.

I deny each of these as inconsistent, because this is a valid inference:

Every proposition is irrelevant to the *positum obligatum* and A is false, therefore it should be denied by you and consequently it ought not to be granted, nor is it the *positum obligatum*, nor does it follow.

⟨5⟩ Fifth argument against rule nine. I posit this to you:

Every proposition except 'You are in Rome' is irrelevant to the *positum obligatum*,

which is to be C. Then:

Only C is the *positum obligatum*.

This should be granted because it is true and irrelevant. Then:

You are in Rome.

Either this should be granted or it should be denied. If ⟨you say⟩ it should be denied, I argue against ⟨you⟩:

This is a possible false proposition which is neither irrelevant nor inconsistent; therefore either it follows or it is the *positum obligatum*; and all such propositions should be granted; therefore this should be granted.

If you say that it should be granted, I argue against you:

This is false and does not follow; therefore it should be denied.

The premiss is obvious because this is not a valid inference:

Every proposition except 'You are in Rome' is irrelevant to the *positum*

obligato, igitur tu es Romae.

Confirmatur:

> Ante casum fuit neganda et ex casu non sequitur quod sit concedenda, igitur adhuc est neganda.

Consequentia tenet et antecedens probatur, quoniam non sequitur:

> Omnis propositio praeter illam 'Tu es Romae' est impertinens posito obligato, igitur 'Tu es Romae' est concedenda,

quia cum toto antecedente staret quod

> Tu es Romae

esset repugnans posito obligato. Quare[23] etc.

Respondetur admittendo positum. Et cum primo proponitur

> Tantum C est positum obligatum,

concedo[24]. Deinde:

> Tu es Romae.

Nego[25], quia est[26] falsa et non sequens. Et tunc ad argumentum

> Illa[27] est falsa possibilis non impertinens nec repugnans, igitur sequens,

concedo consequentiam et consequens, et consequenter concedo quod

> Tu es Romae

est concedendum. Et tunc ad argumentum

> Non sequitur 'Omnis propositio praeter istam "Tu es Romae" est impertinens, igitur tu es Romae'

dico quod si mihi proponitur ista consequentia nego eam, et concedo ipsam[28] esse bonam quia sequens est ipsam esse bonam. Nam sequitur:

> Tantum C est tibi positum obligatum et ista, videlicet 'Tu es Romae', est sequens ex posito obligato[29], igitur illa consequentia est bona.

Si tamen primo proponitur[30]

> 'Tu es Romae' est sequens,

nego. Deinde:

> 'Tu es Romae' est repugnans.

Concedo[31] quia sequens[32]. Sequitur enim:

---

[23] Quare]*om.*E
[24] concedo]concedendo M
[25] Nego]neganda est M
[26] est]*om.*M
[27] Illa . . . argumentum]*om.*M
[28] ipsam]istam E
[29] obligato]*om.*M
[30] proponitur]proponatur E
[31] Concedo]concedendo M
[32] sequens]sequitur M

obligatum; therefore you are in Rome.

A supporting argument:

Before the case was stated it ⟨sc. 'You are in Rome'⟩ should have been denied, and it does not follow from the case that it should be granted; therefore it should still be denied.

The inference holds and the premiss can be proved because

Every proposition except 'You are in Rome' is irrelevant to the *positum obligatum*; therefore 'You are in Rome' should be granted

is an invalid inference because it is consistent with the complete premiss that

You are in Rome

should be inconsistent with the *positum obligatum*. Therefore etc.

I reply by admitting the *positum*. And when

Only C is the *positum obligatum*

is proposed first, I grant it. Then:

You are in Rome.

I deny it because it is false and does not follow. ⟨In reply⟩ to the argument

This is a possible false proposition which is neither irrelevant nor inconsistent; therefore it follows,

I grant the inference and the conclusion, and as a result I grant that

You are in Rome

should be granted. ⟨In reply⟩ to the argument

'Every proposition except "You are in Rome" is irrelevant; therefore you are in Rome' is an invalid inference

I say that if this inference is proposed to me I will reject it, and I will grant that it is valid, because it follows that it is valid. This is a valid inference:

Only C is the *positum obligatum* and this, namely 'You are in Rome', follows from the *positum obligatum*; therefore the above inference is valid.

However if

'You are in Rome' follows

is proposed first, I deny it. Then:

'You are in Rome' is inconsistent.

I grant it because it follows. This is a valid inference:

Tantum C est positum et omnis propositio praeter illam est impertinens, et ista non est sequens, igitur est repugnans.

Si tamen antequam proponatur[33] ista

 Tantum C est positum obligatum

proponatur

 'Tu es Romae' est sequens

vel

 'Tu es Romae' est repugnans,

utrumque est negandum. (230^{vb}M) Deinde

 Tantum C est positum obligatum

negatur, quia tunc est sequens quod

 Tu es Romae

est positum obligatum. Quare etc.

⟨*Contra Regulam Decimam*⟩

Decima regula est ista. Omne falsum non sequens scitum esse tale infra tempus obligationis est negandum et omne verum non repugnans concedendum.

Et licet argumenta contra aliam regulam militent contra istam, tamen adhuc in speciali arguo pluribus mediis valentibus ad utramque, quia non potest fieri argumentum contra istam regulam quod non sit contra aliam et e contra.

⟨1⟩ Arguo ergo primo sic. Sit rei veritas quod unum A sit omne A et[34] quod sit ista

 Tu curris.

Deinde pono tibi istam sic quod nihil aliud ponatur tibi,

 A est concedendum a te,

quae sit B; et C eius contradictorium. Tunc proponatur B. Si conceditur[35], contra:

---

[33] proponatur]proponetur E
[34] et]*om.*E
[35] conceditur]concedatur M

Only C is the *positum* ⟨*obligatum*⟩ and every proposition except this one is irrelevant, and this does not follow; therefore it is inconsistent.
However, if before
   Only C is the *positum obligatum*
was proposed, either
   'You are in Rome' follows
or
   'You are in Rome' is inconsistent
was proposed, each should be denied. Then:
   Only C is the *positum obligatum*
is denied, because then it follows that:
   You are in Rome
is the *positum obligatum*. Therefore etc.

⟨*Against Rule Ten*⟩
The tenth rule is this: Every false proposition which does not follow and is known to be such should be denied during the period of the *obligatio*; and every true proposition which is not inconsistent should be granted.

Although the arguments against the other rule ⟨sc. rule nine⟩ serve against this one, I will still argue ⟨against it⟩ in particular by offering a number of two-pronged arguments which can be used against both rules, for one cannot produce an argument against this rule which will not work against the other, and vice versa.

⟨1⟩ First argument against rule ten. Let it be true in fact that one A is every A, and that A is this:
   You are running.
Then I posit this to you in such a way that nothing else is posited to you:
   A should be granted by you,
which is to be B; and C is its contradictory.[82] Then let B be proposed. If you grant it, I argue against you:

---

[82] This sophism, without the letters B and C, is found in Strode, op.cit., fols. 82vb–83rb. Paul follows Strode's text fairly closely.

Nullum falsum non sequens est a te concedendum, sed omne A est falsum et[36] non sequens, igitur nullum A est a te concedendum,

quod est C, oppositum B. Consequentia patet[37] cum maiori, et minorem probo quia non sequitur

A est a te concedendum, igitur tu curris,

nec potest negari B quia positum et admissum[38].

Respondetur admittendo casum; et ulterius dico quod A sequitur ex B. Contra: non sequitur

A est concedendum a te, igitur tu curris.

Dico quod argumentum est bonum, quia sequitur ex casu illam consequentiam esse bonam. Non tamen concedo consequentiam istam, sicut in casu concederem illam consequentiam esse bonam

Deus est, igitur homo est asinus,

numquam tamen concederem istam. Si autem dematur illa particula quod nihil aliud tibi ponatur, admitto casum et nego quod A est[39] falsum et non sequens.

Et si dicitur 'Pro qua parte?' non respondeo quousque proponantur mihi partes sigillatim. Quod si fiet, primam primo loco propositam concedam et secundam negabo, quia[40] si statim post istam

A est falsum et non sequens

proponatur

A est non[41] sequens,

conceditur; et ista

A est falsum,

negatur. Illa enim non stant simul

A est concedendum a te et non est sequens et tamen est falsum.

Si autem primo loco proponatur

A est falsum,

respondeatur sicut dictum est; et hoc communiter contingit de copulativa facta ex duobus[42] contingentibus veris et impertinentibus repugnante[43].

---

[36] et]*om*.E
[37] patet]tenet E
[38] et admissum]*om*.E
[39] est]sit E
[40] quia]ut E
[41] est non]*transp*.E
[42] duobus]duabus E
[43] repugnante]repugnantibus   E

No false proposition which does not follow should be granted by you, but every A is a false proposition which does not follow; therefore no A ought to be granted by you,

but ⟨this conclusion⟩ is C, the opposite of B. The inference is obvious, as is the major premiss; and I can prove the minor premiss, because

A should be granted by you; therefore you are running

is an invalid inference. Nor can B be denied, because it is the *positum* and *admissum*.

I reply by admitting the case, and I say further that A follows from B. One can argue against this by saying that

A should be granted by you; therefore you are running

is an invalid inference. I say that the argument is valid, because it follows from the case that this inference is valid. I do not, however, grant the inference itself, just as given a certain case I might grant that this inference

There is a God; therefore a human being is a donkey

is valid, although I would never grant ⟨the inference itself⟩. However, if the stipulation that nothing else was posited to you is removed, I grant the case, and I deny that A is false and does not follow.

And if someone says 'On account of which clause?' I do not reply until the clauses are proposed to me separately. If this is done, I grant the first which is proposed in the first place and I deny the second. If immediately after

A is false and does not follow,

A does not follow

is proposed, I grant it; and this:

A is false

is denied. These propositions are not mutually consistent:

A should be granted by you and it does not follow and yet it is false.

But if

A is false

were proposed in the first place, one should reply in the way described. This commonly happens in the case of a conjunction which is formulated from two irrelevant contingent truths and which is itself inconsistent ⟨with what

Eodem modo dico de disiunctiva eius opposita, unde pars primo loco proposita est neganda et secunda concedenda. (188ᵛᵃE)

Concesso igitur quod A est sequens, contra:

Non sequitur ex tibi posito.

Nego. Probo. Non sequitur

'Tu curris' est a te concedendum, igitur tu curris.

Concedo; et ulterius concedo[44]

Non sequitur quin sequatur[45] ex posito.

Illa enim consequentia non valet:

A non sequitur ex isto antecedente, et illud antecedens est tibi positum, igitur A non sequitur ex tibi posito.

Arguitur enim ab inferiori ad suum superius[46], negatione praeposita[47].

Et si dicatur 'Quis est ille alius casus tibi positus?' dicatur quod stat quod sit A vel B. Haec[48] non est determinanda quaestio.

Sed forte quis posset variare casum et ordinem proponendi sic. Pono quod tantum illa

Tu curris

sit a te concedenda, quae sit quodlibet A. Qua admissa, tunc proponitur tibi

Tu curris.

Si[49] conceditur, cedat tempus et ostenditur quod in rei veritate A fuit falsum non sequens, igitur non concedenda. Negata ideo[50] ista

Tu curris,

cum proponitur infra tempus; contra:

Tu negas A et A est a te concedendum, igitur male respondes.

Negatur copulativa antecedens. Et si quaeritur pro qua parte, dicatur quod[51] pro prima ex quo secunda sequitur ex casu. Si tamen primo proponitur consequens, negatur quia falsum et non (231ʳᵃM) sequens. Et similiter negatur[52] ista

Tu negas A

quia repugnans, licet in rei veritate sit vera. Similiter e converso si primo loco proponitur prima pars illius copulativae, conceditur consequenter quod

---

[44] concedo]*om.* E
[45] sequatur]sequitur E
[46] superius]propositam *add.* M
[47] praeposita]*om.* M
[48] Haec]hic E
[49] Si conceditur]*om.* M,E *Add.* M² *in marg.*
[50] ideo]igitur E
[51] quod]*om.* E
[52] similiter negatur]consimiliter negetur M

precedes it⟩. I say the same about the disjunction opposite to this conjunction ⟨sc. the disjunction formed from the negated conjuncts⟩. Here the clause proposed in the first place should be denied, and the second should be granted.

Having granted that A follows, one can argue against this:

It does not follow from a *positum*.

I deny ⟨this claim⟩. Proof: this is an invalid inference:

'You are running' should be granted by you; therefore you are running.

I grant this; and further I grant

It does not follow unless it follows from a *positum*.

⟨However,⟩ this inference is not valid:

A does not follow from this premiss, and this premiss was a *positum*;
therefore A does not follow from a *positum*,

because it argues from an inferior term ⟨sc. 'premiss'⟩ to its superior ⟨sc. '*positum*'⟩, with a negation preceding.

And if someone says 'What other case was it that was posited to you?', one can say that it could be A or B. This question is not to be settled.

But perhaps someone might vary the case and the order of proposing like this. I posit that only this

You are running

should be granted by you, and that this proposition is to be every A. When it has been admitted, then

You are running

is proposed to you. If it is granted, let the period come to an end, and it will be shown that in fact A was a false proposition which did not follow; therefore it ought not to have been granted. But when

You are running

is denied when it is proposed during the period of the *obligatio*, one can argue against this denial:

You deny A and A should be granted by you; therefore you reply incorrectly.

The conjunctive premiss is denied, and if someone asks on account of which clause, one should say on account of the first, because the second follows from the stated case. However if the conclusion is proposed first, it is denied because it is false and does not follow. And similarly

You deny A

is denied, because it is inconsistent, although it is true in fact that it is true. Similarly ⟨one can argue⟩ the converse. If the first clause of that conjunction is

concluditur, scilicet quod male respondes ut sequens, licet sit falsum.

⟨2⟩ Secundo principaliter arguitur sic. Et[53] pono quod concedas primum propositum a me post istud positum. Si non admittitur, contra:

> Casus est scitus a te esse possibilis, igitur per primam regulam est admittendus.

Poteris enim sicut constat concedere qualemcumque propositionem quae proponetur a me sive fuerit possibilis sive impossibilis.

Admisso ergo casu, propono:

> Tu male respondes.

Si concedis, cedat tempus et arguitur quod infra tempus concessisti falsum non sequens, igitur male respondisti vel regula[54] non est vera. Non enim sequitur

> Tu concedis primum propositum aut[55] proponendum a me, igitur male respondes.

Similiter arguitur si dubitatur[56]. Si negatur ergo quod[57] male respondes, proponitur:

> Hoc est primum propositum a me post illud positum.

Conceditur quia verum et[58] non repugnans. Deinde arguitur:

> Tu negas istam et illa est primum propositum a me post positum, igitur negas primum propositum a me post positum et concedis primum propositum a me per casum; igitur idem concedis et negas et infra idem tempus obligationis et in una obligatione; igitur male respondes,

quod erat negatum, etc.

Respondetur ut prius donec proponitur

> Tu negas istam,

quod negatur[59]. Tamen quandocumque proponitur mihi illud primo propositum[60], scilicet

> Tu male respondes,

negatur et nego me negare istam quia repugnans. Sed si proponitur

> Tu concedis eam,

---

[53] Et]*om.*M
[54] regula]secunda E
[55] aut]vel E
[56] dubitatur]dubitetur E
[57] quod]*om.*E
[58] et]*om.*E
[59] negatur tamen]*transp.*E
[60] primo propositum]post positum E

proposed in the first place, one should consequently grant the conclusion, namely that you reply incorrectly, as following even though it is false.

⟨2⟩ Second argument against rule ten. I posit that you grant the first proposition proposed by me after this *positum*.[83] If you do not admit this, I argue against you:

>The case is known by you to be possible; therefore it should be admitted in accordance with the first rule.

As is agreed, you are able to grant any proposition which is proposed by me, whether it was possible or impossible.

Thus when the case has been admitted, I propose:

>You reply incorrectly.

If you grant it, let the period of the *obligatio* come to an end. I argue that during the period you granted a false proposition which did not follow; therefore you replied incorrectly, or the rule is not true. This is not a valid inference:

>You grant the first proposition proposed or to be proposed by me; therefore you reply incorrectly.

I argue similarly if you doubt it. If you therefore deny that you reply incorrectly, I propose:

>This is the first proposition proposed by me after that *positum*.

This is granted because it is true and not inconsistent. Then I argue:

>You deny this, and this is the first proposition proposed by me after the *positum*; therefore you deny the first proposition proposed by me after the *positum*. But according to the stated case you grant the first proposition proposed by me; therefore you grant and deny the same proposition during the same period of *obligatio* and in one *obligatio*; therefore you reply incorrectly.

But this ⟨conclusion⟩ was denied above.

I reply as above until

>You deny this

is proposed. I deny it. However, whenever the proposition which was first proposed to me, namely

>You reply incorrectly

is proposed, I deny it and I deny that I deny it, because this ⟨sc. 'I deny "You reply incorrectly"'⟩ is inconsistent. But if

>You grant it

---

[83] This sophism is found in Strode, op.cit., fol. 83^(rb)–^(va). Paul follows Strode's text very closely.

concedo, quia quod concedo illam sequitur ex posito obligato cum bene concesso. Sequitur enim

> Tu concedis primum propositum a me, sed hoc est primum propositum a me, igitur tu concedis illam.

Et si dicitur

> Tu negas proprium actum dum proponitur illa infra tempus,

negatur, nam cum concedo me concedere quod male respondeo, non nego proprium actum, quia me negare illam

> Tu male respondes

repugnat. Si tamen dicatur

> Cedat tempus,

et proponitur

> Infra tempus negasti actum tuum proprium,

conceditur[61]; nec hoc[62] est inconveniens dummodo sequitur[63], sicut pluries est recitatum.

⟨3⟩ Tertio principaliter arguitur sic. Et pono tibi istam

> 'Tu curris' est vera et impertinens.

Qua admissa, propono tibi illam

> Tu curris.

Si concedis eam[64], cedat tempus, et arguo quod tu concessisti falsum non sequens, igitur male, vel regula[65] est falsa. Quod autem ista sit falsa patet, et quod non sit sequens probatur, quia[66] non sequitur

> 'Tu curris' est vera et impertinens, igitur tu curris,

nam oppositum consequentis stat cum antecedente, secundum quod alias declaratum est. Si ergo[67] negas istam

> Tu curris,

contra:

> Ista est vera et impertinens, ergo non est a te neganda, et tu negas eam, ergo male.

Respondetur admittendo positum, et cum proponitur

---

[61] conceditur]igitur M
[62] hoc]haec M
[63] sequitur]sequatur M
[64] eam]*om*.E
[65] regula]secunda E
[66] quia]nam E
[67] ergo]vero E

is proposed, I grant this because that I grant it ⟨sc. 'I grant "You reply incorrectly"'⟩ follows from the *positum obligatum* together with a correctly granted proposition. This is a valid inference:

> You grant the first proposition proposed by me, but this is the first proposition proposed by me; therefore you grant it.

And if someone says

> You deny your own action when it is proposed during the period,

I deny this, for when I grant that I grant that I reply incorrectly, I do not deny my own action, because for me to deny

> You reply incorrectly

is inconsistent. However, if someone were to say

> Let the period come to an end,

and then propose

> During the period you denied your own action,

I would grant this. Nor is ⟨my denial⟩ awkward so long as it follows, as I have explained many times.

⟨3⟩ Third argument against rule ten. I posit this to you:

> 'You are running' is true and irrelevant.

When this has been admitted, I propose this to you:

> You are running.

If you grant it, let the period come to an end and I will argue that you granted a false proposition which did not follow; therefore either you replied incorrectly or the rule is false. That the ⟨proposition⟩ is false is obvious, and that it does not follow can be proved, for this is not a valid inference:

> 'You are running' is true and irrelevant; therefore you are running.

The opposite of the conclusion is consistent with the premiss, in accordance with what I have explained elsewhere. If you therefore deny:

> You are running

I argue against you:

> This is true and irrelevant; therefore it ought not to be denied by you, and you deny it; therefore you reply incorrectly.

I reply by admitting the *positum* and when

> Tu curris,

nego eam, et cum dicitur

> Est vera et impertinens, igitur non est neganda,

concedo[68] consequentiam et consequens. Et ulterius:

> Tu negas eam.

Concedo.

> Tu male respondes.

concedo[69] tamquam sequens. Si tamen in principio proponatur

> Tu male respondes,

nego quia falsum et impertinens. Deinde:

> Tu negas illam 'Tu curris'.

Nego quia repugnans. Sequitur enim

> Ista non est a te neganda et non male respondes, igitur non negas eam.

⟨4⟩ Quarto arguitur sic. Et pono quod quandocumque A ponitur a parte subiecti alicuius propositionis quod illa propositio sit vera, et quandocumque B ponitur a parte praedicati quod (188^{vb}E) illa propositio sit falsa. Isto admisso, propono tibi[70]

> A est B,

quod sit C; et quaero utrum C sit verum vel falsum. Si verum, probo quod est falsum, quia quandocumque ponitur B a parte (231^{rb}M) praedicati illa propositio est falsa, sed in C, B ponitur a parte praedicati, igitur C est falsum. Si vero conceditur quod C est falsum, contra: quandocumque in aliqua propositione ponitur A a parte subiecti ista propositio est vera, sed in C ponitur A a parte subiecti, igitur C propositio est vera, quod erat negatum. Oportet ergo dicere quod C nec[71] est concedendum nec negandum, et tamen est propositio non sequens, igitur ad ipsam non est respondendum secundum sui qualitatem.

Dicendum admittendo casum non de virtute sermonis sed gratia disputationis, et cum proponitur C, quaerendo[72] utrum sit verum aut falsum, nego C et dico ipsum esse falsum ex quo non est facta mentio de significatione A

---

[68] concedo]concedendo M
[69] concedo]concedendo M
[70] tibi]*om.*E
[71] nec]non E
[72] quaerendo]*om.*E

    You are running

is proposed, I deny it. And when someone says

    It is true and irrelevant; therefore it ought not to be denied,

I grant the inference and the conclusion. And further:

    You deny it.

I grant this.

    You reply incorrectly.

I grant this as following. However, if

    You reply incorrectly

were proposed at the beginning, I would deny it because it is false and irrelevant. Then:

    You deny 'You are running'.

I deny this because it is inconsistent. This is a valid inference:

    This ought not to be denied by you, and you do not reply incorrectly; therefore you do not deny it.

⟨4⟩ Fourth argument against rule ten. I posit that whenever A is put as the subject of some proposition, that proposition is true, and whenever B is put as the predicate, the proposition is false. When this has been admitted, I propose to you:

    A is B,

which is C. I ask whether C is true or false. If it is true, I can prove that it is false, because whenever B is put as the predicate, that proposition is false; but in C, B is put as the predicate; therefore C is false. However, if you grant that C is false, I argue against you. Whenever A is put as the subject in some proposition, that proposition is true, but in C, A was put as the subject; therefore the proposition C is true, which was denied above. Therefore one must say that C should neither be granted nor denied. But it is a proposition which does not follow; therefore one does not have to reply to it in accordance with its status.

One can reply by admitting the case, not as taken literally, but for the sake of the disputation. When C is proposed, and it is asked whether it is true or false, I deny C, and I state that it is false on the grounds that no mention has been made of the signification of A or of B. ⟨In reply⟩ to the argument I deny

vel B. Et tunc ad argumentum nego quod in C a parte subiecti ponatur A, tamquam repugnans. Sequitur enim:

    Quandocumque in aliqua propositione ponitur[73] A[74] a parte subiecti illa propositio est vera, sed C propositio est falsa, igitur in C propositione non ponitur A.

Et si quaeritur quod est subiectum C propositionis, dico quod stat quod[75] A vel B. Talis quaestio non est determinanda usque ad finem obligationis.

    Item si antequam quaeratur[76] an C sit verum vel falsum, proponatur
    Subiectum C est ly .A.,

conceditur, et consequenter quod C est verum. Et si proponitur ulterius

    Praedicatum C est ly .B.,

negatur tamquam repugnans. Unde[77] cum adiutorio positi sequitur[78]

    Subiectum C est ly .A., igitur est verum, igitur non est[79] falsum, igitur praedicatum eius non est B.

Si tamen primo proponeretur

    Praedicatum[80] C est ly .B.,

concederetur tamquam verum et impertinens et negaretur[81] consequenter quod subiectum C est ly[82] .A..

    Ex praedictis potest solvi una obligatio communis, videlicet

    Pono quod quandocumque A ponitur a parte subiecti illa propositio sit[83] vera, et quandocumque ponitur a parte praedicati ista propositio sit[84] falsa.

Deinde capitur talis propositio

    A est Sortes,

quae sit B, et proponitur[85]

    Subiectum B est A.

Conceditur tamquam verum et impertinens. Deinde:

    B est verum.

Conceditur tamquam sequens. Deinde proponitur:

    Sortes est A,

---

[73] ponitur] *om.* E
[74] A] est *add.* E
[75] quod] *om.* E
[76] quaeratur] proponatur M,E, *correxi*
[77] Unde] *om.* E
[78] sequitur] enim *add.* E
[79] est] *om.* E
[80] Praedicatum] Subiectum M,E, *correxi*
[81] negaretur] negatur E
[82] ly] *om.* E
[83] sit] est E
[84] sit] est E
[85] proponitur] proponatur E

as inconsistent ⟨the claim⟩ that A was put as the subject in C. This is a valid inference:

> Whenever A is put as the subject of some proposition, that proposition is true, but the proposition C is false; therefore A is not put ⟨as subject⟩ in the proposition C.

And if someone asks what is the subject of the proposition C, I say that it might be A or B. This question should not be settled until the end of the *obligatio*.

Likewise if

> The subject of C is the expression 'A'

were proposed before it was asked whether C was true or false, it would be granted, and consequently ⟨it would be granted⟩ that C is true. And if someone proposes further:

> The predicate of C is the expression 'B',

this is denied as inconsistent. With the help of the *positum*, this is a valid inference.

> The subject of C is the expression 'A', therefore C is true; therefore C is not false; therefore the predicate of C is not B.

However if

> The predicate of C is the expression 'B'

were proposed first, it would be granted as true and irrelevant, and as a result it would be denied that the subject of C is the expression 'A'.

From what has been said above, one can solve a common *obligatio*, namely

> I posit that whenever A is put as the subject ⟨of some proposition⟩, that proposition is true, and whenever it is put as the predicate, that proposition is false.[84]

Then one takes a proposition such as this:

> A is Socrates,

which is B, and proposes

> The subject of B is A.

This is granted as true and irrelevant. Then:

> B is true.

This is granted as following. Then:

> Socrates is A

---

[84] I have not found this sophism elsewhere, though there is a somewhat similar one in Strode, op.cit., fols. 91vb–92ra. First he posited that when A was subject it signified 'human being' and when A was predicate it signified 'donkey'. Then he proposed: 'A is a human being'. Then he raised the problem of conversion.

et quaeritur utrum sit verum vel falsum. Dato quod concessum sit suum praedicatum esse A, dico quod B est falsum. Contra:

    A est Sortes, igitur Sortes est A.

Ista consequentia est bona et antecedens est verum, igitur et consequens. Dicitur concesso quod illa est antecedens

    A est Sortes,

et ista, consequens

    Sortes est A,

negando[86] istam consequentiam esse bonam quia repugnat. Sequitur enim

    Antecedens est verum et consequens falsum, igitur ista consequentia non valet ad bonum intellectum.

Et si dicitur quod[87] ista est conversio simplex, nego propter repugnantiam. Contra:

    Ibi de subiecto fit praedicatum et de praedicato subiectum, manente eadem quantitate et qualitate, igitur est conversio simplex.

Nego antecedens. Et si dicitur 'Pro qua parte?' dico quod proponantur partes et bene numerentur, et omnes[88] praeter ultimam concedantur[89] quia repugnat illis et prioribus concessis. Quare etc.

⟨5⟩ Quinto ad principale arguitur sic.

    Aliqua est propositio non sequens in obligatione positionis quae non est concedenda, neganda[90] nec dubitanda, igitur regula falsa.

Antecedens probatur. Et pono quod Sortes concedat illam

    Deus est,

et Plato neget illam[91] et Cicero dubitet eam, et[92] quod omne concedens illam bene respondeat, et quod[93] omne negans aut dubitans eam male respondeat. Et sumo istam propositionem

    Ille male respondet,

quae sit A, et demonstro per ly .ille. in illa propositione

    Ille male respondet,

illum qui totaliter respondet ad illam

---

[86] negando]concedo E
[87] quod]*om*.M
[88] et omnes]*om*.E
[89] concedantur]ultima conceditur E
[90] neganda]*om*.M
[91] illam]*om*.E
[92] et . . . respondeat]*om*.E
[93] quod]*om*.M

is proposed, and one asks whether it is true or false. Given that it was granted that its predicate is A, I say that B is false. One can argue against this:

A is Socrates; therefore Socrates is A.

This inference is valid and the premiss is true; therefore the conclusion is also true. One can reply, having granted that

A is Socrates

is the premiss and

Socrates is A

is the conclusion, by denying as inconsistent ⟨the claim⟩ that the inference is valid. This is a valid inference:

> The premiss is true and the conclusion is false; therefore this inference is not valid when correctly understood.

If someone says that it is an example of simple conversion, I deny this because it is inconsistent. One can argue against this:

> ⟨In the example⟩ the subject becomes the predicate and the predicate the subject, while the proposition retains its quantity and quality; therefore it is ⟨a case of⟩ simple conversion.

I deny the premiss. And if someone says 'On account of which clause?', I say that the clauses should be proposed and counted, and all except the last may be granted. The last is inconsistent with the others together with propositions granted earlier. Therefore etc.

⟨5⟩ Fifth argument against rule ten.

> Some proposition exists in an *obligatio* of the *positio* type which does not follow and which ought not to be granted, denied or doubted; therefore the rule is false.

Proof of the premiss. I posit that Socrates grants this:

There is a God,

and Plato denies it and Cicero doubts it, and that everyone who grants it replies correctly, while everyone who denies or doubts it replies incorrectly.[85]
I take this proposition:

He replies incorrectly

which is A, and by the word 'he' in the proposition

He replies incorrectly

I indicate the one who replies to

---

[85] For this sophism, see Fland, op.cit., p. 46, §21. Cf. Peter of Mantua, op.cit., sig.G iiii^ra. Paul's treatment is different.

Deus est

sicut tu respondes ad A. Isto posito, patet quod A est non sequens (231^{va}M) et quod non sit concedenda, neganda, nec dubitanda. Probatur. Et propono tibi A. Si dubitetur, contra:

> Tu scis quod nullus similiter respondet ad illam 'Deus est' sicut tu respondes ad A nisi Cicero, et Cicero male respondet, igitur tu male respondes.

Si negas[94] eam, arguitur similiter de Platone. Si autem concedis eam, igitur respondes consimiliter ad istam sicut Sortes ad illam

> Deus est.

Sed Sortes bene respondet, igitur tu bene respondes et solum concedis illam

> Ille male respondet,[95]

et per ly .ille. demonstratur Sortes, igitur Sortes male respondet, quod est oppositum positi[96]. Quare etc.

Ad istud respondetur negando consequentiam in principio factam, sed oportuit sic argui

> Aliqua est propositio falsa non sequens vel vera non repugnans non concedenda, neganda, nec dubitanda, igitur oppositum regulae.

Unde talem propositionem

> Ille male respondet,

ex quo est impertinens debet responderi (189^{ra}E) sicut extra. Sed extra non concederetur nec negaretur nec dubitaretur nec distingueretur quousque non[97] diceretur quid demonstratur per ly[98] .ille.; igitur sic in proposito debet responderi. Cum ergo proponitur

> Ille male respondet,

quaero quid demonstres[99] per ly .ille., et si dicitur quod demonstro istum etc. sicut prius, et ego respondeo tibi sicut ille quem demonstras, ita quod numquam respondeatur concedendo, negando, nec dubitando quousque non fuerit certificatum quid demonstratur per ly .ille.. Tamen gratia disputationis ad remittendum clamorem opponentis[1], potest A dubitari. Et tunc[2] ad

---

[94] negas]neges E
[95] Ille . . . respondet]tu male respondes M
[96] positi]oppositi M,E, *correxi*
[97] non]*om*.E
[98] ly]*om*.M
[99] demonstres]demonstratur E
[1] opponentis]oppositis E
[2] tunc]*om*.E

There is a God

in exactly the same way as you reply to A. When this has been posited, it is obvious that A does not follow, and that it ought not to be granted, denied, or doubted. Proof: I propose A to you. If you doubt it, I argue against you:

> You know that no one except Cicero replies to the proposition 'There is a God' in the way that you reply to A, and Cicero replies incorrectly; therefore you reply incorrectly.

If you deny it, I present a similar argument about Plato. But if you grant it, then you reply to A in the same way as Socrates replies to

There is a God.

But Socrates replies correctly; therefore you reply correctly. The only thing you grant is:

He replies incorrectly,

and the word 'he' indicates Socrates. Therefore Socrates replies incorrectly, which is the opposite of the *positum*. Therefore etc.

I reply to this by denying the inference which was constructed at the beginning. One ought to have argued like this:

> There is some false proposition which does not follow or some true proposition which is not inconsistent, and which ought not to be granted, denied or doubted. Therefore the opposite of the rule ⟨holds⟩.

From this it follows that a proposition such as

He replies incorrectly

should be replied to as it would be replied to outside ⟨the period of the *obligatio*⟩, because it is irrelevant. But outside ⟨the period⟩ it would not be granted, or denied, or doubted, or made the subject of a distinction, until someone had said who was indicated by the word 'he'. Therefore one ought to reply like this in the proposed case. Therefore when

He replies incorrectly

is proposed, I ask who you indicate by the word 'he'. If you say 'I indicate he who etc.', as before, and I reply to you in the way adopted by the person you indicate, then I shall never ⟨be able to⟩ reply by granting, denying or doubting until I have been satisfied about who is indicated by the word 'he'. However, for the sake of the disputation and to gain relief from the opponent's shouting, one can doubt A. And then in reply to the argument, after I have

argumentum concessis illis partibus sigillatim concedam³ tamquam⁴ sequens quod male respondeo.

⟨*Contra Regulam Undecimam*⟩
Undecima regula fuit ista. Possibili obligato licet falso non propter hoc est negandum necessarium per se nec est concedendum impossibile per se.
⟨1⟩ Contra istam regulam arguitur sic. Et pono tibi istam
    'Homo est asinus' est tibi positum obligatum.
Qua admissa, arguo sic.
    Ex isto possibili posito est concedendum impossibile, igitur regula falsa.
Antecedens arguo sic. Et propono tibi illam
    Homo est asinus.
Si concedis et bene respondes, habeo intentum. Si negas, contra:
    Omne positum obligatum est a te concedendum, sed 'Homo est asinus' est tibi positum obligatum, igitur 'Homo est asinus' est a te concedendum.
Et tu negas ipsum, igitur tu male respondes. Maior est regula et minor est⁵ tibi posita, igitur consequens est a te concedendum.
⟨1.1⟩ Quod si conceditur, videlicet
    'Homo est asinus' est a te concedendum,
arguo sic:
    'Homo est asinus' est a te concedendum, sed 'Homo est asinus' est impossibile per se, igitur per se impossibile est a te concedendum, et tantum possibile est tibi⁶ positum, igitur posito possibili⁷ est impossibile per se⁸ concedendum.
⟨1.2⟩ Item sic:
    'Homo est asinus' est concedendum⁹ et non nisi infra tempus obligationis, igitur¹⁰ infra tempus obligationis est concedendum; sed infra

---

³ concedam]concedatur M
⁴ tamquam sequens]*om*.M
⁵ est]*om*.M
⁶ tibi]*om*.E
⁷ possibili]positum *add*.E
⁸ per se]*om*.E
⁹ concedendum]negandum M
¹⁰ igitur . . .]*om*.M

granted all these clauses taken separately, I shall grant that I reply incorrectly as following.

⟨Against Rule Eleven⟩
The eleventh rule was this: A proposition which is necessary *per se* should not be denied because of an *obligatum* which is possible, even if it is false, nor should a proposition which is impossible *per se* be granted.
⟨1⟩ First argument against rule eleven. I posit this to you:
'A human being is a donkey' is the *positum obligatum* put to you.[86]
When this has been admitted, I argue like this:
On the basis of this possible *positum* an impossible proposition ought to be granted; therefore the rule is false.
I argue for the premiss like this. I propose this to you:
A human being is a donkey.
If you grant it and thereby reply correctly, I have made my point. If you deny it, I argue against you:
Every *positum obligatum* should be granted by you but 'A human being is a donkey' is the *positum obligatum* put to you; therefore 'A human being is a donkey' should be granted by you.
But you deny it; therefore you reply incorrectly. The major premiss is a rule, and the minor premiss is the *positum* put to you, therefore the conclusion should be granted by you.
⟨Arguments against the conclusion⟩:
⟨1.1⟩ If you grant the ⟨conclusion⟩, namely
'A human being is a donkey' should be granted by you,
I argue like this:
'A human being is a donkey' should be granted by you, but 'A human being is a donkey' is impossible *per se*; therefore a proposition which is impossible *per se* should be granted by you, and only a possible proposition was posited to you; therefore on the basis of a possible *positum* a proposition which is impossible *per se* should be granted.
⟨1.2⟩ Likewise ⟨I argue⟩ like this:
'A human being is a donkey' should be granted, and this should happen only during the period of the *obligatio*; therefore it should be granted during the period of the *obligatio*. But it should be denied during the

---

[86] For this sophism see Albert, op.cit., fol. 49vb; Buser, op.cit., fol. 76va; Marsilius, op.cit., fol. 87^{r-v}; Wyclif, op.cit., p. 73; *Lat.misc.e 79*, fol. 19va; and *Lib.Soph.Oxon.*, sig.C vi^r. The usual statement of the sophism ends with the conclusion (1.11) '"Homo est asinus" est a te concedendum'. Paul's discussion is considerably more elaborate than that found in these sources.

tempus est negandum; igitur idem est concedendum et negandum infra tempus obligationis[11].

Quod autem

    Homo est asinus

est[12] negandum infra tempus obligationis[13], probo, quia negas[14] eam infra tempus bene respondendo; sed non negas non negandum bene respondendo, igitur ista est a te neganda.

⟨1.3⟩ Item si

    Homo est asinus

est concedendum et nihil est concedendum nisi verum vel sequens, sed non est verum quia est impossibile, igitur est sequens. Et per consequens ex possibili sequitur impossibile, quod est contra Philosophum in multis locis.

⟨1.4⟩ Item si

    Homo est asinus

est concedendum infra tempus, tunc cedat tempus et arguo sic.

    'Homo est asinus' fuit concedendum infra tempus, et non concessisti illam infra tempus quando fuit proposita, igitur male respondisti.

⟨1R⟩ Ad istud solet responderi dicendo quod illa

    Homo est asinus

non est a me concedenda[15]. Et tunc ad (231^{vb}M) argumentum

    Omne tibi[16] positum obligatum est a te concedendum, sed 'Homo est asinus'

est tibi positum obligatum, igitur 'Homo est asinus' est a te concedendum, dubitatur minor, eo quod potest esse propositio posita obligata vel talis propositio sumpta sub universali propositione praedicti syllogismi. Si sit propositio posita, consequentia non valet quia non praedicatur subiectum maioris de propositione posita obligata. Sed ad hoc quod consequentia valeat oporteret[17] sic arguere:

    Omne tibi positum obligatum est a te concedendum, sed 'Homo est asinus' est tibi positum obligatum, igitur '"Homo est asinus" est positum[18] obligatum' est a te concedendum.

---

[11] . . . . obligationis]*om*.M
[12] est]sit E
[13] obligationis]*om*.E
[14] negas]negares E
[15] concedenda]neganda E
[16] tibi]*om*.E
[17] oporteret]oportet E
[18] positum . . . est]*om*.E

period; therefore the same proposition should be granted and denied during the period of the *obligatio*.

I can prove that the proposition

A human being is a donkey

should be denied during the period of the *obligatio*, because when you deny it during the period you reply correctly, but one cannot deny what ought not to be denied when one replies correctly; therefore the proposition ought to be denied by you.

⟨1.3⟩ Likewise ⟨assume that⟩

A human being is a donkey

should be granted. Nothing should be granted unless it is true or it follows; but this proposition is not true, because it is impossible, therefore it follows. As a result an impossible proposition follows from a possible proposition, which is contrary to what Aristotle said in many places.[87]

⟨1.4⟩ Likewise, if

A human being is a donkey

should be granted during the period, let the period come to an end. I argue like this:

'A human being is a donkey' should have been granted during the period, and you did not grant it during the period when it was proposed; therefore you replied incorrectly.

⟨1⟩ ⟨Reply to the main argument⟩. People are accustomed to reply by saying that

A human being is a donkey

ought not to be granted by me. And then ⟨in reply⟩ to the argument:

Every *positum obligatum* put to you should be granted by you, but 'A human being is a donkey' is the *positum obligatum* put to you; therefore 'A human being is a donkey' should be granted by you,

the minor premiss is doubted. It could be the proposition which is the *positum obligatum*, but ⟨it could also be⟩ a proposition of the sort referred to by the universal proposition ⟨which is the major premiss⟩ of the aforesaid syllogism. If it is the posited proposition, then the inference is invalid because the subject of the major premiss is not predicated of the proposition which is the *positum obligatum*. In order for the inference to be valid, one would have to argue like this:

Every *positum obligatum* put to you should be granted, but 'A human being is a donkey' is the *positum obligatum* put to you; therefore '"A human being is a donkey" is the *positum obligatum*' should be granted by you.[88]

---

[87] E.g. Aristotle, *Metaphysics* IX.4. 1047 b15–30, *Prior Analytics* I.13. 32 a18–20.
[88] This point was made by Wyclif, op.cit., p. 73, and *Lib.Soph.Oxon.*, sig.C vi^r.

Si vero minor fuerit haec propositio

    Homo est asinus,

sumpta sub universali propositione, concedenda est consequentia, sed negatur antecedens.

  Distinctio ista non est ad propositum eo quod casus ponit quod ista

    Homo est asinus

sit posita obligata.

  Item, si sit propositio posita obligata, syllogismus adhuc est[19] necessarius eo quod subiectum maioris vel sibi proportionabile praedicatur in minori, et maior extremitas praedicatur de minori in conclusione.

  Item, ponatur cum toto casu quod illa

    Homo est asinus,

sumatur sub subiecto illius universalis, quo posito stabit argumentum ut prius sine solutione.

  Ideo est aliter dicendum, negando istam

    Homo est asinus,

quotienscumque proponitur. Et tunc ad argumentum, concedo[20] quod illa est a me concedenda et quod nego eam et consequenter quod male respondeo, non tamquam verum sed quia sequens.

⟨1.1R⟩ Et tunc ad argumenta probantia quod illa non est a me concedenda, respondetur ad primum. Cum dicitur

    'Homo est asinus' est a te concedendum et 'Homo est asinus' est per se
      impossibile, igitur per se impossibile est a te concedendum,

nego minorem tamquam repugnantem. Sequitur enim

    'Homo est asinus' est a te concedendum, igitur 'Homo est asinus' non est
      per se impossibile,

sicut apparebit infra. Verumtamen concesso quod 'Homo est asinus' est per se impossibile non habetur intentum, quia nego istam:

    Tantum possibile est positum,

quia repugnat. Sequitur enim

---

[19] est]esset E
[20] concedo]concedendo M

If indeed the minor premiss was this proposition

A human being is a donkey

taken as an example of the sort referred to by the universal proposition, then the conclusion should be granted but the premiss is denied.

This distinction does not address itself to the issue, given that the case states that

A human being is a donkey

is the *positum obligatum*.

Again, if ⟨'A human being is a donkey'⟩ is the proposition which is the *positum obligatum*, the syllogism is still necessary, given that the subject of the major premiss or something analogous to it is predicated in the minor premiss and the major term is predicated of the minor in the conclusion.

Again, it is given as part of the case that

A human being is a donkey

is included under the subject-term of that universal proposition. But when this is posited the argument remains as before, without a solution.

Hence one must reply in another way, by denying

A human being is a donkey,

however often it is proposed. Then ⟨in reply⟩ to the argument I grant that it ⟨sc. 'A human being is a donkey'⟩ should be granted by me, and that I deny it and as a result ⟨I grant that⟩ I reply incorrectly, not as true but as following.

⟨1.1R⟩ Then ⟨I turn⟩ to the arguments which ⟨tried to⟩ prove that the proposition ought not to be granted by me. Reply to the first argument: When it is said,

> 'A human being is a donkey' should be granted by you, but 'A human being is a donkey' is impossible *per se*; therefore a proposition which is impossible *per se* should be granted by you,

I deny the minor premiss as inconsistent. This:

> 'A human being is a donkey' should be granted by you; therefore 'A human being is a donkey' is not impossible *per se*,

is a valid argument, as will be shown below. Nevertheless, these people do not make their point ⟨even if⟩ one grants that 'A human being is a donkey' is impossible *per se*, for I deny this:

Only a possible proposition was posited

as inconsistent. This is a valid inference:

'Homo est asinus' est per se (189^rbE) impossibile et est positum, igitur non tantum possibile est positum.

⟨1.1RO⟩ Sed forte contra istam responsionem arguitur[21] sic, ponendo quod C sit tota ista propositio:

'Homo est asinus' est tibi positum obligatum.

Tunc arguitur sic:

Tantum C est tibi positum obligatum, sed C est propositio possibilis, igitur tantum possibile est tibi positum obligatum.

Praeterea cedat tempus, et arguo sic:

Tunc nullum impossibile fuit tibi positum, igitur etc.

Antecedens probatur, quia tantum C propositio possibilis fuit tibi posita.

⟨1.1ROR⟩ Respondetur negando quod tantum C sit mihi positum tamquam repugnans. Sequitur enim.

'Homo est asinus' est tibi positum, ergo non tantum C est tibi positum.

Et cum[22] dicitur

Cedat tempus,

admitto; et nego quod

Homo est asinus

fuit mihi positum infra tempus, et concedo[23] quod tantum C fuit mihi positum infra tempus; et nego quod aliquod impossibile fuit mihi positum infra tempus. Omnia ista tamen fuerunt falsa, sed sequentia, et ideo infra tempus concedenda.

Et si arguitur sic

Tantum possibile fuit positum et impossibile fuit concedendum infra[24]

tempus, igitur propter possibile positum fuit impossibile concedendum, consequentia patet et antecedens etiam, quia omne positum obligatum fuit concedendum infra tempus, sed

Homo est asinus

fuit positum obligatum, igitur

Homo est asinus

---

[21] arguitur]arguo E
[22] cum]si E
[23] concedo]concedendo M
[24] infra ... concedendum]om.M

'A human being is a donkey' is impossible *per se* and it is the *positum*; therefore it is not the case that only a possible proposition was posited.

⟨1.1RO⟩ But perhaps someone might argue against this reply as follows, by positing that C is this entire proposition:

'A human being is a donkey' is the *positum obligatum* put to you.

Then it is argued:

Only C is the *positum obligatum* put to you, but C is a possible proposition; therefore only a possible proposition is the *positum obligatum* put to you.

Furthermore, let the period come to an end, and I argue like this:

No impossible proposition was posited to you then; therefore etc.

The premiss can be proved, because only C, which is a possible proposition, was posited to you.

⟨1.1ROR⟩ I reply by denying as inconsistent ⟨the claim⟩ that only C was posited to me. This is a valid inference:

'A human being is a donkey' is the *positum* put to you; therefore it is not the case that only C was posited to you.

And when someone says

Let the period come to an end,

I admit it; and I deny that

A human being is a donkey

was posited to me during the period; and I grant that only C was posited to me during the period; and I deny that some impossible proposition was posited to me during the period. All these claims were false, but they did follow, and for that reason they were to be granted during the period.

And if someone argues like this:

Only a possible proposition was posited to you, and an impossible proposition should have been granted during the period; therefore an impossible proposition should have been granted on account of a possible *positum*,

the inference is obvious, as is the premiss, because every *positum obligatum* should have been granted during the period, but

A human being is a donkey

was the *positum obligatum*; therefore

A human being is a donkey

fuit concedendum infra tempus. Sed
> Homo est asinus

est, et tunc fuit impossibile. Igitur etc.

Dicitur negando quod impossibile fuit concedendum infra tempus obligationis, et concedo quod omne positum obligatum (232^{ra}M) fuit concedendum infra tempus, et nego quod
> Homo est asinus

fuit positum obligatum infra tempus. Si tamen talis propositio fuisset mihi proposita infra tempus, ipsam concessissem quia fuisset mihi posita.

⟨1.2R⟩ Ad aliud principale quando dicebatur[25] quod
> Homo est asinus

est a me negandum, nego; et nego quod negem ipsam[26] bene respondendo. Unde si proponitur
> Tu negas eam,

concedo. ⟨Deinde⟩
> Tu male respondes.

Concedo[27]. Si in principio proponitur
> Tu male respondes,

nego. ⟨Deinde⟩
> Tu negas eam.

Nego quia repugnat.

⟨1.3R⟩ Ad aliud dicitur negando quod omne concedendum sit concedendum aut quia verum aut quia sequens, quia etiam est concedendum quia positum obligatum. Concesso tamen[28] isto antecedente, potest concedi consequenter quod
> Homo est asinus

est sequens sed non ex possibili.

⟨1.4R⟩ Ad aliud cum dicitur
> Cedat tempus,

admitto; et nego quod

---

[25] dicebatur]dicitur E
[26] ipsam]eam E
[27] Concedo]concedendo M
[28] tamen]ergo E

should have been granted during the period. But
> A human being is a donkey

is impossible and was impossible then. Therefore etc.

I reply by denying that an impossible proposition should have been granted during the period of the *obligatio*. I grant that every *positum obligatum* should have been granted during the period, and I deny that
> A human being is a donkey

was the *positum obligatum* during the period. However, if such a proposition ⟨sc. "'A human being is a donkey" was the *positum obligatum*'⟩ had been proposed to me during the period, I would have granted it because it had been posited to me.

⟨1.2R⟩ Reply to the second argument. When it was said that
> A human being is a donkey

should be denied by me, I deny it; and I deny that I would reply correctly if I were to deny it. Hence if
> You deny it

is proposed, I grant it. ⟨Then⟩
> You reply incorrectly.

I grant it. ⟨But⟩ if at the beginning
> You reply incorrectly

is proposed, I deny it. ⟨Then⟩
> You deny it.

I deny it because it is inconsistent.

⟨1.3R⟩ Reply to the third argument. I deny that everything which should be granted should be granted either because it is true or because it follows. It may also have to be granted because it is the *positum obligatum*. However, if the premiss had been granted one could as a result grant that
> A human being is a donkey

does follow, though not from a possible proposition.

⟨1.4R⟩ Reply to the fourth argument. When someone says
> Let the period come to an end,

I admit it; and I deny that

Homo est asinus

fuit concedendum infra tempus et tota causa dicta est[29]. Quare etc.

Sed adhuc fortius arguitur contra regulam et contra responsionem. Et pono tibi istam

'Homo est asinus' est tibi positum obligatum et haec 'Homo est asinus' est per se impossibilis.

Casus est[30] possibilis, quia possibile est quod tibi ponatur per se impossibile et quod[31] tu admittis[32] illud. Admisso ergo isto casu[33], propono tibi

'Homo est asinus' est a te concedendum.

Si negas, contra:

'Homo est asinus' est tibi positum obligatum, igitur 'Homo est asinus' est a te concedendum.

Si concedis[34], arguitur quod

Homo est asinus

est a te negandum, nam

'Homo est asinus' est per se impossibile, igitur 'Homo est asinus' est a te negandum.

Probatur consequentia. Sequitur enim[35]

'Homo est asinus' est per se impossibile et aliquid[36] est tibi positum obligatum, igitur repugnat tibi posito obligato, sed omne repugnans tibi posito obligato est a te negandum, igitur 'Homo est asinus' est a te negandum.

Respondetur admittendo casum, et cum proponitur

'Homo est asinus' est a te concedendum[37],

nego. Contra:

'Homo est asinus' est tibi positum obligatum, igitur 'Homo est asinus' est a te concedendum.

Concedo consequentiam et concesso quod illud sit antecedens et illud consequens, nego quod antecedens sit concedendum a me. Et si dicitur contra:

---

[29] est]*om*.M
[30] est]*om*.M
[31] quod]*om*.E
[32] admittis]admittas E
[33] casu]*om*.E
[34] concedis]conceditur M
[35] enim]*om*.M
[36] aliquid]aliud E
[37] concedendum]negandum M

A human being is a donkey

should have been granted during the period, for reasons which have been given in full. Therefore etc.

But one can argue even more strongly against the rule and against the ⟨usual⟩ reply. I posit this to you:

'A human being is a donkey' is the *positum obligatum* put to you, and 'A human being is a donkey' is impossible *per se*.

The case is possible, because it is possible for someone to posit a proposition which is impossible *per se* to you, and for you to admit it. When therefore the case has been admitted, I propose to you:

'A human being is a donkey' should be granted by you.

If you deny it, I argue against you:

'A human being is a donkey' is the *positum obligatum* put to you; therefore 'A human being is a donkey' should be granted by you.

If you grant it, I argue that

A human being is a donkey

should be denied by you, for

'A human being is a donkey' is impossible *per se*; therefore 'A human being is a donkey' should be denied by you.

This inference can be proved. This is a valid inference:

'A human being is a donkey' is impossible *per se* and there is something which is the *positum obligatum* put to you; therefore it ⟨sc. 'A human being is a donkey'⟩ is inconsistent with the *positum obligatum*, but everything inconsistent with the *positum obligatum* put to you should be denied by you; therefore 'A human being is a donkey' should be denied by you.

I reply by admitting the case. When

'A human being is a donkey' should be granted by you

is proposed, I deny it. One can argue against ⟨the denial⟩:

'A human being is a donkey' is the *positum obligatum* put to you; therefore 'A human being is a donkey' should be granted by you.

I grant the inference, and having granted that this is the premiss and this the conclusion, I deny that the premiss should be granted by me. And if someone argues against this:

Omne positum obligatum est concedendum a te, sed 'Homo est asinus' est positum obligatum, igitur 'Homo est asinus' est concedendum a te,
nego maiorem tamquam repugnantem. Et si dicitur
    Ista est regula,
nego. Pro quo[38] est[39] notandum quod omnes regulae obligationum habent intelligi sine obligatione contraria, quoniam omnes antedictae regulae sunt verae propositiones non necessariae, igitur cuiuscumque regulae talis est oppositum possibile, et per consequens potest admitti vel concedi ex aliquo antecedente ipsum. Verbi gratia, pono[40] quod tu concedas repugnans posito obligato et bene respondeas ad illud solummodo respondendo; istud est possibile, ideo admittendum. Quo admisso, fiat haec consequentia:
    Tu concedis repugnans posito obligato, igitur male respondes.
Conceditur consequentia sicut etiam conceditur antecedens quotienscumque proponitur. Non tamen conceditur ipsum esse[41] concedendum, quia tunc consequens esset concedendum, et sic concedendum esset te male respondere et te bene respondere respectu eiusdem. Ita in proposito est obligatio contraria cum ponitur quod illa
    Homo est asinus
sit posita[42] obligata cum hoc quod sit impossibile per se. In eo enim[43] quod est impossibilis (189^{va}E) per se sequitur quod est neganda, et per consequens non concedenda. Quare etc[44]. (232^{rb}M)

⟨*Contra Regulam Duodecimam*⟩
Duodecima regula et ultima fuit ista. Qualibet parte copulativae concessa, concedenda est copulativa cuius illae vel consimiles sunt partes principales.
⟨1⟩ Contra istam regulam[45] arguitur per motivum oppositum tenentium. Nam pono tibi illam
    Aliquis homo est Romae.
Sit tamen rei veritas quod nullus homo sit Romae. Qua admissa, propono tibi istam:

---

[38] quo]qua E
[39] est]*om*.E
[40] pono]posito M
[41] esse]omne E
[42] posita]et *add*.E
[43] enim]*om*.E
[44] Quare etc.]*om*.E; Et sic est finis huius capituli. Incipit duodecima regula] *add*.M
[45] regulam]*om*.M

Every *positum obligatum* should be granted by you, but 'A human being is a donkey' is the *positum obligatum*; therefore 'A human being is a donkey' should be granted by you,

I deny the major premiss as inconsistent. And if someone says

This is a rule,

I deny it. Here one should note that all the rules for *obligationes* should be understood ⟨as to be granted only⟩ in the absence of a contrary *obligatio*, since all the aforesaid rules are true propositions, but not necessary.[89] Therefore the opposite of any such rule is also possible, and as a result it can be admitted or granted as following from some premiss. For instance, I posit that you grant something inconsistent with the *positum obligatum* and you reply correctly in making this single reply. This is possible; therefore it should be admitted. When it has been admitted, let this inference be constructed:

You grant something inconsistent with the *positum obligatum*; therefore you reply incorrectly.

The inference is granted, as the premiss is also granted whenever it is proposed. However, one does not grant that ⟨the premiss⟩ should be granted because then the conclusion should be granted, and thus one should grant that you reply incorrectly and you reply correctly with respect to the same ⟨reply⟩. Thus in the proposed case there is a contradictory *obligatio* when it is posited that

A human being is a donkey

is the *positum obligatum* and that it is impossible *per se*. Insofar as it is impossible *per se*, it follows that it ought to be denied, and as a result that it ought not to be granted. Therefore etc.

⟨*Against Rule Twelve*⟩

The twelfth and last rule was this: When each clause of a conjunction has been granted, the conjunction of which these or equiform propositions are the principal clauses should be granted.

⟨1⟩ ⟨First argument against rule twelve⟩. This argument is based on the view of those who hold the opposite of the rule. I posit this to you:

Some human being is in Rome.

Let it be true in fact that no human being is in Rome. When ⟨the *positum*⟩ has been admitted, I propose this to you:

---

[89] The point that the rules themselves were contingent propositions was made by Buser, op.cit., fol. 74ra and Marsilius, op.cit., fol. 76^v.

> Aliquis homo est Romae et tu es homo.

Haec propositio est falsa et impertinens, igitur neganda; et tamen quaelibet eius pars est concedenda. Probatur. Haec est concedenda

> Aliquis homo est Romae,

quia[46] posita obligata; et haec etiam est concedenda

> Tu es homo,

quia vera et impertinens, et tamen ut apparet copulativa est neganda; igitur non ad concessionem cuiuslibet partis copulativae est concedenda copulativa.

Respondetur admittendo positum. Et quando[47] proponitur

> Aliquis homo est Romae et tu es homo,

nego illam copulativam tamquam falsam et impertinentem. Et quando[48] dicitur

> Utraque pars est concedenda,

dicitur quod prima est concedenda et non secunda[49]. Vera est, sed repugnans posito et opposito bene negati, quia eius contradictorium est sequens. Sequitur enim

> Nullus homo est Romae vel tu non es homo, sed aliquis homo est Romae, igitur tu non es homo.

Si vero proponatur copulativa per alium modum concedenda est quia sequens, ut si statim post positum proponeretur illa

> Tu es homo,

quae esset concedenda quia vera et impertinens. Quare etc.

Similiter[50] est[51] dicendum si proponeretur[52] sicut solet proponi[53] quod omnis homo currat. Qua admissa, proponitur

> Omnis homo currit[54] et tu es homo.

Negetur[51] illa et respondeatur ut prius.

⟨2⟩ Secundo principaliter contra regulam arguitur sic. Et pono tibi illam[56]:

> Omnis homo est Romae.

Qua posita et admissa propono tibi

> Tu es homo et tu es Romae.

---

[46] quia]eo quod M
[47] quando]cum E
[48] quando]cum E
[49] secunda]quae *add*.E
[50] Similiter]consimiliter M
[51] est]*om*.E
[52] proponeretur]responderetur E
[53] proponi]poni E
[54] currit]est Romae E
[55] Negetur]negatur E
[56] illam]*om*.E

ON *OBLIGATIONES*

Some human being is in Rome and you are a human being.[90]

This proposition is false and irrelevant; therefore it should be denied. However, each of its clauses should be granted. Proof: this:

Some human being is in Rome

should be granted, because it is the *positum obligatum*; and this:

You are a human being,

should also be granted, because it is true and irrelevant. However, as appears, the conjunction should be denied. Therefore a conjunction should not be granted when each of its clauses has been granted.

I reply by admitting the *positum*. And when

Some human being is in Rome and you are a human being

is proposed, I deny that conjunction as false and irrelevant. And when someone says

Each clause should be granted,

I say that the first should be granted but not the second. The latter is true, but it is inconsistent with the *positum* and the opposite of a correctly denied proposition, because its contradictory follows. This is a valid inference:

Either no human being is in Rome or you are not a human being, but some human being is in Rome; therefore you are not a human being.

If indeed the conjunction is proposed in some other way, it should be granted because it follows. For instance, ⟨it should be granted⟩ if this

You are a human being

were proposed immediately after the *positum*, for then ⟨this proposition⟩ would have to be granted because it is true and irrelevant. Therefore etc.

A similar reply should be made if, as is customary, it were proposed that every human being was running. When this has been admitted, this is proposed:

Every human being is running and you are a human being.

This should be denied, and one should reply as above.

⟨2⟩ Second argument against rule twelve. I posit this to you:

Every human being is in Rome.

When this has been posited and admitted, I propose to you:

You are a human being and you are in Rome.

---

[90] For another discussion of the same example, see Part 1, section 3, rule 12. Cf. Strode, op.cit., fol. 79^{rb-va}.

Neganda est quia falsa et impertinens. Deinde propono tibi

    Tu es homo.

Concedenda est quia vera et impertinens. Non enim videtur cui repugnet[57] vel ad quid[58] sequatur. Deinde propono tibi

    Tu es Romae.

Si concedis habeo intentum quia negasti copulativam et concessisti quamlibet eius partem. Si negas, contra:

    Tu negas sequens ex posito obligato et concesso, igitur male.

Antecedens probatur, quia sequitur[59]

    Omnis homo est Romae, tu es homo, igitur tu es Romae.

    Respondetur admisso casu, negando istam copulativam. Et cum proponitur

    Tu es homo,

nego eam[60] quia repugnat posito et opposito bene negati, nam[61] suum oppositum sequitur. Probo, nam sequitur

    Omnis homo est Romae, et[62] tu non es homo vel tu non es Romae, igitur tu non es homo.

Probo istam consequentiam, nam bene sequitur

    Omnis[63] homo est Romae et[64] tu non es homo, ergo tu non es homo[65].

Similiter sequitur

    Omnis homo est Romae, tu non es Romae, igitur tu non es homo.

Arguitur[66] igitur sic:

    Haec 'Tu non es homo' sequitur ex posito et qualibet parte illius disiunctivae, ergo sequitur ex eodem posito et tota disiunctiva.

Patet consequentia ex hoc quia disiunctiva infertur ex qualibet eius parte.

    Item sequitur

    Tu es homo et omnis homo est Romae, igitur tu es homo et tu es Romae.

Ista consequentia est bona et oppositum consequentis est et cuiuslibet partis antecedentis. Similiter igitur ex opposito consequentis cum minori sequitur oppositum maioris, et sic habetur intentum.

⟨3⟩ Tertio contra regulam arguitur sic. Et pono tibi illam[67]

---

[57] repugnet]repugnat M
[58] quid]quod E
[59] sequitur]*om.* M
[60] eam]*om.* E
[61] nam]cum M
[62] et]*om.* E
[63] Omnis]*om.* E
[64] et]*om.* E
[65] homo]Romae E
[66] Arguitur]arguo E
[67] illam]*om.* E

This should be denied because it is false and irrelevant. Then I propose to you:
> You are a human being.

This should be granted because it is true and irrelevant. One cannot see what it might be inconsistent with, or from what it might follow. Then I propose to you:
> You are in Rome.

If you grant it I have made my point because you denied the conjunction and granted each of its clauses. If you deny it, I argue against you:
> You deny what follows from the *positum obligatum* and a previously granted proposition; therefore you reply incorrectly.

Proof of the premiss: this is a valid inference:
> Every human being is in Rome, you are a human being; therefore you are in Rome.

When the case has been admitted, I reply by denying this conjunction. And when
> You are a human being

is proposed, I deny it because it is inconsistent with the *positum* and the opposite of a correctly denied proposition, for its opposite follows. Proof: this is a valid inference:
> Every human being is in Rome and either you are not a human being or you are not in Rome; therefore you are not a human being.

Proof of the inference: this is a valid inference:
> Every human being is in Rome and you are not a human being; therefore you are not a human being.

Similarly this is a valid inference:
> Every human being is in Rome, you are not in Rome; therefore you are not a human being.

⟨On the basis of these two inferences⟩ one can argue like this:
> 'You are not a human being' follows from the *positum* together with each clause of that disjunction; therefore it follows from the same *positum* together with the whole disjunction.

This inference is obvious, because a disjunction is inferred from each of its clauses.

⟨Another proof of the inference⟩: Likewise this is a valid inference:
> You are a human being, and every human being is in Rome; therefore you are a human being and you are in Rome.

This inference is valid and the opposite of the conclusion exists, as does each clause of the premiss. Similarly therefore from the opposite of the conclusion together with the minor premiss there follows the opposite of the major premiss, and thus I prove my point.

⟨3⟩ Third argument against rule twelve. I posit this to you:

Omnis homo currit[68].

Qua admissa et concessa, cedat tempus et propono tibi talis copulativa
'Omnis homo currit[69] et tu es homo' fuit a te concedenda.

Si conceditur, contra:
Ista fuit falsa et impertinens, igitur.

Si dicitur (232^{va}M) quod fuit neganda et, ut patet, quaelibet eius pars fuit concedenda, igitur oppositum regulae[70].

Ad istud argumentum respondet unus magister dicens admittendo positum et quod illa copulativa fuit a me neganda et quaelibet pars principalis pro tunc fuit concedenda. Nec incidit, ait idem[71], haec[72] responsio in rationes[73] tenentium oppositum regulae praedictae; quia non obstante conclusione nunc concessa non est respondendum ad copulativam ipsam negando et utramque eius partem concedendo; sed postquam negabitur copulativa negetur[74] altera pars copulativae[75] ut repugnans posito cum bene concesso vel opposito bene negati.

Puto quod huius magistri intentio bona sit; tamen verba non recte procedunt. Arguo namque sic

Haec copulativa non fuit proposita infra tempus obligationis, nec aliquod oppositum ipsius sequens ex aliquo posito obligato aut concesso vel quovis alio modo, igitur ista non fuit neganda.

Idem argumentum (189^{vb}E) sit probando quod nulla eius pars fuit concedenda cum non fuit proposita, et[76] consequentia patet capiendo 'concedendum' et[77] 'negandum' pro 'digno concedi vel negari', nominaliter et non participialiter.

Secundo non videtur mihi quare illa copulativa fuit neganda quin etiam consimili ratione fuit concedenda, quod negat iste magister. Patet consequentia quia sicut potuit proponi immediate post[78] positum ita etiam[79] post illam

Tu es homo.

Tertio arguitur sic. In eodem tempore obligationis fuit ista copulativa neganda et quaelibet eius pars concedenda et praecise una obligatio fuit, igitur copulativa ista non significavit ut suae partes, aut non sequebatur ex eisdem.

---

[68] currit]est Romae E
[69] currit]est Romae E
[70] regulae]*om*.E
[71] idem]ibidem E
[72] haec]habeo E
[73] rationes]responsione E
[74] negetur]negatur E
[75] copulativae]*om*.M
[76] et]*om*.E
[77] et]vel E
[78] post]*om*.M
[79] etiam]et M

Every human being is running.

When this has been admitted and granted, let the period come to an end. I propose a conjunction such as this to you:

'Every human being is running and you are a human being' should have been granted by you.[91]

If you grant this, I argue against you:

This ⟨conjunction⟩ was false and irrelevant; therefore ⟨it should have been denied⟩.

If someone says that it should have been denied and, as is obvious, each of its clauses should have been granted; then, therefore, the opposite of the rule holds.

One master replies to this argument by admitting the *positum* and saying that the conjunction should have been denied by me, but that each principal clause should have been granted at that time.[92] The same person says that this reply does not collapse into the arguments of those who hold the opposite of the aforesaid rule, because notwithstanding the thesis now granted, one should not reply to that conjunction by denying it while granting each of its clauses. After a conjunction has been denied, one of its clauses is to be denied as inconsistent with the *positum* together with a correctly granted proposition or the opposite of a correctly denied proposition.

I think that the intention of this master is correct; but his words do not do him justice. For this reason I argue like this:

This conjunction was not proposed during the period of the *obligatio*, nor did any opposite ⟨of the conjunction⟩ follow from any *positum obligatum* or from a previously granted proposition or from any other kind of proposition; therefore it was not a proposition which should be denied.

The same argument can be used to prove that none of its clauses was a proposition which should be granted, since none was proposed. The inference is obvious if one takes 'should be granted' and 'should be denied' as meaning 'worthy to be granted or denied', i.e. nominally and not participially.

Second, I do not see why that conjunction was a proposition which should be denied, when by an equally good reason ⟨it could have been viewed as⟩ a proposition which should be granted; yet this master denies the latter claim. The inference is obvious, for just as one was able to posit ⟨the conjunction⟩ immediately after the *positum*, one could also have posited it after:

You are a human being.

Third, one can argue like this. During the period of one *obligatio* this conjunction was a proposition which should be denied, and each of its clauses was a proposition which should be granted, and there was just one *obligatio*. Therefore, either this conjunction did not signify in the same way as its

[91] See Strode, op.cit., fols. 85vb–86ra.
[92] 'Unus magister' could be Richard Billingham or Albert of Saxony. Billingham, op.cit., fol. 92^v, wrote 'notandum est quod licet utraque categorica alicuius copulativae sit concedenda, non

Non est dicendum primum ut patet, igitur secundum, cuius oppositum ponitur[80]. Et sic incidit in opinionem illorum quos porcinos[81] vocat.

Est igitur aliter dicendum quod ista copulativa nec fuit concedenda nec neganda nec dubitanda, dato quod non fuerit prolata nec alicubi scripta. Si tamen fuisset in anima vel scripta, respondeo sicut[82] non fuisset mihi proposita ab aliquo et circa ipsam considerassem. Si prius circa copulativam quam secundam partem illa fuisset a me neganda et consequenter secunda pars. Si vero prius direxissem[83] oculum ad secundam partem copulativae, ipsam concedendo concederem brevissime[84] copulativam.

Et ita dico si ab aliquo mihi proposita fuisset ista copulativa. Si immediate post positum proposuisset[85] eam, neganda fuisset et consequenter eius secunda pars. Si vero secunda pars immediate post positum fuisset proposita, concedenda fuisset et consequenter copulativa totalis. Quare etc.

⟨4⟩ Quarto arguitur sic. Et pono tibi illam
    Tu curris.
Qua admissa, propono tibi
    Tu curris et tu moveris.
Neganda est quia falsa ut patet, et non sequens, cum a parte copulativae ad totam non valet[86] argumentum. Deinde propono tibi
    Tu curris.
Concedenda est, quia positum obligatum. Ulterius
    Tu moveris.
Concedenda est quia sequens ex posito obligato, et sic patet quod copulativa est neganda et quaelibet eius pars est concedenda.

Respondetur admittendo positum, et concedo[87] istam copulativam
    Tu curris et tu moveris,
et dico quod est sequens ex posito. Pro quo regulariter observandum est quod quandocumque ponitur et admittitur aliquid et[88] deinde proponitur copulativa cuius quaelibet pars sequitur ex posito obligato, concedenda est

---

[80] ponitur] ponit M, E *correxi*
[81] porcinos]porciones M
[82] sicut]quod si M
[83] direxissem]dirixem M
[84] concedendo ... brevissime]concedo

concedere debuisset E
[85] proposuisset]proposuissem E
[86] valet]valeat M
[87] concedo]concedendo M
[88] et]*om*.M

---

tamen propter hoc tota copulativa est concedenda.' He was followed by other versions of the *Logica Oxoniensis*, e.g. *Lat.misc.e 79*, fol. 20ʳᵇ: 'Et nota quod licet utraque pars copulativae sit concedenda, non tamen tota copulativa est concedenda.' Albert of Saxony had raised the matter in an earlier chapter of his *Perutilis Logica*, entitled *De propositionibus hypotheticis*, op.cit., fol. 19ʳᵇ, where he wrote: 'Ad hoc autem quod aliqua copulativa sit ab aliquo concedenda non sufficit unam eius partem esse concedendam, unde in casu quaelibet pars copulativae est concedenda et tamen copulativa est neganda'. Strode reported the view, op.cit., fols. 85ᵛᵇ–86ʳᵃ. In an earlier passage, op.cit., fol. 79ᵛᵃ, he commented that because one could not grant 'Omnis homo currit et tu es homo' immediately after the *positum* 'Omnis homo currit', 'per talem ergo ordinem proponendi putaverunt se multi velut inevitabiliter ex regulis omnibus demonstrare quod copulativa esset neganda, sicut iam proponebatur, cuius tamen quaelibet pars esset concedenda'. The intention of the rule was made plain by *Lib.Soph.Oxon.*, sig.C viiʳ: 'Et nota quod licet

clauses, or it did not follow from them. The first claim should not be made, as is obvious, therefore the second ⟨must be granted⟩, although its opposite is posited. Hence his view does collapse into the view of those whom he calls swinish.[93]

Therefore one should reply in another way, saying that this conjunction was not a proposition which should be granted, or denied, or doubted, given that it had not been uttered or written down anywhere. However, if it had existed in someone's mind, or in writing, I would reply as if it had not been proposed to me by anyone, but I had considered it carefully. If ⟨I had considered⟩ the conjunction before its second clause, it would have been a proposition which should be denied and so, as a result, would its second clause ⟨when it was proposed⟩. But if I had first directed my gaze to the second clause of the conjunction and had granted it I would, in short, then grant the conjunction.

And if the conjunction had been proposed to me by somebody, I would reply like this. If it had been proposed immediately after the *positum*, it would have been a proposition which should be denied, and as a result so would its second clause. But if the second clause had been proposed immediately after the *positum*, then it would have been a proposition which should be granted and as a result, so would the entire conjunction. Therefore etc.

⟨4⟩ Fourth argument against rule twelve. I posit this to you:

You are running.

When this has been admitted I propose to you:

You are running and you are moving.

This should be denied because it is false, as is obvious, and it does not follow, since the argument from one clause of a conjunction to the whole conjunction is not valid. Then I propose to you:

You are running.

This should be granted because it is the *positum obligatum*. Further:

You are moving.

This should be granted because it follows from the *positum obligatum*; and thus it is obvious that a conjunction should be denied while each of its parts should be granted.

I reply by admitting the *positum*, and I grant this conjunction:

You are running and you are moving,

and I say that it does follow from the *positum*. One can offer as a rule that whenever something is posited and admitted and then a conjunction is proposed each of whose clauses follows from the *positum obligatum*, that

---

utraque pars copulativae sit concedenda per se, non tamen sequitur quod copulativa sit concedenda antequam proponantur ambae partes'. Cf. the pair of rules in John of Holland, op.cit., fol. 102ʳ: 'Aliqua tota copulativa est neganda cuius utraque pars est concedenda. . . . Omnis copulativa est concedenda cuius quaelibet pars est prius concessa'.

[93] For discussion of Swyneshed, see Part 1, section 3, rule 12. I do not know the source of Paul's remark.

copulativa tamquam sequens; et sic est in proposito, ut patet consideranti. Idem dico si poneretur illa

    Tu curris[89],

⟨qua⟩ admissa, proponeretur

    Tu curris et deus est.

Debet concedi quia sequens ratione (232^{vb}M) suarum partium, quarum[90] prima sequitur convertibiliter, secunda quia per se necessaria et simpliciter.

Similiter si ponitur aliqua propositio, qua[91] admissa, proponitur aliqua propositio quae potest esse indifferenter copulativa aut[92] disiunctiva; et copulativa esset sequens, disiunctiva vero non[93], non debet responderi affirmative aut negative ad talem quousque non[94] fiat certificatio an sit copulativa aut disiunctiva. Verbi gratia, pono tibi istam:

    Tu curris vel tu[95] moveris localiter.

Deinde propono tibi illam:

    Tu curris vel tu non curris[96] et tu moveris localiter.

Tota copulativa concedatur quia sequens; sed disiunctiva negetur[97] quia falsa et impertinens.

---

[89] curris]deinde *add*.E
[90] quarum]*om*.M
[91] qua . . .propositio]*om*.E
[92] aut]vel E
[93] non]*om*.E
[94] non]*om*.E
[95] tu]*om*.M
[96] curris]moveris E
[97] negetur]negatur E

conjunction should be granted as following. The proposed case is of this sort, as is obvious to anyone who considers the matter carefully. I would say the same if this:

You are running

were posited and then, when it had been admitted, this:

You are running and God exists

were proposed. ⟨This conjunction⟩ should be granted because it follows by virtue of its clauses. The first follows because it is interchangeable ⟨with the *positum*⟩; and the second because it is necessary *per se* and simply.

Similarly if some proposition is posited, and after it has been admitted some proposition which could either be interpreted as a conjunction or as a disjunction is proposed, and the conjunction follows but the disjunction does not, one should not reply affirmatively or negatively to such a proposition until one has been assured that it is a conjunction, or a disjunction. For instance, I posit this to you:

You are running or you are moving with local motion.

Then I propose this to you:

You are running or you are not running and you are moving with local motion.

The whole conjunction may be granted because it follows; but the disjunction is to be denied because it is false and irrelevant.[94]

---

[94] Something has gone wrong here. On the manuscript reading, the disjunction does follow, since it is impossible for the premiss to be true and the conclusion false. 'A v B' is true only if either A or B is true. If A is true then 'A v (-A & B)' is true. If A is false, then -A is true and B is also true. Hence (-A & B) is true, and so is 'A v (-A & B)'. On the reading from the edition, the conjunction does not follow.

⟨*Capitulum Secundum: De Copulativis*⟩

In materia copulativarum solet multipliciter obligari.

⟨1⟩ Et primo sic. Pono tibi istam:

> Omnis homo currit et nihil est tibi positum.

Qua admissa, propono tibi illam[1]:

> Omnis homo currit.

Haec est concedenda quia sequens. Sequitur enim:

> Omnis homo currit et nihil est tibi positum; igitur omnis homo currit,

cum quaelibet pars copulativae sequatur[2] ex tota copulativa. Deinde propono tibi istam:

> Tu non es obligatus.

Haec est concedenda tamquam sequens. Sequitur enim:

> Nihil est tibi positum; igitur tu non es obligatus.

Deinde propono iterum illam:

> Omnis homo currit.

Si negas et prius concessisti, igitur male. Eodem modo arguitur si dubitas. Si concedis, concedis falsum non obligatus, igitur male respondes[3].

Ad istud respondetur admittendo positum; et quando proponitur:

> Omnis homo currit,

concedo eam tamquam sequentem. Et quando proponitur illa:

> Tu non es obligatus,

negatur, quia non sequitur:

> Nihil est tibi positum; igitur tu non es obligatus.

Posses enim esse obligatus per depositionem aut suppositionem.

Tamen aliqui dicunt negando consequentiam, quia[4] posses esse obligatus per dubitationem aut petitionem. Patet quod haec ratio non est sufficiens cum omnis dubitatio vel petitio sit positio ut in principio fuit ostensum.

Non obstante hac responsione, revertitur difficultas principaliter intenta, quia pono tibi illam:

> Omnis homo currit et nihil est tibi positum, suppositum, aut depositum.

---

[1] illam]*om*.E
[2] sequatur]sequitur E
[3] respondes]*om*.E
[4] quia]quod E

⟨Chapter Two: On Conjunctions⟩

It is usual to produce many different *obligationes* when dealing with the topic of conjunctions.[1]

⟨1⟩ First *obligatio*. I posit this to you:
   Every human being is running and nothing is posited to you.[2]
When this has been admitted I propose this to you:
   Every human being is running.
This should be granted because it follows. This inference:
   Every human being is running and nothing is posited to you; therefore every human being is running
is valid, since each clause of a conjunction follows from the whole conjunction. Then I propose this to you:
   You are not obligated.
This should be granted as following. This is a valid inference:
   Nothing is posited to you; therefore you are not obligated.
Then I propose:
   Every human being is running
a second time. If you deny it and you granted it earlier, then you reply incorrectly. If you doubt it, the same argument can be put forward. If you grant it, you grant a false proposition without being obligated to do so; therefore you reply incorrectly.

I reply to this by admitting the *positum*, and when
   Every human being is running
is proposed, I grant it as following. And when
   You are not obligated
is proposed, I deny it because this:
   Nothing is posited to you; therefore you are not obligated,
is an invalid inference. You could be obligated by a *depositio* or a *suppositio*.

However, some people reply by denying the inference on the grounds that you might be obligated by a *dubitatio* or a *petitio*.[3] It is obvious that this reason is not adequate, since every *dubitatio* or *petitio* is a *positio*, as was shown at the beginning.

Notwithstanding this reply, the main difficulty returns, because ⟨I can re-phrase the *positum*⟩ and posit this to you:
   Every human being is running and nothing is posited to you, assumed, or deposited.

---

[1] Paul follows Marsilius and Buser by plunging straight into the discussion of sophisms: for references, see note 2.
[2] This sophism is found in Albert, op.cit., fol. 50rb–va; Marsilius, op.cit., fols. 93v–94r; and Buser, op.cit., fol. 77rb. Both Marsilius and Buser rejected Albert's solution, which was to disallow the *positum* as inconsistent. Paul omits this discussion, as he also omits an initial clause specifying that no men are in fact running. Otherwise, he follows his sources closely.
[3] Where Paul writes 'some people say' (*aliqui dicunt*), Marsilius has 'one can reply' (*respondetur*) and Buser has 'it can be denied that' (*potest negari*). The objection may well be Buser's own.

Quo admisso, arguatur ut prius. Ideo iam concedo quod non (190^{ra}E) sum obligatus, et concedo ut prius illam:

    Omnis homo currit.

Et tunc ad argumentum:

    Concedis falsum non obligatus; igitur male respondes,

concedo consequentiam et consequens infra tempus, non tamquam verum sed tamquam sequens.

⟨2⟩ Secundo obligatur sic. Et pono tibi illam[5]:

    Omnis homo est Romae et nulla copulativa est tibi posita, supposita, vel[6] deposita.

Qua admissa, propono tibi illam[7]:

    Tu non es obligatus.

Haec est concedenda quia sequens ex secunda parte copulativae[8]. Deinde propono tibi[9]:

    Omnis homo est Romae.

Si negas vel dubitas, contra: tu negas vel dubitas sequens ex copulativa posita obligata; igitur male. Si concedis, contra:

    Tu concedis falsum non sequens, igitur male.

Antecedens probatur, nam quod sit falsum patet, et[10] quod non sit[11] sequens probatur, quia tu non es obligatus, igitur illa non est sequens.

    Respondetur admittendo positum et quando proponitur:

    Tu non es obligatus,

nego quia falsum et impertinens. Et nego quod sequatur[12] ex secunda parte copulativae, quia non sequitur:

    Nulla copulativa est tibi posita, deposita, vel supposita; igitur tu non es obligatus,

quia potes obligari per categoricam vel simplicem obligationem[13].

    Si tamen ponatur cum prima parte copulativae illa:

    Tu non es obligatus

et proponatur

---

[5] illam] *om.* E
[6] vel]aut E
[7] illam] *om.* E
[8] copulativae] *om.* E
[9] propono tibi]proponitur E
[10] et]sed E
[11] non sit]*transp.* E
[12] sequatur]sequitur E
[13] categoricam . . . obligationem]per simplicem obligationem ad categoricum E

When this has been admitted, one can argue as before. For this reason I immediately grant that I am not obligated, and I grant

> Every human being is running

as before. ⟨In reply⟩ to the argument

> You grant a false proposition without being obligated to do so; therefore you reply incorrectly,

I grant the inference and the conclusion during the period, not as true but as following.

⟨2⟩ Second *obligatio*. I posit this to you:

> Every human being is in Rome and no conjunction is posited to you, assumed, or deposited.[4]

When this has been admitted, I posit this to you:

> You are not obligated.

This should be granted because it follows from the second clause of the conjunction. Then I propose:

> Every human being is in Rome

to you. If you deny or doubt it, I argue against you: you deny or doubt something which follows from a conjunction which is the *positum obligatum*; therefore you reply incorrectly. If you grant it, I argue against you:

> You grant a false proposition which does not follow; therefore you reply incorrectly.

Proof of the premiss: it is obvious that the proposition is false, and it can be proved that it does not follow. Because you are not obligated, therefore it does not follow.

I reply by admitting the *positum*.[5] When

> You are not obligated

is proposed, I deny it because it is false and irrelevant. And I deny that it follows from the second clause of the conjunction, because this

> No conjunction is posited to you, deposited, or assumed; therefore you are not obligated,

is an invalid inference, given that you might be obligated by means of a categorical or simple *obligatio*.

However, if

> You are not obligated

is posited together with the first clause of that conjunction, and

---

[4] This sophism is found in Albert, op.cit., fol. 50ᵛᵃ (with 'Omnis homo currit' in place of 'Omnis homo est Romae'); Marsilius, op.cit., fol. 94ʳ (with 'Sortes currit'); and Buser, op.cit., fol. 77ʳᵇ. Cf. *Lat.misc.e 79*, fol. 20ᵛᵃ and *Lib.Soph.Oxon.*, sig.C viiʳ.

[5] Paul's solution is taken from Buser. Marsilius had followed Albert more closely in suggesting that although one could argue 'No conjunction has been posited to you and I have posited nothing other than a conjunction, therefore you are not obligated', this inference did not hold. The reason given by both Albert and Marsilius, and referred to in passing by Buser, was that in positing a conjunction one thereby posited each of its parts and could not, therefore, be said to posit nothing other than a conjunction. Albert also remarked that within an obligational disputation one would have to deny the proposition that in fact some conjunction had been posited, since this was inconsistent with 'No conjunction has been posited to you.'

> Omnis homo est Romae

conceditur. Et cum dicitur

> Tu concedis falsum non sequens; igitur male

conceditur[14] consequentia et consequens. (233^{ra}M)

⟨3⟩ Tertio obligatur sic. Et pono tibi illam:

> Tu respondes ad falsum et solum respondes ad A,

et sit A prima pars principalis istius copulativae, scilicet:

> Tu respondes ad falsum.

Qua admissa, propono tibi illam[15]:

> Tu solum respondes ad A.

Concedenda est tamquam sequens cum sit altera pars copulativae. Deinde propono tibi istam:

> Tu respondes ad falsum.

Si negas, negas sequens cum sit pars principalis copulativae; igitur male. Eodem modo arguitur si dubitas[16]. Si concedis; igitur tu respondes ad falsum et solum respondes ad A; igitur A est falsum. Sed A est ista:

> Tu respondes ad falsum,

igitur haec est falsa:

> Tu respondes ad falsum.

Dicitur admittendo positum et quando[17] proponitur:

> Tu respondes ad falsum,

concedo eam tamquam sequentem. Et quando arguitur:

> Tu respondes ad falsum et solum respondes ad A; igitur A est falsum,

concedo consequentiam et consequens, scilicet quod illa est falsa:

> Tu respondes ad falsum.

Cum hoc tamen bene concedo illam[18]:

> Tu respondes ad falsum.

Nam non est inconveniens in arte obligatoria infra tempus obligationis concedere aliquam propositionem et tamen negare ipsam esse veram sicut secunda demonstravit conclusio.

---

[14] conceditur]concedo E
[15] tibi illam]*om*.E
[16] si dubitas]sicut prius E
[17] quando]est E
[18] illam]quod E

> Every human being is in Rome

is proposed, I grant it.[6] And when someone says

> You grant a false proposition which does not follow; therefore you reply incorrectly,

I grant the inference and the conclusion.

⟨3⟩ Third *obligatio*. I posit this to you:

> You reply to a false proposition, and you reply only to A,

and let A be the first principal clause of this conjunction, namely

> You reply to a false proposition.[7]

When this has been admitted, I propose this to you:

> You reply only to A.

This should be granted as following, since it is one clause of the conjunction. Then I propose this to you:

> You reply to a false proposition.

If you deny it, you deny a proposition which follows, since it is a principal clause of the conjunction; therefore you reply incorrectly. If you doubt it, one can argue in the same way. If you grant it, then you reply to a false proposition and you only reply to A; therefore A is false. But A is this:

> You reply to a false proposition;

therefore this is false:

> You reply to a false proposition.

I reply by admitting the *positum*, and when

> You reply to a false proposition

is proposed, I grant it as following. And when it is argued

> You reply to a false proposition and you only reply to A; therefore A is false,

I grant the inference and the conclusion, namely that

> You reply to a false proposition

is false. However, I can also correctly grant

> You reply to a false proposition.

In the art of *obligatio* it is not awkward to grant some proposition during the period of the *obligatio* and yet to deny it to be true, as the second thesis pointed out.

---

[6] The final clause is Paul's own.

[7] This sophism is found in Albert, loc.cit. (in fourth place); Marsilius, op.cit., fol. 94^{r-v}; and Buser, op.cit., fol. 77^{rb-va}. Albert took it from Burley, op.cit., 3.123–124, and offered the same solution, i.e. that the *positum* could not be admitted because it was inconsistent. Both Marsilius and Buser explicitly rejected this solution, offering in its place the one adopted by Paul.

⟨4⟩ Quarto sic obligatur. Pono tibi istam:

> Aliquis homo est Romae et nullus alius a te est Romae.

Qua admissa, propono tibi istam:

> Tu es Romae.

Si negas, negas sequens ex posito obligato; igitur male. Antecedens probatur, nam[19] sequitur:

> Aliquis homo est Romae et nullus alius a te est Romae; igitur tu es Romae.

Si concedis, concedis falsum et impertinens; igitur male respondes, quia non sequitur:

> Aliquis homo est Romae et nullus alius a te est Romae; igitur tu es Romae,

quia cum toto antecedente stat quod tu non sis.

Respondetur admittendo positum et nego[20] illam:

> Tu es Romae.

Et ad probationem[21] dico quod non sequitur ex posito, sed deberet sic argui:

> Aliquis homo est Romae et nullus alius a te est Romae et tu es homo; igitur tu es Romae.

Consequentia est bona; sed negatur ista:

> Tu es homo

tamquam repugnans. Si tamen immediate post positum proponeretur ista:

> Tu es homo,

concederem eam tamquam veram et impertinentem; et secundario concederem illam:

> Tu es Romae

tamquam sequentem ex posito et uno concesso, ut dictum est. Quare etc.

---

[19] nam . . . respondes] *om.* M
[20] nego] negando E
[21] ad probationem] cum dicitur E

⟨4⟩ Fourth *obligatio*. I posit this to you:

Some human being is in Rome and no one other than you is in Rome.[8]

When this has been admitted, I propose this to you:

You are in Rome.

If you deny it, you deny a proposition which follows from the *positum obligatum*; therefore you reply incorrectly. Proof of the premiss: this is a valid inference:

Some human being is in Rome and no one other than you is in Rome; therefore you are in Rome.

If you grant it, you grant a proposition which is false and irrelevant; therefore you reply incorrectly, because this:

Some human being is in Rome and no one other than you is in Rome; therefore you are in Rome,

is an invalid inference. It is consistent with the entire premiss that you do not exist.[9]

I reply by admitting the *positum* and I deny this:

You are in Rome.

⟨In reply⟩ to the proof I say that ⟨'You are in Rome'⟩ does not follow from the *positum*. The argument ought to go like this:

Some human being is in Rome, and no one other than you is in Rome, and you are a human being;[10] therefore you are in Rome.

The inference is valid, but ⟨the extra premiss⟩

You are a human being

is denied as inconsistent. However, if

You are a human being

were proposed immediately after the *positum*, I would grant it as true and irrelevant; and secondly I would grant

You are in Rome

as following from the *positum* and a previously granted proposition, as has been explained. Therefore etc.

---

[8] This sophism is not found in Buser. Paul follows Albert, op.cit., fol. 50va (in third place), and Marsilius, op.cit., fol. 94^v (with *Parisius* in place of *Romae*). Cf. *Lat.misc.e* 79, fol. 20va and *Lib.Soph.Oxon.*, op.cit., sig. C vii^r.

[9] The author of *Lat.misc.e* 79 explained that 'No one other than you is in Rome' has to be true when you do not exist, since its contradictory, 'Someone other than you is in Rome' is false. This explanation can be understood in the light of Albert's remark that for two things to be related by otherness, they must both exist (. . . quod inter quaecumque habet esse alienitas, oportet quod illa sint). In other words, if X does not exist, the description 'other than X' is empty. We must also remember the late medieval convention that affirmative statements with non-referring subjects are false. Given this convention, an interpretation can be found which makes the premisses of the proposed argument true and the conclusion false.

[10] Albert and Marsilius both suggested the extra premiss.

⟨*Capitulum Tertium: De Disiunctivis*⟩
De disiunctivis pauca sunt dicenda.

⟨*Regulae*⟩
⟨1⟩ Verumtamen est[22] primo regulariter observandum quod nulla disiunctiva cuius quaelibet pars est impossibilis est admittenda.

Patet[23] quia quaelibet talis est impossibilis, sed nullum impossibile per se est admittendum ut patet per primam regulam; igitur, etc.

⟨2⟩ Secunda regula est ista. Si ponitur disiunctiva cuius quaelibet pars est vera sed alteri impertinens ubicumque proponitur[24] aliqua eius pars, concedatur.

Patet quia quaelibet talis est vera[25] et impertinens disiunctivae ubicumque proponatur. Verbi gratia: pono tibi istam:

Tu es homo vel tu es albus.

Qua admissa, propono tibi[26]:

Tu es homo.

Concedenda est, quia vera et impertinens. Deinde:

Tu es albus.

Concedenda est propter causam dictam.

⟨3⟩ Tertia regula (190rbE) est ista. Si ponitur disiunctiva cuius quaelibet pars est possibilis sed falsa et quaelibet cuilibet impertinens[27], semper quae primo proponitur est neganda et altera concedenda. Verbi gratia: pono tibi illam:

Tu curris vel tu es Romae.

Qua admissa, propono tibi[28]:

Tu[29] curris.

Neganda est, quia falsa et impertinens. Deinde:

Tu es Romae.

Concedenda est, quia sequens ex posito et opposito bene negati. Sequitur enim:

---

[22] est]in *add*.E
[23] Patet . . . etc.]*om*.M
[24] proponitur]proponatur   E
[25] vera et]*om*.E
[26] tibi]*om*.E
[27] cuilibet impertinens]cuiuslibet impertinentis E
[28] tibi]*om*.E
[29] Tu]*om*.E

⟨Chapter Three: On Disjunctions⟩

There are a few things which should be said about disjunctions.[1]
⟨*Rules*⟩
⟨1⟩ First rule. No disjunction of which each clause is an impossible proposition should be admitted.

This is obvious because every such ⟨disjunction⟩ is itself impossible, but no proposition which is impossible *per se* ought to be admitted by virtue of the first ⟨main⟩ rule. Therefore etc.

⟨2⟩ Second rule. If a disjunction is posited each of whose clauses is true but irrelevant to the other clause, then whenever one of these clauses is proposed it should be granted.

This is obvious because each such clause is true and irrelevant to the disjunction whenever it is proposed. For instance, I posit this to you:

Either you are a human being or you are white.

When this has been admitted I posit to you:

You are a human being.

This should be granted because it is true and irrelevant. Then

You are white.

This should be granted for the reason given.

⟨3⟩ Third rule. If a disjunction is posited each of whose clauses is possible but false, and each ⟨of whose clauses⟩ is irrelevant to the other, then the first to be proposed should always be denied and the other should be granted. For instance, I posit this to you:

Either you are running or you are in Rome.

When this has been admitted, I propose to you:

You are running.

This should be denied, because it is false and irrelevant. Then:

You are in Rome.

This should be granted because it follows from the *positum* and the opposite of a correctly denied proposition. This is a valid inference:

---

[1] While the doctrines and examples of this section are all familiar, neither Paul's arrangement of the material into ten rules nor the sophism is found in the sources I am acquainted with. Cf. Albert, op.cit., fols. 50vb–51ra; Marsilius, op.cit., fols. 95^{r}–96^{r}; Buser, op.cit., fol. 77va; Strode, op.cit., fols. 88vb–89ra; *Lat.misc.e* 79, fols. 20vb–21rb; *Lib.Soph.Oxon.*, sig.C vii^{r-v}.

Tu curris vel tu es Romae, sed tu non curris; igitur tu es Romae. Similiter si haec:

Tu es Romae

primo proponeretur neganda esset et altera

Tu curris

secundo loco proposita foret[30] concedenda.

⟨4⟩ Quarta regula est ista. Si ponitur disiunctiva cuius quaelibet pars est dubia et[31] impertinens alteri, admittenda est. Qua admissa, disiunctiva semper est concedenda ubicumque proponatur et semper quaelibet pars (233^{rb}M) dubitetur. Verbi gratia: pono tibi illam:

Rex sedet vel Papa est Romae.

Qua admissa, semper concedatur ista et quotienscumque proponitur ista:

Rex sedet

aut illa[32]:

Papa est Romae,

dubitetur, quia dubia et impertinens.

⟨5⟩ Quinta regula est ista. Si ponitur disiunctiva de partibus impertinentibus cuius una pars est falsa et reliqua dubia, si prius proponatur[33] falsa quam dubia, negatur falsa et concedatur dubia. Verbi gratia: pono tibi illam:

Tu curris vel rex sedet.

Qua admissa, propono tibi[34]

Tu curris.

Neganda est, quia falsa et impertinens. Deinde:

Rex sedet.

Concedatur[35], quia sequens ex posito et opposito bene negati.

Ex ista regula sequitur quod non est inconveniens eandem propositionem primo dubitare et postmodum concedere, sicut non est inconveniens quod eadem propositio primo sit impertinens et postmodum sit sequens. Unde facta admissione, si[36] proponetur[37] illa

Rex sedet,

---

[30] foret]*om*.M
[31] et . . . est]*om*.M
[32] illa]*om*.E
[33] proponatur]proponitur E
[34] tibi]*om*.E
[35] Concedatur]conceditur E
[36] si]*om*.E
[37] proponetur]proponeretur E

Either you are running or you are in Rome, but you are not running; therefore you are in Rome.

Similarly if this

You are in Rome

were proposed first, it should be denied, and the other:

You are running

when proposed in the second place, would have to be granted.

⟨4⟩ Fourth rule. If a disjunction is posited each of whose clauses is uncertain and irrelevant to the other clause, it should be admitted. When it has been admitted, the disjunction should always be granted wherever it is proposed, and each clause should always be doubted. For instance, I posit this to you:

Either a king is sitting down or the Pope is in Rome.

When this has been admitted, it should always be granted. However often this

A king is sitting down

or this

The Pope is in Rome

is proposed, it is doubted because it is uncertain and irrelevant.

⟨5⟩ Fifth rule. If a disjunction is posited whose clauses are irrelevant but one of whose clauses is false while the other is uncertain, and if the false clause is proposed before the uncertain clause, then the false clause should be denied and the uncertain clause should be granted. For instance, I posit this to you:

Either you are running or a king is sitting down.[2]

When this has been admitted I propose

You are running

to you. It should be denied because it is false and irrelevant. Then:

A king is sitting down.

This should be granted because it follows from the *positum* and the opposite of a correctly denied proposition.

It follows from this rule that it is not awkward to doubt a proposition at first and afterwards to grant the same proposition, just as it is not awkward for the same proposition to be irrelevant at first and afterwards to follow.[3] Hence, when the *admissio* has been completed, if

A king is sitting down

---

[2] See also Part 2, chapter 1, against rule 8, sophism 2.
[3] This corollary of rule 5 was explicitly accepted by Albert, op.cit., fol. 50vb; Marsilius, op.cit., fols. 95^v–96^r; *Lat.misc.e 79*, fol. 21ra; *Lib.Soph.Oxon.*, sig.C vii^r. Peter of Mantua, however, raised some doubts: Peter of Mantua, op.cit., sig.G v^{vb}–G vi^{ra}.

dubitanda esset quia dubia et impertinens. Deinde secundo loco proposita[38] negaretur illa:

Tu curris

quia falsa et impertinens. Sed[39] tertio loco concederetur[40] illa[41]:

Rex sedet

quae prius dubitatur, quia facta est pertinens sequens ex posito et opposito bene negati, ut patet[42].

⟨6⟩ Sexta regula est ista. Si ponitur una disiunctiva cuius quaelibet pars est possibilis licet falsa, sed una sequens ad aliam, pars non sequens est neganda et pars sequens est concedenda ubicumque et quandocumque proponitur. Verbi gratia: pono tibi istam:

Antichristus est albus vel Antichristus est coloratus.

Qua admissa, ubicumque et quandocumque proponitur illa:

Antichristus est albus

negatur et alia concedatur

Antichristus est coloratus.

Si enim negaretur illa:

Antichristus est coloratus,

oporteret[43] concedere istam:

Antichristus est albus,

quia sequens ex posito et opposito bene negati. Qua concessa, oporteret concedere istam:

Antichristus est coloratus,

quae prius fuisset negata, quia sequeretur formaliter ex illa concessa:

Antichristus est albus.

⟨7⟩ Septima regula est ista. Si ponitur aliqua[44] disiunctiva cuius quaelibet pars est possibilis falsa sed quaelibet ad alteram sequens, concedenda est quaelibet istarum quotienscumque infra tempus obligationis proponitur. Verbi gratia: pono[45] tibi istam:

Antichristus est homo vel Antichristus est risibilis.

---

[38] proposita]*om*.M
[39] Sed]in *add*.E
[40] concederetur]concedatur M
[41] illa . . . sedet]*om*.M
[42] ut patet]*om*.M
[43] oporteret]oportet E
[44] aliqua]una M
[45] pono]propono E

is proposed, it should be doubted because it is uncertain and irrelevant. Then when

   You are running

has been proposed in the second place, it should be denied because it is false and irrelevant. But

   A king is sitting down

will be granted when it is ⟨proposed⟩ in the third place, even though it was doubted at first, because it has become a relevant proposition by virtue of following from the *positum* and the opposite of a correctly denied proposition, as is obvious.

⟨6⟩ Sixth rule. If a disjunction is posited each of whose clauses is possible but false, and one clause follows from the other, the clause which does not follow should be denied and the clause which does follow should be granted wherever and whenever it is proposed. For instance, I posit this to you:

   Either Antichrist is white or Antichrist is coloured.[4]

When this has been admitted,

   Antichrist is white

is denied wherever and whenever it is proposed and the other,

   Antichrist is coloured,

is granted. If one were to deny

   Antichrist is coloured

one would have to grant

   Antichrist is white,

because it follows from the *positum* and the opposite of a correctly denied proposition. When it had been granted, one would have to grant

   Antichrist is coloured,

which was denied earlier, because it follows formally from

   Antichrist is white,

which has been granted.

⟨7⟩ Seventh rule. If some disjunction is posited each of whose clauses is false but possible, and each ⟨of whose clauses⟩ follows from the other, each clause should be granted however often it is proposed during the period of the *obligatio*. For instance, I posit this to you:

   Either Antichrist is a human being or Antichrist is able to laugh.

---

[4] This example was standard in the Oxford logic: see Billingham, op.cit., fol. 93^v; *Lat.misc.e 79*, fol. 21rb; *Lib.Soph.Oxon.*, sig.C vii^v.

Qua admissa, oporteret[46] concedere quamlibet illarum propositam[47]:
>Antichristus est homo,
>Antichristus est risibilis,

quia non posset negari una quin contingeret[48] eandem concedere infra idem[49] tempus obligationis.

⟨8⟩ Octava regula est ista. Si ponitur disiunctiva facta ex parte possibili et ex[50] parte per se impossibili semper pars possibilis est concedenda et pars[51] per se impossibilis neganda. Verbi gratia: pono tibi illam:
>Tu curris vel homo est asinus.

Qua admissa, propono tibi illam:
>Tu curris.

Si concedis, habeo intentum. Si negas, propono tibi illam:
>Homo est asinus.

Si negas, contra: tu negas sequens ex posito et opposito bene negati; igitur male. Si concedis, cedat tempus obligationis et probo quod in tempore concessisti per se impossibile admisso possibili; igitur male.

Sed forte arguitur quod ista:
>Tu curris

primo loco proposita non debet concedi, quia est falsa ut patet, et non sequens.

Dicitur quod est sequens, quia sequitur ex qualibet parte disiunctivae. Ex prima namque convertibiliter; (233^{va}M) ex secunda vero[52] quia per se impossibilis.

⟨9⟩ Nona regula: Si ponitur aliqua disiunctiva cuius una pars est[53] necessaria per se et altera possibilis, semper pars per se necessaria est concedenda, et ad alteram est respondendum secundum sui qualitatem. Verbi gratia: pono tibi illam:
>Deus est vel tu es homo.

Semper quaelibet istarum est concedenda. Sed si ponatur haec:
>Deus est vel Antichristus est,

---

[46] oporteret] oportet E
[47] propositam] om. E
[48] contingeret] negare add. E
[49] idem] om. E
[50] ex] om. M
[51] pars] om. M
[52] vero] vera E.
[53] est] sit M

When this has been admitted, one ought to grant each of these

    Antichrist is a human being,

    Antichrist is able to laugh,

when it has been proposed, because one cannot deny one without also having to grant it during the period of the same *obligatio*.[5]

⟨8⟩ Eighth rule. If a disjunction is posited which has been formulated from one clause which is possible and one clause which is impossible *per se*, the clause which is possible should always be granted and the clause which is impossible *per se* should be denied. For instance, I posit this to you:

    Either you are running or a human being is a donkey.

When this has been admitted, I propose this to you:

    You are running.

If you grant it, I have made my point. If you deny it, I propose this to you:

    A human being is a donkey.

If you deny it, I argue against you: you deny something which follows from the *positum* and the opposite of a correctly denied proposition; therefore you reply incorrectly. If you grant it, let the period of the *obligatio* come to an end and I will prove that during the period you granted a proposition which was impossible *per se* on the basis of a possible *admissum*; therefore you replied incorrectly.

But perhaps someone will argue that

    You are running

should not be granted when proposed in the first place because it is false, as is obvious, and does not follow.

I reply that it does follow, for it follows from each clause of the disjunction. It follows from the first ⟨clause⟩ because this is interchangeable with it, and from the second ⟨clause⟩ because this is impossible *per se* ⟨and hence implies anything⟩.

⟨9⟩ Ninth rule. If some disjunction is posited one of whose clauses is necessary *per se* while the other is possible, the clause which is necessary *per se* should always be granted, and one should reply to the other in accordance with its status. For instance, I posit this to you:

    Either there is a God or you are a human being.

Each of these clauses should always be granted. But if I posit

    Either there is a God or Antichrist exists,

---

[5] If 'A or B' is posited and A is denied, then B follows. But if A and B imply each other then B yields A, and we have the contradiction 'A and not A'.

semper concedatur ista:

> Deus est

tamquam sequens tam ex prima quam ex secunda parte[54] disiunctivae. Altera vero, videlicet 'Antichristus est', semper negetur[55] quia falsa et impertinens.

⟨10⟩ Decima regula: Si ponitur una disiunctiva cuius una pars est possibilis falsa et altera per accidens impossibilis, respondeatur sicut quaelibet (190^{va}E) istarum esset possibilis et falsa. Verbi gratia: pono tibi istam:

> Antichristus est vel Adam non fuit.

Si primo loco proponitur illa[56]:

> Antichristus est,

negetur[57] et consequenter concedatur illa:

> Adam non fuit,

quia sequens ex posito et opposito bene negati. Non enim est inconveniens concedere impossibile per accidens. Si autem primo proponeretur ista:

> Adam non fuit,

negaretur, et secundo loco concederetur ista:

> Antichristus est

tamquam sequens. Quare[58] etc.

⟨*Sophisma*⟩

Iuxta praedicta solet sic obligari: pono tibi istam:

> Homo est asinus vel omne tibi positum est impossibile.

Si non admittitur[59], dicendo quod casus est impossibilis, tunc sic:

> Ille casus est impossibilis et ille casus est omne tibi positum; igitur omne tibi positum est impossibile.

Consequentia bona, antecedens est possibile, igitur et consequens. Tunc sic:

> Omne tibi positum est impossibile; igitur homo est asinus vel omne tibi positum est impossibile.

Consequentia tenet a parte disiunctivae ad totam disiunctivam[60] et antecedens est possibile; igitur et consequens. Tunc arguitur[61] sic:

> Consequens est possibile et consequens est tibi positum; igitur tibi

---

[54] parte]*om*.M
[55] negetur]negatur E
[56] illa]*om*.E
[57] negetur]negatur E
[58] Quare]*om*.E
[59] admittitur]casus *add*.M
[60] disiunctivam]*om*.M
[61] arguitur]*om*.E

this:
> There is a God

should always be granted as following from both the first and the second clauses of the disjunction. But the other clause, namely 'Antichrist exists', is always denied because it is false and irrelevant.

⟨10⟩ Tenth rule. If a disjunction is posited one of whose clauses is false but possible, while the other is impossible *per accidens*, one should reply as if each clause were possible and false. For instance, I posit this to you:
> Either Antichrist exists or Adam did not exist.

If
> Antichrist exists

is proposed in the first place, it is denied and consequently this:
> Adam did not exist,

is granted, because it follows from the *positum* and the opposite of a correctly denied proposition. It is not awkward to grant a proposition which is impossible *per accidens*. But if this
> Adam did not exist

were proposed first, it would be denied, and this:
> Antichrist exists

would be granted as following ⟨when it is proposed⟩ in the second place. Therefore etc.

⟨*Sophism*⟩

It is usual to present this kind of *obligatio* in relation to what has been said above. I posit this to you:
> A human being is a donkey or everything posited to you is impossible.

If you do not admit it, saying that the case is impossible, then ⟨I argue⟩ like this:
> This case is impossible, and this case is everything posited to you; therefore everything posited to you is impossible.

The inference is valid, the premiss is possible; therefore the conclusion is also possible. Then I argue like this:
> Everything posited to you is impossible; therefore either a human being is a donkey or everything posited to you is impossible.

The inference from one clause of a disjunction to the whole disjunction holds, and the premiss is possible; therefore the conclusion is too. Then I argue like this:
> The conclusion is possible and the conclusion is the *positum* put to you;

positum est possibile, et non admittis illud; igitur male.

Ideo si admittitur casus, propono tibi illam:

Homo est asinus.

Hoc oportet negare iuxta octavam regulam. Tunc propono:

Omne tibi positum est impossibile.

Concedendum est, quia sequens ex posito cum[62] opposito bene negati. Tunc sic:

Omne tibi positum est impossibile, iste casus est tibi positus; igitur iste casus est impossibilis et tu admisisti istum; igitur male respondebas[63].

Respondetur admittendo positum; et cum proponitur

Omne tibi positum est impossibile,

concedo[64]. Et tunc ad argumentum:

Omne tibi positum est impossibile, et[65] iste casus est tibi positus; igitur ille casus est impossibilis[66],

nego istam copulativam. Et si dicitur 'Pro qua parte?' pro secunda, quia repugnat uni concesso et opposito bene negati. Si tamen partes illae categoricae proponantur, concedatur[67] ultimate et[68] quod male admissi vel respondebam, non tamquam verum sed tamquam sequens[69].

⟨*Capitulum Quartum: De Similibus et Dissimilibus*⟩

Materiam intricatam et intricantem de[70] similibus propositionibus ac dissimilibus expedit declarare ut finem habeat genus positionum.

⟨*Sophismata*⟩

⟨1⟩ Sit ergo rei veritas quod tu[71] sis Parisius, et pono tibi illam:

'Tu es Parisius' et 'Tu es Romae' sunt similia.

Et intelligo per[72] 'propositiones esse similes' ipsas esse similes in veritate aut in[73] falsitate. Qua admissa, propono tibi illam:

Tu es Parisius.

---

[62] cum]et E
[63] respondebas]respondisti E
[64] concedo]concedendo M
[65] et]sed E
[66] ille . . . impossibilis]etc.M
[67] concedatur]conceditur E
[68] et]*om.*E
[69] sequens]etc. *add.*E
[70] de . . . dissimilibus]*om.*E
[71] tu]*om.*E
[72] per]*om.*E
[73] in]*om.*E

therefore the *positum* is possible, and you do not admit it; therefore you reply incorrectly.

If the case is admitted for this reason, I propose this to you:

A human being is a donkey.

This ought to be denied in accordance with the eighth ⟨main⟩ rule. Then I propose

Everything posited to you is impossible.

This should be granted, because it follows from the *positum* together with the opposite of a correctly denied proposition. Then ⟨I argue⟩ like this:

Everything posited to you is impossible, but this case is posited to you; therefore this case is impossible, and you admitted it; therefore you replied incorrectly.

I reply by admitting the *positum*, and when

Everything posited to you is impossible

is proposed, I grant it. And ⟨in reply⟩ to the argument

Everything posited to you is impossible, and this case is posited to you; therefore this case is impossible,

I deny this conjunction. And if someone asks 'On account of which clause?', ⟨I reply⟩ on account of the second because it is inconsistent with a previously granted proposition and the opposite of a correctly denied proposition. However, if the clauses are proposed as separate categorical propositions, the last one to be proposed is granted, and ⟨I also grant⟩ that I admitted or replied incorrectly, not as true but as following.

⟨Chapter Four: On Similars and Dissimilars⟩

I must now explain the confused and confusing topic of similar and dissimilar propositions so that I can being my discussion of *positio* to an end.[1]

⟨*Sophisms*⟩

⟨1⟩ ⟨First sophism⟩. Let it be true in fact that you are in Paris. I posit this to you:

'You are in Paris' and 'You are in Rome' are similars.[2]

By the phrase 'propositions are similar' I understand that they are similar in truth or in falsehood. When the case has been admitted, I propose this to you:

You are in Paris.

---

[1] Strode put this topic at the very end of his treatise, and showed how little he thought of it by writing: 'Solet difficultas assignari in ponendo propositiones esse similes vel dissimiles, quam partem obligatoriam reputo frustra fore vel inanem.' Strode, op.cit., fol. 92vb.

[2] This sophism is found in Marsilius, op.cit., fols. 89^r–90^r (with 'in Monte Pessulano' and 'in Avinione'); and Buser, op.cit., fols. 76vb–77ra (with 'Avinione' and 'Vercellis'). With certain omissions, to be noted below, Paul follows Marsilius and Buser in essence, but his presentation is less complex.

Si negas vel dubitas eam, contra:

    Ipsa est⁷⁴ vera et impertinens, igitur concedenda.

Quod sit vera, patet⁷⁵. Quod sit impertinens probatur, quia non sequitur nec repugnat, ut patet intuenti. Si ergo concedis eam, propono tibi illam: (233ᵛᵇM)

    Tu es Romae.

Si negas eam et concessisti utramque partem, igitur male. Consequentia patet per duodecimam regulam. Si concedis eam, cedat tempus obligationis et arguo quod concessisti impossibile facta obligatione possibili, igitur male. Quod autem illa copulativa sit impossibilis cuilibet notum est cum non sit possibile naturaliter aliquem⁷⁶ esse in duobus adaequatis locis.

    Dimissis ergo fantastibilibus multorum quibus ars⁷⁷ ista tenebrosa existit, respondeo admittendo positum; et cum proponitur

    Tu es Parisius,

concedo quia verum et impertinens. Deinde:

    Tu es Romae.

Nego, quia falsum non sequens. Nam non sequitur:

    'Tu es Parisius' et 'Tu es Romae' sunt similia⁷⁸, sed tu es Parisius, igitur tu es Romae,

sicut non sequitur:

    'Deus est' et 'Homo est asinus' convertuntur, sed Deus est, igitur homo est asinus.

Et tunc ad argumentum:

    Tu negas illam et concessisti alteram similium, igitur male,

non valet argumentum, sicut non sequitur:

    Tu negas illam: 'Homo est asinus' et concessisti⁷⁹ secum convertibilem, igitur male respondes.

Propterea si in principio proponeretur:

    Haec est vera: 'Tu es Parisius'

concedo⁸⁰ quia verum et impertinens. Deinde:

---

⁷⁴ est]*om.*M
⁷⁵ Quod . . . patet]quia vera E
⁷⁶ aliquem]aliquid   E
⁷⁷ ars]arguere E
⁷⁸ similia]consimilia E
⁷⁹ concessisti]concedis E
⁸⁰ concedo]concedendo M

This sophism, like many others, hinges on the relation between mention and use. In "'You are in Paris" and "You are in Rome" are similar' two sentences are mentioned, and there is no need to assume that they are ascribed any particular meaning. In turn, there is no need to assume that the claim has the truth value which would be ascribed to it under normal circumstances. Similarly, in "'You are in Paris" is true', something is being said of a sentence, of a set of sounds or symbols which may or may not have their conventional meaning; and, accordingly, the claim may or may not have its expected truth value. On the other hand, when a sentence is used, as in the utterance 'You are in Paris', it must have its conventional meaning and hence will bear the expected truth value.

If you deny or doubt it, I argue against you:

It is true and irrelevant; therefore it should be granted.

It is obvious that it is true. It can be proved that it is irrelevant, because it neither follows nor is inconsistent, as is obvious to anyone who considers the matter carefully. If, therefore, you grant it, I propose this to you:

You are in Rome.

If you deny it and you granted each clause, then you reply incorrectly.[3] The inference is obvious, by virtue of rule twelve. If you grant it, let the period of the *obligatio* come to an end, and I will argue that you granted an impossible proposition on the basis of a possible *obligatio*; therefore you replied incorrectly. It is clear to everyone that the conjunction ⟨sc. 'You are in Paris and you are in Rome'⟩ must be impossible since it is not possible in the order of nature for anyone to be in two distinct places.

After dismissing the fantasies of many[4] to whom this art is in a shadowy state, I reply by admitting the *positum*. When

You are in Paris

is proposed, I grant it because it is true and irrelevant. Then:

You are in Rome.

I deny it because it is false and does not follow. This is an invalid inference:

'You are in Paris' and 'You are in Rome' are similars, but you are in Paris; therefore you are in Rome,

just as this is invalid:

'There is a God' and 'A human being is a donkey' are interchangeable, but there is a God; therefore a human being is a donkey.

Then ⟨in reply⟩ to the argument:

You deny this and you granted the other similar proposition; therefore you reply incorrectly,

⟨I say that⟩ the argument is invalid, just as this is an invalid inference:

You deny 'A human being is a donkey' and you granted a proposition which is interchangeable with it; therefore you reply incorrectly.

Therefore, if

'You are in Paris' is true

were proposed at the beginning, I would grant it because it is true and irrelevant. Then:

---

[3] Marsilius and Buser explain that to deny 'You are in Rome' here involves a violation of the common rule that when one similar is denied the other must also be denied, and when one similar is granted the other must also be granted. By 'concessisti utramque partem' Paul means: You have granted both 'P and Q are similars' and P, hence you have granted P and Q.

[4] At this point in the argument both Marsilius and Buser examined an argument which stemmed from Burley. Burley had laid down two rules, op.cit., 3.95: 'Si possint esse similia in veritate tantum, utrumque primo loco propositum est concedendum. Si possint esse similia in falsitate tantum, utrumque primo loco propositum est negandum.' These rules are also to be found in *Lat.misc.e 79*, fol. 21va and *Lib.Soph.Oxon.*, sig. C viii^r. Given these rules one can argue that 'You are in Paris' and 'You are in Rome' can be similar only in falsehood; and when 'You are in Paris' is proposed, it will be denied. Marsilius and Buser reject this argument on two grounds. (1) 'You are in Paris' is strictly speaking irrelevant to the *propositum* and, since by hypothesis it is true, it must be granted. (2) The sentences mentioned in the *propositum* may have been given a new meaning.

Haec est vera: 'Tu es Romae'.

Concedo[81], quia sequens. Sequitur enim:

Illae[82] sunt similes, sed haec est vera: 'Tu es Parisius', igitur haec est vera: 'Tu es Romae.'

Et[83] si arguitur sic:

Haec est vera: 'Tu es Romae' et haec adaequate significat te esse Romae, igitur tu es Romae. Et tu es Parisius, igitur simul es in duobus locis,

videatur hic an primo sit[84] concessa illa:

Tu es Parisius

vel[85] non. Si sic, negetur[86] quod ista:

Tu es Romae

significet adaequate te esse Romae, quia repugnat. Sequitur enim:

Tu es Parisius, igitur tu non es Romae

et ultra:

Tu non es Romae et haec est vera: 'Tu es Romae', igitur ipsa non significat adaequate te esse Romae.

Si autem non sit illa in principio concessa

Tu es Parisius

sed (190^{vb}E) solum quod ipsa est vera, concedo[87] in ultima deductione quod tu es Romae et nego quod tu es Parisius tamquam repugnans. Et consequenter dicatur ut prius quod illa:

Tu es Parisius

non significat adaequate te esse Parisius. Et si quaeritur quid adaequate significat, dicatur quod haec quaestio non est determinanda.

Item si in principio proponatur:

Haec est vera: 'Tu es Romae'

negetur[88], quia falsa et impertinens. Deinde:

Haec est vera: 'Tu es Parisius'

negetur[89], quia repugnans posito et opposito bene negati. Sequitur enim:

---

[81] concedo]concedendo M
[82] Illae]*om.*E
[83] Et . . . Romae]*om.*E
[84] sit]est M
[85] vel]an E
[86] negetur]negatur E
[87] concedo]concedendo M
[88] negetur]negatur E
[89] negetur]negatur E

'You are in Rome' is true.

I grant it because it follows. This is a valid inference:

> These are similars, but 'You are in Paris' is true; therefore 'You are in Rome' is true.

And if someone argues like this:

> 'You are in Rome' is true, and it adequately signifies that you are in Rome;[5] therefore you are in Rome. You are also in Paris; therefore you are in two places at once,

one should see whether

> You are in Paris

has been granted first or not. If it has, one may deny that

> You are in Rome

does adequately signify that you are in Rome. It is inconsistent because this is a valid inference

> You are in Paris; therefore you are not in Rome,

and further

> You are not in Rome and 'You are in Rome' is true; therefore this proposition does not adequately signify that you are in Rome.

But if

> You are in Paris

has not been granted at the beginning, but only that it is true, in the above deduction I grant that you are in Rome and I deny that you are in Paris as inconsistent. Consequently one may say, as above, that

> You are in Paris

does not adequately signify that you are in Paris. And if someone asks what it does adequately signify, one may say that this question should not be settled.

Again, if

> 'You are in Rome' is true

were proposed at the beginning, it would be denied because it is false and irrelevant. Then

> 'You are in Paris' is true

is denied because it is inconsistent with the *positum* and the opposite of a correctly denied proposition. This is a valid inference:

---

[5] The clause 'adaequate significat' is used here to ensure conventional meaning. Marsilius uses such phrases as 'significando sicut nunc significant.' Cf. Part 1, section 2, note 7.

Ista sunt similia et haec non est vera: 'Tu es Romae', igitur nec ista: 'Tu es Parisius.'

⟨2⟩ Consimiliter dicatur ad unum aliud forte sophisma, cum ponitur quod 'Tibi concluditur' et 'Tu[90] nescis tibi concludi' sint similia. Quo admisso, propono[91]:

Tibi concluditur.

Negatur, quia falsa et impertinens. Deinde:

Tu nescis tibi concludi.

Concedo quia verum non repugnans. Sed si in principio[92] proponitur:

Haec est falsa: 'Tibi concluditur'

concedo. Deinde:

Haec est falsa: 'Tu nescis tibi concludi'.

Concedo quia sequens. Ulterius propono:

Hoc est suum oppositum[93] vel saltem convertibile cum ipso, 'Tu scis tibi concludi.'

Concedo gratia disputationis. Deinde:

Haec est vera: 'Tu scis tibi concludi.'

Concedo. Tunc arguitur sic:

Tu scis tibi concludi, igitur concluditur,

quod negasti. Concedo consequentiam et nego antecedens. Propter hoc quod concedam illam esse veram, non tamen concedo ipsam.

Et si arguitur ut prius:

Illa est vera et significat adaequate quod tu scis tibi concludi, igitur[94] tu scis tibi concludi,

nego minorem (234ra M) tamquam repugnantem, quia suum oppositum sequitur ex duobus concessis. Quia sequitur:

Haec est vera: 'Tu scis tibi concludi' et tu nescis tibi concludi, igitur ipsa non adaequate sic significat, etc.

⟨Regulae de Similibus⟩

Pro maiori[95] horum evidentia pono aliquas regulas.

---

[90] Tu]om.E
[91] propono]proponitur M
[92] principio]tibi add.E
[93] oppositum]contradictorium add.E
[94] igitur . . . concludi]om.E
[95] maiori]ergo add.E

These are similars and 'You are in Rome' is not true; therefore 'You are in Paris' is not true either.

⟨2⟩ ⟨Second Sophism⟩ One can reply in a similar manner to another very forceful sophism, in which it is posited that 'The argument goes against you' and 'You do not know that the argument goes against you' are similars.[6] When this has been admitted, I propose.

The argument goes against you.

It is denied because it is false and irrelevant. Then:

You do not know that the argument goes against you.

I grant it because it is true and not inconsistent. But if

'The argument goes against you' is false

is proposed at the beginning, I grant it. Then:

'You do not know that the argument goes against you' is false.

I grant it because it follows. Further I propose

The above is the opposite of 'You know that the argument goes against you' or at least, it is interchangeable with it.

I grant this for the sake of the disputation. Then:

'You know that the argument goes against you' is true.

I grant it. Then I argue like this:

You know that the argument goes against you; therefore the argument goes against you;

but you denied ⟨the conclusion of this inference⟩. I grant the inference and I deny the premiss. Just because I grant a proposition to be true, it does not follow that I grant that proposition.

And if someone argues as before:

This is true and it adequately signifies that you know that the argument goes against you; therefore you know that the argument goes against you,

I deny the minor premiss as inconsistent, because its opposite follows from two previously granted propositions. This is a valid inference:

'You know that the argument goes against you' is true, and you do not know that the argument goes against you; therefore that proposition does not adequately signify ⟨that you know the argument goes against you⟩.

⟨Rules for Similars⟩

I will give some rules in order to make these matters clearer.[7]

---

[6] Compare the discussion here with the subsequent discussion of the same example in the context of Rule 4. The sophism is found in Burley, op.cit., 3.96–97; Albert, op.cit., fols. 49vb–50ra, Lat.misc.e 79, fols. 21vb–22ra; Lib.Soph.Oxon., sig.C viii^r; Marsilius, op.cit., fol. 90^{r-v}; Buser, op.cit., fol. 77^{ra-rb}; and Strode, op.cit., fol. 93ra.

The sophism as presented by all but Buser and Marsilius is found in essence on p. 356, lines 12–20, under Rule 4. Most authors explained that what we have here is a case in which P and Q can be similar only in truth because P is the conclusion and 'You don't know that P' is the

⟨1⟩ Prima regula⁹⁶ est ista. Quandocumque ponuntur duae propositiones esse similes absque mentione sui adaequati significati, respondeatur ad eas concedendo vel negando vel dubitando infra tempus obligationis sicut responderetur⁹⁷ extra tempus eiusdem. Verbi gratia: pono tibi illam:

'Tu curris' et 'Tu sedes' sunt similia.

Qua admissa, semper concedatur ista:

Tu sedes

si ita est in rei veritate et⁹⁸ negetur⁹⁹ ista:

Tu curris.

Et ita de omnibus aliis dicatur sive sint possibiles sive¹ impossibiles, necessariae² vel contingentes.

⟨2⟩ Secunda regula est illa. Quandocumque ponuntur duae propositiones esse similes non faciendo mentionem de adaequato significato³, ad primo propositam esse veram vel falsam respondeatur sicut extra et consequenter ad aliam sic sumptam. Verbi gratia: pono tibi istam:

'Tu es homo' et 'Antichristus est' sunt similia.

Qua admissa, propono:

Haec est vera: 'Tu es homo.'

Concedatur⁴ quia vera et impertinens. Deinde:

Haec est vera: 'Antichristus est.'

Concedatur⁵ quia sequens ex posito et concesso. Sequitur enim:

Illae sunt similes et prima est vera, igitur et secunda.

Si igitur⁶ primo proponeretur ista:

Antichristus est,

quaerendo⁷ an sit vera vel falsa, dicatur quod est falsa, quia verum et impertinens et consequenter dicatur quod ista est falsa:

Tu es homo.

Et si prius non est concessum quod⁸ tu es homo, concedatur quod illa adaequate significat te esse hominem, et quod tu non es homo. Si autem

---

⁹⁶ regula]*om*.E
⁹⁷ responderetur]respondetur M
⁹⁸ et]*om*.E
⁹⁹ negetur]negatur E
¹ sive]sint *add*.E
² necessariae]*om*.E
³ significato]semper *add*.E
⁴ Concedatur]conceditur E
⁵ Concedatur]conceditur E
⁶ Si igitur]similiter M
⁷ quaerendo]*om*.E
⁸ quod]*om*.M

---

negation of the premiss of the valid inference 'You know that P, therefore P'. If both P and 'You don't know that P' were false, then there would be a valid inference with a true premiss and a false conclusion, which is impossible. Paul splits the sophism into two parts because, unlike Burley, Albert and Strode, he does not assume that mentioned sentences bear their conventional signification, and, unlike the author(s) of *Lat.misc.e 79* and *Lib.Soph.Oxon.*, who both specified that the sentences were taken 'primarie significando', he wants to consider all alternatives. In this he is following Buser and Marsilius, both of whom treated the sophism in one place but gave two solutions, one Burley's for the case in which, as Marsilius put it, the sentences are posited to be similar 'sic significando praecise sicut semper ante hoc instans obligationis communiter significabant', Marsilius, op.cit., fol. 90ᵛ, corrected from edition, sig.C iiiiʳᵃ; and the other that given by Paul here.

⟨1⟩ First rule. Whenever two propositions are posited to be similar without any mention of an adequate significate, one should reply to them by granting denying or doubting during the period of the *obligatio* just as one would respond outside the period of the *obligatio*. For instance, I posit this to you:

'You are running' and 'You are sitting down' are similars.

When this has been admitted, this:

You are sitting down

should always be granted if it is in fact true, and this:

You are running

should be denied. All other examples should be treated in the same way, whether they are possible or impossible, necessary or contingent.

⟨2⟩ Second rule. Whenever two propositions are posited to be similar without any mention being made of an adequate significate, one should reply to the first claim that one ⟨of them⟩ is true or false as one would outside the period, and one should reply to a similar claim about the other in accordance with one's first reply. For instance, I posit this to you:

'You are a human being' and 'Antichrist exists' are similars.

When this has been admitted, I propose:

'You are a human being' is true.

It may be granted, because it is true and irrelevant. Then:

'Antichrist exists' is true.

This may be granted because it follows from the *positum* and a previously granted proposition. This is a valid inference:

These are similars, and the first is true; therefore the second is too.

Therefore if

Antichrist exists

were the first to be proposed, in answer to the question whether it is true or false, one should say that it is false, because this ⟨sc. '"Antichrist exists" is false'⟩ is true and irrelevant. Consequently one may say that

You are a human being

is false. And if it has not previously been granted that you are a human being, one may grant that the proposition adequately signifies that you are a human being, and ⟨one may grant⟩ that you are not a human being. But if it has been previously granted that you are a human being, this minor premiss ⟨sc. '"You

---

Paul has simplified his presentation of the sophism by omitting some of the subsidiary arguments about, e.g., what could be said if the first sentence proposed ('Tibi concluditur') had been granted.

I owe the translation of 'tibi concluditur' to Paul Spade.

[7] While there is nothing new in the content of his rules, no such neat package is offered by any of the authors I have looked at. It will be noticed that Paul is careful to specify whether the case allows the possibility of new meanings for mentioned sentences or not. If conventional meaning is specified, then the logical relations of the mentioned sentences have to be considered carefully.

prius concessisti quod tu es homo, negetur[9] ista minor tamquam repugnans. Et consequenter in aliis dicatur[10].

⟨3⟩ Tertia regula est ista. Quandocumque ponuntur duae propositiones esse similes sic significando adaequate quarum una sit per se necessaria et reliqua per se impossibilis vel adinvicem repugnantes aut altera casui repugnans non admittendus est casus, ut si ponantur tales esse similes:

'Deus est' et 'Homo est asinus',
'Rex sedet' et 'Nullus rex sedet',
'Homo est asinus' et 'Quaelibet propositio est dissimilis isti.'

Repugnat enim quod illae sint[11] similes sic adaequate significando et quod quaelibet propositio sit dissimilis illi. Quod autem primus casus sit impossibilis, probo. Quia si non, admittatur igitur illas[12] esse similes[13] sic adaequate significando:

'Homo est asinus' et 'Deus est.'

Qua admissa, propono illam:

Homo est asinus.

Vel concedis vel negas. Si concedis, cedat tempus et arguo quod concessisti per se impossibile facta obligatione possibili. Si negas, arguo sic:

Homo non est asinus et haec: 'Homo est asinus' adaequate significat hominem esse asinum, igitur ipsa est falsa.

Tunc ultra:

Ipsa est falsa et ipsa[14] est similis huic 'Deus est'; igitur haec est falsa: 'Deus est.' Sed ipsa significat adaequate deum esse ut ponit casus; igitur falsum est deum esse,

quod est impossibile, cum sit simpliciter necessarium. Et ita patet quod si ponuntur[15] ambae esse falsae sequitur (191^{ra}E) quod deus non est. Si vero ponerentur ambae esse verae[16], nunc sequitur[17] hominem esse asinum, sicut potest deduci ex praedictis. Et ita consequenter in aliis casibus nominatis ostendatur praedicta regula.

⟨4⟩ Quarta regula est ista. Quandocumque ponuntur duae propositiones esse

---

[9] negetur]negatur E
[10] dicatur]est dicendum E
[11] sint]sunt M
[12] illas]illam E
[13] similes]similem E
[14] ipsa]*om.*M
[15] ponuntur]ponantur E
[16] verae]*om.*E
[17] nunc sequitur]*om.*M

are a human being" adequately signifies that you are a human being') is to be denied as inconsistent. As a result similar remarks should be made about other examples.

⟨3⟩ Third rule. Whenever two propositions are posited to be similar, given their adequate signification, and one of them is necessary *per se* and the other impossible *per se*, or they are mutually inconsistent, or one is inconsistent with the case, then the case should not be admitted. For instance ⟨this rule would apply⟩ if such propositions as these were posited to be similar:

'There is a God' and 'A human being is a donkey',
'A king is sitting down' and 'No king is sitting down',
'A human being is a donkey' and 'Every proposition is dissimilar to the former proposition'.

It is inconsistent that these propositions should be similar, given their adequate signification, and that every proposition should be dissimilar to ⟨'A human being is a donkey'⟩. Proof that the first case is impossible: if it is not, then let it be admitted that

'A human being is a donkey' and 'There is a God'

are similar, given their adequate signification. When this has been admitted, I propose this:

A human being is a donkey.

Either you grant it or you deny it. If you grant it, let the period come to an end and I will argue that you granted a proposition which is impossible *per se* on the basis of a possible *obligatio*. If you deny it, I argue like this:

A human being is not a donkey, and 'A human being is a donkey' adequately signifies that a human being is a donkey; therefore it is false.

Then further:

It is false and it is similar to 'There is a God'; therefore 'There is a God' is false. But this adequately signifies that there is a God, as the case posits; therefore it is false that there is a God.

But this conclusion is impossible since ⟨'There is a God'⟩ is simply necessary. Thus it is obvious that if both propositions are posited to be false it follows that there is no God. But if both propositions were posited to be true, it would now follow that a human being was a donkey, as can be deduced from the previous remarks. As a result one can show how the aforesaid rule applies to the other cases which were mentioned.

⟨4⟩ Fourth rule. Whenever two propositions are posited to be similar, given their adequate signification, and one or both of them follow from the

similes sic significando adaequate quarum una vel quaelibet sequitur ad contradictorium alterius, istae sunt similes in veritate, et ubicumque et quandocumque proponuntur, sunt concedendae, ut patet posito quod ponam tales esse similes sic significando (234^{rb}M) adaequate:

'Tibi concluditur' et 'Tu nescis tibi concludi',
'Tu es Romae' et[18] 'Tu nescis te esse Romae',
'Tu non curris' et 'Tu moveris',
'Quilibet homo est coloratus' et 'Aliquis homo non est albus.'

Probatur. Nam admisso primo casu, quaero utrum illae[19]:

'Tibi concluditur' et 'Tu nescis tibi concludi'

sint similes in veritate vel in falsitate. Si primum, habeo intentum. Si secundum, sequitur quod ista est falsa:

Tu nescis tibi concludi.

Cum ergo ipsa significet adaequate te nescire tibi concludi, et suum contradictorium est, quod[20] sit illud

Tu scis tibi concludi,

igitur ipsum est verum. Et significat adaequate[21] te scire tibi concludi; igitur tu scis tibi concludi; igitur tibi concluditur. Tunc sic:

Tibi concluditur et haec: 'Tibi concluditur' significat adaequate tibi concludi per casum; igitur ipsa est vera; et prius dixisti ipsam esse falsam; igitur male.

Et eodem modo potest argui quod non sit aliqua harum[22] neganda, sed quaelibet concedenda[23], et ita proportionabiliter in aliis exemplis[24] dicatur.

Ex ista regula sequitur ista conclusio: quod si ponantur duae propositiones esse similes in[25] significando adaequate quarum quaelibet est necessaria vel una necessaria et altera contingens, quaecumque istarum proposita est concedenda; et non possunt esse similes sic adaequate significando nisi in veritate, ut:

'Deus est' et 'Homo est',
'Deus est[26]' et 'Tu curris'[27],
'Homo est' et 'Nullus homo est ⟨asinus⟩.'

⟨5⟩ Quinta regula est ista. Quandocumque ponuntur[28] duae propositiones esse similes sic significando adaequate ex quarum una sequitur oppositum alterius,

---

[18] et]*om.*E
[19] illae]]*om.*M
[20] quod]cum E
[21] adaequate]*om.*E
[22] harum]earum E
[23] concedenda]concedere E
[24] exemplis]*om.*E
[25] in]*om.*E
[26] 'Deus est' et]*om.*M
[27] curris]et *add.*M
[28] ponuntur]proponuntur E

contradictory of the other, they are similar in truth. They should be granted whenever and wherever they are proposed, as is obvious if one posits that such propositions as the following are similar, given their adequate signification:

'The argument goes against you' and 'You do not know that the argument goes against you'.

'You are in Rome' and 'You do not know that you are in Rome',

'You are not running' and 'You are moving',

'Each human being is coloured' and 'Some human being is not white'.

Proof: when the first case has been admitted, I ask whether these:

'The argument goes against you' and 'You do not know that the argument goes against you'

are similar in truth or in falsehood.[8] If the first, then I have made my point. If the second, it follows that

You do not know that the argument goes against you

is false. But since it adequately signifies that you do not know that the argument goes against you, and its contradictory exists, namely this:

You know that the argument goes against you,

it follows that this ⟨contradictory⟩ is true. But it adequately signifies that you know that the argument goes against you; therefore you know that the argument goes against you; therefore the argument goes against you. Then I argue like this:

The argument goes against you, and this proposition 'The argument goes against you' adequately signifies that the argument goes against you by virtue of the case, therefore this proposition is true; and you said previously that it was false; therefore you reply incorrectly.

In the same way one can argue that none of these propositions should be denied, but each should be granted; and the same remarks apply analogously to the other examples.

This thesis follows from the rule: if two propositions are posited to be similar, given their adequate signification, and each of them is necessary, or one of them is necessary and the other is contingent, then each of them should be granted when it has been proposed; and, given their adequate signification, they can only be similar in truth. Some examples are:

'There is a God' and 'A human being exists',

'There is a God' and 'You are running',

'A human being exists' and 'No human being is ⟨a donkey⟩'.

⟨5⟩ Fifth rule. Whenever two propositions are posited to be similar, given their adequate signification, and the opposite of one of them follows from the

---

[8] See note 6.

illae sunt similes in falsitate et quaecumque proposita est neganda, ut posito quod istae essent[29] similes sic adaequate significando:

'Tibi non concluditur' et 'Tu scis tibi concludi',
'Tu scis te esse Romae vel hominem' et 'Tu non es[30] Romae vel homo',
'Tu es homo' et 'Tu non es animal',
'Tu es albus' et 'Tu non es coloratus',
'Tu curris' et 'Tu non moveris'.

Quaelibet istarum cum proponitur neganda est et adserenda falsa. Nam admisso primo casu, quaero numquid illae sint similes[31] simul falsae vel simul verae:

'Tibi non concluditur' et 'Tu scis tibi concludi.'

Si primum, habeo intentum. Si secundum, igitur ista est vera:

Tu scis tibi concludi,

et significat adaequate te scire tibi concludi per casum; igitur tu scis tibi concludi; igitur tibi concluditur, et haec:

Tibi concluditur,

quae est contradictoria illius, sic adaequate significat, igitur ipsa est vera. Et illa similiter est vera:

Tibi non concluditur,

ut concessum est; igitur duo contradictoria sunt simul vera. Idem sequitur[32] si dicitur[33] aliquam istarum esse concedendam sicut potest patere volenti ex praemissis deducere.

Ex ista regula sequitur ista conclusio, quod si ponuntur duae propositiones esse similes sic adaequate significando quarum quaelibet est impossibilis per se vel una impossibilis et altera contingens, quaecumque illarum proposita est neganda, ut[34]:

'Homo est asinus' et 'Nullus deus est',
'Homo est asinus' et 'Tu es homo.'

Quare etc.

⟨6⟩ Sexta regula et ultima est ista. Quandocumque ponuntur duae propositiones esse similes sic adaequate significando[35] quarum nulla sequitur ex contradictorio

---

[29] essent]sunt E
[30] es ... non moveris]*om*.M aliquot exempla *add*. M² *in marg*.
[31] similes]*om*.E
[32] sequitur]dicitur M
[33] dicitur]dicatur E
[34] ut]*om*.E
[35] sic ... significando]*om*.E

other, they are similar in falsehood, and whichever is proposed should be denied. ⟨This rule applies to such examples as the following⟩, when it is posited that they are similar, given their adequate signification:

'The argument does not go against you' and 'You know that the argument goes against you'.

'You know that either you are in Rome or you are a human being' and 'Either you are not in Rome or you are not a human being',

'You are a human being' and 'You are not an animal',

'You are white' and 'You are not coloured',

'You are running' and 'You are not moving'.

Each of these should be denied when it is proposed and it should be claimed to be false. When the first case has been admitted, I ask whether these are similars which are both false or which are both true:

'The argument does not go against you' and 'You know that the argument goes against you'.

If the first, then I have made my point. If the second, then this is true:

You know that the argument goes against you,

and, according to the case, it adequately signifies that you know that the argument goes against you; therefore you know that the argument goes against you; therefore the argument goes against you, and this is adequately signified by

The argument goes against you,

which is the contradictory of the other similar, and which must be true. But

The argument does not go against you

is similarly true, as was granted; therefore two contradictories are true at the same time. The same ⟨conclusion⟩ follows if one says that one of these propositions should be granted, as can be made plain to anyone wishing to deduce it from the premisses.

This thesis follows from the rule: If two propositions are posited to be similar, given their adequate signification, and each of them is impossible *per se*, or one of them is impossible and the other contingent, then each of them should be denied when it is proposed. For instance:

'A human being is a donkey' and 'There is a God',

'A human being is a donkey' and 'You are a human being'.

Therefore etc.

⟨6⟩ Sixth and last rule: Whenever two propositions are posited to be similar, given their adequate signification, and neither of them follows from the

alterius nec ex aliqua istarum sequitur contradictorium alterius, respondendum est[36] concedendo et negando iuxta modum primae propositae; ita quod si primo proposita fuerit falsa negetur[37] quaelibet istarum, et dicatur quaelibet istarum esse[38] falsa; ut posito quod illae sint similes sic adaequate significando:

'Tu curris' et 'Tu es homo',
si primo loco proponitur illa[39]:
    Tu curris
negetur[40] quia falsa et impertinens, et similiter ista:
    Tu es homo.
Et si primo loco proponitur illa:
    Tu es homo,
concedatur[41] quia vera et impertinens, et alia similiter:
    Tu curris.
Et sic per omnia est in aliis dicendum. Quare etc[42].

⟨*Regulae de Dissimilibus*⟩

Ex praedictis possunt[43] regulae de dissimilibus deduci absque ulteriori scriptura. Tamen propter maiorem vitandum laborem sit haec regula prima:
⟨1⟩ Quandocumque ponuntur duae propositiones esse dissimiles, non faciendo mentionem de adaequato significato, respondeatur ad eas concedendo (234^{va}M) vel[44] negando vel dubitando infra tempus obligationis sicut[45] respondetur extra tempus obligationis[46] eiusdem. Verbi gratia: pono tibi istam:

'Tu es homo' et (191^{rb}E) 'Tu es albus' sunt dissimilia.

Concedatur[47] quaelibet istarum cum proponitur, quia concederetur[48] extra; et infra quaelibet istarum ubicumque proposita[49] est impertinens, igitur etc.
⟨2⟩ Secunda regula est ista. Quandocumque ponuntur duae propositiones esse dissimiles, non faciendo mentionem de adaequato significato, semper ad

---

[36] est]in *add*.M
[37] negetur]negatur E
[38] esse]*om*.M
[39] illa]*om*.E
[40] negetur]negatur E
[41] concedatur]conceditur E
[42] Quare etc.]*om*.M
[43] possunt]possent E
[44] vel]*om*.M
[45] sicut]sic E
[46] obligationis]*om*.M
[47] Concedatur]conceditur E
[48] concederetur]conceduntur M
[49] proposita]*om*.E

contradictory of the other, nor does the contradictory of either follow from the other, then one should reply by granting and denying in accordance with the status of the first to be proposed. Thus if the first to be proposed was false, each of them is denied and each is said to be false. For instance, if it is posited that
  'You are running' and 'You are a human being'
are similar, given their adequate signification, then if
  You are running
is proposed in the first place, it is denied because it is false and irrelevant; and likewise this
  You are a human being
⟨is denied⟩. And if
  You are a human being
is proposed in the first place, it is granted because it is true and irrelevant, and likewise this
  You are running
⟨is granted⟩. Exactly the same should be said of other examples. Therefore etc.

⟨*Rules for Dissimilars*⟩
From what has been said above one can deduce rules for dissimilars without any further discussion. However, ⟨I will give some rules⟩ in order to avoid a greater effort ⟨on your part⟩.
⟨1⟩ First rule. Whenever two propositions are posited to be dissimilar, and no mention is made of the adequate significate, one should reply to them during the period of the *obligatio* by granting or denying or doubting, just as one would reply outside the period of the *obligatio*. For instance, I posit this to you:
  'You are a human being' and 'You are white' are dissimilars.
Each should be granted when it is proposed, because it would be granted outside; and during the period each of them is irrelevant wherever it is proposed. Therefore etc.
⟨2⟩ Second rule. Whenever two propositions are posited to be dissimilar, and no mention is made of the adequate significate, one should always reply as

primo propositam esse veram vel falsam respondeatur sicut extra, et ad aliam dissimiliter secundario sumptam. Verbi gratia: pono quod illae sint dissimiles:

'Tu es homo' et 'Tu es albus.'

Deinde[50] propono:

Haec est vera: 'Tu es homo.'

Concedo. Deinde propono[51]:

Haec est falsa: 'Tu es albus.'

Concedo. Si in principio proponeretur:

Haec est vera: 'Tu es albus',

concederem, et dicerem consequenter illam esse falsam: 'Tu es homo.'

⟨3⟩ Tertia regula est ista. Quandocumque ponuntur duae propositiones esse dissimiles, sic significando adaequate, quarum quaelibet est necessaria vel impossibilis vel sunt convertibiles vel[52] altera casui[53] repugnans, non est admittendus casus; ut posito quod tales sint dissimiles sic adaequate significando:

'Deus est' et 'Homo est',

'Nullus deus est' et 'Homo est asinus',

'Tu es homo' et 'Tu es risibilis vel animal rationale',

'Tu es capra' et 'Quaelibet propositio est similis isti.'

⟨4⟩ Quarta regula est ista. Si ponuntur duae propositiones esse dissimiles sic adaequate significando, quarum una est necessaria et reliqua impossibilis vel contingens, propositio necessaria ubicumque et quandocumque proponitur est concedenda, impossibilis vero vel contingens est neganda; ut:

'Deus est' et 'Tu es asinus',

'Deus est' et 'Tu es homo.'

Immo si una istarum est[54] impossibilis et alia necessaria vel contingens, impossibilis est neganda et[55] necessaria est concedenda, et contingens similiter, sive vera fuerit sive falsa, ut:

'Tu es asinus' et 'Deus est' vel[56] 'Tu curris.'

⟨5⟩ Quinta regula est ista. Si ponuntur duae propositiones contingentes esse dissimiles sic significando adaequate quarum una antecedit ad reliquam et non e

---

[50] Deinde . . . Concedo]om.E
[51] propono]om.M
[52] vel]aut M
[53] casui]casu E
[54] est]fuerit M
[55] et]om.M
[56] vel]et E

one would outside to the one which is first proposed to be true or false. To the other which is taken in the second place ⟨one must reply⟩ dissimilarly. For instance, I posit that:

'You are a human being' and 'You are white'

are dissimilar. Then I propose:

'You are a human being' is true.

I grant it. Then I propose:

'You are white' is false.

I grant it. If

'You are white' is true

were proposed at the beginning, I would grant it, and as a result I would say that 'You are a human being' was false.

⟨3⟩ Third rule. Whenever two propositions are posited to be dissimilar, given their adequate signification, and each of them is necessary or impossible, or they are interchangeable, or one is inconsistent with the case, the case should not be admitted.[9] ⟨This rule applies⟩ when it is posited that such propositions as the following are dissimilar, given their adequate signification:

'There is a God' and 'A human being exists',

'There is no God' and 'A human being is a donkey',

'You are a human being' and 'You are able to laugh, or are a rational animal',

'You are a goat' and 'Every proposition is similar to the former proposition'.[10]

⟨4⟩ Fourth rule. If two propositions are posited to be dissimilar, given their adequate signification, and one of them is necessary and the other is impossible or contingent, then the necessary proposition should be granted whenever and wherever it is proposed, and the impossible or contingent proposition should be denied. For instance:

'There is a God' and 'You are a donkey',

'There is a God' and 'You are a human being'.

On the other hand, if one is impossible and the other is necessary or contingent, then the impossible ⟨proposition⟩ should be denied and the necessary ⟨proposition⟩ should be granted, and so should the contingent ⟨proposition⟩, whether it is true or false. For instance:

'You are a donkey' and 'There is a God', or 'You are running'.

⟨5⟩ Fifth rule. If two contingent propositions are posited to be dissimilar, given their adequate signification, and one of them is a premiss to the other,

---

[9] Cf. Strode, op.cit., fol. 93ra for similar remarks.

[10] The examples here (as with the list given above under rule 3) are strongly reminiscent of two sophisms found in the *Logica Oxoniensis*, and only there, so far as I know: '"Deus est" et "Omnis homo est animal" sunt dissimiles' and '"Homo est asinus" et "Quaelibet propositio est similis illi" sunt dissimiles'. See *Lat.misc.e 79*, fol. 22rb and *Lib.Soph.Oxon.*, sig.C viii^v. The second sophism is not in Billingham.

contra, antecedens ubicumque et quandocumque proponitur est negandum et consequens concedendum, ut posito quod illae sint dissimiles sic adaequate significando:

'Tu curris' et 'Tu moveris',

haec:

Tu curris,

semper est neganda et ista:

Tu moveris,

continue est concedenda. Idem dicatur de illis:

'Tibi non concluditur' et 'Tu non scis tibi concludi',

quarum prima semper debet negari et secunda concedi.

Et notanter dicitur 'et non e contra', quia si propositiones essent convertibiles, negaretur casus ut prius dicebatur.

⟨6⟩ Sexta regula et ultima est ista. Si ponuntur duae propositiones esse dissimiles sic adaequate significando non se habentes aliquo praedictorum modorum, respondendum est ad eas sicut ad impertinens, ita quod si primo proposita fuerit vera concedatur et alia negetur[57]; et si primo proposita fuerit falsa, negetur, et alia concedatur; ut posito quod illae sint dissimiles sic adaequate significando:

'Tu curris' et 'Tu es Parisius',

quaecumque istarum primo proponatur[58] debet negari et alia concedi. Idem dicitur de istis:

'Tibi concluditur' et 'Tu nescis tibi concludi'.

Prima primo proposita negetur et secunda concedatur. Si tamen secunda prius proponeretur deberet[59] negari et altera postmodum[60] proposita concedi.

Item notandum quod illae propositiones dicuntur dissimiles quarum una est vera et reliqua[61] falsa; et ubi una esset necessaria et alia vera sed contingens non propter hoc dicuntur dissimiles, quia similitudo et dissimilitudo non (234^{vb}M) sumuntur[62] in proposito nisi pro similitudine in veritate aut falsitate aut pro dissimilitudine sic sumpta similiter. Ubi tamen

---

[57] negetur]negatur E
[58] proponatur]proponitur E
[59] deberet]debent E
[60] postmodum]primo modo E
[61] reliqua]est *add*.M
[62] sumuntur]sumitur E

but not the reverse, the premiss should be denied wherever and whenever it is proposed, and the conclusion should be granted.[11] For instance, if it is posited that

'You are running' and 'You are moving'

are dissimilars, given their adequate signification, then

You are running

should always be denied and

You are moving

should always be granted. The same should be said of these

'The argument does not go against you' and 'You do not know that the argument goes against you'.

Here the first ought always to be denied and the second granted.

It should be noted that I say 'but not the reverse', for if the propositions were interchangeable, the case would be denied as was said before.

⟨6⟩ Sixth and last rule. If two propositions are posited to be dissimilar, given their adequate signification, and they are not related in any of the aforesaid ways, then one should reply to them as if to an irrelevant proposition. Thus if the first to be proposed were true, it would be granted and the other would be denied; and if the first to be proposed were false, it would be denied and the other would be granted. For instance, if it is posited that

'You are running' and 'You are in Paris'

are dissimilars, given their adequate signification, then whichever of these is proposed first ought to be denied and the other granted. The same is said of these:

'The argument goes against you' and 'You do not know that the argument goes against you'.

The first proposition when it is proposed first is denied and the second is granted. However, if the second were proposed before ⟨the other⟩, it ought to be denied, and the other, when it is proposed afterwards, ought to be granted.

Again, it should be noted that propositions are called dissimilar when one is true and the other false. They are not called dissimilar on the grounds that one is necessary and the other true but contingent, because similarity and dissimilarity with respect to the present topic are taken ⟨to refer⟩ only to similarity or dissimilarity in truth or falsehood. However, where the

---

[11] Marsilius, op.cit., fol. 93^{r-v}, gives this rule explicitly with the rubric 'dummodo nova impositio sit exclusa'.

opponens vellet similitudinem et dissimilitudinem magis ad suum placitum ampliare aliter oporteret[63] respondere, qualiter non est declarandum quia sine dubio inutile foret. Quare etc.

Ex praedictis sequitur quod si ponitur et admittitur ista:

Tu es Romae;

qua posita et admissa proponitur:

Istae sunt dissimiles: 'Tu es Romae' et 'Tu es episcopus',

debet negari, quia[64] quaelibet istarum est falsa. Si tamen immediate post positum admissum proponeretur ista:

'Tu es Romae' significat adaequate te esse Romae,

concedendum est, quia verum et impertinens. Deinde illa:

'Tu es Romae' est vera

conceditur tamquam sequens. Ulterius proponitur[65]:

'Tu es Romae' et 'Tu es episcopus' sunt dissimiles.

Conceditur. Deinde:

Ista est falsa: 'Tu es episcopus.'

Conceditur.

Similiter si iam proponeretur:

'Tu curris' et 'Tu es homo' sunt dissimiles,

concedatur quia verum et impertinens. Deinde:

Ista est falsa: 'Tu es homo.'

Conceditur tamquam sequens. Sequitur enim:

Illae sunt dissimiles et ista 'Tu curris' est vera, igitur ista est falsa 'Tu es homo'; etc. (191^{va}E)

---

[63] oporteret]oportet E
[64] quia]et M
[65] proponitur]proponatur E

opponent wishes to broaden ⟨the types of⟩ similarity and dissimilarity ⟨allowed⟩ more in accordance with his own desire, one would have to reply in a different way. How one would go about this will not be explained here, because it would doubtless be a pointless exercise. Therefore etc.

From what has been said it follows that if this:
> You are in Rome

is posited and admitted, and when it has been posited and admitted this:
> 'You are in Rome' and 'You are a bishop' are dissimilar

is proposed, then it should be denied, because each of these propositions is false. However, if one were to propose
> 'You are in Rome' adequately signifies that you are in Rome

immediately after the *positum*, it should be granted because it is true and irrelevant. Then this:
> 'You are in Rome' is true

is granted as following. Further:
> 'You are in Rome' and 'You are a bishop' are dissimilar

is proposed. It is granted. Then:
> 'You are a bishop' is false.

It is granted.

Similarly if this were now proposed:
> 'You are running' and 'You are a human being' are dissimilar,

it may be granted because it is true and irrelevant. Then:
> 'You are a human being' is false.

It is granted as following. This is a valid inference:
> These are dissimilar and 'You are running' is true; therefore 'You are a human being' is false.

⟨PARS TERTIA: DE DEPOSITIONE⟩

⟨*Capitulum Primum: Regulae.*⟩

Praedicta de positione dicenda ostenduntur[1] in depositione, quoniam species oppositae dicuntur modo opposito per omnia se habentes intrinsece[2]. Verumtamen pro maiori evidentia sit haec regula prima.

⟨1⟩ Nullum necessarium per se aut simpliciter, scitum esse tale, in depositione est admittendum.

Patet quia si tale[3] admitteretur oporteret concedere per se impossibile et negare per se necessarium, cuius oppositum dictum est.

⟨2⟩ Secunda regula est ista. Omne possibile contingens aut per accidens necessarium vel impossibile quovis modo scitum esse tale in depositione est admittendum.

Patet quia admisso tali non sequitur aliquod inconveniens, sicut nec si poneretur.

⟨3⟩ Tertia regula est ista. Omne depositum sub forma depositi tempore suae depositionis propositum scitum esse tale est negandum. Verbi gratia: si deponatur talis propositio:

    Aliquis homo est Romae,

qua deposita et admissa proponatur eadem, neganda est.

⟨4⟩ Quarta regula. Omne antecedens ad depositum scitum esse tale infra tempus obligationis est negandum. Verbi gratia: deposita et admissa tali propositione:

    Homo currit,

proponatur ista:

    Iste homo currit.

Quocumque demonstrato[4], neganda est quia si concederes istam oportet[5] concedere sequens ex ipsa. Cum ergo depositum sit sequens ex ipsa, oporteret[6] concedere depositum, quod est contra tertiam regulam.

---

[1] ostenduntur]ostendunt M
[2] intrinsece]intrinseca M
[3] tale]*om*.E
[4] demonstrato]adaequato E
[5] oportet]te *add*.E
[6] oporteret]oportet te E

⟨PART THREE: CONCERNING *DEPOSITIO*⟩

⟨Chapter One: Rules⟩
What has been said about *positio* shows what ought to be said about *depositio* since opposite species are described in an opposite way with respect to all their essential characteristics. However, for greater clarity, ⟨I will give some rules⟩:

⟨1⟩ First rule. No proposition which is necessary *per se* or simply and is known to be such, ought to be admitted in a *depositio*.[1]

This is obvious, because if such were admitted, one would have to grant the impossible *per se* and deny the necessary *per se*, ⟨but⟩ the opposite of this has been stated ⟨as a rule⟩.

⟨2⟩ Second rule. Every possible proposition which is contingent or necessary *per accidens*, ⟨and every⟩ impossible proposition no matter what kind, ⟨whether *per accidens* or *per se*⟩, and which is known to be such, should be admitted in a *depositio*.

This is obvious because when such a proposition has been admitted no awkward results will follow, any more than if the proposition had been posited.[2]

⟨3⟩ Third rule. Every *depositum* which is proposed in the form of the *depositum* during the period of its *depositio*, and is known to be such, should be denied.[3] For instance, if a proposition such as this is deposited:

Some human being is in Rome,

and when it has been deposited and admitted, the same proposition is proposed, then it should be denied.

⟨4⟩ Fourth rule. Every premiss from which a *depositum* can be inferred, which is known to be such, should be denied during the period of the *obligatio*.[4] For instance, when

A human being is running

has been deposited and admitted, let

This human being is running

be proposed. Whoever is indicated, this proposition should be denied, because if it were granted one would have to grant what follows from it. Since the *depositum* follows from it, one would have to grant the *depositum*, which violates the third rule.

---

[1] For the contents of rules 1 and 2, which were not always put in the form of rules, see *Lat.misc.e 79*, fol. 23ra; Marsilius, op.cit., fol. 99^r (rule 3); and Strode, op.cit., fol. 89^{ra-rb}. Peter of Candia, op.cit., fol. 69rb, merely said that the necessary was not to be admitted. Strode remarked: 'quasi pro vitio reputaretur deponere impossibile, non tamen respectu respondentis sed arguentis sicut et ponere necessarium'. Strode, op.cit., fol. 89rb, text corrected from MS, fol. 44rb. Paul's position may be compared with that found in Martinus, op.cit., fol. 130^v: 'Unde sciendum quod in depositione non debet admitti propositiones nisi contingentes'; and Fland, op.cit., p. 49, §40: 'numquam debent aliquae propositiones admitti in depositione nisi propositiones verae contingentes vel propositiones dubiae'.

[2] Paul must have meant to exclude the impossible *per se* from this remark.

[3] For this rule, see Albert, rule 1, op.cit., fol. 51rb; Marsilius, rule 1, op.cit., fol. 99^r; *Lat.misc.e 79*, rule 1, fol. 23ra; *Lib.Soph.Oxon.*, rule 1, sig.D i^r; Buser, op.cit., fol. 77vb; Peter of Candia, rule 1, op.cit., fol. 69rb. Albert and Marsilius omitted the phrase 'scitum esse tale'.

[4] See Albert, rule 3, op.cit., fol. 51rb; Marsilius, rule 4, op.cit., fol. 99^r; *Lat.misc.e 79*, rule 4, fol. 23^{ra-rb}; *Lib.Soph.Oxon.*, rule 3, sig.D i^r; Peter of Candia, rule 2, op.cit., fol. 69rb; Strode, rule 1, op.cit., fol. 89rb.

⟨5⟩ Quinta regula est ista. Omne contradicens deposito scitum esse tale infra tempus obligationis est concedendum. Verbi gratia: deposita et admissa tali propositione

> Homo est Romae,

si haec proponatur:

> Nullus[7] homo est Romae,

concedenda est quia ex quo negatur unum contradictorium, reliquum debet concedi.

⟨6⟩ Sexta regula est ista. Omne sequens ad contradictorium depositi scitum esse tale infra tempus obligationis est concedendum. Verbi gratia: depono tibi istam:

> Sortes est.

Qua deposita et admissa, proponatur eadem. Negatur. Deinde propono tibi istam:

> Sortes non loquitur.

Concedenda est, quia sequitur ad contradictorium depositi, nam bene sequitur:

> Nullus Sortes est, igitur nullus Sortes loquitur.

⟨7⟩ Septima regula est ista. Omne repugnans opposito contradictorio depositi scitum esse tale infra tempus obligationis est negandum. Verbi gratia: deposita et admissa tali propositione:

> Sortes non est Romae,

si proponatur illa[8]:

> Sortes non est,

haec est neganda quia repugnans contradictorio depositi. Haec enim repugnat[9]:

> Omnis Sortes est Romae et Sortes non est.

⟨8⟩ Octava regula est ista. Omne sequens ex contradictorio depositi et bene concesso vel bene concessis, opposito bene negati (235^{ra}M) vel bene negatorum, scitum esse tale, est concedendum. Verbi gratia: deposita et admissa tali propositione:

---

[7] nullus]non M.
[8] illa]haec E
[9] repugnat]repugnant M

⟨5⟩ Fifth rule. Every proposition which contradicts the *depositum* and is known to do so, should be granted during the period of the *obligatio*.[5] For instance, when a proposition of this sort:

A human being is in Rome

has been deposited and admitted, then if

No human being is in Rome

is proposed, it should be granted because when one contradictory has been denied the other ought to be granted.

⟨6⟩ Sixth rule. Every proposition which follows from the contradictory of a *depositum* and is known to do so, should be granted during the period of the *obligatio*.[6] For instance, I deposit this to you:

Socrates exists.

When this has been deposited and admitted, let the same proposition be proposed. It is denied. Then I propose this to you:

Socrates is not speaking.

This should be granted, because it follows from the contradictory of the *depositum*. This is a valid inference:

Socrates does not exist; therefore Socrates is not speaking.

⟨7⟩ Seventh rule. Every proposition which is inconsistent with the contradictory of the *depositum*, and is known to be such, should be denied during the period of the *obligatio*.[7] For instance, when a proposition of this sort

Socrates is not in Rome

has been deposited and admitted, then if

Socrates does not exist

is proposed, it should be denied because it is inconsistent with the contradictory of the *depositum*. This ⟨conjunction⟩ is inconsistent:

Socrates is in Rome and Socrates does not exist.

⟨8⟩ Eighth rule. Every proposition which follows from the contradictory of the *depositum* together with a correctly granted proposition or propositions or the opposite of a correctly denied proposition or propositions and is known to be such, should be granted.[8] For instance, when a proposition of this sort

---

[5] See Albert, rule 2, op.cit., fol. 51rb; *Lat.misc.e* 79, rule 6, fol. 23rb; *Lib.Soph.Oxon.*, rule 2, sig.D ir; Marsilius, rule 2, op.cit., fol. 99r; Buser, rule 2, part 1, op.cit., fol. 77vb; Peter of Candia, rule 3, op.cit., fol. 69rb. Albert's formulation is careless since he uses the word 'repugnans'. As Burley had pointed out, op.cit., 4.02, not every inconsistent proposition need be granted 'quia repugnantia possunt simul esse falsa'.

[6] See Buser, rule 2, part 2, op.cit., fol. 77vb. A marginal note, apparently in the same hand, in Peter of Candia, op.cit., fol. 69rb, gives this as an alternative version of Peter's rule 4, and uses the same examples as appear in Paul. The rule also appears in Peter's main text on fol. 69va without the examples, but with the corollary: 'omne contradicens sequenti ex contradictorio depositi est negandum'.

[7] See Peter of Candia, op.cit., fol. 69vb. The examples are the same.

[8] See Peter of Candia, op.cit., fol. 69vb. The examples are the same.

Aliquis homo non est Romae,
proponatur illa:
Tu es aliquis homo.
Concedenda est[10] quia vera et impertinens. Deinde si proponatur
Tu es Romae,
concedenda est quia bene sequitur:
Quilibet homo est Romae, tu es aliquis homo, igitur tu es Romae.
⟨9⟩ Nona regula est ista. Omne repugnans contradictorio depositi et bene concesso vel bene concessis, opposito bene negati vel oppositis[11] bene negatorum, scitum esse tale, infra tempus obligationis est negandum. Verbi gratia: deposita et admissa tali propositione
Aliquis homo non currit,
proponatur illa:
Tu es aliquis homo.
Concedenda est quia vera et impertinens. Deinde si proponatur illa:
Tu non curris,
neganda est quia repugnans contradictorio depositi et concesso, sicut ostensum est in priori regula.
⟨10⟩ Decima regula est ista. Omne antecedens ad depositum cum concesso vel concessis, opposito bene negati vel oppositis bene negatorum, scitum esse tale, infra tempus obligationis est negandum. Verbi gratia: depono tibi istam:
Aliquis homo non currit.
Qua admissa, propono
Tu es homo.
Concedenda est quia vera et impertinens. Deinde
Tu non[12] curris.
Neganda est quia antecedens cum uno concesso ad ⟨depositum⟩[13]. Sequitur enim:
Tu es aliquis homo et tu[14] non curris, igitur aliquis homo non currit.

---

[10] est]*om*.E
[11] oppositis]*om*.E
[12] non]*om*.E
[13] depositum]oppositum depositi M,E, *correxi*
[14] tu]*om*.M

> Some human being is not in Rome,

has been deposited and admitted, let

> You are some human being

be proposed. This should be granted because it is true and irrelevant. Then if this

> You are in Rome

is proposed, it should be granted, because this is a valid inference:

> Every human being is in Rome, you are some human being; therefore you are in Rome.

⟨9⟩ Ninth rule. Every proposition which is inconsistent with the contradictory of the *depositum* together with a correctly granted proposition or propositions, or the opposite of a correctly denied proposition or propositions, and is known to be such, should be denied during the period of the *obligatio*.[9] For instance, when a proposition of this sort

> Some human being is not running

has been deposited and admitted, let this

> You are some human being

be proposed. This should be granted because it is true and irrelevant. Then if this

> You are not running

is proposed, it should be denied because it is inconsistent with the contradictory of the *depositum* and a previously granted proposition, as was shown in ⟨the discussion of⟩ the earlier rule.

⟨10⟩ Tenth rule. Every proposition which is a premiss from which, together with a previously granted proposition or propositions, or the opposite of a correctly denied proposition, or the opposites of correctly denied propositions, the *depositum* can be inferred, and which is known to be such, should be denied during the period of the *obligatio*.[10] For instance, I deposit this to you:

> Some human being is not running.

When this has been admitted, I propose

> You are a human being.

This should be granted because it is true and irrelevant. Then

> You are not running.

This should be denied because it is a premiss from which, together with a previously granted proposition, ⟨the *depositum*⟩ can be inferred. This is a valid inference:

> You are some human being and you are not running; therefore some human being is not running.

---

[9] See Peter of Candia, op.cit., fol. 69ᵛᵇ. The examples are the same.

[10] See *Lat.misc.e 79*, rule 7, fol. 23ʳᵇ; *Lib.Soph.Oxon.*, rule 3, sig.D iʳ. This is the only one of Paul's rules not found in Peter of Candia. It should be noted that Peter only numbered his first four rules, and that all the unnumbered rules appeared later, after his sophisms. *Lib.Soph.Oxon.*, loc.cit., added as rule 4 the corollary that the contradictory of any such proposition should be granted.

Si enim concederetur quaelibet istarum, oporteret[15] necessario concedere depositum.

Item si in principio proponeretur ista:

Tu non curris,

concedenda esset, quia vera et impertinens. Deinde

Tu es homo

neganda, quia antecedit ad depositum cum concesso, ut patet.

Similiter si immediate post depositum proponeretur ista:

Tu non es homo,

neganda esset quia falsa et impertinens. Deinde

Tu non curris

neganda est quia antecedit ad depositum cum opposito bene negati. Sequitur enim ut prius:

Tu non curris et tu es aliquis homo, igitur aliquis homo non currit.

⟨11⟩ Undecima regula est ista. Propositio impertinens est[16] ista quae nec est sequens ex (191^{vb}E) deposito, nec[17] antecedens ad ipsum, nec repugnans deposito, nec sequens ex opposito depositi, nec repugnans opposito depositi. Verbi gratia: deposita et admissa ista:

Sortes currit,

proponitur:

Plato currit.

Haec propositio est impertinens, cum non se habeat aliquo praedictorum[18] modorum.

⟨12⟩ Duodecima et ultima regula[19] est ista. Ad omne sequens et ad omne impertinens et ad omne repugnans quod non est contradictorium nec convertibile cum contradictorio depositi scitum esse tale infra tempus obligationis respondendum est secundum suam[20] qualitatem. Verbi gratia: deposita et admissa tali propositione

Sortes currit,

deinde[21] proponatur[22] illa:

---

[15] oporteret]oportet E
[16] est . . . quae]in hac specie obligationis dicitur esse quia E
[17] nec . . . ipsum]*om*.M
[18] praedictorum]dictorum E
[19] regula]*om*.E
[20] suam]sui E
[21] deinde]*om*.M
[22] proponatur]proponitur E

If each of these propositions were granted, one would necessarily have to grant the *depositum*.

Likewise if

You are not running

were proposed at the beginning, it should be granted because it is true and irrelevant. Then:

You are a human being

should be denied because it is a premiss from which, together with a previously granted proposition, the *depositum* can be inferred, as is obvious.

Similarly if

You are not a human being

were proposed immediately after the *depositum*, it would have to be denied because it is false and irrelevant. Then

You are not running

should be denied because it is a premiss from which, together with the opposite of a correctly denied proposition, the *depositum* can be inferred. As before, this is a valid inference:

You are not running and you are some human being; therefore some human being is not running.

⟨11⟩ Eleventh rule. An irrelevant proposition is one which neither follows from the *depositum* nor is a premiss to it nor is inconsistent with it nor follows from the opposite of the *depositum* nor is inconsistent with the opposite of the *depositum*.[11] For instance, when this

Socrates is running

has been deposited and admitted, this

Plato is running

is proposed. This proposition is irrelevant, since it is not related ⟨to the *depositum*⟩ in any of the aforesaid ways.

⟨12⟩ Twelfth and last rule. During the period of the *obligatio* one should reply to every proposition which follows from or is irrelevant ⟨to the *depositum*⟩ and to every inconsistent proposition which is not the contradictory ⟨of the *depositum*⟩ nor interchangeable with the contradictory of the *depositum*, and which is known to be such, in accordance with its status.[12] For instance, when a proposition of this sort,

Socrates is running,

has been deposited and admitted, then let this

---

[11] See Peter of Candia, op.cit., fol. 69^{va-vb}. The example is the same, but with 'est' for 'currit' on p. 374, line 2 from bottom. As Paul Spade pointed out to me, the definition of 'irrelevant' here is different from that given earlier: see Part 1, section 1, definition 11. A proposition (I) was characterized as irrelevant to the *positum* (P) if and only if neither it nor its negation followed from P (where P → -I is equivalent to 'P & I' is inconsistent). Thus both P → I and P → -I must be false. Here we are told that all of the following are false: D → I, D → -I, -D → I and -D → -I. What seems to have happened is that a proposition is defined as irrelevant both to the *depositum* D and to the negation of D, i.e. the proposition which is to be granted. This may reflect the confusion in the literature about which proposition, D or 'Not D', was to be taken as the *obligatum*: see Part 3, chapter 2, note 2. Other sources defined an irrelevant proposition as one which was not a premiss to the *depositum* and whose contradictory was not a premiss either. That is, both I → D and -I → D were false, and so were their equivalents -D → I and -D → -I.

Non homo est.

Illa est repugnans deposito; non tamen est contradictorium depositi, nec convertibile cum eo. Ideo respondendum est[23] secundum sui qualitatem, scilicet eam negando. Nec est aliquod inconveniens duas propositiones repugnantes negare, nam istae duae repugnant

'Quilibet homo est albus' et 'Nullus homo est albus',

et tamen ambae sunt negandae ut patet intuenti.

Item si in casu isto proponatur illa

Sortes[24] est,

non propter hoc est neganda, quia negata fuit ista

Sortes currit.

Nam in consequentia bona et formali conceditur consequens et negatur antecedens, ut:

Homo est asinus[25], igitur homo est.

Ideo non est inconveniens negare illam:

Sortes currit,

et concedere istam:

Sortes est.

Iterum[26] si proponitur ista:

Deus est,

vel quaecumque alia impertinens, respondendum est[27] secundum sui qualitatem ac si nulla obligatio facta fuisset, scilicet concedendo, negando vel[28] dubitando secundum quod materia requirit. Unde necessarium per se quocumque loco propositum est concedendum quia sequens ex contradictorio (235^{rb}M) depositi. Ideo ad istam:

Deus est

respondendum est concedendo. Si vero proponatur talis:

Homo est asinus,

neganda est quia per se impossibilis, et per consequens repugnans[29] contradictorio depositi secundum quod alias declaratum est. Et ita respondeatur ad quodlibet aliud per se impossibile. Quare etc[30].

[23] est]*om*.E
[24] Sortes]non *add*.E
[25] asinus]albus E
[26] Iterum]item E
[27] est]ad eam *add*.E
[28] vel]*om*.E
[29] repugnans]repugnat E
[30] Quare etc.]*om*.E

See *Lib.Soph.Cant.*, sig.C iii^r; *Lib.Soph.Oxon.*, sig.D i^r; *Lat.misc.e* 79, fol. 23rb.

[12] See Peter of Candia, rule 4, op.cit., fol. 69^{rb-va}. The examples are the same, as is most of the wording. In the printed text at least, Albert, op.cit., fol. 51^{rb-va}, said that every proposition following formally from the *depositum* was to be denied, but no one else made this mistake. Cf. Burley, op.cit., 4.02. See also *Lat.misc.e* 79, fol. 23ra; rule 2 is that the 'sequentes' need not be denied.

It is not the case that a human being exists

be proposed. It is inconsistent with the *depositum*, but it is not the contradictory of the *depositum*, nor is it interchangeable with ⟨the contradictory⟩. Therefore we should reply to it in accordance with its status, that is, by denying it. Nor is there any awkwardness in denying two inconsistent propositions, for these two:

'Every human being is white' and 'No human being is white'

are inconsistent; yet both should be denied, as is obvious to anyone who considers the matter.

Likewise if in this case

Socrates exists

is proposed, it should not be denied on the grounds that

Socrates is running

has been denied. One can grant the conclusion and deny the premiss of a formally valid inference, as with:

A human being is a donkey; therefore a human being exists.

For that reason it is not awkward to deny

Socrates is running

and to grant

Socrates exists.

Again if

There is a God

or some other irrelevant proposition is proposed, one should reply to it in accordance with its status as if no *obligatio* has been brought into being, that is by granting, denying or doubting it as the topic requires. Hence a proposition which is necessary *per se* should be granted, no matter where it is proposed, because it follows from the contradictory of the *depositum*. Thus one should reply to

There is a God

by granting it. But if this

A human being is a donkey

were proposed, it should be denied because it is impossible *per se* and as a result is inconsistent with the contradictory of the *depositum*, in accordance with what was explained elsewhere. One should reply in the same way to any other proposition which is impossible *per se*. Therefore etc.

⟨*Capitulum Secundum: Conclusiones*⟩
Ex praedictis sequuntur aliquae breves conclusiones.
⟨1⟩ Prima est ista[31]. Non omne obligatum ab aliquo admissum et eidem infra tempus obligationis propositum, scitum[32] esse tale, est ab eodem concedendum.
⟨2⟩ Secunda conclusio. Non omne sequens ex obligato scitum esse tale est[33] concedendum.
⟨3⟩ Tertia conclusio. Aliquod repugnans obligato scitum esse tale est concedendum.
⟨4⟩ Quarta conclusio. Non omne repugnans obligato scitum esse tale infra tempus obligationis est negandum.

Patet quaelibet harum conclusionum eo quod sicut positum in positione est obligatum, ita depositum in depositione, licet quam plurimi oppositum dicant[34], putantes contradictorium depositi esse obligatum, quod tamen est falsum. Sicut enim in positione positi oppositum non est obligatum sed[35] ipsum positum ita in depositione. Unde potest fieri tale argumentum:

> In depositione oppositum depositi non est depositum, ut patet; nec positum nec suppositum, quia non per signa positionis aut suppositionis; igitur non est obligatum.

Patet consequentia, quia omne obligatum aut est suppositum, positum, vel depositum sicut in secundo articulo fuit ostensum[36].

⟨*Capitulum Tertium: Sophismata*⟩
Circa praedictam speciem depositionis plura declarabo sophismata ut regularum veritas perfectius innotescat.
⟨1⟩ Primum ergo sophisma sit tale. Depono tibi istam:

> Aliquis homo non est Romae.

Qua admissa, propono illam:

> Quilibet homo est Romae.

Concedenda est quia contradictorium depositi. Deinde propono tibi istam:

---

[31] ista]*om*.M
[32] scitum]*om*.E
[33] est]ab eodem *add*.E
[34] dicant]dicunt E
[35] sed]secundum E
[36] ostensum]etc. *add*.E

⟨Chapter Two: Theses⟩
Some short theses follow from what has been said above.[1]
⟨1⟩ First thesis. It is not the case that every *obligatum* which has been admitted by someone and proposed to him during the period of the *obligatio*, and is known by him to be such, should be granted by that person.
⟨2⟩ Second thesis. It is not the case that every proposition which follows from an *obligatum* and is known to do so, should be granted.
⟨3⟩ Third thesis. Something which is inconsistent with the *obligatum* and is known to be such, should be granted.
⟨4⟩ Fourth thesis. It is not the case that every proposition which is inconsistent with the *obligatum* and is known to be such should be denied during the period of the *obligatio*.

Each of these theses is obvious because just as the *positum* is the *obligatum* in a *positio*, so the *depositum* ⟨is the *obligatum*⟩ in a *depositio*, although many people say the opposite in their belief that the contradictory of the *depositum* is the *obligatum*.[2] This belief is false. Just as in a *positio* the opposite of the *positum* is not the *obligatum*, but rather the *positum* itself ⟨is the *obligatum*⟩, so it is in a *depositio*. Hence one can construct an argument like this:

> In a *depositio* the opposite of the *depositum* is not the *depositum*, as is obvious, nor is it a *positum* or a *suppositum*, because ⟨it is⟩ not ⟨governed⟩ by the marks of a *positio* or a *suppositio*; therefore it is not an *obligatum*.

The inference is obvious, because every *obligatum* is either a *suppositum* or a *positum* or a *depositum*, as was shown in the second section ⟨of Part One⟩.

⟨Chapter Three: Sophisms⟩
I will explain a number of sophisms which have to do with the aforesaid species of *depositio* so that the truth of the rules may be more perfectly known.
⟨1⟩ First sophism. I deposit this to you:
> Some human being is not in Rome.[1]

When this has been admitted, I propose this:
> Every human being is in Rome.

This should be granted because it is the contradictory of the *depositum*. Then I propose this to you:

---

[1] These *conclusiones* were given by Marsilius, op.cit., fol. 71^v, and Buser, op.cit., fol. 72rb.

[2] There are several authors Paul could have had in mind here. Albert, op.cit., fol. 51va, wrote: 'cum aliquid deponitur, eius contradictorium ponitur'. Marsilius, op.cit., fol. 99^r, write: 'In omni depositione formaliter respondendum ac si oppositum esset positum'. Strode, op.cit., fol. 89ra, wrote: 'Depositio sit alicuius propositionis quasi positio sui contradictorii, et tantum valet "Depono tibi 'Tu curris'" ac si dicerem "Pono quod non curras".' *Lat.misc.e 79*, fol. 23rb, had added: 'per hoc apparet quod illa species obligationis est reducibilis ad speciem positionis'. Cf. Part 1, section 1, note 20.

[1] This is the first sophism given by Albert, op.cit., fol. 51va (though the printed text has 'rationalis' for 'Romae'); and by Marsilius, op.cit., fol. 99^{r-v} (with 'Parisius' instead of 'Romae'); it is the first sophism in *Lat.misc.e 79*, fol. 23va and *Lib.Soph.Oxon.*, sig.D i^r; and it is the only sophism for *Depositio* in Buser, op.cit., fols. 77vb–78ra. Paul's only minor alteration is at the end. Albert, Marsilius, and Buser argued 'You are a human being' was to be denied because 'You are

Tu es Romae.

Neganda est quia falsa et impertinens ut patet ex dictis in undecima regula. Deinde propono tibi istam:

Tu es aliquis homo.

Si negas, negas verum et impertinens, igitur male. Si concedis, iterum propono tibi illam:

Tu es Romae.

Si concedis et prius negasti, igitur male. Si negas, negas sequens ex concessis, igitur male. Sequitur enim:

Quilibet homo est Romae, tu es aliquis homo, igitur tu es Romae.

Respondetur admittendo depositum, et quando proponitur[37] eius contradictorium, concedo. Et nego istam:

Tu es Romae;

et istam similiter:

Tu es aliquis homo,

dupliciter: primo, quia repugnat uni concesso et opposito bene negati; secundo, quia antecedit ad depositum cum opposito bene negati. Sequitur enim:

Tu non es Romae[38] et tu es aliquis homo, igitur aliquis homo non est Romae[39].

⟨2⟩ Secundum sophisma est istud. Depono tibi istam:

Tu es Romae[40] vel aliquis homo est animal.

Qua deposita et admissa, propono istam:

Tu es Romae.

Si negas[41], contra: ipsa est vera, supposito quod tu[42] sis Romae, et impertinens quia non sequitur nec repugnat, ut patet intuenti. Si concedis[43], contra dupliciter: primo, quia antecedit ad depositum, igitur male respondes concedendo eam; (192^{ra}E) secundo, nam capio oppositum depositi et arguo sic:

Tu non es Romae et nullus homo est animal, igitur tu non es Romae.

Consequentia patet a tota[44] copulativa affirmativa ad alteram partem principalem; et antecedens est concedendum cum sit contradictorium depositi, igitur conse-

---

[37] proponitur]propositum M
[38] es Romae]curris M,E *corr.M² s.lin.*
[39] est Romae]currit M,E *corr.M²s.lin.*
[40] Romae]homo E
[41] negas]negatur M
[42] tu]*om*.M
[43] concedis]conceditur M
[44] a tota]*om*.M

---

not a human being' followed from 'Every human being is in Rome and you are not in Rome.' Buser added that because this was so, 'You are a human being' was inconsistent: cf. Paul's first point. Paul's second point is found in *Lib.Soph.Oxon.*: 'Negetur, quia illud cum opposito bene negati est antecedens ad depositum, sic arguendo: "Vos estis aliquis homo et vos non estis Romae, ergo aliquis homo non est Romae".'

You are in Rome.

This should be denied because it is false and irrelevant, as is obvious from what was said in rule eleven. Then I propose this to you:

You are some human being.

If you deny this, you deny a proposition which is true and irrelevant; therefore you reply incorrectly. If you grant it, I propose

You are in Rome

to you once more. If you grant it and you previously denied it, then you reply incorrectly. If you deny it, you deny what follows from previously granted propositions, therefore you reply incorrectly. This is a valid inference:

Every human being is in Rome, you are some human being; therefore you are in Rome.

I reply by admitting the *depositum* and when its contradictory is proposed, I grant it. And I deny this:

You are in Rome;

and similarly ⟨I deny⟩ this:

You are some human being

for two reasons: first, because it is inconsistent with a previously granted proposition and the opposite of a correctly denied proposition; second, because it is a premiss from which, together with the opposite of a correctly denied proposition, the *depositum* can be inferred. This is a valid inference:

You are not in Rome and you are some human being; therefore some human being is not in Rome.

⟨2⟩ Second sophism. I deposit this to you:

You are in Rome or some human being is an animal.[2]

When this has been deposited and admitted, I propose this:

You are in Rome.

If you deny this, I argue against you. The proposition is true, assuming that you are in Rome, and irrelevant, because it does not follow, nor is it inconsistent, as is obvious to anyone who considers the matter carefully. If you grant it, I argue against you in two ways. First, because it is a premiss from which the *depositum* can be inferred; therefore in granting it you reply incorrectly. Second, because I can take the opposite of the *depositum* and argue like this:

You are not in Rome and no human being is an animal; therefore you are not in Rome.

The inference is obvious because it proceeds from an affirmative conjunction to one of its principal clauses; and the premiss should be granted because it is the contradictory of the *depositum*; therefore the conclusion should be

---

[2] This is the second sophism given by Peter of Candia, op.cit., fol. 69va. Peter omits Paul's argument on p. 380, lines 25–26. He says that 'You are in Rome' is not irrelevant because its negation follows from the contradictory of the *depositum*. This is logically equivalent to Paul's explanation (p. 382, lines 5–6) that it is a premiss to the *depositum*, since P → Q if and only if -Q → -P.

quens est concedendum, et tu concessisti[45] contradictorium consequentis, igitur male.

Respondetur admittendo depositum; et quando proponitur

Tu es Romae,

nego eam. Et cum dicitur quod est vera et impertinens, nego quod[46] sit impertinens cum antecedit ad depositum.

⟨3⟩ Tertium sophisma est istud. Depono tibi istam:

Aliquae propositiones non sunt verae.

Quo admisso, propono

Istae (235^{va}M) sunt propositiones,

demonstratis illis:

'Tu curris' et 'Tu non curris.'

Concedendum est quia scitum esse verum non antecedens ad depositum. Stat enim cum opposito depositi utramque istarum significare convertibiliter deum esse. Deinde propono:

Duo mutuo contradictoria sunt duo vera.

Si negatur, contra: omnes propositiones sunt verae, sed istae duae, scilicet

'Tu curris' et 'Tu non curris',

sunt propositiones; igitur illae sunt verae; et istae mutuo contradicunt, igitur duo invicem contradictoria sunt duo vera.

Respondetur omnino sicut si poneretur quod omnes propositiones sint[47] verae. Unde, concesso opposito depositi, velut repugnans negatur quod illa sint[48] contradictoria; immo illud aperte antecedit ad depositum.

⟨4⟩ Quartum sophisma. Depono tibi istam:

Aliquae propositiones non sunt similes.

Qua admissa, propono

'Deus est' et 'Homo est asinus' sunt propositiones.

Concedendum est, quia verum et impertinens. Deinde:

---

[45] tu concessisti]concedenti E
[46] quod . . . impertinens]om.M
[47] sint]sunt M
[48] sint]sunt M

granted. But you granted the contradictory of this conclusion; therefore you replied incorrectly.

I reply by admitting the *depositum*, and when

> You are in Rome

is proposed, I deny it. And when it is said that it is true and irrelevant, I deny that it is irrelevant, because it is a premiss from which the *depositum* can be inferred.

⟨3⟩ Third sophism. I deposit this to you:

> Some propositions are not true.[3]

When this has been admitted, I propose

> These are propositions,

indicating these:

> 'You are running' and 'You are not running'.

The proposition should be granted because it is known to be true and is not a premiss from which the *depositum* can be inferred. It is consistent with the opposite of the *depositum* that each of these propositions should signify interchangeably that there is a God. Then I propose

> Two mutually contradictory propositions are two truths.

If this is denied, I argue against ⟨the denial⟩: All propositions are true, but these two, namely:

> 'You are running' and 'You are not running'

are propositions; therefore they are true. They are mutually contradictory; therefore two propositions which are mutually contradictory are two truths.

I reply altogether as if it were posited that all propositions were true. Hence, having granted the opposite of the *depositum*, I deny ⟨the claim⟩ that they are contradictories as inconsistent. Indeed, ⟨the claim⟩ is clearly a premiss from which the *depositum* can be inferred.

⟨4⟩ Fourth sophism. I deposit this to you:

> Some propositions are not similar.[4]

When this has been admitted, I propose

> 'There is a God' and 'A human being is a donkey' are propositions.

This should be granted, because it is true and irrelevant. Then

---

[3] This sophism is found in Strode, op.cit., fol. 89rb, and Paul reproduces Strode's text with only minor alterations. Strode had used the sophism to illustrate the rule 'Omne antecedens ad tibi depositum est negandum et similiter omne falsum non sequens ad oppositum depositi.' He referred to the second clause in explaining why 'Duo mutuo contradictoria sunt duo verae' had to be denied. For an earlier discussion of the same sophism see John of Holland, op.cit., fol. 107^r. Peter of Mantua uses the sentence 'Aliquae propositiones non sunt verae' but his sophism is quite different: op.cit., sig.G viii^{ra-rb}.

[4] This is the second sophism in Albert, op.cit., fol. 51va; and in Marsilius, op.cit., fol. 99^v (in the form 'Aliquae propositiones sunt dissimiles'). Paul follows their arguments. The sentence 'Aliquae propositiones non sunt similes' appears in *Lat.misc.e 79*, fol. 23^{rb-va}, and *Lib.Soph.Oxon.* sig.D i^r, but the sophism is quite different.

'Deus est' et 'Homo est asinus' sunt similes.

Si concedis, concedis falsum et impertinens, igitur male. Si negas, contra: eius oppositum antecedit deposito cum uno concesso, igitur male. Antecedens probatur, quia bene sequitur:

> Istae non sunt similes, et istae[49] sunt aliquae propositiones, igitur aliquae propositiones non sunt similes

quod est depositum.

Dicitur concedendo illam[50] secundo propositam:

> 'Deus est' et 'Homo est asinus' sunt similes;

et nego quod sit impertinens: immo sequens ex opposito depositi et uno concesso.

⟨5⟩ Quintum sophisma. Depono tibi istam:

> Deus est et aliquod depositum est negandum a te.

Quo admisso et negato, proponitur

> Deus est.

Concedendum est, quia per se necessarium. Deinde proponitur:

> Aliquod tibi depositum est negandum a te.

Quo negato, quia cum praecedente concesso antecedit ad depositum, arguo sic:

> Illa copulativa est neganda a te et illa est aliquod tibi depositum, igitur aliquod tibi depositum est negandum a te.

Breviter negatur haec copulativa quae sumitur pro antecedente. Et si dicitur 'Pro qua parte?' dico quod propositis partibus semper concedam primo propositam et alteram negabo tamquam repugnantem concesso et opposito bene negati.

⟨6⟩ Sextum sophisma. Depono tibi istam:

> Tu es homo et omne tibi depositum est negandum a te[51].

Quo admisso et negato, propono

> Omne tibi depositum est negandum a te.

Si conceditur, propono istam:

> Tu es homo;

et patet quod est neganda quia cum priori concesso[52] antecedit ad depositum. Deinde propono:

---

[49] istae]*om*.M
[50] illam]*om*.E
[51] a te]*om*.M
[52] concesso]*om*.E

'There is a God' and 'A human being is a donkey' are similar.

If you grant this, you grant a proposition which is false and irrelevant; therefore you reply incorrectly. If you deny it, I argue against you. The opposite of this is a premiss from which, together with a previously granted proposition, the *depositum* can be inferred; therefore you reply incorrectly. Proof of the premiss: this is a valid inference:

> These are not similars, and these are some propositions; therefore some propositions are not similars,

and ⟨this conclusion⟩ is the *depositum*.

I reply by granting that second proposition which was proposed:

'There is a God' and 'A human being is a donkey' are similars,

and I deny that it is irrelevant. On the contrary, it follows from the opposite of the *depositum* together with a previously granted proposition.

⟨5⟩ Fifth sophism. I deposit this to you:

> There is a God and some *depositum* should be denied by you.[5]

When this has been admitted and denied,

> There is a God

is proposed. It should be granted because it is necessary *per se*. Then

> Some *depositum* which was put to you should be denied by you,

is proposed. When this has been denied, because it is a premiss from which, together with the preceding proposition which was granted, the *depositum* can be inferred, I argue like this:

> That conjunction should be denied by you, and it is some *depositum* which was put to you; therefore some *depositum* which was put to you should be denied by you.

In short, the conjunction which serves as the premiss is to be denied. And if someone asks 'On account of which clause?' I say that when the clauses have been proposed I will always grant the first to be proposed, and I will deny the other as inconsistent with a previously granted proposition and the opposite of a correctly denied proposition.

⟨6⟩ Sixth sophism. I deposit this to you:

> You are a human being and every *depositum* put to you should be denied by you.[6]

When this has been admitted and denied, I propose

> Every *depositum* put to you should be denied by you.

If this is granted, I propose

> You are a human being.

It is obvious that it should be denied because together with the previously granted proposition it is a premiss from which the *depositum* can be inferred. Then I propose:

---

[5] This sophism is in Strode, op.cit., fol. 89^{rb-va}, as the first of two sophisms for conjunction. Paul's treatment is essentially the same except at the very end where Strode explains his denial of the second conjunct by saying: 'non quod sit falsa, sed quia antecedit deposito cum bene concesso.'

[6] This sophism is in Strode, op.cit., fol. 89va, as the second of two sophisms for conjunction.

Tu non es homo.

Concedendum est. Deinde:

Nullum tibi depositum est.

Concedendum est tamquam sequens, quia sequitur

Tu non es homo, igitur nullum tibi depositum est.

Ultimo propono tibi[53]:

Non omne tibi depositum est a te[54] negandum.

Si concedis et etiam concessisti suum contradictorium, igitur male. Si negas, negas sequens ex concesso, igitur male. Antecedens patet, nam sequitur

Nullum tibi depositum est, igitur nullum tibi depositum est a te[55] negandum.

Negatur breviter quod omne tibi depositum est a te negandum, quia antecedit ad depositum. Sequitur enim

Omne tibi depositum est negandum a te, ergo omne tibi depositum est a te negandum et tu es homo.

Et si arguitur contra:

Omne depositum admissum est negandum, igitur male respondes,

nego consequentiam, quia ex eodem antecedente non sequitur quod omne mihi depositum sit[56] negandum a me.

⟨7⟩ Septimum sophisma. Depono tibi istam:

Aliquod verum non est tibi depositum obligatum vel aliquod falsum non est tibi positum (235^{vb}M) obligatum.

Quo admisso, propono tibi[57] illam:

Omne verum est tibi depositum obligatum.

Concedenda est quia sequens ad oppositum depositi. Deinde:

Haec est vera: 'Deus est.'

Concedendum est quia impertinens, ut patet inquirenti. Deinde:

Ipsa est deposita obligata.

Concedendum quia sequens ex duobus concessis. Deinde arguo sic:

Ipsa est tibi deposita obligata, igitur est a te neganda; et est per se necessarium, igitur per se necessarium est a te negandum; quod implicat.

---

[53] tibi]om.E
[54] a te]om.E
[55] a te]om.E
[56] sit]est M
[57] tibi]om.M

Paul gives a fuller explanation of the arguments than did Strode. In particular, Paul brings out the point that you must exist in order for it to be true that you are participating in an obligational disputation. Hence the second clause of the *depositum* implies the first.

You are not a human being.
This should be granted. Then:
Nothing is deposited to you.
This should be granted as following, since this is a valid inference:
You are not a human being; therefore nothing is deposited to you.
Finally I propose to you:
Not every *depositum* put to you should be denied by you.
If you grant it, and you have already granted its contradictory, then you reply incorrectly. If you deny it, you deny what follows from a previously granted proposition; therefore you reply incorrectly. The premiss is obvious, because this is a valid inference:
Nothing is deposited to you; therefore no *depositum* put to you should be denied by you.
In short, I deny that every *depositum* put to you should be denied by you, because this is a premiss from which the *depositum* can be inferred. This is a valid inference:
Every *depositum* put to you should be denied by you; therefore every *depositum* put to you should be denied by you and you are a human being.
And if someone argues against this:
Every *depositum* which has been admitted should be denied; therefore you reply incorrectly,
I deny this inference, because from the same premiss it does not follow that every *depositum* put to me should be denied by me.

⟨7⟩ Seventh sophism. I deposit this to you.
Some true proposition is not the *depositum obligatum* put to you, or some false proposition is not the *positum obligatum* put to you.[7]
When this has been admitted, I propose this to you:
Every true proposition is the *depositum obligatum* put to you.
This should be granted because it follows from the opposite of the *depositum*. Then:
'There is a God' is true.
This should be granted because it is irrelevant, as is obvious to anyone who investigates the matter. Then:
That proposition is a *depositum obligatum*.
This should be granted because it follows from two previously granted propositions. Then I argue like this:
That proposition is the *depositum obligatum* put to you; therefore it should be denied by you; but it is necessary *per se*; therefore a proposition which is necessary *per se* should be denied by you, which leads to ⟨a contradiction⟩.

---

[7] I have found no other discussion of this sophism.

Eodem modo arguitur ex altera parte oppositi (192^{rb}E) depositi, quod aliquod per se impossibile est concedendum.

Deinde[58] dicendum concedendo quod ista:

> Deus est

est a me neganda; et negando[59] quod sit per se necessaria tamquam repugnans. Et ita dicendum de ista:

> Homo est asinus,

quod est a me concedenda. Numquam tamen concedam eam[60]; et negabo quod sit per se impossibile tamquam repugnans similiter[61].

⟨8⟩ Octavum et ultimum sophisma. Depono tibi istam:

> Tu es asinus vel aliquod impossibile antecedit tibi deposito.

Quo admisso quia contingens, propono:

> Aliquod impossibile antecedit tibi deposito.

Quo negato quia antecedit tibi deposito, propono

> Haec est impossibilis: 'Homo est asinus.'

Concedendum est quia verum et impertinens. Tunc arguitur sic:

> Haec[62] 'Homo est asinus' est impossibilis et antecedit ad tibi depositum, igitur aliquod impossibile antecedit ad tibi depositum.

Dicitur negando minorem tamquam repugnantem. Et si dicitur contra:

> Tu es asinus, igitur tu es asinus vel aliquod impossibile antecedit tibi[63] deposito,

ubi constat quod antecedens est illa

> Tu es asinus

et consequens tibi depositum; respondetur concedendo quod ista consequentia valet, et quod antecedens est ista:

> Tu es asinus;

et negando[64] tamquam repugnantem[65] quod illud consequens aut illa disiunctiva sit mihi deposita. Sequitur enim:

> Nullum impossibile antecedit tibi deposito, sed ista: 'Homo est asinus' et[66] est impossibilis et antecedit ad istam disiunctivam et ad illud

---

[58] Deinde]om.E
[59] negando]nego M
[60] eam]ipsam M
[61] similiter]simpliciter E
[62] Haec]illa M
[63] tibi deposito]ad tibi depositum M
[64] negando]nego M
[65] repugnantem]repugnans M
[66] et]om.E

In the same way one can argue on the basis of the other clause of the opposite of the *depositum* that a proposition which is impossible *per se* should be granted.

One should reply by granting that this:

>There is a God

should be denied by me, and by denying that it is necessary *per se* as inconsistent. And thus one should say that

>A human being is a donkey

should be granted by me. However, I will never grant that proposition, and similarly I will deny that it is impossible *per se* as inconsistent.

⟨8⟩ Eighth and last sophism. I deposit this to you:

>You are a donkey or some impossible proposition is a premiss to the *depositum* put to you.[8]

When this has been admitted because it is contingent, I propose:

>Some impossible proposition is a premiss to the *depositum* put to you.

When this has been denied because it is a premiss to the *depositum* put to you, I propose:

>'A human being is a donkey' is impossible.

This should be granted because it is true and irrelevant. Then I argue like this:

>'A human being is a donkey' is impossible and it is a premiss to the *depositum* put to you; therefore some impossible proposition is a premiss to the *depositum* put to you.

I reply by denying the minor premiss as inconsistent. And if someone argues against this:

>You are a donkey; therefore you are a donkey or some impossible proposition is a premiss to the *depositum* put to you,

where it is agreed that the premiss is

>You are a donkey

and the conclusion is the *depositum* which was put to you, I reply by granting that the inference is valid, and that the premiss is

>You are a donkey;

but I deny as inconsistent that that conclusion or that disjunction was posited to me. This is a valid inference:

>No impossible proposition is a premiss to the *depositum* put to you, but the proposition 'A human being is a donkey' is both impossible and a premiss to this disjunction and to that conclusion, therefore neither that

---

[8] This sophism is in Strode, op.cit., fol. 89va, as the only sophism for disjunction. Paul's explanation of the arguments is slightly fuller than Strode's.

consequens, igitur nec illa disiunctiva nec illud consequens est tibi depositum.

Ut praedicti casus cum suis responsionibus clarius videantur est in copulativis regulariter observandum quod[67] cum deponitur copulativa cuius utraque pars est falsa, admittitur et negatur utraque pars. Si una pars sit vera et alia falsa, conceditur verum et negatur falsum. Sed si una pars est necessaria et alia contingens, conceditur necessarium et negatur contingens sive verum sive falsum. Si sit utraque pars vera contingens et una pars sit consequens ad aliam, pars antecedens negatur et consequens conceditur. Si neutra sequitur[68] ad aliam, conceditur pars primo proposita et negatur secundo loco proposita.

In disiunctivis vero regulariter teneatur quod cum deponitur disiunctiva cuius una pars est necessaria vel cuius oppositum est per se impossibilis[69] copulativa sicut sunt istae:

Tu es asinus vel deus est,

Tu non curris vel tu non sedes,

Sortes est vel Sortes non est,

Homo non currit vel aliquod animal movetur,

istarum nulla debet admitti in depositione, quia sunt omnes necessariae.

Admissa vero disiunctiva debet quaelibet eius[70] pars principalis negari quia[71] quaelibet antecedit ad depositum.

Item notandum quod in materia positionum vel depositionum nullum[72] casum posui pertinentem ad (236^{ra}M) scire et dubitare quia ipsos posui in prima parte tractatus de modalibus ubi propriam tractavi materiam.

Ultimo sciendum quod licet multae regulae et multae sophismata de hac specie possent[73] formari, tamen quia in omnibus similiter[74], licet opposito modo, regulae et sophismata debent deduci et solvi in depositione sicut in positione, ubi diffusa argumenta sunt quae hic possunt[75] adaptari, ideo gratia brevitatis dimitto huiusmodi ut ars ista calculatoria citius finem recipiat etc[76].

---

[67] quod]et E
[68] sequitur]sequatur M
[69] impossibilis]impossibile M
[70] eius]*om.*E
[71] quia]et E
[72] nullum]unum E
[73] possent]possunt E
[74] similiter]similantur E
[75] possunt]possent E
[76] etc.]Deo toti caelesti curiae triumphanti gratiarum actiones refero *add.*M

disjunction nor that conclusion is the *depositum* which was put to you.

So that the aforesaid cases and the replies made to them may be more clearly understood, one should take notice of some rules which govern conjunctions.[9] When a conjunction each of whose clauses is false is deposited it should be admitted and each clause should be denied. If one clause is true and the other false, the true ⟨clause⟩ should be granted and the false denied. But if one clause is necessary and the other contingent, the necessary ⟨clause⟩ should be granted and the contingent denied, whether it is true or false. If each clause is a contingent truth and one clause follows from the other, the clause which is a premiss is to be denied and the conclusion is to be granted. If neither follows from the other, the clause proposed first should be granted and the clause proposed in the second place is to be denied.

Rule for disjunctions:[10] When a disjunction is deposited of which one clause is necessary, or whose opposite is a conjunction which is impossible *per se*, as in the following examples:

You are a donkey or there is a God;

Either you are not running or you are not sitting down;

Socrates exists or Socrates does not exist;

Either some human being is not running or some animal is moving,

none of these should be admitted in a *depositio* because they are all necessary propositions.

But when a disjunction has been admitted, each of its principal clauses should be denied because each is a premiss to the *depositum*.

Likewise one should note that when dealing with the topic of *positio* and *depositio* I did not put forward any cases to do with knowing and being uncertain. I have put these cases forward in the first part of the tract on modal propositions, where I dealt with this particular topic.[11]

Finally one should know that although many rules and many sophisms can be formulated about this species ⟨sc. *depositio*⟩ because they are completely analogous, albeit as opposites, to the rules and sophisms presented in ⟨the section on⟩ *positio*, they should be set out and solved in the same way as in ⟨the section on⟩ *positio*.[12] In my treatment of *positio*, arguments are set out at much greater length, all of which can be adapted ⟨to *depositio*⟩. Hence for the sake of brevity I leave the matter here, so that this calculatory art may more quickly be brought to an end.

---

[9] See Strode, op.cit., fol. 89rb. Paul makes only minor verbal changes.

[10] See Strode, op.cit., fol. 89va. Paul makes only minor verbal changes.

[11] See *Logica Magna Part I Fascicule 7*.

[12] These remarks about the relationship of *depositio* to *positio* and the corresponding lack of need for an extended treatment of *depositio* echo Paul's sources: see Marsilius, op.cit., fol. 99^v; Buser, op.cit., fol. 78ra; Peter of Candia, op.cit., fol. 69vb.

BIBLIOGRAPHY

I. OBLIGATIONS TREATISES.

1. *Manuscripts and early printed texts*

Albert of Saxony, *Perutilis Logica* (Venetiis, 1522. Reprinted: Hildesheim, New York: Georg Olms, 1974).

Anonymous, [Obligationes] Oxford, Bodleian Library MS *Lat.misc.e* 79, fols. 18ra–24ra.

Anonymous, *De Obligationibus*. In *Libellus Sophistarum ad Usum Oxoniensium* (Londoniis, 1510). Oxford, Bodleian Library, Vet.A 1 e 60. See also Cambridge, Corpus Christi College MS 378, fols. 48^r–57^r; Cambridge, Corpus Christi College MS 244 (245), fols. 13^v–18^v.

Anonymous, *De Obligationibus*. In *Libellus Sophistarum ad Usum Cantabrigiensium* (Londoniis, 1524). Oxford, Bodleian Library 4° S 38 Art. Seld. See also Cambridge, Gonville and Caius College MS 182/215, pp. 42–47.

Anonymous, *Tractatus Obligatoriorum*. In *Copulata super omnes tractatus parvorum logicalium Petri hispani ac super tres tractatus modernorum*. . . . ([Cologne: Quentell], 1493). London, British Library IA 4595. For a translation (very unreliable) see Peter of Spain. *Tractatus Syncategorematum and Selected Anonymous Treatises*. Translated by J.P. Mullally. (Milwaukee, Wisc.: The Marquette University Press, 1964).

John of Holland, *Obligationes*. Cracow, Biblioteka Jagiellońska MS 2132, fols. 101^v–107^v. See also Cracow, Biblioteka Jagiellońska MS 2045, fols. 192^v–209^v.

Marsilius of Inghen, *Tractatus de Obligationibus*. Cracow, Biblioteka Jagiellońska MS 2602, fols. 70^r–101^r. See also *Tractatus de arte obligandi. Editus a magistro Petro de Alliaco* (Parisius, 1489). Cambridge, University Library Inc.5 D 1 20.

Martinus Anglicus, [Obligationes] Cracow, Biblioteka Jagiellońska MS 2602, fols. 127^r–131^r. See also Vienna, Oesterreichische Nationalbibliotek MS VPL 4698, fols. 71^r–78^v.

Paul of Venice, *Logica* ([Venice] 1472. Reprinted: Hildesheim, New York: Georg Olms, 1970). Cited as: *Logica Parva*.

Peter of Candia, *Obligationes*. Oxford, Bodleian Library MS Canon.Class.Lat.278, fols. 65ra–69vb. Apparently copied by Almerico da Seravalle, student of arts at Padua: see William Buser.

Peter of Mantua, *Logica* ([Venice: Bonetus Locatellus], 1492). Oxford, Bodleian Library, Auct.2 Q V 1.

Ralph Strode, *Obligationes* in *Consequentie Strodi etc.* (Venetiis, 1517). Cambridge, University Library G* 11.42 (D). See also Oxford, Bodleian Library MS Canon. misc.219 fols. 37ra–47ra. According to fol. 47ra the manuscript was written by Almerico da Seravalle, student of arts at Padua. He copied the preceding tract in 1393: see fol. 36va.

Richard Billingham, *Ars Obligatoria*. Salamanca University MS 1735, fols. 89^r–95^v.

William Buser, *Obligationes*. Oxford, Bodleian Library MS Canon.Class.Lat.278, fols. 72^{ra-rb}. According to fol. 78rb this manuscript was copied by Almerico da Seravalle, student of arts at Padua, in 1391.

William Heytesbury, *Casus Obligationis*. Oxford, Bodleian Library MS Canon.Class. Lat.278, fol. 70^{ra-rb}. Apparently copied by Almerico da Seravalle: see William Buser.

2. *Editions*

John Buridan: Johannes Buridanus, *Sophismata*. Critical edition with an introduction by T.K. Scott. *Grammatica Speculativa, Band* I (Stuttgart-Bad Cannstatt; Frommann Holzboog, 1977). Translated as: *Sophisms on Meaning and Truth*. Translated and with an introduction by T.K. Scott (New York: Appleton-Century-Crofts, 1966).

John Wyclif: Johannis Wyclif, *Tractatus de Logica*. Now first edited from the Vienna and Prague mss. (Vienna 4352; Univ.Prag. V.E.14) by M.H. Dziewicki. Volume I (London: Trübner & Co., 1893. Reprinted: New York: Johnson Reprint Corporation, Frankfurt am Main: Minerva G.m.b.H., 1966).

Paul of Pergula: *Logica and Tractatus de Sensu Composito et Diviso*, edited by Sister Mary Anthony Brown (St. Bonaventure, N.Y.: The Franciscan Institute, 1961).

Richard Lavenham: Paul Vincent Spade, 'Richard Lavenham's *Obligationes*. (Edition and comments by Paul Vincent Spade).' *Rivista Critica di Storia della Filosofia*, 33 (1978), 225–242.

Robert Fland: Paul Vincent Spade, 'Robert Fland's *Obligationes*: an edition.' *Mediaeval Studies*, 42 (1980), 41–60.

Roger Swyneshed: Paul Vincent Spade, 'Roger Swyneshed's *Obligationes*: edition and comments.' *Archives d'histoire doctrinale et littéraire du moyen âge*, 44 (1977), 243–285.

Walter Burley: Romuald Green, *The Logical Treatise 'De Obligationibus': An Introduction with Critical Texts of William of Sherwood and Walter Burley* (St. Bonaventure, N.Y.: The Franciscan Institute. Forthcoming).

William Ockham: *Summa Logicae*, edited by Philotheus Boehner, Gedeon Gál, Stephen Brown. Opera Philosophica I (St. Bonaventure, N.Y.: The Franciscan Institute, 1974).

Addendum

Since the work for this edition was completed, John of Holland's *Obligationes* has been edited: see John of Holland, *Four Tracts on Logic (Suppositiones, Fallacie, Obligationes, Insolubilia)*, edited by E.P. Bos. Artistarium 5. Nijmegen: Ingenium Publishers, 1985.

II. OTHER SOURCES

CH. *The Cambridge History of Later Medieval Philosophy*, edited by Norman Kretzmann, Anthony Kenny, Jan Pinborg (Cambridge: Cambridge University Press, 1982).

Angelelli, Ignacio, 'The techniques of disputation in the history of logic'. *The Journal of Philosophy*, 67 (1970), 800–815.

Aristotle, *Aristoteles Latinus VI 1–3. De Sophisticis Elenchis*, edited by Bernard G. Dod (Leiden: E.J. Brill, Bruxelles: Desclée de Brouwer, 1975).

Ashworth, E.J., 'The doctrine of exponibilia in the fifteenth and sixteenth centuries', *Vivarium*, 11 (1973), 137–167.

Ashworth, E.J., '"I promise you a horse": A second problem of meaning and reference in late fifteenth and early sixteenth century logic', *Vivarium*, 14 (1976), 62–79; continued, Ibid., 14 (1976), 139–155.

Ashworth, E.J., 'The "Libelli Sophistarum" and the use of medieval logic texts at Oxford and Cambridge in the early sixteenth century', *Vivarium*, 17 (1979), 134–158.

Ashworth, E.J., 'Mental language and the unity of propositions: a semantic problem discussed by early sixteenth century logicians', *Franciscan Studies*, 41 (1981), 61–96.

Ashworth, E.J., 'The problems of relevance and order in obligational disputations: some late fourteenth century views', *Medioevo*, 7 (1981), 175-193.
Ashworth, E.J., 'Renaissance man as logician: Josse Clichtove (1472-1543) on disputations', *History and Philosophy of Logic*, 7 (1986), 15-29.
Ashworth, E.J., 'English *Obligationes* texts after Roger Swyneshed: The tracts beginning "Obligatio est quaedam ars"', in *The Rise of British Logic*, edited by P. Osmund Lewry O.P., pp. 309-333. Papers in Mediaeval Studies, 7 (Toronto: Pontifical Institute of Mediaeval Studies, 1985).
Averroes, *Aristotelis de Physico Auditu libri octo cum Averrois Cordubensis variis in eosdem Commentariis. Aristotelis Opera cum Averrois Commentariis*. Vol. IV. (Venetiis, 1562. Reprinted Frankfurt am Main: Minerva G.m.b.H., 1962).
Boethius of Dacia, *Boethii Daci Opera. Topica. Opuscula. Vol. 6, Pars 1. Quaestiones super Librum Topicorum*, edited by N.J. Green-Pedersen and Jan Pinborg (Hauniae: G.E.C. Gad, 1976).
Bos, E.P., 'Peter of Mantua's tract on *Appellatio* and his interpretation of immanent forms' in *English Logic in Italy in the 14th and 15th Centuries*, edited by Alfonso Maierù, pp. 231-252 (Napoli: Bibliopolis, 1982).
Bottin, Francesco, 'Alcune correzioni ed aggiunte al censimento dei codici di Paolo Veneto', *Quaderni per la Storia dell' Università di Padova*, 14 (1981), 57-60.
Bottin, Francesco, 'Paolo Veneto e il problema degli universali' in *Aristotelismo Veneto e Scienza Moderna. Saggi e Testi*, 17, pp. 459-468 (Padova: Antenore, 1983).
Bottin, Francesco, 'Logica e filosofia naturale nelle opere di Paolo Veneto' in *Scienza e Filosofia all'Università di Padova nel Quattrocento*, edited by A. Poppi, Contributi alla storia dell'università di Padova, 15, pp. 85-124 (Trieste: Lint, 1983).
Brown, Sister Mary Anthony, 'The role of the *Tractatus de obligationibus*' in mediaeval logic', *Franciscan Studies*, 26 (1966), 26-55.
Green-Pedersen, N.J., 'Early British treatises on consequences', in *The Rise of British Logic*, edited by P. Osmund Lewry, O.P., 285-307. Papers in Mediaeval Studies, 7 (Toronto: Pontifical Institute of Mediaeval Studies, 1985).
Hamblin, Charles Leonard, *Fallacies*, (London: Methuen, 1970).
Kenny, Anthony and Jan Pinborg, 'Medieval Philosophical Literature', in *CH*, pp. 11-42.
Kneepkens, C.H., 'The mysterious Buser again: William Buser of Heusden and the *Obligationes* tract *Ob Rogatum*' in *English Logic in Italy in the 14th and 15th Centuries*, edited by Alfonso Maierù, pp. 147-166 (Napoli: Bibliopolis, 1982).
Knuuttila, Simo, 'Modal logic', in *CH*, pp. 342-357.
Lewy, Casimir, *Meaning and Modality*, (Cambridge: Cambridge University Press, 1976).
Lohr, Charles H., 'Medieval Latin Aristotle commentaries: Authors Narcissus-Richardus', *Traditio*, 28 (1972), 281-396.
Lohr, Charles H., 'A note on manuscripts of Paulus Venetus, *Logica*', *Bulletin de philosophie médiévale*, 15 (1973), 145-6.
Maier, Anneliese, *Codices Vaticani Latini, Codices 2118-2192* (Città del Vaticano: In Bibliotheca Vaticana, 1961).
Nardi, Bruno, *Saggi sull'aristotelismo padovano dal secolo xiv al xvi* (Firenze: Sansoni, 1958).
Pardo, Jerónimo, *Medulla Dyalectices* (Parisius, 1505).
Paul of Venice, *Quadratura* (Venetiis, 1493).
Paul of Venice, *Sophysmata* (Venetiis, 1493).
Paul of Venice, *Logica Magna. Part II. Fascicule 6. [Tractatus de Veritate et Falsitate Propositionis et Tractatus de Significato Propositionis]*, edited with notes on the sources by Francesco del Punta. Translated into English with explanatory

notes by Marilyn McCord Adams (Oxford: Published for the British Academy by the Oxford University Press, 1978).

Paul of Venice. *Logica Magna. Part I. Fascicule 1. [Tractatus de Terminis]* edited with an English translation and notes by Norman Kretzmann (Oxford: Published for the British Academy by the Oxford University Press, 1979).

Paul of Venice. *Logica Magna. Part I. Fascicule 7. [Tractatus de Scire et Dubitare]*, edited with an English translation and notes by Patricia Clarke (Oxford: Published for the British Academy by the Oxford University Press, 1981).

Perreiah, Alan R., 'A biographical introduction to Paul of Venice', *Augustiniana*, 17 (1967), 450–461.

Perreiah, Alan R., 'Insolubilia in the *Logica Parva* of Paul of Venice', *Medioevo*, 4 (1978), 145–171.

Perreiah, Alan R., '"Obligationes" in Paul of Venice's "Logica Parva"', *Analecta Augustiniana*, 45 (1982), 89–116.

Prior, A.N., 'Now', *Noûs*, 2 (1968), 101–119.

Prior, A.N., 'Recent advances in tense logic', *The Monist*, 53 (1969), 325–339.

Rijk, Lambertus Marie de, 'Some thirteenth century tracts on the game of obligation', *Vivarium*, 12 (1974), 94–123; continued, ibid., 13 (1975), 22–54; ibid., 14 (1976), 26–49.

Rijk, Lambertus Marie de, 'Logica Cantabrigiensis – a fifteenth century Cambridge manual of logic', *Revue internationale de philosophie: Grabmann*, 29e année, 113 (1975), 297–315.

Rijk, Lambertus Marie de, '*Logica Oxoniensis*. An attempt to reconstruct a fifteenth century Oxford manual of logic', *Medioevo*, 3 (1977), 121–164.

Rijk, Lambertus Marie de, editor, *Die mittelalterlichen Traktate De modo opponendi et respondendi. Einleitung und Ausgabe der einschlägigen Texte. Beiträge zur Geschichte der Philosophie und Theologie des Mittelalters. Neue Folge Band 17* (Münster: Aschendorff, 1980).

Rijk, Lambertus Marie de, editor, *Some 14th Century Tracts on the Probationes Terminorum. Martin of Alnwick O.F.M., Richard Billingham, Edward Upton and Others*, Artistarium 3, (Nijmegen: Ingenium Publishers, 1982).

Risse, Wilhelm, *Bibliographia Logica. Verzeichnis der Druckschriften zur Logik mit Angabe ihrer Fundorte. Band I. 1472–1800* (Hildesheim: Georg Olms, 1965).

Spade, Paul Vincent, 'Three theories of *obligationes*: Burley, Kilvington and Swyneshed on counterfactual reasoning', *History and Philosophy of Logic*, 3 (1982), 1–32.

Spade, Paul Vincent, 'Obligations: B. Developments in the fourteenth century', in *CH*, 335–341.

Spade, Paul Vincent, 'Logic in late medieval Oxford 1330–1500', in *The History of the University of Oxford. Volume II* (forthcoming).

Spade, Paul Vincent and Eleonore Stump, 'Walter Burley and the *Obligationes* attributed to William of Sherwood', *History and Philosophy of Logic*, 4 (1983), 9–26.

Stump, Eleonore, 'William of Sherwood's Treatise on Obligations', *Historiographia Linguistica*, 7 (1980), 249–264.

Stump, Eleonore, Review of: L.M. de Rijk (ed.) *Die mittelalterlichen Traktate De modo opponendi et respondendi*, in *History and Philosophy of Logic*, 3 (1982), 213–216.

Stump, Eleonore, 'Obligations: A. From the beginning to the early fourteenth century', in *CH*, 315–334.

Stump, Eleonore, 'Roger Swyneshed's theory of obligations', *Medioevo*, 7 (1981), 135–174.

Sylla, Edith Dudley, 'The Oxford calculators', in *CH*, 540–563.

Weidemann, Hermann, 'Ansätze zu einer Logik des Wissens bei Walter Burleigh', *Archiv für Geschichte der Philosophie*, 62 (1980), 32–45.

Weisheipl, James A., 'The interpretation of Aristotle's *Physics* and the science of motion', in *CH*, 521–536.

Zippel, Giuseppe, *Le Vite di Paolo II di Gaspare da Verona e di Michele Canensi. Rerum Italicarum Scriptores* T.III, P.XVI (Città di Castello, 1904).

INDEX OF SOPHISMS

Part One. Section One
'Deus est' et 'Homo est asinus' convertuntur: p. 28. See also Section Four, p. 74.

Part One. Section Three
Reliquum istorum est verum: p. 52.
Tu numquam respondisti ad 'Deus est': p. 66.

Part One. Section Four
A est aliquid et tamen nihil est A: p. 92.
A est B et tamen nullum B est A: p. 92.
A et B convertuntur et tamen nec A est B nec B est A: p. 92.
A est B et tamen B existente, impossibile est A esse: p. 92.
A videt B et tamen B non videtur ab A: p. 94.
A differt a B et tamen <non> B differt ab A: p. 94.
Pono quod A sit illa: Deus est; A est verum: p. 96.
Imponit quod A significet tantum praecise sicut una illarum: 'Rex sedet' et 'Nullus rex sedet'; tu scis A esse verum: p. 96.
Sit quod A significet alteram istarum 'Deus est' et 'Homo est asinus', te sciente; et sit A in rei veritate illa 'Deus est', sed hoc lateat te. Tunc proponit: A est verum: p. 98.

Part Two. Chapter One
I.1. Pono tibi omne possibile: p. 100.
I.2. A convertitur cum illo termino 'asinus' in propositione vera et cum illo termino 'homo' in propositione falsa, et cum illo disiuncto 'homo vel non homo' in propositione dubia: p. 104.
I.3. A significare omne quod non est A est possibile: p. 108.
I.4. A converti cum illa propositione 'Deus est' est possibile: p. 110.
I.5. Et pono quod tu sis A si primum tibi propositum sit falsum, et quod tu non sis A si primum tibi propositum sit verum: p. 112.
I.6. Pono quod A sit primum instans in quo proponetur tibi falsum; propono tibi 'A est': p. 114.
I.7. Pono quod ly. hominem est. convertatur cum illa 'Deus est': p. 118.
'Deus est' et 'Deum esse' convertuntur: p. 122.
II.1. Pono tibi illam propositionem de qua cogito: p. 122.
II.2. Pono tibi alterum illorum quae scis invicem contradicere, scilicet 'Rex sedet' et 'Nullus rex sedet': p. 126.
II.3. Sint tantum tres propositiones categoricae verae scilicet A, B, C, sic quod A sit unum illorum 'Rex sedet' et 'Nullus rex sedet' quod scias esse tibi dubium; deinde pono copulativam factam <ex A, B, C> significantem ut eius partes praetendunt: p. 136.
II.4. Sint A, B, C omnes categoricae verae ita quod A sit illa 'Rex sedet' vel ista 'Nullus rex sedet' sic quod scias A esse hanc vel hanc, sic quod hanc vel hanc scias esse A, et tibi positam obligatam: p. 140.
III.1. Pono tibi istam, quae sit A: 'Nullum tibi positum est a te concedendum', et hoc est tibi positum (demonstrato A): p. 146.
III.2. Tu es Romae et oppositum cuiuslibet talis est a te concedendum: p. 148.
III.3. Tu curris et 'Tu non curris' est a te concedendum: p. 152.
III.4. Pono quod illa copulativa sit tibi posita obligata 'Aliquid sequitur ex posito et nullum sequens ex posito est concedendum': p. 156.
III.5. A est aliqua propositio posita obligata et sit A ista 'Nulla propositio est tibi posita': p. 162.
'Nihil est tibi positum' <est tibi positum> et admissum: p. 162.
III.6. Tu negas necessarium simpliciter: p. 164.
III.7. Pono tibi istam: Tu concedis istam 'Homo est asinus': p. 168.
IV.1. Nihil est tibi positum: p. 170. Cf. Part One, Section Three, p. 84.
Tu nihil admittis: p. 170.

INDEX OF SOPHISMS

Tu non es: p. 170. Cf. Part One, Section Three, p. 84.
Tu non es obligatus: p. 172.
IV.2. Tu es Romae et omne repugnans huic propositioni 'Tu es Romae' est a te concedendum: p. 176.
IV.3. Omnis homo est Romae; 'Homo non est Romae' est a te concedenda: p. 180.
IV. 4. Nihil est repugnans posito; aliquid est repugnans posito: p. 180.
IV.5. Sit rei veritas quod tu sis albus, et pono tibi illam 'Tu es niger' quae praecise maneat tibi posita donec proponatur tibi aliquod a te negandum, et non ultra sis obligatus ad istam: p. 184.
IV.6. Tu non es obligatus: p. 186.
IV. 7. Quodcumque istorum contradictoriorum 'Rex sedet' et 'Nullus rex sedet' tibi primo propono, sit tibi positum et admissum: p. 188.
IV. 8. Nulla propositio est tibi dubia: p. 190.
V. 1. 'Deus est' et 'Homo est asinus' convertuntur: p. 194.
V. 2. Omnis homo currit; tu es homo; haec 'Tu curris' est a te concedenda: p. 208.
V. 3. Quandocumque profertur propositio universalis, omne currens sit asinus, et quandocumque profertur propositio singularis, tu sis currens: p. 212.
V. 4. Omnis homo est Romae; haec propositio est impertinens 'Tu es Romae': p. 216.
VI. 1. Omnis homo currit; tu es homo; 'Tu non curris' est a te concedenda: p. 222.
VI. 2. Omnis homo currit et omne repugnans aliquibus praemissis est a te concedendum: p. 224.
VI. 3. Omnis homo currit et pono tibi 'Tu non curris': p. 226.
VII. 1. Admisso quocumque contingente falso sit quodlibet aliud contingens falsum et impertinens concedendum: p. 234.
VII. 2. Tu es Romae vel 'Tu es Romae' est concedendum: p.236.
VII. 3. Sit rei veritas quod Sortes et Plato et Cicero sint omnes homines et quilibet istorum sedeat; isto supposito, pono tibi istam: Aliquis homo currit: p. 240.
Sit rei veritas quod non sint nisi tres homines in mundo, scilicet Sortes, Plato et Cicero, et quod solus Sortes loquatur: p. 244.
VIII. 1. Omnis homo currit; tu curris; 'Tu es homo' est a te concedenda: p. 248.
VIII. 2. Tu curris vel rex sedet; nullus rex sedet: p. 250.
VIII. 3. 'Tu curris' est a te concedendum; utrumque istorum est a te concedendum: 'Tu curris' et 'Tu es homo': p. 252.
VIII. 4. Tantum homo est asinus est tibi positum: p. 256.
IX. 1. Tu es Romae; tu es Romae in hoc instanti: p. 260
IX. 2. Omnis propositio est vera; haec est vera 'Homo est asinus': p. 272.
IX. 3. Rex sedet et nulla obligatio tibi fit: p. 276.
IX. 4. Omnis homo est Romae et quaelibet propositio est impertinens posito et obligato; omnis homo est Romae: p. 278.
IX 5. Omnis propositio praeter istam 'Tu es Romae' est impertinens posito obligato (quae sit C); tantum C est tibi positum obligatum: p. 280.
X.1. Sit rei veritas quod unum A sit omne A et quod sit ista 'Tu curris'; A est concedendum a te: p. 284.
X. 2. Pono quod concedas primum propositum a me post istud positum; tu male respondes: p. 290.
X. 3. 'Tu curris' est vera et impertinens; tu curris: p. 292.
X. 4. Pono quod quandocumque A ponitur a parte subiecti alicuius propositionis quod illa propositio sit vera, et quandocumque B ponitur a parte praedicati quod illa propositio sit falsa; A est B: p. 294.
Pono quod quandocumque A ponitur a parte subiecti illa propositio sit vera, et quandocumque ponitur a parte praedicati ista propositio sit falsa: p. 296.
X. 5. Pono quod Sortes concedat illam 'Deus est' et Plato neget illam et Cicero dubitet eam, et quod omne concedens illam bene respondeat, et quod omne negans aut dubitans eam male respondeat; sumo 'Ille male respondet', quae sit A, et demonstrato per ly .ille. in illa propositione illum qui totaliter respondet ad illam 'Deus est' sicut tu respondes ad A: pp. 298–300.
XI. 1. 'Homo est asinus' est tibi positum obligatum; homo est asinus: p. 302.
XII. 1. Aliquis homo est Romae; aliquis homo est Romae et tu es homo: pp.314–316.
XII. 2. Omnis homo est Romae; tu es homo et tu es Romae: p. 316.
XII. 3. Omnis homo currit; 'Omnis homo currit et tu es homo' fuit a te concedenda: p. 320.
XII. 4. Tu curris; tu curris et tu moveris: p. 322.

Part Two. Chapter Two
1. Omnis homo currit et nihil est tibi positum: p. 326.
2. Omnis homo est Romae et nulla copulativa est tibi posita, supposita vel deposita: p. 328.
3. Tu respondes ad falsum et solum respondes ad A; sit A 'Tu respondes ad falsum'; tu solum respondes ad A: p. 330.
4. Aliquis homo est Romae et nullus alius a te est Romae; tu es Romae: p. 332.

Part Two. Chapter Three
1. Homo est asinus vel omne tibi positum est impossibile: p. 342.

Part Two. Chapter Four
1. 'Tu es Parisius' et 'Tu es Romae' sunt similia: p. 344.
2. 'Tibi concluditur' et 'Tu nescis tibi concludi' sunt similia: p. 350.

Part Three
1. Aliquis homo non est Romae; quilibet homo est Romae; tu es Romae: p. 376.
2. Tu es Romae vel aliquis homo est animal; tu es Romae: p. 380.
3. Aliquae propositiones non sunt verae; istae sunt propositiones 'Tu curris' et 'Tu non curris': p. 382.
4. Aliquae propositiones non sunt similes; 'Deus est' et 'Homo est asinus' sunt propositiones; p. 382.
5. Deus est et aliquod depositum est negandum a te: p. 384.
6. Tu es homo et omne tibi depositum est negandum a te: p. 384.
7. Aliquod verum non est tibi depositum obligatum vel aliquod falsum non est tibi positum obligatum: p. 386.
8. Tu es asinus vel aliquod impossibile antecedit tibi deposito: p. 388.

INDEX OF NAMES

Note: anonymous works have been entered under their short title. Full references will be found in the bibliography.

When a name appears in the text as well as in footnotes, the page reference is given twice: e.g. 'ix; ix n. 5'.

Adams, M.M. ix n.8; 35 n.7; 396.
Albert of Saxony. xi; xii; xiv; 3 n.1; 14 n.13; 19 n.19, n.20; 21 n.24; 23 n.27; 23–24 n.28; 25 n.29; 29 n.30; 37 n.10; 41 n.14; 45 n.16; 51 n.2; 57 n.6; 63 n.9; 67 n.13; 69–70 n.15; 77 n.4; 81 n.8; 83 n.9; 86–87 n.12; 93 n.17; 97 n.23; 99 n.24; 105–106 n.4; 109 n.8; 111 n.10; 113 n.11, n.12; 115 n.14; 119 n.15; 123 n.16; 171 n.27, n.28; 173 n.29; 185 n.34; 195 n.39; 243 n.64; 245 n.65, n.66; 247 n.68; 251 n. 71; 303 n.86; 321–322 n.92; 327 n.2; 329 n.4, n.5; 331 n.7; 333 n.8, n.9, n.10; 335 n.1; 337 n.3; 351–352 n.6; 369 n.3, n.4; 371 n.5; 376 n.12; 379 (chapter 2) n.2; 379–380 (chapter 3) n.1; 383 n.4; 393.
Almerico da Seravalle. 393.
Angelelli, I. 394.
Aristotle. 7 n.6; 15; 33 n.3; 35 n.6; 61 n.8; 65 n.11; 305 n.87; 394.
 Categories. c.6 4 b20–25: 7 n.6.
 Metaphysics. Bk.9 c.4 1047 b15–30: 65 n.11; 305 n.87.
 Physics. Bk.3 c.1 201 a10: 15.
   Bk.4 c.4 212 a20: 15.
   Bk.5 c.2 226 a23 226 b9: 61 n.8
 Prior Analytics. Bk.1 c.13 32 a18–20: 61 n.11; 305 n.87.
 De Sophisticis Elenchis. 165 bl–10: 33 n.3. 165 b14–16: 35 n.6.
Ashworth, E.J. xi n.18; xiv n.28; 69 n.15; 93 n.17; 129 n.20; 259 n.75; 394–395.
Averroes. 15; 15 n.17; 395.
Billingham: see Richard Billingham.
Boehner, P. 15 n.14; 394.
Boethius of Dacia. 33 n.3; 395.
Bos, E.P. 188 n.36; 394; 395.
Bottin, F. vii n.1; viii n.3, n.4; ix; ix n.5, n.6, n.7, n.8, n.9; xvi; 395.
Broadie, A. xvi.
Brown, M.A. 394; 395.
Brown, S. 15 n. 14; 394.
Buridan: see John Buridan.
Burley: see Walter Burley.
Buser: see William Buser.
Cambridge Corpus Christi College MS 378 (Anonymous, De obligationibus): 86 n.12; 393.

Cambridge Gonville and Caius College MS 182/215 (Anonymous, De obligationibus): xi; 393.
Cittadini da Faenza, Antonio. ix n.6.
Clarke, P. xv; 98 n.23; 396.
Copulata (Anonymous, Tractatus Obligatoriorum): 65–66 n.11; 105 n.4; 393.
Dod, B.G. 33 n.3; 394.
Dziewicki, M.H. 13 n.12; 394.
Fland: see Robert Fland.
Gál, G. 15 n.14; 394.
Gaspar of Verona. vii; vii n.2.
Geach, P.T. xiv; xvi; 90 n.16; 95 n.18.
Green, R. x n.13, n.16; 15 n.14; 394.
Green-Pedersen, N.J. xi n.17; 33 n.3; 395.
Hamblin, C.L. 395.
Heytesbury: see William Heytesbury.
John Buridan. 89 n.14; 105–106 n.4; 111 n.10; 394.
John Dumbleton: see Pseudo-Dumbleton.
John of Holland. xi; 12 n.11; 25 n.29; 37 n.11; 53 n.4; 83 n.9; 105–106 n.4; 171 n.27; 173 n.28; 195 n.39; 235 n.61; 243 n.64; 323 n.92; 383 n.3; 393; 394.
John Tarteys. x n.16.
John Wyclif. xi; 13 n.12; 33 n.3; 37 n.11; 173 n.28; 303 n.86; 305 n.88; 394.
Kenny, A. x n.13; 23 n.26; 394; 395.
Kneepkens, C.H. xii n.20, n.21, n.22; xvi; 395.
Knuuttila, S. 51 n.2; 395.
Kretzmann, N. x n.13, n.16; 23 n.26; 394; 395; 396.
Lat.misc.e 79, Oxford Bodleian Library MS (Anonymous, Obligationes): 13 n.12;33 n.3; 37 n.11; 51 n.2; 53 n.4; 63 n.9; 86 n.12; 88 n.14; 171 n.28; 257 n.74; 261 n.76; 303 n.86; 322 n.92; 329 n.4; 333 n.8, n.9; 335 n.1; 337 n.3; 339 n.4; 347 n.4; 351–352 n.6; 363 n.10; 369 n.1, n.3, n.4; 371 n.5; 373 n.10; 376 n.11, n.12; 379 (chapter 2) n.2, (chapter 3) n.1; 383 n.4; 393.
Lavenham: see Richard Lavenham.
Lewry, P.O. xi n.17; 394; 395.
Lewy, C. 76–77 n.3; 395.
Lib.Soph.Cantab. (Anonymous, De Obligationibus): xi; xi n.18, n.19; 13 n.12; 33

n.3, n.4; 88 n.14; 376 n.11; 393.
Lib.Soph. Oxon.. (Anonymous, *De Obligationibus*): xi; xi n.18; 13 n.12; 33 n.3; 37 n.11; 86 n.12; 88 n.14; 171–172 n.28; 257 n.74; 261 n.76; 303 n.86; 305 n.88; 322–323 n.92; 329 n.4; 333 n.8; 335 n.1; 337 n.3; 339 n.4; 347 n.4; 351–352 n.6; 363 n.10; 369 n.3, n.4; 371 n.5; 373 n.10; 376 n.11; 379–380 (chapter 3) n.1; 383 n.4; 393.
Lohr, C.H. vii n.1; viii n.3; ix n.8; 16 n.17; 395.
Maier, A. ix n.8; 395.
Maierù, A. xii n.20; 188 n.36; 395.
Marsilius of Inghen. xii; xii n.22; 3 n.1; 7 n.5; 9 n.8; 11 n.10; 11–12 n.11; 13 n.12; 13–14 n.13; 15 n.14, n.16; 19 n.19, n.21, n.22; 21 n.24; 23 n.27; 25 n.29; 29 n.30; 31 n.1; 34 n.5; 37 n.10, n.11; 39 n.12, n.13; 41 n.14, n.15; 51 n.2; 67 n.13; 69–70 n.15; 72 n.19; 73 n.20; 75–76 n.3; 77 n.5; 79 n.6, n.7; 81 n.8; 83 n.9; 85 n.11; 88 n.14; 93 n.17; 96 n.19; 97 n.22, n.23; 99 n.24; 105–106 n.4; 107 n.7; 109–110 n.8; 111 n.10; 113 n.11; 115 n.13; 119 n.15; 123 n.16; 126 n.18; 171 n.27; 172 n.28; 173 n.29, n.30; 175 n.32; 185 n.34; 195 n.39, n.40; 239 n.63; 243 n.64; 245 n.66; 257 n.74; 303 n.86; 315 n.89; 327 n.1, n.2, n.3; 329 n.4, n.5; 331 n.7; 333 n.8, n.10; 335 n.1; 337 n.3; 345 n.2; 347 n.3, n.4; 349 n.5; 351–352 n.6; 365 n.11; 369 n.1, n.3, n.4; 371 n.5; 379 (chapter 2) n.1, n.2; 379–380 (chapter 3) n.1; 383 n.4; 391 n.12; 393.
Martinus Anglicus. x–xi; xi n.17, n.18; 13 n.12; 37 n.11; 53 n.4; 69 n.15; 71 n.17; 86 n.12; 88 n.14; 369 n.1; 393.
Mullally, J.P. 393.
Nardi, B. ix n.6; 395.
Ockham: see William Ockham.
Pardo, Jerónimo. 262 n.76; 395.
Paul of Pergula. 394.
Paul of Venice.
  Life vii–viii.
  Works viii–x.
  Expositio super VIII libros Physicorum. 16 n.17.
  Logica Parva. viii–ix; 14 n.13; 37 n.11; 95 n.18; 393.
  Logica Magna. viii–ix; ix n.8, n.9; 31 n.1; 33; 33 n.2; 35 n.7; 51; 51 n.2, n.3; 67; 67 n.14; 90 n.16; 95 n.18; 97–98 n.23; 99 n.24; 126 n.18; 129 n.20; 247; 247 n.69; 259 n.75; 269 n.78; 391; 391 n.11; 395–396.
    I.2. De suppositionibus terminorum. 90 n.16; 129 n.20; 247; 247 n.69.
    I.3. De terminis confundentibus. 95 n.18.
    I.4. De dictionibus exclusivis. 259 n.75.
    I.18. De incipit et desinit. 269 n.78.
    II.9. De hypotheticis propositionibus. 33; 33 n.2; 51; 51 n.3; 126 n.18.
    II.12. Tractatus de necessitate, contingentia, possibilitate et impossibilitate propositionum. 31 n.1; 51 n.2.
      Part I Fascicule 1. 396.
      Part I Fascicule 7. 97–98 n.23; 99 n.24; 391; 391 n.11; 396.
      Part II Fascicule 6. 35 n.7; 67; 67 n.14; 395–396.
  Quadratura. ix; ix n.11; 395.
  Sophysmata. ix–x; 395.
  Sources xii–xiii.
Percival, W.K. vii n.2.
Perreiah, A. vii n.1; 396.
Peter of Candia. xii; 5 n.4; 12 n.11; 33 n.3; 37 n.11; 69 n.15; 71 n.17; 83 n.9, n.10; 97–98 n.23; 99 n.24; 165 n.24; 169 n.25; 171 n.27; 175 n.31, n.32; 217 n.59; 219 n.60; 261 n.76; 273 n.79; 275 n.81; 369 n.1, n.3, n.4; 371 n.5, n.6, n.7, n.8; 373 n.9, n.10; 375 n.11; 376 n.12; 381 n.2; 391 n.12; 393.
Peter of Mantua. xii; 7 n.7; 9 n.8; 11 n.9; 34 n.5; 35 n.8, n.9; 37 n.11; 39 n.12; 51 n.2; 69 n.15; 73 n.22; 83 n.9; 88 n.14; 101 n.2; 123 n.17; 188 n.36; 235 n.61; 299 n.85; 337 n.3; 383 n.3; 393.
Peter of Spain. 188 n.36; 393.
Pinborg, J. x n.13; 23 n.26; 33 n.3; 394; 395.
Poppi, A. vii n.1; 395.
Prior, A.N. 263 n.76; 396.
Pseudo-Dumbleton. x n.16.
Punta, F. del. ix n.8, n.9; 35 n.7; 395.
Ralph Strode. xi; xii; xiii; xiv; 4 n.3; 12 n.11; 21 n.24, n.25; 33 n.3, n.4; 34 n.5; 35 n.6, n.8, n.9; 37 n.11; 65 n.10; 69–70 n.15; 71 n.17; 72 n.18; 73 n.21; 75 n.1, n.2; 79 n.6; 83 n.9, n.10; 85 n.11, n.12; 87 n.13; 88–89 n.14; 89 n.15, n.16; 96 n.21; 99 n.24; 101 n.2; 105–106 n.4; 107 n.5; 119 n.15; 123 n.17; 127 n.19; 137 n.21; 153 n.22; 163 n.23; 169 n.25; 171 n.27; 172 n.28; 173 n.30; 185 n.34; 187 n.35; 187–188 n.36; 188 n.37; 197 n.41, n.43; 199 n.47; 205 n.55; 213 n.57; 215 n.58; 235 n.61; 237 n.62; 239 n.63; 247 n.67; 251 n.71; 251–252 n.72; 253 n.73; 261–262 n.76; 263 n.77; 285 n.82; 291 n.83; 297 n.84; 317 n.90; 321 n.91; 322 n.93; 335 n.1; 345 n.1; 351–352 n.6; 363 n.9; 369 n.1, n.4; 379 (chapter 2) n.2; 383 n.3; 385 n.5, 385–386 n.6; 389 n.8, 391 n.9, n.10; 393.
Richard Billingham. xi; 37 n.11; 86 n.12; 171 n.28; 321–322 n.92; 339 n.4; 363 n.10; 393.
Richard Brinkley. x n.16; 89 n.14.
Richard Lavenham. xi; 11–12 n.11; 19 n.20; 25 n.29; 37 n.11; 69 n.15; 70 n.16; 86

INDEX OF NAMES

n.12; 87 n.14; 105 n.4; 107 n.7; 171 n.27; 394.
Rijk, L.M. de. x n.12; xi n.17, n.18, n.19; 15 n.14; 33 n.4; 396.
Risse, W. viii n.3; ix n.9, n.10; 396.
Robert Fland. xi; 69 n.15; 71 n.17; 86 n.12; 88 n.14; 105 n.4; 107 n.7; 111 n.10; 123 n.16; 299 n.85; 369 n.1; 394.
Roger Swyneshed. x; x n.14, n.15; xi; xii; xiii; xiv; 11 n.11; 25 n.29; 37 n.11; 50 n.19; 57 n.7; 69 n.15; 70 n.16; 73 n.21; 83 n.9; 86–87 n.12; 87–88 n.14; 99 n.24; 105 n.4; 107 n.7; 119 n.15; 123 n.16; 171 n.27; 195 n.39; 201 n.48; 323 n.93; 394.
Scott, T.K. 89 n.14; 394.
Spade, P.V. x n.13, n.14, n.15, n.16; xiii; xiv n.25, n.26; xvi; 11 n.11; 69 n.15; 89 n.14; 171 n.27; 201 n.48; 352 n.6; 375 n.11; 394; 396.
Strode: see Ralph Strode.
Stump, E, x n.13, n.14; xiv; xiv n.26, n.27; xvi; 34 n.6; 41 n.14; 50 n.19; 67 n.13; 69 n.15; 99 n.24; 237 n.62; 239 n.63; 396.
Swyneshed: see Roger Swyneshed.
Sylla, E.D. xiii; xiii n.24; 396.
Tarski, A. 76–77 n.3.
Thomas Manlevolt (Maulvelt). 106 n.4.
Tomasi, Pietro. ix.
Walter Burley. x; x n.13; xi; xii; xiv; 15 n.14; 23 n.27; 33 n.3; 34 n.5; 35 n.8; 41 n.14; 45 n.16; 53 n.4; 57 n.6; 63 n.9; 67 n.13; 81 n.8; 83 n.9, n.10; 105–106 n.4; 109 n.8; 113 n.11, n.12; 115 n.14; 125–126 n.18; 171 n.27; 185 n.34; 235 n.61; 237 n.62; 239 n.63; 243 n.64; 245 n.65; 331 n.7; 347 n.4; 351–352 n.6; 371 n.5; 394.
Weidemann, H. 57 n.6; 396.
Weisheipl, J.A. 61 n.8; 397.
William Buser. xii n.20, n.22; xii–xiii; 3 n.1; 7 n.5; 9 n.8; 11 n.10; 11–12 n.11; 13 n.12; 13–14 n.13; 15 n.14; n.16; 19 n.19, n.21, n.22; 21 n.24; 23 n.27; 25 n.29; 29 n.30; 31 n.1; 33 n.3; 34 n.5; 37 n.10, n.11; 41 n.14; 41–42 n.15; 45 n.16; 51 n.2; 53 n.4; 55 n.5; 67 n.13; 69 n.15; 72 n.19; 73 n.20; 75–76 n.3; 77 n.5; 79 n.6, n.7; 81 n.8; 83 n.9; 85 n.11; 88 n.14; 93 n.17; 96 n.19, n.20, n.21; 97 n.22, n.23; 99 n.24; 105–106 n.4; 107 n.7; 113 n.11; 115 n.13; 171 n.27; 172 n.28; 173 n.29, n.30; 175 n.32; 185 n.34; 195 n.39, n.40; 197 n.43; 199 n.44, n.45, n.46; 201 n.48; 203 n.50; 203–204 n.51; 205 n.52, n.53, n.54; 239 n.63; 243 n.64; 245 n.66; 247 n.67; 257 n.74; 303 n.86; 315 n.89; 327 n.1, n.2, n.3; 329 n.4, n.5; 331 n.7; 333 n.8; 335 n.1; 345 n.2; 347 n.3, n.4; 351–352 n.6; 369 n.3, 371 n.5, n.6; 379 (chapter 2) n.1; 379–380 (chapter 3) n.1; 391 n.12; 393.
William Heytesbury. 96 n.21; 97–98 n.23; 99 n.24; 130 n.20; 393.
William Ockham. 15 n.14; 33 n.4; 41 n.14; 49 n.18; 83 n.9, n.10; 126 n.18; 171 n.27; 173 n.28; 175 n.31; 394.
Wood, R. xvi.
Wyclif: see John Wyclif.
Zippel, G. vii n.2; 397.

INDEX OF DOCTRINES

Note: in some cases (e.g. 'inferences and inconsistent sets') this index is not exhaustive, but seeks only to give a fair sampling of the innumerable places in which there is reference to a particular doctrine.

Act
  obligation to an, 45
  of obligating, 9, 9 n.8
  of the obligater, 11
  of the obligated, 11
  simple or complex, 45–47
Action
  denial of own, 173 n.28, 293
  or passion, category of, 9
Adam, 51 n.2, 53, 269, 343
Admissio
  definition of, 5–7, 5 n.4
  denial of, 85
  made under a condition, 23
  marks of, 5
  not a part of an *obligatio*, 7–9
  not an *obligatio*, 7, 17
  period of, 7 n.7, 9, 23–25, 187
  relevance to, 27
  without an *obligatio*, 53
Admissiones, two, 233–235
Admissum
  can be an *obligatum*, 17
  definition of, xv, 5, 7
  explicit existence of, 7
  implicit existence of, 5–7
Antichrist, 37, 49, 63, 63 n.9, 263 n.76, 269–271, 339–343, 353
Appellation, 187, 187–188 n.36
Art
  calculatory, 391
  disputatory, 173
  obligatio is an, 13
  of *obligatio*, ix n.11, 33, 35, 83, 85, 331
'Begins' and 'ceases' (*incipit* and *desinit*), 269, 269 n.78
Bologna, University of, vii, xii
Case (*casus*), 49 n.18, 103, 139, 291, 307, 313, 343, 363
Cases, two, 231, 275
Categories, 7–11
Certificatio, 4 n.3
Cicero, Marcus Tullius, 57, 57 n.6
Conditional
  end-clause, 191
  proposition, 191
  see also Proposition, conditional
Conjunction

Billingham on, xi, 321–323, 321–323 n.92
  meaning of whole and parts, 73, 137, 321–323
  order of denial, 161, 193
  positing of parts, 179, 329 n.5
  propositional rules for, 139, 151, 323, 327, 381
  relation to disjunction, 69, 70 n.16, 235, 289, 325, 325 n.94, 391
  rules for *depositio* of, 391
  rules for *positio* of, 69–75, 161, 193, 287–289
  sophisms for, 147–161, 177–181, 225–231, 277–281, 315–325, 327–333, 385–387, 385 n.5, 385–386 n.6.
  Swyneshed on, x, 69–75, 70 n.16, 323
  truth and modalities of, 193, 391
Connotation, 265, 267
Constantia, 110 n.9
  see also Non-referring subject
Contingent falsehoods, proof of, 235–237, 235 n.61
Contradiction, everything to be admitted which does not imply a, 51
Contradictories
  as both true, 383, 383 n.3
  not to be granted, 33, 35, 53, 151, 231
  rule for, 371
Conversion, 297 n.84
  simple, 299
  see also Propositions, interchangeable
Counterfactual reasoning, xiii-xiv, xiv n.25, n.26
Definition (*descriptio*)
  informal, 15
  strict, 15
De Morgan's Laws, 69, 70 n.16, 235, 289
Depositio
  definition of, 5
  marks of, 5
  not an *obligatio*, 7, 17
  reducible to *positio*, 379 (chapter 2) n.2
  rules for, 369–377
  sophisms for, 379–391
  species of *obligatio* 37, 37 n.11
Depositum
  definition of, xv, 5
  is an *obligatum*, 17, 19, 19 n.20, 379

'Differs' (*differt*), 95, 95 n.18
   see also Exponibilia
Disjunction
   and doubt, 51, 337–339
   meaning of whole and parts, 73
   propositional rules for, 65, 71, 157, 237, 319, 341, 341 n.5, 343, 391
   relation to conjunction, 69, 70 n.16, 235, 289, 325, 325 n.94, 391
   rules for *depositio* of, 391
   rules for *positio* of, 73, 287–289, 335–343
   sophisms for, 237–239, 343–345, 381–383, 387–391, 389 n.8
   Swyneshed on, 70 n.16
   truth and modalities of, 335–343
Disjunction elimination rule, 319
Disjunctive phrase, 105
Disposition
   obligation to a, 45–47
   simple or complex, 45–47
Disputation, doctrinal, xiv n.28
Disputation, misleading, 49
   not produced by *suppositio*, 49
Disputation, obligational
   disruptions in a, 23, 23 n.26, 301
   distinct from a doctrinal disputation, xiv n.28
   purpose of, xiii-xiv, 33, 33 n.3, 49, 79–81
Disputations, obligational, two at once, 49–51, 49–50 n.19
Distinction, making a, 301, 307
   see also Propositions, modes of upholding
Doubt
   and denying or granting, 129–131, 145–147, 251–253, 337–339
   and disjunctions, 51, 337–339
   and necessary propositions, 107
   during and after the disputation, 127
   epistemic conditions for, 125
   rules for, 121, 125, 125–126 n.18, 127, 129
   sophisms for, 123–127, 127–137, 191–193, 251–253
   see also Dubitatio
Dubie positio, 12 n.11, 37 n.11, 39 n.12
   see also Dubitatio
Dubitatio, 19 n.19, 39, 41, 43, 45, 45 n.16, 327
   is a *positio*, 39, 327
   rules for, 125, 125–126 n.18, 127, 129
   see also Doubt
Equiforms
   of signs, 89
   of statements or propositions, 7, 69, 315
   of discourse, 217
'Except' (*praeter*), 281–285
   see also Exponibilia
Exclusive
   end-clause, 257–261
   proposition, 257–259

   see also 'Only'
Existential premiss (*constantia*), 109, 110 n.9
   see also Non-referring subject; Proposition, singular
'Exists' in inference, 179, 371, 377, 386 n.6
   see also 'Exist, you do not'
'Exist, you do not', 85, 85 n.11, 85–86 n.12, 87 n.13, 119, 171–173, 171–173 n.28, 175, 177, 333, 333 n.9
Exponibilia, 95 n.18, 257
   see also 'Differs'; 'Except'; 'Only'
Grammatical failings (*incongruitas*), 119, 119 n.15
   see also Reply not to be given
Granting an inference and granting an inference to be valid, 77–79, 211– 213, 283, 287
Granting and denying the same proposition, 219, 219 n.60, 231, 275
Granting P and granting P to be true, 99
   in a *positio*, 37, 47, 47 n.17, 49, 75–79, 95, 107, 119, 331, 351
   in a *suppositio*, 37, 49
   see also Truth, Tarski's adequacy criterion of; Use and mention
Granting P and granting that P ought to be granted, 147, 151, 153–155, 163, 203, 227, 239 n.63, 389
   sophisms concerning, 147–165, 237–239, 249–251
'If' (*si*), inferential and conditional interpretations of, 113
Impositio, 12 n.11, 75–76 n.3, 77 n.5, 89–99, 115 n.14, 195–209, 195 n.39, 197 n.41
   authentic, 87, 89 n.16, 99
   dependent, 113 n.11, 113–119
   for A and B, 90 n.16
   Logica Cantabrigiensis on, xi
   new, 87–99, 89 n.16, 197 n.41
   not an *obligatio*, 17
   rules for, 87–89 n.14, 87–91
   species of *obligatio*, is, 37 n.11, 39, 39 n.13, 43, 45, 47
   species of *positio*, is, 39
Impositum, 97, 99
Impossible, anything whatever follows from what is, 51 n.3, 53, 67 n.12, 341
Inconsistency
   and denial, 377
   and *depositio*, 371, 371 n.5, 373, 375, 377, 379
   and inference, 31, 73–75
   and relevance, 25, 85, 85 n.11, 85–87 n.12
   types of, 85, 85–87 n.12, 171–173 n.28, 173
   which debars an *obligatio*, 11
   with the case, 355, 363
Induction, 143
Inferences
   and granting, 197, 377
   and inconsistent sets, 31, 59, 61, 63, 73–75, 115

and a necessary link, 77
and *obligationes*, 33
and the conjunction of premisses, 73
invalid, 85, 275
valid, 203–204 n.51, 271, 319
Insolubles and *obligationes*, ix n.11, xiv
Intentional verbs, 129 n.20
Intentions, first and second, 75 n.3, 109–110 n.8, 115 n.13
Knowing and being uncertain, 43, 137, 147, 391
Knowing and granting, 55, 57
Knowing that P, 351, 351–352 n.6, 357, 359, 365
'Let the period of the *obligatio* come to an end' (*cedat tempus*), 21–25, 79–81
Logica Cantabrigiensis, xi
Logica Oxoniensis, xi, xii, 70 n.15, 322 n.92, 339 n.4, 363 n.10
Marks (*signa*), 3–7, 11–17, 39
Material names (*nomina materialia*), 89, 90 n.16
Meaning
conventional, 75 n.3, 352 n.6, 353 n.7
natural, 75 n.3
see also Signification
Merton College, Oxford, xi
Modalities of propositions, 31
see also Proposition, contingent; Proposition, impossible; Proposition, necessary; Proposition, possible
Modality, statistical interpretation of, 51 n.2
Moment (*instans*)
first, 115–119
this, 9, 261–263 n.76, 261–273
until a, 23
Moments, two, are neither continuous nor contiguous, 271
Motion, 15, 61, 61 n.8, 325
Natural philosopher, 15
Nature, the order of, 347
Necessary, every proposition implies what is, 67, 67 n.12, 77, 199, 325, 343, 377
Non-referring subject, 110 n.9, 247 n.67, n.70, 333 n.9
Obligated, the, 11
Obligater, the, 11
Obligatio
absence of impeding conditions needed for an, 177, 261
as a relation, xii, 7–15, 17
definition of, 3–4 n.1, 7–15
definition in *Logica Parva*, ix, 13–14 n.13
is not an *admissio, depositio,* or *positio*, 7
is not an art, 13
is not an existent statement, 11
is not an *oratio*, 11–13
is not a preface to a statement, 15
in other contexts, xv

marks of an, 13, 15–17, 187
period of, 9, 21–25
species of, 37–49
temporal relations of to *positio* and *admissio*, 9
Obligatio (as type of *positio*), 17–19, 39, 39 n.12
Obligationes, two, 21, 49–51, 231–235
Obligatum
belongs to the genus of relation, 17
definition of, xv, 15–21, 15 n.15
is an *admissum*, 17
is a *positum* or *depositum*, 17, 379
is a *suppositum*, 379
is not part of an *obligatio*, 19
is not the opposite of a *depositum*, 19
requires an *admissio*, 15
two senses of, 17
Oblique contexts, 263 n.76
'Only' (*tantum*), 257–261, 259 n.75, 281–285
see also Exclusive proposition; *Exponibilia*
Opponent, 13, 13 n.12, 133, 231, 367
death of, 23
Order of denying and granting, 121, 145, 155, 161, 193, 243, 259, 287–289, 323, 335, 361
Order of doubting and granting or denying, 251–253, 337–339
Order of propositions in a disputation (*est ordo maxime attendendus*), 83 n.10, 83–85, 115, 117, 121, 207, 219–221
'Other' (*reliquum*), 53–55, 55 n.5
'Other than' (*alius a*), 333, 333 n.9
Oxford, University of, vii, ix, xi, xiii
Padua, University of, vii
Paradoxes, xiv
Paris, University of, vii, xi-xii
Period of the *obligatio* (*tempus obligationis*), 9, 53–55
definition of, 21–25
outside the, 35, 35 n.8, 73, 79–81, 95–99, 115, 145, 205, 213
see also 'Let the period of the *obligatio* come to an end'
Period of the *suppositio*, 49–51
Period of two *obligationes*, 49–51
Petitio, 12 n.11, 17, 39, 39 n.13, 41 n.14, 41–42 n.15, 41–43, 45– 47, 327
and an impossible proposition, 41 n.14, 41–42 n.15, 41–43
as an inferior species of *positio*, 39 n.13
is a *positio*, 39, 39 n.13, 327
Petitum, 43
Phoenix, 267
Places, one cannot be in two at once, 347
Posita, two, 50 n.19, 71, 72 n.19
Positio
as a genus, 39, 39 n.13
Billingham on, xi
cadens, 23, 23 n.27, 185 n.34, 185–187
definition of, 3–4 n.1, 3–5

INDEX OF DOCTRINES

denial of, 85
dependens, 11, 23, 23 n.27, 185 n.34, 185–187
  inconsistent with *positum*, 85, 85–87 n.12, 171–173 n.28, 173
  marks of, 3
  not an *obligatio*, 7, 17
  not part of an *obligatio*, 7–9
  period of, 7 n.7, 23–25
  preceded by *suppositio*, 41
  renascens, 23 n.27
  rules, 51–75
  species of *obligatio*, 37, 37 n.11, 45
Positiones, two, 231, 233–235, 275
Positum
  can be *positio*, 5
  definition of, xv, 3, 5
  false, 33, 33 n.4, 37
  impossible, 41 n.14, 43, 313
  inconsistent with *positio*, 85–87, 85–87 n.12, 173
  is an *obligatum*, 17, 379
  may be true, 33, 33 n.4
  proposed in the form of the *positum* (*sub forma positi*), 53–55, 57 n.6
  unknown, 127, 133, 143
  see also Proposition, unknown
Possible, possible conclusion implied by what is, 51, 167, 275, 305, 343
Prague, University of, xi
Preface to statement (*Praefixio alicuius enuntiabilis*), 15, 15 n.14, n.15, 19 n.22, 19–21
'Promise', 129–131 n.20, 131, 135
Pronouns, demonstrative, 89, 95–97, 299–301
  see also 'This'
Propositio, as a move in an obligational disputation, 5 n.4
Proposition
  as an occurrent sentence, 75 n.3, 129, 137, 273 n.80, 273–277, 323
  as something (*aliquid*), 171, 173–175
  categorical, quality of, 299
    quantity of, 217
  causal, 259
  conditional, 113, 113 n12, 191, 201, 203–204 n.51
  see also Conditional; 'If'
  contingent, 357, 359, 363–365, 369, 389
    and false, proof of, 235 n.61, 235–237
  see also Rules of *obligatio* are contingent
  determinate, 133
  see also Proposition, unknown
  exclusive, 257–261, 259 n.75
  functionalizable (*officiabilis*), 257–261
  has subject, predicate and copula, 111–113
  impossible, 169, 169 n.25, 291, 369
    and disjunction, 335, 391
    and *petitio*, 41 n.14, 41–42 n.15, 41–43
    and *positum*, 41 n.14, 43, 313
    does not follow from a possible proposition, 51, 275, 305
    implies everything, 51 n.3, 53, 67 n.12, 341
    is inconsistent with every proposition, 67, 377
    per accidens, 51, 51 n.2, 67, 101, 343
    per se, 67, 195, 355, 377, 389
    simpliciter, 51–53
    sophisms for, 169, 303–315, 343–345, 389–391
  indefinite, in relation to singular, 243
  irrelevant (*impertinens*), 25
    and order, 83, 219–221, 337
    false, 65
    sophisms for, 235–237, 279–285
    to *depositum*, 375–377, 375–376 n.11
    true, 65
    uncertain, 65
  mental, 75 n.3, 323
    sophism for, 123–127
  necessary
    and conjunction, 391
    and disjunction, 391
    and *suppositio*, 37, 37 n.11
    follows from everything, 67, 67 n.12, 77, 199, 325, 343, 377
    not to be doubted, 107
    per accidens, 67, 369
    per se, 65, 67, 377, 389
    per se and *simpliciter* 325, 355, 369
    simpliciter 77, 165, 193, 195
    sophism for, 165–169
  particular, in relation to singular, 243–245
  possible, 31 n.1, 51
    implies only possible propositions, 167, 275, 305
    sophism for, 101–105
  relevant (*pertinens*), 25–31, 83–87, 85 n.11
    and order, 83, 219–221, 337
    as following (*pertinens sequens*), 25, 25 n.29
    as inconsistent (*pertinens repugnans*), 25, 25 n.29
    Swyneshed's view of, 25 n.29, 57 n.7, 83 n.9
  singular, 241–247, 247 n.70
  universal, in relation to singular, 245–247
  unknown, 123–127, 131 n.20, 133
    not to be admitted, 127, 133, 143
Propositions
  dissimilar
    definition of, 365
    rules for, 361–365
  interchangeable (*convertibiles*)
    and dissimilar propositions, 363
    and doubt, 121
    rules for, 201, 201 n.48
    sophisms for, 75–79, 111–113, 119–123, 195–209

modes of upholding
    affirmatively or negatively, 7, 15, 19–21, 119
    four, 301
    with uncertainty (*dubitative*), 7 n.5, 15, 119
    see also Replies, types of
proposed as categorical or hypothetical, 203, 211–213, 227, 239, 279, 345
similar
    definition of, 345
    rules for, 347 n.3, n.4, 351–361
    sophisms for, 345–351, 383–385
Puzzle-cases, 33
Quality, category of, 9
    statement belongs to the, 17
Quality of categorical propositions, 299
Quantity, category of, 7
Quantity of categorical propositions, 217, 299
Question, reply by posing a, 125, 133, 143, 145
Questions, no straight answer should be given to, 81, 81 n.8, 157, 225, 243, 247, 273, 289, 297, 349
    see also Reply not to be given
Redargutio, 33, 34–35 n.6
Relation, category of, xii, 7–15, 17
Replies
    inconsistent pairs of, 35, 251–253, 337, 337 n.3
    referred to one moment, 33, 34 n.5, 251
    types of, 37–39, 125, 147
    see also Propositions, modes of upholding; Question, reply by posing a; Reply not to be given
Reply, no reason to be given for, 177, 197
Reply not to be given, 121, 123, 147, 177, 213
    see also Grammatical failings; Questions, no straight answer should be given to
Replying incorrectly, 79–81
Respondent, 13, 13 n.12, 33, 129 n.20, 161
    death of, 23
Responsio
    antiqua, x
    nova, xi
Rules of *obligatio* are contingent, 79 n.7, 315, 315 n.89
Sense
    composite and divided, 103, 103 n.3, 131, 135–137, 261 n.76
    exclusive and inclusive, 23, 23–24 n.28, 185 n.34
    indefinite and relative, 55
    nominal, 35, 35 n.9, 249, 321
    participial, 35, 35 n.9, 135, 321
Significate
    adequate, 35, 35 n.7, 67, 269, 353, 361

distinct from term, 109
    of terms, 31
    unknown, 107, 109, 113–115
Signification, 90 n.16
    adequate, 53, 355, 357, 359, 361, 363, 365
    distinct, 113
    fixed or variable, 89–91, 89 n.16, 99
    see also Impositio; Meaning
Signify
    adequately, 47, 89, 109, 209, 247, 349, 349 n.5, 351, 353, 355, 357, 359, 367
    in a confused way, 107
    interchangeably (*convertibiliter*), 383
Sit verum, 39, 39 n.13, 41, 43–47, 45 n.16
    as inferior species of *positio*, 39 n.13
Sophisms, x-xiii, 135–137
    physical, xiii
    see also Index of Sophisms
Speech (*oratio*), 7, 7 n.6
    obligatio is not a, 11–13
Subject, non-referring, 51 n.2, 110 n.9, 386 n.6
    see also Existential premiss
Substance, category of, 7
Suppositio (species of *obligatio*), 81, 189, 273, 327, 379
    and *casus*, 49 n.18
    and two obligational disputations, 49–50 n.19, 49–51
    definition of, 37
    does not produce a misleading disputation, 49
    genus of other species, 39–41
    marks of, 37
    not a *positio* or *depositio*, 47
    period of, 49–51
    rule for, 49
    species of *obligatio*, 37, 37 n.11, 43
    virtually precedes *positio*, 41
Suppositio (theory of), 95 n.18
    material, 89–91, 90 n.16
    merely confused, 131 n.20, 135
    of part for whole, 175 n.31
Suppositum, 37, 49, 137, 241
    is an *obligatum*, 379
Swinish logicians, 323
Syllogism, 305, 307
    definition of, 73
    in Baroco, 61
    in Darii, 59, 211
Temporal indexicals, 262–263 n.76, 265–271
    see also Moment
Temporal priority, 17, 23
Temporal relations in an obligational disputation, 11, 11 n.9, 13, 17, 23– 25
Temptativa, disputatio, 33 n.3, 78
Terms
    common and singular, 265
    inferior and superior, 289

interchangeable, sophisms for, 93–95, 105–109, 111–113
relative, 135
simple and complex, 111 n.10, 111–113
syncategorematic, 93 n.17
synonymous, 57
see also Intentions, first and second
'This' (*hoc*), 89, 95–97, 96 n.21, 141–143, 191, 261–262 n.76, 261–273
Token-type distinction, 263 n.76
Truth
 must be told outside the period of an *obligatio*, 35
 not an issue, xiv, xiv n.28
 Tarski's adequacy condition of, 76–77 n.3
'Until' (*donec*), inclusive and exclusive senses of, 23, 23–24 n.28, 185 n.34
Use and mention, xiv, 47 n.17, 75–77 n.3, 107 n.6, n.7, 181 n.33, 191 n.38, 197 n.41, 203 n.49, 346 n.2, 352 n.6
 see also Granting P and Granting P to be true
Vienna, University of, xi
'Whenever' (*quandocumque*), 215, 215 n.58